The Nature of Supply Networks

Advance Praise for *The Nature of Supply Networks*

"*The Nature of Supply Networks* takes us through the fascinating world of supply networks, using an interdisciplinary lens from complexity science and operations management. The result is a unique and powerful combination of firm-level perspectives, complex triadic relationships, and the wider, emergent ecosystems. This is a timely and important book that guides a research agenda for supply chain management in an increasingly volatile world. A must-read for both scholars and practitioners."

—**Alexandra Brintrup**, University of Cambridge

"Business resilience is anchored on having a solid supply network. Choi provides the foundational framework combined with new theoretical developments and practical insights on how to build a first-class supply network. Understanding the complex supply networks and building collaborative relationships can enable companies to orchestrate the supply network for resilience, and managing it as an adaptive system allows the network to jointly become an engine of innovation and value creation. This is a great book for supply chain leaders, practitioners, and researchers."

—**Hau Lee**, Stanford University

"I have been excited about this book since first hearing about it. The concept of supply networks developed in this book is important. In fact, it is a much better construction of the relationships we call supply chain management than supply chains themselves. *The Nature of Supply Networks* is a spellbinding examination of wider, emergent ecosystems told in a clear and concise manner. It is an important work for practitioners and academics."

—**Dale Rogers**, Arizona State University

"Hardly any organization could create value for its customers without the input from its suppliers and other stakeholders in the wider ecosystem. Hence, the understanding of how suppliers and the interaction among them create value is of utmost importance. This book contains a critical analysis of supply network structures and management practices. It is research-based and forward-looking. Many firms—from small firms to multinationals—still have to understand and take up many of the practices discussed in the book."

—**Stephan M. Wagner**, ETH Zurich

"Today, companies are, more than ever before, embedded into global supply networks. Developing collaborative relationships with supply chain partners and integrating processes though digital technologies are crucial for achieving competitive advantages. This book addresses these issues by applying the network concepts and complex adaptive systems theory. It presents best practices for supply base management and supply network design. All supply chain researchers and practitioners should read it."

—**Xiande Zhao**, China Europe International Business School

The Nature of Supply Networks

THOMAS Y. CHOI

OXFORD
UNIVERSITY PRESS

OXFORD
UNIVERSITY PRESS

Oxford University Press is a department of the University of Oxford. It furthers
the University's objective of excellence in research, scholarship, and education
by publishing worldwide. Oxford is a registered trade mark of Oxford University
Press in the UK and certain other countries.

Published in the United States of America by Oxford University Press
198 Madison Avenue, New York, NY 10016, United States of America.

Library of Congress Cataloging-in-Publication Data
Names: Choi, Thomas Y., author.
Title: The nature of supply networks / Thomas Y. Choi.
Description: New York, NY : Oxford University Press, [2023] |
Includes bibliographical references and index.
Identifiers: LCCN 2023011439 (print) | LCCN 2023011440 (ebook) |
ISBN 9780197673249 (hardback) | ISBN 9780197673263 (epub) |
ISBN 9780197673270
Subjects: LCSH: Business logistics. | Industrial procurement
Classification: LCC HD38.5.C396 2023 (print) | LCC HD38.5 (ebook) |
DDC 658.7—dc23/eng/20230323
LC record available at https://lccn.loc.gov/2023011439
LC ebook record available at https://lccn.loc.gov/2023011440

DOI: 10.1093/oso/9780197673249.001.0001

Printed by Integrated Books International, United States of America

I dedicate this book to the late Bill Richards, who took me into his home and taught me social networks and social network analysis. At the time, I was a graduate student and a stranger to networks. This book is also dedicated to Dave Nelson, who was EVP at Honda of America when I first met him. I was still a young assistant professor, and he opened the door for me at Honda and allowed me to learn from its cutting-edge practices. I also dedicate this book to two close colleagues in my department—Kevin Dooley for being a partner in my intellectual journey and introducing me to the world of complex adaptive systems, and Dale Rogers for encouraging me to take on this book and for being more than a colleague, a friend. At a personal level, I dedicate this book to my wife, Sarah Choi, for staying with me every step of the way as I took on each chapter and wrote each page. I dedicate this book to our two children, Joshua and David, for providing constant encouragement throughout this book-writing process.

Contents

Preface

The exact date of this event escapes me. In those days, we did not have Outlook calendars or mobile devices. We all carried calendar planner books, which are used less often now. To the best of my recollection, it was sometime in the mid-1990s. At the time, the talk of the town was this newfangled thing called materials resource planning (MRP) from companies like Manugistics and SAP.

I remember the location of this event clearly: Bloomington, Indiana. Indiana University's business school invited people to attend their conference on supply chain linkages. Even then, I fancied myself researching the upstream side of supply chains and was intrigued by the topic. They also offered to pay for my travel, so how could I refuse? I was a young assistant professor with limited resources.

I recall how the conference was full of people from a leading MRP company. My guess was that the company might have bankrolled the conference, including my travel expenses. Some of the company's people—I think they had to be sales types—were boasting about their product's integrative capability over organizations' supply chains. One such person said, "Imagine how you would be able to control the activities of an entire supply chain with a click of a button from your office!"

The entire supply chain . . . control . . . a click of a button . . . Some of those words kept reverberating through my head. I felt ill, but I did not know why.

Thus, I began an intellectual walkabout. I wanted to find out why I responded so negatively to what this salesperson said. There should be nothing wrong with the company trying to stretch the limits of its product's capabilities. But why was I so bothered by it? This struggle continued for several weeks. Even while driving to visit a relative in Wisconsin, I kept thinking about this issue. Then the answer surfaced. When I woke up in my relative's house the following morning, it dawned on me.

Control in supply chains has two faces: one intended by the buyer, and one that the supplier acknowledges. Although similar, the two are not necessarily the same. I had previously witnessed an incident where a supplier threw out one of their buying firms' forecast and its suggested production target because the supplier did not trust that buying firm. That supplier later told me that the buying firm always gave them inflated projections because it wanted only to protect itself.

In this incident, the supplier decided what to do with what came from the buyer. The buyer could not completely control one first-tier supplier, let alone the entire supply chain. Indeed, this is true in general: no single buyer, no matter how powerful, can control its entire supply chain.

After this realization, additional thoughts came quickly. Products and services arrive at the market with no single entity orchestrating the activities of the whole supply chain. As a phenomenon, when a product appears in the market, we can surmise a supply chain must exist. In this regard, a supply chain manages itself. Further, supply chain changes occur simultaneously and in parallel. As a buyer selects a new supplier, that new supplier may also be in the process of selecting a new supplier unknown to the buyer. The buyer does not know about this new second-tier supplier, and it has no way of controlling activities between the two suppliers. Generally, most buying companies work primarily with their first-tier suppliers, and buyers depend on those first-tier suppliers to manage the suppliers at the next tier down. Eventually, a coherent form of a working supply chain emerges, and products and services begin to appear in the market.

I shared my thoughts with a colleague at Arizona State University, Kevin Dooley, and he uttered a few fateful words, "Tom, what you have captured here is what we call a *complex adaptive system.*" We went on to write a conceptual paper that framed supply chains as complex adaptive systems (Choi, Dooley, and Rungtusanatham 2001). This paper became the foundation for the research group Kevin Dooley and I still co-direct, the Complex Adaptive Supply Networks Research Accelerator (CASN-RA) (see https://research. wpcarey.asu.edu/supply-networks/).

If my academic life were a movie, it would show the ending first and then retrace how we got there. My research career began by framing supply networks as a complex adaptive system. Since then, I have been examining what is inside these systems. I have studied dyads, triads, supply bases, extended supply chains, and supply networks. This book flows in the same sequence—from laying down the groundwork in dyads and triads that make up the supply network to framing the supply network as a complex adaptive system. I conclude by discussing the implications of the current global context, where we anticipate prolonged major supply chain disruptions.

Thus, this book does not have to be read in sequence. Of course, it is perfectly fine to start from the beginning and read to the end. Alternatively, a reader may prefer to jump around. The book's logical flow should be apparent from reading the table of contents. Once the logic is clear, it might make sense to read a bit from each chapter as different aspects of supply networks drive the reader's curiosity. I also think it is acceptable to begin at the end of the book and trek backward. The last chapter addresses some of the current challenges, and the penultimate chapter covers supply networks as a complex adaptive system.

Chronologically, in terms of the publication dates, I first became interested in the multi-tiered nature of supply chains (i.e., Choi and Hartley 1996) about the same time I attended the conference at Indiana University that I referred to above. Subsequently, I wrote the theoretical paper that frames supply networks as a complex adaptive system (Choi, Dooley, and Rungtusanatham 2001). After that, I went to Honda to take on a study to map a real-world supply network (Choi and Hong 2002). From what I learned from Honda came the papers on supplier-supplier relationships (Choi et al. 2002), supply base management (Choi and Krause 2006), various triadic dynamics in a network (Choi and Wu 2009; Li and Choi 2009; Rossetti and Choi 2005; Yang et al. 2022), and multi-tier sourcing issues (Chae et al. 2019).

I published papers on buyer-supplier relationships throughout my career, covering topics such as deep buyer-supplier relationships (Liker and Choi 2004), buyer-supplier relationships embedded in extended ties (Choi and Kim 2008; Kim, Choi, and Skilton 2015), and the dark side of buyer-supplier relationships (Villena, Revilla, and Choi 2011). More recently, I began learning about cybersecurity in supply chains (Rogers and Choi 2018), data analytics and digitization (Handfield, Jeong, and Choi 2019), supply chain financing (Rogers, Leuschner, and Choi 2020), and digital supply chains (Jeong, Oke, and Choi 2022). I wrote many of these papers with my students and colleagues, who brought me new ideas. I am indebted to them. This book would not have been possible without their hard work and support.

1

Introduction

No company exists in isolation. Every company operates in connection with other businesses. As they work together, they become organized into networks. In these networks, nodes are companies, and links are business relationships between companies. This book describes the basic structural elements (i.e., dyads, triads, etc.) and the nature of their relationships (i.e., buyer-supplier relationships, supply bases, extended supply chains, etc.). The book examines how companies set up routines and infrastructure to operate across organizational boundaries and adapt to unexpected changes and how the behavioral patterns of supply networks (i.e., complex adaptive systems) emerge over time. It concludes by anticipating how supply networks will evolve in coming years with increasing extreme events and what issues we need to pay attention to.

Indeed, we are currently living through frequent supply chain disruptions. These disruptions are expected to continue into the foreseeable future. Some use the term "regression to the tail" (Flyvbjerg 2020) to describe the time we live in. We are seeing and experiencing more extreme events than ever before, such that outlier events are more common, and when we stack data, the data points regress to the tail. Thus, we end up with fat tails fattened by more frequent extreme events. We do not have to look too deeply to figure out why. The reasons surround us. Such extreme events are triggered by the global health crisis from COVID-19 and episodic recurrences of the virus; trade tensions around the globe involving major economies (e.g., the United States and China, Australia and China, Brexit and the European Union, among others); military conflicts (i.e., between Russia and Ukraine and in other parts of the world involving other countries); and global warming associated with wildly fluctuating weather patterns across the globe and weather patterns with amplitudes of oscillations seemingly growing larger and larger. We live in a world operating far from equilibrium.

Many popular presses have reported on supply chains, and supply chain management has become a household lexicon. Their reports focus primarily on why goods are not getting to consumers from manufacturers

The Nature of Supply Networks. Thomas Y. Choi, Oxford University Press. © Thomas Y. Choi 2023.
DOI: 10.1093/oso/9780197673249.003.0001

(e.g., Gonchar 2021; Helper and Soltas 2021). For instance, they cover how a product (i.e., cell phone charging unit) made in Vietnam or Taiwan is packaged and put into a container, how this container is placed on an ocean-carrying vessel, how this vessel is now stuck at a harbor (e.g., Long Beach), and how the container is eventually offloaded and placed on a truck to a distribution center and then delivered to a brick-and-mortar retailer for consumers or online sales warehouses. Consumers are interested in under-standing how goods get to them from manufacturers. But that is only half the story and perhaps a smaller one compared to the stories that unfold up-stream to the manufacturers. Figure 1.1 shows the connection between the focal companies (e.g., brand companies) and consumers that occupies just one layer of the overall supply network. The supply networks that lie up-stream to these focal companies are much bigger and more complex. We say "upstream" in terms of the flow of the materials. There, we have companies located around the globe engaged in contracting, sourcing, making, and delivering across many tiers of the supply chains. In this book, we examine the upstream side of the supply chain from focal companies (e.g., Honda, Apple, Boeing, etc.), where there is a vast number of companies working to-gether to bring parts and modules to the focal companies that then assemble them for consumers.

To explain the upstream activity, this book extracts and synthesizes the essence of the papers I have published with various co-authors on the topic of supply networks and integrate them into a coherent whole. Various topics

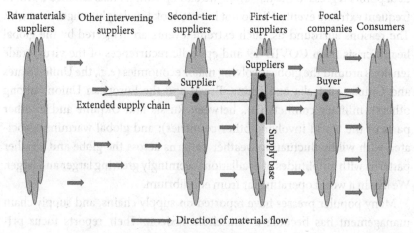

Figure 1.1 Simplified Supply Network Structure

are addressed, including buyer-supplier (B-S) relationships (Liker and Choi 2004), supplier-supplier (S-S) relationships (Choi 2007; Wu and Choi 2005), buyer-supplier-supplier (B-S-S) triads (Choi and Wu 2009b,), supply base management (Choi and Krause 2006), extended supply chains (Choi et al. 2021), supply networks (Choi and Hong 2002), supply networks as a complex adaptive system (Choi, Dooley, and Rungtusanatham 2001), nexus suppliers (Choi, Shao, and Shi 2015; Shao et al. 2018), and intertwined supply networks (Feizabadi, Gligor, and Choi 2021). This book is a culmination of the work I have compiled over my academic career.

One theme that permeates throughout this book is the distributive nature of supply chain management. No one organization or government can completely orchestrate entire supply networks. The U.S. government, a powerful promotor of resilient supply networks, can help coordinate pockets of activities in supply networks by setting appropriate incentives and policies. Implementation of smart contracts (Rogers et al. 2018) and artificial intelligence (AI) (Brintrup 2022) can increase some autonomous activities in supply networks. However, ultimately, the individual companies seeking their own gains make decisions to their benefit. These companies, behaving in a self-seeking way, come together as a supply network with no one entity dictating how they should do that (Choi, Dooley, and Rungtusanatham 2001).

From a single company's perspective, questions are where and at what level should it, as a buying company, try to exert its influence on the supply network to be most effective. These individual businesses eventually form a network, and many supply networks juxtaposed on top of one another are what we call an economy. Thus, every organization or every government with its set of stakeholders might try to manage using its visible hands, but in the end, it is the invisible hand that prevails. The movement of this invisible hand is what the theory of complex adaptive system, applied to supply chain management, informs (Carter, Rogers, and Choi 2015; Choi, Dooley, and Rungtusanatham 2001).

Having a systems perspective of supply networks is essential to understanding how disparate parts come together to create one whole. To understand how a system behaves, we have studied its complexity, including its individual elements and interactions. An organization is a complex system, similar to how a water molecule or a flock of migrating birds is a complex system. However, there is one crucial difference. In a water molecule, oxygen and hydrogen atoms cannot make decisions. They do not have agency. In contrast, an organization or a flock of migrating birds can make decisions and adapt to changes—they have agency. We call this particular type of complex system, in which elements have agency, a complex adaptive system. Supply networks are complex adaptive systems.

Key Points

- The book examines how companies set up routines to operate across organizational boundaries and how the behavioral patterns of supply networks emerge over time.
- The book has a progressive flow—moving across dyads, triads, supply bases, extended supply chains, supply networks, and supply networks as a complex adaptive system.
- The book focuses on the supply network that unfolds with a multitude of supplier companies as we look upstream from the brand manufacturers.
- This book is essentially a compilation of the published papers by the author and his collaborators.

2

Companies, Supply Chains, and Supply Networks

We all have one life to live. To maximize the time given to us, we seek to be good and happy. To help facilitate this goal, we depend on certain goods and services. For example, we rely on our automobiles to go to school, work, grocery stores, and church. We rely on smart devices such as laptops, mobile phones, and tablets to obtain and process information. We rely on building maintenance, transportation infrastructure, vehicle maintenance and repairs, professional cooking, and local hair salons. For these goods and services to reach us as individual consumers trying to live our lives to the fullest possible, there are many organizations that work together and engage in economic activities of buying and supplying. Many of these organizations are companies seeking to maximize their profit. They are organic entities that make decisions to attain their prosperity and survivability.

Ronald Coase (1937) received a Nobel Prize in 1991 for explaining the birth of organizations. He noted that organizations would never have come into existence, had one-on-one bartering been the most efficient form of exchange. Organizations come together because, as a collective, they can provide needed goods and services more efficiently than a single individual can. Within these organizations are elements that work together as a system. Operating under negative entropy as attested by systems theory (e.g., Martínez-Berumen, López-Torres, and Romo-Rojas 2014), these organizations devise boundaries that separate them from the market and ensure their own identity.

Building on Coase's work, Oliver Williamson (1981) received a Nobel Prize in 2009 for theorizing how companies transact with markets. If the governance cost of producing a particular product within the organization is higher than the transaction cost incurred by going to the market, then the organization would buy from the market. As such, no organization exists in isolation, and companies have to acquire resources from the market, to be more precise, from the supply market (i.e., suppliers) that exists upstream to

The Nature of Supply Networks. Thomas Y. Choi, Oxford University Press. © Thomas Y. Choi 2023.
DOI: 10.1093/oso/9780197673249.003.0002

a business. For instance, if we need an automobile or fresh produce, there is a collection of companies through which materials flow so these goods can get to us. Fresh produce requires companies that provide seeds and fertilizers and tilling and planting equipment available for farmers. Take fertilizers, for example; even further upstream in the supply network, other companies refine needed chemicals from raw materials and other businesses that provide containers, shipping services, and so forth. Each company represents a point of convergence of many, many transactions that have procured necessary resources to facilitate needed products in various stages of development (i.e., raw materials, chemicals, parts, components, modules, etc.).

Companies

Figure 2.1 shows that a company receives resources, transforms them, and sends the transformed products to customers. Thompson (2003) offers us a description of an organization as a system of interdependent elements that procures resources from external sources, engages in transformation activities, and delivers the finished products to customers. In supply networks, customers refer to industrial customers; for example, Dell purchases central processing units (CPUs) from Intel, and, as such, Dell is an industrial customer of Intel. To facilitate its transformation process, transactions with the

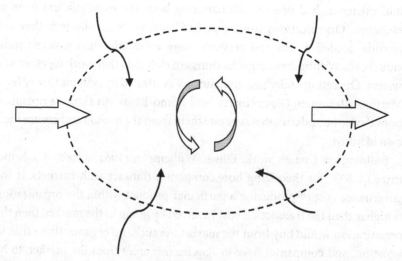

Figure 2.1 The Flow of Materials in an Organization

suppliers occur, and goods flow through its boundary—CPUs from Intel arrive at Dell's receiving dock and are released into Dell's assembly lines. As shown in Figure 2.1, the boundary is depicted as a dotted line to signify its permeability, meaning materials from external companies enter the organization through the permeable boundary.

Two large horizontal arrows indicate resource input and product output—CPUs and other parts are assembled into a Dell laptop. The inputs are *direct* materials that become part of the final product (i.e., CPUs, display screens, keypads, etc.). These inputs are then converted into desirable product forms that customers are willing to purchase. The two arrows moving in a circular fashion in the middle reflect the transformation process of converting materials from one state to another—to cut and bend things, to assemble things together, and so on. In the case of Dell, the transformation process would primarily entail assembly work. To facilitate this transformation process, companies need other resources such as equipment, maintenance-repair-operation (MRO) items, and other *indirect* goods. These resources are catalysts for the transformation process in that they do not undergo a transformation, but they facilitate the transformation of materials into products. These catalysts are represented by the curvy arrows pointing into the organization through its permeable boundary.

Per Coase and Williamson, we know companies exist because they represent an efficient form of organization, but they rely on other businesses for resources. This dynamic means companies have to work together, which means every company engages in make or buy decisions. As a value-creating entity, a company engages in making because it is more efficient to do so as a collective (i.e., transformation process). To do this, companies have to obtain resources from other businesses (i.e., direct and indirect materials). In other words, if the company decides to manufacture its product, work stays inside the organization, and if the decision is to buy, work goes outside to the supply market. When a company decides it would be more efficient to get resources from other businesses, that would be the buying decision. Materials, either direct or indirect, entering the organization are depicted by the arrows pointing into the oval (again, see Figure 2.1).

According to the transaction cost theory proposed by Williamson, companies consider transaction costs, defined as the frictional cost of doing business with outside businesses (i.e., buying from suppliers). If this frictional cost is too high, companies tend to make their goods in-house. Otherwise, they tend to turn to the market and buy. Every company has to purchase something from the market (i.e., their suppliers). Labor-intensive companies, for example, may purchase only 20 to 30% of their total cost of goods sold (COGS) from their suppliers. Design-intensive and assembly-focused companies like Honda buy 80–90% of their COGS from their suppliers. Some companies like Apple and Nike buy close to 100% of their goods and materials from their suppliers.

Supply Chains

As a company engages in a buying activity with a supplier, they form a buyer-supplier pair, and we have the beginnings of a supply chain. The supplier in this buyer-supplier relationship also needs to buy materials from its supplier, who also needs to purchase products from its supplier. When we depict the extension of suppliers across several tiers, we have a supply chain. Figure 2.2 shows a four-tier supply chain. Tiers refer to the progressive levels companies occupy in bringing together a product. For example, as shown in Figure 2.2, the left-most company could be a raw materials supplier, which supplies to a parts supplier, which supplies to a component supplier, and the component supplies to a company that puts together modules. In essence, an output from one company becomes an input for another company.

To engage in value-creating transformation activities, a buying company places an order with a supplier. This fact creates a fundamental supply chain question: How does a buyer know what to order and how much to order? Every company has a core competency; for instance, a laptop manufacturer makes laptops, a grocery store has a list of consumable items that consumers demand, and an airline provides airplanes ready to fly for air travelers. So, what to order may not be so difficult. Each company stands for something (i.e., type of the value-add they provide to their customers), so they would naturally have a list of what items to order from their suppliers. They

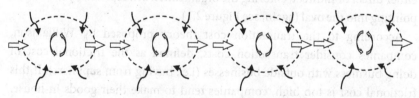

Figure 2.2 A Supply Chain

would just have to look at their bill of materials for the products they produce. Engineers and product designers create the bill of materials. The procurement professionals and cost engineers then work together to engage in make or buy decisions, and if the decision is to buy, it turns to its suppliers. However, how much to order is a different story: This is a very different proposition all together.

The difficulty arises from the fact that it takes time to manufacture things (i.e., lead time), and we simply do not know the level of demand at the time point when the product will be released. Companies do not have crystal balls, so they do the best thing they can—they forecast product demand using various methods. These methods range from qualitative (i.e., Delphi method), quantitative (i.e., time series analysis), and some combination of both qualitative and quantitative (i.e., accurate response method). Once the forecast is created and finalized, it drives the company's subsequent activities. Basically, forecasting examines the past, identifies trends, and attempts to extrapolate past trends into the future. If demand is up, say, by a factor of 5% in the current period, a forecaster would project that increase in the demand trend into the future, and they may predict an increase of 5% for the next period. Forecasting is essential because it takes time to order, pack, transport, and receive goods, and suppliers need lead time to respond to orders. Ultimately, the forecast drives the activities between now and the next period. This process seems straightforward, and maybe this is not that difficult. We just need to figure out the risk of over-forecasting and the risk of under-forecasting to optimize the two.

But not so fast. The fact that all forecasts are always wrong is an issue, but that is just the beginning. Things get really complicated once we line up multiple companies in a supply chain. This increase in demand forecast gets amplified as one moves upstream in a supply chain. This complication means that whatever forecast error there was, to begin with, also gets amplified. Think about how the next supplier in the supply chain uses the increased demand and extrapolates it into their future production: The forecast amplifies more and more as we move further away from the source (i.e., we go further upstream from a downstream source closer to the consumers). Amplified forecasts would lead to overproduction. As overproduced parts and materials arrive at buying companies across the supply chain, demand may shift down, and the forecast points downward. Now, the same thing happens across the supply chain, except this time in the downward direction. Inventories pile up, and companies may have to lay people off. In this confusing state of product demands fluctuating, we cannot forget it takes time for the supply chain as a system to respond to changes. This effect is captured by a well-known phenomenon called the "bull-whip effect" (Lee, Padmanabhan, and Whang 1997). It is called such because demand fluctuations get amplified as one moves further upstream from the consumer market, and the system response is delayed because the lead times are required across the supply chain as information propagates from one tier to the next. Jay Forrester (1999) was the first to recognize this phenomenon, which is referenced as system dynamics. John Sterman (https://web.mit.edu/jsterman/www/SDG/beergame.html) popularized the concept of the bull-whip effect by creating a hands-on supply chain simulation called the "beer game." The game consists of a four-tier supply chain similar to the supply chain shown in Figure 2.2. The right-most node, in this case, is represented by the retailer that faces consumers, and the left-most node is represented by the beer brewer, who manufactures the beer and supplies it to the wholesaler, who then supplies the beer to the distributor, who in turn supplies it to the retailer. This simple model demonstrates the system dynamics of a supply chain and how a group of businesses linked together in this fashion exhibit entirely different dynamics unobserved in individual companies.

Supply Networks

Figure 2.2, as adopted in the beer game, gives us a linear, four-tiered supply chain. In reality, however, there would be multiple beer brewers, wholesalers, distributors, and retailers. Figure 2.3 offers a pictorial rendition of an expanded four-tier supply network. Some companies may be connected in a buyer-supplier relationship, but many may not.

For example, an automobile requires many modules such as an engine, exhaust system, instrument panel, and so forth. The companies that provide these modules would be the first-tier suppliers. Take an instrument panel that requires sub-assemblies made of plastic parts and fasteners. The companies that produce these sub-assemblies would be the second-tier suppliers, and the companies that manufacture plastic molding parts or fasteners would be the third-tier suppliers. Then, these parts manufacturers would need raw materials (i.e., rolled steel and plastic pallets) from their suppliers, who would occupy the fourth tier. They all would have competing companies in the market and engage in business transactions of buying and supplying,

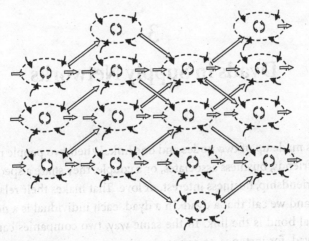

Figure 2.3 A Supply Network

driven by their business goal to maximize economic gain. In the end, we invariably end up with a supply network.

In other words, what we have in reality resembles a network more than a chain. In this regard, supply chains are networks. Supply chains are a simplification of what actually happens. Supply networks are much closer to what is real. There are competing businesses and numerous sourcing arrangements that involve multiple suppliers. In this regard, supply networks, rather than supply chains, are what actually happens in the economy. We consider the nature of supply networks in the remainder of this book.

Key Points

- All companies exist because they create value for their customers, and for that, they need to procure resources from their suppliers.
- If the transaction cost is high, companies tend to choose to manufacture their products in-house, whereas if the transaction cost is low, they turn to the market to buy.
- Every company is a buyer and a supplier. When multiple companies line up as buyers and suppliers, we have a supply chain.
- Every supplier has multiple buyers, and every buyer has multiple suppliers. Therefore, in reality, we have supply networks, and supply chains are a simplification of what actually happens.

3

Dyads in Supply Networks

A dyad is made up of two nodes and one link. When two people meet and become friends, business associates, or a couple, they share a special bond such as friendship, business interest, or love. That makes their relationship distinct, and we call that a dyad. In a dyad, each individual is a node, and the special bond is the link. In the same way, two companies can link to form a dyad, for instance, to engage in a joint venture or to buy or supply goods or services in business-to-business transactions. When companies begin to work together as a buyer and a supplier, a dyad is formed. When multiple dyads come together for a buying company and are stretched out across multiple tiers, they become a supply chain. When several, often overlapping, supply chains with diverse expertise for the purpose of producing and delivering an identifiable product to the market come together, they become a supply network.

In a supply network, there are primarily two types of dyads in operation—the *buyer-supplier* dyad and the *supplier-supplier* dyad. In general, the buyer-supplier dyads occur across different tiers, and the supplier-supplier dyads occur in the same tier. In Figure 3.1, two companies are shown vertically to depict a buyer-supplier relationship and horizontally to depict a supplier-supplier relationship.

During the pandemic, many of us became accustomed to ordering goods online. To facilitate deliveries, corporations like Dell may hire a third-party logistics (3PL) company to handle certain routes. Here, Dell and this 3PL would be in a *buyer-supplier* business relationship. Dell buys the services of the 3PL company, and this 3PL supplies delivery services. In general, a *supplier-supplier* relationship happens when the two suppliers collaborate to share production capacity or capability. The two suppliers may be in competition, or they may provide complementary products or services. For example, to cover all its routes, a buying company like Dell uses several 3PL companies. On occasion, two competing 3PL companies may be asked to share capacity in case one 3PL runs low on capacity so that the other 3PL can step in to cover for them. For this sort of supplier-supplier relationship to

The Nature of Supply Networks. Thomas Y. Choi, Oxford University Press. © Thomas Y. Choi 2023.
DOI: 10.1093/oso/9780197673249.003.0003

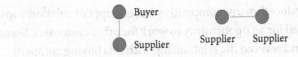

Figure 3.1 Types of Dyads

work, the two suppliers would have to share communications and coordinate their capacity and scheduling activities.

In this chapter, we first discuss the nature of the relationship between a buyer and a supplier as in the buyer-supplier relationship. This particular dyad is fundamental to how companies work together in supply chains. We then add a network perspective to the buyer-supplier relationship to broaden the context. We consider, for instance, how a supplier is embedded in its extended ties and how that affects the nature of buyer-supplier relationships. After that, we address the other type of dyad, namely supplier-supplier relationships. We consider different types of supplier-supplier relationships, first theoretically and then empirically. We discuss the performance implications of different kinds of supplier-supplier relationships. By then, we will be ready to move on to our next chapter on triads.

Buyer-Supplier Relationships

A buyer-supplier relationship is typically characterized in two ways—cooperative or competitive. Toyota and Honda are considered exemplary for having cooperative relationships with their suppliers (Liker and Choi 2004), and the other automakers have often been considered to have more of a competitive relationship with their suppliers. To describe cooperative and competitive buyer-supplier relationships in the automobile industry, Helper (1991) uses the term "voice" to refer to a cooperative relationship and the term "exit" to capture a competitive relationship. Voice espouses a win-win mode of operation, while exit reflects an adversarial approach in a win-lose mode of operation. As an example of an exit relationship, a major U.S. automobile company once had a 3-2-2 program for its suppliers. That meant the suppliers were required to give this buying company a 3% cost reduction in the first year of the program and 2% in each of the following two years. Suppliers resisted because, for many of them, 2% or 3% was their profit margin. Needless to say, this program was implemented in a contentious atmosphere and produced many competitive buyer-supplier relationships. These suppliers looked for an opportunity to work for other customers. Some of them succeeded and severed the relationship with this buying company.

In fact, cost concerns have been the major factor that determines how the buyer-supplier relationship is managed (Choi and Hong 2002). And there is a good reason why a company like this major U.S. auto manufacturer would seek a cost reduction from its suppliers. It is not just this automaker, but also many other buying companies in different industries had similar cost-reduction programs. Some of us working with companies in the high-tech industry heard numbers like 10% or even 30% to 40% cost reductions from suppliers. The reason why these companies seemed obsessed with supplier cost concessions is that a dollar saved from their suppliers on the upstream side of their supply chain usually has a much more significant impact on their return on investment (ROI) compared to a dollar earned on the sales side from the downstream side of their supply chain. It seems a no-brainer that the CEOs of these companies would put pressure on their supply management professionals to get additional cost concessions from the upstream supply side. This is an important underlying motivation we need to understand.

Figure 3.2 shows the basic cost structure leading to a company's ROI. Inventory, accounts receivables, and petty cash together make up current assets. To that, add fixed assets, and we get total assets. Now, to get cost of goods sold (COGS), we need to add up labor, parts and materials, and overhead. By subtracting COGS from sales, we get profit. Finally, we take the ratio between profit and total assets to get our ROI. Following the chart, we see this company is currently enjoying an ROI of 10%, which is pretty good. To this cost structure, suppose we are able to get a 10% cost reduction from the suppliers, which is shown in numbers outside the boxes: then the ROI increases to 20%. That is huge! Compare that to what happens to ROI if we were to sell 10% more on the sales side from downstream. If we work out the numbers, we will see that ROI does increase by 15%—to sell 10% more, inventory increases, accounts receivables (A/R) increases, labor, and parts and materials would all have to increase by about 10%, and there might be other expenses associated with sales promotions. The lesson here is that the 10% cost reduction from the upstream suppliers offers better ROI results than the 10% sales increase from the downstream sales, given the cost structure shown in the figure. In addition, getting a cost concession from suppliers seems a much more expedient and safer venture than conducting a sales promotion.

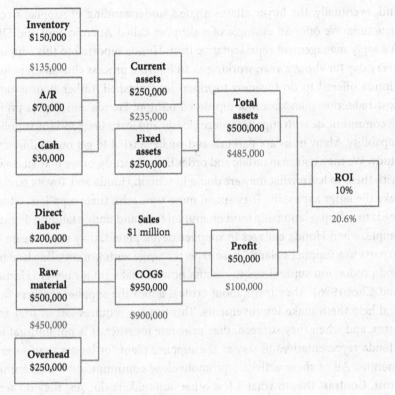

Figure 3.2 Impact of Supply Cost Reductions

Given the upstream effects on ROI as demonstrated, it is not surprising why many buying companies have their supply management professionals focus on getting a cost reduction from their suppliers (Dobler and Burt 1996). Mandating unilateral cost concessions on suppliers has been the hallmark of the competitive buyer-supplier relationship. However, obvious questions arise. Does that mean those buying companies such as Honda and Toyota, known for their cooperative relationship with suppliers, do not impose unilateral cost reductions on suppliers? Do they not care about the cost reductions?

To be clear, they do care. They likewise put pressure on their suppliers to reduce costs. How they approach cost reduction is laid out in Liker and Choi (2004). In their article, a cooperative buyer-supplier relationship is referred to as a "deep" relationship because to cooperate reasonably, the buyer and supplier need to get to know each other well in terms of the business processes, and, eventually, the buyer attains a good understanding of supplier's cost structure. We offer an example of a supplier called Atlantic Tool and Die. A supply management representative from Honda reported to this supplier every day for about a year, working as an internal process consultant before Honda offered to do business together. In a nutshell, rather than issuing cost-reduction mandates in a top-down fashion, Honda and Toyota prefer to communicate with suppliers more closely and learn firsthand the supplier capability. Many of us are parents, and we have tried to get our children to study. We may issue a mandate and order them to study, or we may sit down with them to learn what they are doing in school. Honda and Toyota tend to take the latter approach. They spend more time with their suppliers, which leads to a deep relationship built on mutual trust and understanding. For example, when Honda engages in supplier development, they send a team of experts to a supplier's plant. These experts engage with workers, line leaders, and production supervisors to discuss how to make things better (Hartley and Choi 1996). They learn about critical issues the supplier workers face and help them make improvements. This process requires lots of trial and error, and when they succeed, they celebrate together. It is not unusual for Honda representatives to stay at the supplier plant for longer than several months. All of these activities promote close communication and mutual trust. Contrast that to what a few other automakers do. Yes, they do send their experts to suppliers, and they do engage in joint improvement activities. But they take more of a cookie-cutter approach they call "kaizen-blitz." The team sent to the supplier typically stays for one week and goes through a prescribed improvement activity. The result typically is that they demonstrate savings because they pick the low-hanging fruits. Some of them would then go so far to extend those savings to other areas in the supplier plant and demand additional savings. In the article by Liker and Choi (2004), one supplier working for the U.S. automakers was quoted as saying that "the Big Three set annual cost-reduction targets. To realize those targets, they'll do anything..., a reign of terror, and it gets worse every year."

To capture how to cooperatively work with suppliers, Liker and Choi (2004) propose a satisfaction progression model similar to Maslow's needs hierarchy. We call it the *supplier-partnering hierarchy*. Just as in Maslow's model where a basic need for food must be met before needing to meet a higher order need such as self-esteem, our model attests that understanding how suppliers work must happen first before one can tell suppliers what to do or engage in joint improvement activities. For instance, a big part of understanding how suppliers work is to obtain substantial knowledge about the supplier's cost structure. Once that happens, the buyer and supplier can agree on a price to ensure the supplier covers their costs. In this case, the profit margin is set very tight, but Honda and Toyota help their suppliers make improvements through various supplier-development activities to widen the profit margin. So, both parties gain, and a win-win situation occurs. Thus, it is apparent why Honda and Toyota always get high ratings on supplier surveys (https://www.prnewswire.com/news-releases/toyota-honda-general-motors-finish-1-2-3-in-annual-working-relations-study-301297436.html).

Thus far, we have discussed two types of buyer-supplier relationships and presented supply cost as the driving concern in a buyer-supplier relationship. We have associated competitive relationships with terms like mandates, terror, and so on. In contrast, we have portrayed a cooperative relationship as an open and mutually beneficial relationship. However, there is a dark side to the cooperative buyer-supplier relationship. In some cases, cooperative relationships built on collaboration and communication can become too much of a good thing.

When the buyer and supplier become so close that they share common work processes and work norms, that must be a good thing. Or is it? We hear about the relationship between Toyota and one of its first-tier suppliers, with whom Toyota has had a celebrated, long-term relationship. Toyota makes its bestselling sedan, Toyota Camry, in Georgetown, Kentucky. Also located there is this supplier, which makes a key module for the Camry. These two companies work together so well that the supplier keeps no finished goods inventory. Operating under the Toyota Production System (TPS), both companies have synchronized their tact time so that the finished modules come off the production line at the supplier plant, go directly into the back of a semi-truck, and are delivered to the Toyota Camry plant. Once the truck arrives, the back opens up, and modules flow right into the production process seamlessly. The supplier receives its *Kanban*, that acts as the production signal, from Toyota every morning, and the modules are sequenced based on the production targets for different models of Camry. The supplier produces to the specification on the Kanban. How can this be bad?

What is just described as happening between Toyota and this supplier is what every buyer and supplier would dream of. It is a beautiful thing. I actually saw it work and beheld its beauty when I visited this supplier in person. However, this beautiful thing began to take on a different color when a manager from Toyota came to talk to me in my office at Arizona State University. He said he had a problem involving one of his suppliers. He told me about this supplier with whom Toyota had had a deep relationship. This relationship is so deep that this supplier was being rigid. When Toyota asked the supplier to do certain things, the supplier would refuse and was unwilling to be convinced otherwise. The supplier would even provide the logic based on their deep understanding of TPS. How would you manage the relationship with this supplier? I learned from this visit that a deep buyer-supplier relationship could have a dark side.

Having a dark side, of course, implies there is a bright side. Indeed, a deep buyer-supplier relationship reduces transaction costs because they operate based on shared norms and processes. Trust is built over time so that incoming inspections can be waived and closely monitoring suppliers may not be necessary. However, at a certain point, when there is too much trust, that can manifest in rising supplier opportunism unbeknownst to the buyer. Theoretically speaking, the supplier may take the deep relationship for granted and choose not to give it their best. The supplier might start to cut corners and engage in minimalist behavior. The buyer may begin to suspect something is up; however, the buyer may not want to rock the boat by confronting the supplier. When this occurs, we are in the realm of a dark side of the cooperative buyer-supplier relationship.

Villena, Revilla, and Choi (2011) conduct an empirical study using survey data and secondary performance data to investigate the dark side of buyer-supplier relationships. We find a statistically significant association between the level of buyer-supplier relational capital and the operational performance of the buyer (see Figure 3.3). Relational capital is accrued when the buyer and supplier work together to develop a deep relationship characterized by trust, friendship, and respect. As expected, with increasing relational capital, the buyer's operational performance increases. Still, after a certain point, this positive trend takes a turn and begins to show a downward trend, as shown in Figure 3.3.

In a separate study, we focus on the duality of inter-organizational trust and find the same negative quadratic effect between trust and efficiency (Villena, Choi, and Revilla 2019). As evidence, Automotive News in 2012 reported how some of Toyota's close suppliers went behind Toyota's back and engaged in price-fixing. We articulate where the dark side begins to occur—when the buyer begins to lose objectivity, when the supplier starts to behave opportunistically, and when the buyer begins to detect knowledge redundancy where

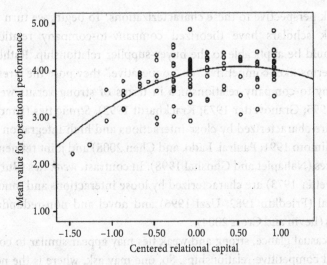

Figure 3.3 Empirical Evidence of the Dark Side of Deep Buyer-Supplier Relationships
Source: Villena, Revilla, and Choi 2011

no new ideas are being exchanged. In response, we propose a few strategies a buyer can consider to combat the dark side—that is, to continuously set up challenging goals, implement rotation policies for their supply professionals, and install explicit languages in contracts with the supplier (Villena, Choi, and Revilla 2015). Villena, Choi, and Revilla (2021) conduct a formal study examining these mitigating mechanisms and find empirical support for challenging goals and contractual explicitness. It appears that, while rotation policies are standard for sales professionals, rotation policies for supply management may not be as widespread. While we suspect rotation policies for the supply management professionals would still be helpful in combating the dark side, there are just not enough data points to ascertain it.

Buyer-Supplier Relationships from a Network Perspective

As previously discussed, the buyer-supplier relationship is typically categorized as competitive or cooperative, based mainly on the literature in supply chain management. A competitive relationship is characterized as short term, arm's length, and win-lose, whereas a cooperative relationship is characterized as long term, deep, and win-win. We now apply the network perspective to these characterizations. To begin, we turn to how network scholars have theorized company-to-company relationships that would be applicable to the buyer-supplier relationship. Rather than using terms like "competitive" or "cooperative," they pose the strength of company-to-company relationships in terms of strong versus weak ties (Burt 1995; Granovetter 1973; Krackhardt 1992). *Strong* ties (Krackhardt 1992) are characterized by close interactions and high integration (Clark and Fujimoto 1991; Paulraj, Lado, and Chen 2008) and joint refinement of resources (Nahapiet and Ghoshal 1998). In contrast, *weak* ties (Burt 1995; Granovetter 1973) are characterized by loose interactions and innovation potential (Friedkin 1982; Uzzi 1996) and novel and non-redundant resources (Levin and Cross 2004).

At a casual glance, strong and weak ties may appear similar to cooperative and competitive relationships. So, one may ask, where is the network perspective? There are profound network implications in these ties. Think of it this way. Conceptualization of the strong and weak ties considers other extended ties connected to the nodes. Imagine two colleagues who work together all the time and are very successful in publishing together. They have a strong tie. They understand each other, trust each other, and work together very efficiently. However, strong ties have a dark side. They tend to recycle more or less the same ideas. This is because nodes in a strong tie become beholden to each other, and they are not likely to venture out to explore new ideas from other external nodes. This happened to those suppliers that belonged to a *keiretsu* in postwar Japan (Womack, Jones, and Roos 2014)— a *keiretsu* represents a business practice referring to a group of firms that have organized themselves around a powerful manufacturing organization. Notable examples are Toyota keiretsu and Fuji keiretsu. A supplier belonged to one keiretsu with a close relationship with the lead manufacturing company. They worked together very efficiently (i.e., short product development time). At the same time, they did not do business with other firms outside their given keiretsu; consequently, suppliers under the umbrella of a keiretsu became comfortable and isolated. Of course, although there may still be lingering tendencies, Japanese suppliers primarily do not operate this way anymore, but some economists attribute this particular business structure to the prolonged recession Japan has suffered. The point here is that a business tie between a buyer and a supplier is profoundly related to how the extended ties are attached to the nodes in a relationship. Therein lies the network perspective.

In a weak-tie relationship, both companies are less constrained by the existing tie and are freer to venture out to work with other businesses. The automobile companies in the U.S. used to be a highly vertically integrated organization. They had under their corporate umbrella a car stereo company, tire company, and so on. However, under such a strong tie arrangement, these subsidiaries were comfortable and not particularly motivated to innovate (Womack, Jones, and Roos 2014). Therefore, as part of their corporate downsizing initiative, the auto companies, such as General Motors, spun off these subsidiaries; essentially, they turned strong ties into weak ties. Now, these subsidiaries had to fend for themselves by exploring other extended ties to find new buyers and new suppliers. An important point is that both strong and weak ties have redeeming qualities for the buying company. Kim and Choi (2018) offer empirical evidence that both strong and weak ties are much more effective in value creation compared to the ties of intermediate strength.

What this all means is that, for the buying company, how a supplier is *embedded* in its extended ties is important (Choi and Kim 2008). The concept of "embeddedness" is attributed to Polanyi (2001) and Granovetter (1985), and it refers to "the contextualization of economic activity in ongoing patterns of social relations and captures the contingent nature of an economic actor's activities . . . in a larger social structure" (Choi and Kim 2008, p. 8). When a girl brings a boy home to meet her father, some questions the girl's father may ask the boy are where he works, where he comes from, what his parents do, and so on. What the father is probing for is the boy's extended ties because he instinctively knows these extended ties will affect how well the boy will do in his career and life. Choi and Kim (2008) argue that in much the same way, a supplier's performance would be dependent on its extended ties. Here are two examples we offer—in both examples, the source of the problem comes from other companies the supplier is doing business with. An aerospace corporation onboarded a new supplier for their technical capability, but soon they ran into a quality problem. From the buying firm's perspective, the problem came from the supplier. But upon further investigation, the source of the problem was this supplier's supplier. Another example involves a well-known Japanese automaker that was working with a large, U.S.-based first-tier auto parts supplier. This supplier started to miss production targets and ran into other problems. The buying company then learned the source of the problem was actually another well-known U.S. automaker that was having financial problems. The first example illustrates how a

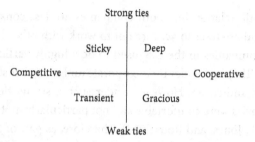

Figure 3.4 Network-Inspired Buyer-Supplier Relationships
Source: Kim and Choi 2015

supplier's supplier can be the source of the problem, while the second points to the supplier's other buyer as the source of the problem.

Kim and Choi (2015) subsequently bring into a single framework the dimensions of strong vs. weak ties and competitive vs. cooperative relationships. We pose that a strong- or weak-tie relationship can be either competitive or cooperative (see Figure 3.4). Using the data we collected from a major Japanese automaker and their direct-parts suppliers in North America, we offer empirical support for the orthogonality of these two dimensions. From there, four new types of buyer-supplier relationships are articulated, as shown in Figure 3.4. The *deep* relationship, as has been discussed, offers stability (i.e., well-established just-in-time, JIT, operations) but may suffer from supplier rigidity because the buyer and supplier are beholden to each other and are set in their ways. The *sticky* relationship is like a bad marriage. The buyer and supplier are stuck in an adversarial and long-term relationship. There is little synergy but ample opportunism between the two companies. The buyer and supplier in the *transient* relationship seek short-term gains at the expense of the other company (i.e., price advantage). The relationship tends to be temporary and governed by contractual terms. The buyer and supplier are not committed to their current relationship, and as a consequence, they enjoy relational flexibility. The buyer in a *gracious* relationship with a supplier would have little leverage or control over the supplier. However, the opportunity for supplier innovation is high. Business deals between the two companies may happen occasionally, but the two corporations keep each other in high regard.

One may then wonder how realistic these new relationship types might be. Would we encounter them in the real world? The answer is a resounding yes. As mentioned above, data comes from a well-known Japanese automaker operating in the U.S. (Kim and Choi 2015). The automaker offered us the list of its 241 core suppliers in North America, and we successfully gathered the data from 163 supplier companies. For collecting matching data from the buying firm, we were asked to limit the number. In the end, we ended up collecting the buyer-side data on 32 suppliers and were able to ascertain a close match in terms of how the two sides of the dyad view their working relationships. Once that was done, we analyzed the data primarily from the suppliers. The results are shown in Figure 3.5.

This particular Japanese automaker is well known for its deep relationship with its suppliers. So, initially, we were concerned about whether we would see suppliers in quadrants other than the deep relationship quadrant. As evidenced in Figure 3.5, to our delight, our concern did not materialize. This buying firm has a well-balanced number of suppliers across all four quadrants.

We have now presented empirical evidence that these relationship types exist in the real world. Yet, another lingering question has to do with their utility. How would these new relationship types help us manage our suppliers better? When we apply the network-based embeddedness concept to the buyer-supplier relationship, each new supplier type takes on the *dual outcome* implications. Kim and Choi (2021) present a detailed analysis of dual outcomes for each of the four types.

The *deep* relationship leads to stability, which then partially induces supplier rigidity. Stability exists within the dyad, but rigidity comes from the fact that given the strong-tie relationship, the supplier has little opportunity to venture out and explore other external relationships. Thus, the information in the dyad becomes redundant, and the supplier becomes set in its ways. The *sticky* relationship is signified by the buyer's exploitation strategy. Consequently, within the dyad, there is little synergy between the two companies. Given the strong-tie context, with the buyer prone to exerting its power, the most obvious recourse the supplier has is to look for ways to behave opportunistically. The major thrust behind the *transient* relationship is the buyer's intention to keep the supplier on its toes. Therefore, the buyer may prefer to keep the relationship in an ambiguous state with no definite commitment. The buyer would tend to engage in competitive tendering and aggressive negotiation. With a weak-tie relationship in the dyad, the supplier can maintain options available in its extended ties and leverage its flexibility to choose alternative options when necessary. In a *gracious* relationship, the buyer and supplier remain positive and available

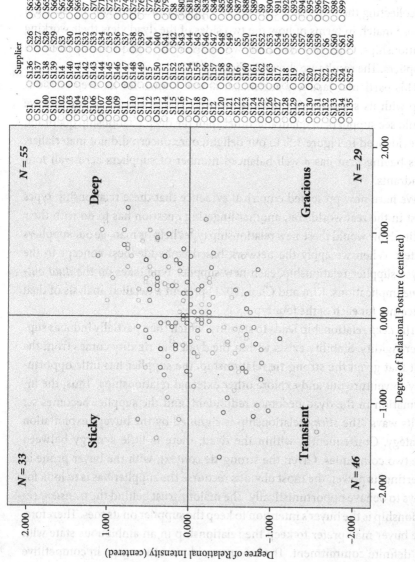

Figure 3.5 Presence of Suppliers in Different Relationship Types

Source: Kim and Choi 2016

to each other's business needs. They tend to engage in intermittent projects, and the buyer has little leverage over the supplier. Because of this condition, the supplier can readily explore with other companies in its extended ties, which often means they come across diverse and innovative ideas. Given the positive stance with the buyer, the supplier may often share innovative ideas.

Among the four types of relationships, the most interesting type is perhaps not the deep relationship that has been the subject of admiration and many publications (i.e., Liker and Choi 2004) but the gracious relationship associated with supplier innovation (Kim, Choi, and Skilton 2015). One of the reasons why the deep relationship has been the subject of admiration is because the closely tied, cooperative relationship is often credited to supplier innovation. The simple logic is that after establishing a close relationship, only then would a supplier open up to share innovative ideas with the buyer (Moran 2005; Noordhoff et al. 2011). What has been overlooked, however, is that in a closely tied, or strong-tie, relationship, the two companies become beholden to each other, and their knowledge tends to be redundant. Notably, the relationship has to entail a weak-tie relationship for the supplier to expose itself to non-redundant, innovative ideas. Couple the weak tie with the cooperative relationship, in what we call the gracious relationship, the supplier would be willing to become a bridge to relay innovative ideas (Uzzi and Lancaster 2003).

One remaining question in this regard then, might be, what would be the differences in the type of innovation coming from the deep versus gracious relationships? Kim, Choi, and Skilton (2015) inform that a deep relationship would tend to lead to gray-box and systemic innovations, whereas a gracious relationship would lead to black-box and modular innovations for the buying company. This is so because, in a deep relationship, the two businesses work closely together, involving intense interactions through strategic supplier alliances (Ellram 1995; Oliver 1990; Whipple and Frankel 2000). Therefore, this relationship would likely lead to gray-box and more all-encompassing systemic innovations. In contrast, the gracious relationship resembles "sustained contingent collaboration" (Herrigel and Wittke 2005). The two companies work together intermittently, maintaining autonomy, and this condition would be more conducive to black-box innovations. The scope of the innovation would be less all-encompassing and more modularized, but the novelty of innovation would be more intense.

Performance Implications of Buyer-Supplier Relationships

A supplier's performance is tracked just like any other company. The supplier tracks its own business performance, and others, such as its financial and government stakeholders and its potential investors, would as well. In particular, its performance is tracked and controlled by the buying company, its industrial customer. At a casual glance, there appears nothing unusual about this. However, the buying company often imposes additional demands that the supplier must comply with (i.e., measures for worker safety, process quality, sustainability, etc.). When a new performance requirement is imposed in the buyer-supplier context, a supplier often engages in a rather strange behavior. We call that an *institutional* response as opposed to a technical response (Choi and Eboch 1998; Shi et al. 2018). Its primary motivation for complying with the buyer's mandates is to maintain goodwill with the buyer (i.e., institutional logic) rather than increase efficiency (i.e., technical logic). The state of institutional response is "loosely coupled" with the state of technical logic (Meyer and Rowan 1977; Choi and Wasti 1995). This is an intriguing supplier behavior we should consider more deeply (Barratt and Choi 2009; Bhakoo and Choi 2013; Choi and Eboch 1998; Fernandez-Giordano et al. 2022; Shi et al. 2018).

To state the obvious, let us consider briefly the types of activities the buying company conducts to manage supplier performance. The buying company conducts a supplier evaluation to reveal opportunities for improvement or to qualify new sources. When a supplier is evaluated, the buyer typically measures the supplier's performance via key performance indicators (KPIs), and they usually involve financial conditions, consistency in quality and delivery, relationship orientation, flexibility, technological capability, support from sales representatives, production or service reliability, and low initial price (see Carter and Choi 2008; Choi and Hartley 1996). Additional areas of evaluation are risk, innovation, and sustainability. A summary of a supplier's performance on KPIs are shown on a supplier scorecard. These scorecards are sent to the supplier on a regular basis. Honda of America, for example, sends supplier scorecards once a month to all its core suppliers. Other buying companies may do that less frequently. Also, supplier performance is discussed at executive round tables where top executives from both sides meet to discuss performance history. These discussions also include the buying company's future plans; potential technical capabilities the buyer may need from the supplier in coming years; new areas of KPIs, such as environment, social, and (corporate) governance (ESG); and cybersecurity concerns.

It is one thing to measure how the supplier engages in its core transformational activities through how well it manages cost, quality, and delivery. However, it is an entirely different thing if the buyer demands evidence for worker suggestion programs or environmentally friendly practices. From visiting suppliers, they have told me about the "flavor of the month" programs initiated by the buying companies. From the supplier's perspective, it has a difficult task at hand. It has to keep up with its own operational goals and meet its industrial customers' KPI's, which vary from customer to customer. It now has to deal with additional mandates from the buyer. For example, the supplier may not immediately see how keeping track of sustainability practices might be related to its internal operational goals, but it knows it has to comply with this mandate. Thus, suppliers have to manage these two conflicting activities—one to meet its internal goals, and another to comply with external mandates.

On the one hand, a supplier must manage its operations to the best of its abilities, working with the inputs it receives and transforming them into products that its customers need. On the other hand, its customers or buying companies may continue to place additional burdens, for example, supplier certification requirements, implementing quality control mechanisms such as statistical process control systems or quality control circles, worker safety requirements, and more. From the buying company's perspective, these additional demands are imposed on the supplier for the betterment of supplier performance. It wants to ensure timely and quality inputs from its suppliers with minimum cost.

So, what does a supplier do? The suppliers typically consider these two sets of activities as being separate from each other and, therefore, manage them separately (Choi and Eboch 1998). Organizations want to maintain doing what they know best in the transformation process, promoting efficiency, and at the same time, but separately, they comply with the exogenous demands from their stakeholders in order to promote legitimacy and goodwill (Meyer and Rowan 1977). Suppose a stamping company in the automotive industry receives a request from its customer (e.g., General Motors or Toyota) to submit statistical process control charts of its processes in a required format. This stamping company has been performing well, so based on its own engineering assessment, it does not see the need for an additional statistical process control. However, because a customer demands it,

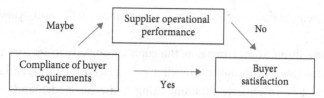

Figure 3.6 Buyer Requirements and Supplier Performance
Source: Choi and Eboch 1998

the stamping company is compelled to oblige. It may now have to invest in additional resources to acquire new technology and training to prepare the charts in the required format. This type of organizational response is well laid out in the institutional theory (Meyer and Rowan 1977; DiMaggio and Powell 1983; Zucker 1987; Scott 1987; Choi and Wasti 1995). When organizations face exogenous pressures initiated by their external stakeholders (i.e., industrial customers, professional associations, government agencies, etc.), they choose to create a state of "loose decoupling" between their technical cores that are engaged in value-adding transformation processes and the administrative responses that are set up to comply with these exogenous requirements (Meyer and Rowan 1977).

In the buyer-supplier context, this type of loose coupling manifests in how the implementation of the new practice demanded by the buying company affects the supplier's operational performance versus customer satisfaction (i.e., satisfying the buyer by complying with its demands). It seems like customer satisfaction should be affected by both complying with the buyer's requirements and the supplier's operational performance. However, there is empirical evidence that this is *not* the case. In fact, there is a loose coupling between suppliers' operational performance and customer satisfaction. The empirical evidence comes from a study by Choi and Eboch (1998) that investigates the state of loose coupling for the case of total quality management (TQM) practices required by the buying companies (see Figure 3.6). The TQM practices represent an overarching management approach that includes process quality, human resources (i.e., worker involvement), strategic quality planning, and information analysis. These practices have been promoted by the industrial customers in various forms (i.e., lean manufacturing, six sigma, etc.) to their suppliers.

The supplier's compliance with buyer requirements has a direct impact on buyer satisfaction. Whether the buyer promotes TQM or sustainability practices, the supplier is interested in complying with this requirement because it depends on the company for resources (i.e., new contracts). As articulated in the institutional literature, organizations seek legitimacy and goodwill from powerful external stakeholders (Meyer and Rowan 1977; DiMaggio and Powell 1983; Zucker 1987; Scott 1987) to ensure the continued flow of needed resources. From the buying company's perspective, the visible compliance by the supplier leads to its satisfaction. However, for supplier compliance to have an impact on its performance, the supplier requires fortuitous matching between some aspects of the required practices by the buyer and the technical needs of its company (Choi and Eboch 1998). Interestingly, Choi and Eboch find only a moderate level of empirical support for the connection between supplier compliance and operational performance (i.e., the arrow labeled "maybe" in Figure 3.6). Further, their study finds no statistical correlation between the supplier's operational performance as induced by the particular compliance and buyer satisfaction. This effect is, in fact, predicted based on the institutional logic in that the small amount of supplier performance benefited from the compliance is loosely coupled with the buyer's satisfaction by observing the compliant behavior. Choi and Behling (1997) explain this effect further. They point out this type of response happens when the supplier's main orientation driven by the top management is tactically focused primarily on meeting and satisfying the customer's requirements. Here, the temporal focus is the present, and the image of the buyer is a demanding customer. Apparently, the participating companies in the Choi and Eboch's study would fall into this category. However, at least in theory, the supplier's main orientation can be elevated to being developmental. Here, the supplier is willing to take the initiative to make necessary changes and behave as a full-fledged partner in the buyer-supplier relationship. The focus in this case on the supplier's part is growing its business and relationship with the buying company, and the temporal focus is the future.

Choi and Eboch (1998) suggest that supplier compliance leads to a statistically significant impact on customer satisfaction, but the supplier's operational performance as affected by the compliance shows no statistical connection to customer satisfaction, as predicted by the institutional theory. What has not been predicted well by the institutional theory is the moderate connection between supplier compliance and supplier's operational performance. This particular result clarifies that institutional conformance is not necessarily decoupled from the activities of the technical core but rather is loosely coupled, meaning there may be some impact. Choi and Liker (1992) articulate how some of the mandates that come down from the corporate office can lead to "internalization" at the plant-level conformance. When this happens, it leads to internal pressure to act out the mandate at the worker level. Another example is the mandated implementation of radio frequency identification (RFID) technology (Barratt and Choi 2009). When decentralized business units under a large defense contractor were mandated to implement RFID technology by the U.S. Department of Defense, different business units responded differently by showing varied responses in terms of how much coupling they would allow between the institutional conformance at the administrative level and the operational activities at the technical core.

One strategy Toyota has used to drive closer coupling between the two is by engaging in *Gemba*, which means "go and see." When a supplier is pressed to implement statistical process control (SPC) on a process it has been operating successfully for many years without SPC, its institutional response is to implement the technology, compile the data, and ship it off to the customer, without really using the technology to affect the work at the technical core. However, when the buying company's representatives come to see how the implementation has been done, the supplier would now need to internalize the new technology and integrate it into their daily operational activities rather than merely placate and try to assuage their demanding customer (Choi and Behling 1997). From the supplier's perspective, it has many conflicting demands on its performance. For example, for worker safety practices, one customer (e.g., GM) has a specific requirement, and another (e.g., Ford) requests a different way. Even the government (e.g., OSHA) may require it differently. For the suppliers, their institutional environment is stratified (i.e., Fernandez-Giordano et al. 2022), and, in general, when they respond with changes at the administrative level, they gain market growth, whereas if they internalize and respond with changes at the technical core they enhance their business' operational performance (Shi et al. 2018).

Supplier-Supplier Relationships

Another important dyad in supply networks is the supplier-supplier relationship. Wu and Choi (2005) reference Asanuma (1985) as the first to articulate the importance of the supplier-supplier relationship. Some Japanese companies bring their suppliers together to collaborate on a joint project, while those same companies keep the suppliers away from one another to compete on a job. This competition exists when responding to a request for quotation (RFQ), and it can also occur when engaged in design work. Kamath and Liker (1994) explain how Japanese companies would request competing suppliers to send their engineers to compete on a design project side by side. Therefore, the relationship between suppliers matters because sometimes the buyer would want the suppliers to work together, as in a new product development project or to share production capacity; other times, the buyer would not want the suppliers to even talk to each other, especially when they are bidding on the same contract (Choi 2007). Therefore, how the suppliers work together or do not work together affects the buying firm.

Yet, many buying companies seem to assume the supplier would do what they are told to do. If they are told to work together, they would need to do so. Well, not exactly. Consider the following example. A large buying firm had been working with a plastic-molding supplier for over 10 years. A deep relationship would best characterize their business relationship. However, at some point, the buying company decided it needed a second plastic-molding supplier. After some effort, it selected a new supplier, and this supplier had more capacity and capability than the first supplier. So, the buying company involved the second supplier in design engineering and manufacturing. By the way, the buying company did not hide its new venture with the new supplier from its first supplier. The first supplier was watching all that was going on and was uncomfortable and even a little upset that the buying firm was giving the new supplier design work because this first supplier always wanted to be involved in the design. From the buying firm's perspective, everything was going well—it kept open communications. It had informed the first supplier what was going on, and it looked like it was building a good supplier relationship with the second supplier. However, once the buying company felt it had successfully onboarded the second supplier, it asked the first supplier to share certain information and help bring this new supplier up to speed. The first supplier resisted. When the buying firm asked the first supplier to send the parts to the second supplier, there were shipment delays and a lack of communication. In the meantime, the second supplier did not show much respect for the first supplier because it had more resources and the first supplier was a much smaller supplier. The second supplier felt that it should not have to go begging for information or cooperation. The new equipment the second supplier had acquired required the help of the first supplier, but the help never came. Besides, the parts from the first supplier never arrived on time. Consequently, the working relationship with the second supplier never really panned out as expected. In the end, the buying company had to sever

Table 3.1 Comparing Supplier-Supplier Relationships

	Competitive	Cooperative	Co-opetitive
Information about the other supplier	Objective	Subjective	Guarded
Time orientation	Short term	Long term	Varied
Dominant relationship focus	Self-centered	Trust based	Strategic interest based
Supplier switching cost for the buyer	Low	High	Moderate

Source: Adapted from Choi et al. 2002

the relationship with the second supplier and return to the first supplier with more business.

To manage business relationships between suppliers, we begin by understanding different types of supplier-supplier relationships. Choi et al. (2002) first proposed three types of supplier-supplier relationships—competitive, cooperative, and co-opetitive. Their basic characteristics are shown in Table 3.1. In a competitive supplier-supplier relationship, the two suppliers may know about each other and generally do not maintain a direct line of communication. Even if communication were to occur, it would happen on a short-term basis in a very focused context and, typically, under the auspices of the buying company. They do not engage in mutualistic behaviors toward each other, and their behaviors would tend to be self-centered. From the buyer's perspective, these suppliers are expendable and are evaluated mainly based on how well they respond to an RFQ or how quickly they respond to problems that emerge. For instance, a high-tech company has products with very short product life cycles. One type of supplier is substrate suppliers. With short product life cycles, the buyer cannot change these suppliers once the production process begins. For this reason, the buying company chooses two suppliers after a competitive bidding process. One supplier does not know who the other supplier is, but both suppliers are aware of the presence of the other company. They know if one of them falls behind in performance, it can potentially lose the business to the other supplier. So, like a race horse with its blinders on, they forge ahead knowing they are in competition.

In a cooperative supplier-supplier relationship, two suppliers cooperate for a shared purpose, either as directed by the buying company or on their own to solve a problem common to both. They may exchange improvement ideas or share production capacity and capability. They may even enter a joint venture project or organize a manufacturing network together. A large aircraft engine manufacturer had been downsizing its supply base and eventually succeeded in working with a smaller number of suppliers. The aftermath of this supply-base downsizing effort had a small number of suppliers that were retained and became the manufacturer's first-tier suppliers, while a large group of suppliers were discontinued by the buying company. To survive, those suppliers that were downsized came together and formed what they called a manufacturing network. Together, these suppliers were able to offer this engine manufacturer integrated, collective capacity and capability. The suppliers would cooperate when an RFQ came from the buying company. There was a lead supplier that put the quotation together by communicating with the other suppliers. If selected, they would then do the work together, pooling their resources. The suppliers were working together in a long-term and trusted relationship. Thus, it would be difficult for the buyer to replace one supplier with another because of the cooperative relationship they all operated under.

Co-opetition describes a relationship that is both cooperating and competing at the same time (Bengtsson and Kock 2000; Brandenburger and Nalebuff 1996). This type of relationship is in disequilibrium: both suppliers realize they are in competition, but they also know they have to share ideas and work together toward a common goal. A semiconductor company needed to have its suppliers collaborate to design capital equipment that tests microprocessors. The suppliers sent their engineers to participate in brainstorming sessions first. They were then given performance specifications to come up with a design collectively. The design work took several months, and once that was done, all suppliers that participated in the design were given the opportunity to submit their cost estimations for manufacturing the equipment. They knew they would be competing for the job in the end, and how they contributed to the design work would affect how the buyer would perceive them. While their engineers collaborated, all the suppliers at the company level would take a guarded stance on how they shared information with the other suppliers. Their collaboration would be project based with a predefined duration. The primary motivation for collaborating would be driven by the decision to bid on the manufacturing job eventually. From the buyer's perspective, it would prefer to have suppliers stay on the job, but if some were to drop out, that would not necessarily derail the project.

Among the three types of supplier-supplier relationships, the co-opetitive relationship has been proposed as instrumental in instilling resilience and overcoming disruptions in supply chains (Durach, Wiengarten, and Choi 2020). From the buying company's perspective, resilience is a multidimensional "capability of the firm to be alert, to adapt to, and quickly respond to changes brought by a supply chain disruption" (Ambulkar, Blackhurst, and Grawe 2015, p. 112). While resilience has been viewed as capability that a company would hold, Durach, Wiengarten, and Choi (2020) propose that the capability to withstand a disruption that comes through a supply chain does not have to lie inside the four walls of a company. It can be attained in conjunction with the first-tier suppliers that compete and cooperate simultaneously (Brandenburger and Nalebuff 1996). With the involvement of suppliers in a co-opetitive relationship, a company's capacity to withstand a supply chain disruption can reside across its boundaries involving suppliers. For instance, a corporate buyer can promote information flow across businesses and reduce information asymmetry (Wakolbinger and Cruz 2011). One of Toyota's suppliers, Aisin Seiki, which manufactures proportioning valves, had a fire and saw its production lines go down (Nishiguchi and Beaudet 1998; Dyer and Hatch 2006). To avert the disruption for Toyota, other suppliers came together in a co-opetitive effort. They made decisions to divide the work among themselves and to help make repairs to damaged production lines at Aisin Seiki.

Performance Implications of the Supplier-Supplier Relationship

Wu, Choi, and Rungtusanatham (2010) examine the supplier performance implications of supplier-supplier relationships. The focus is on the co-opetitive relationship between the suppliers. The data are collected from a large aerospace buying corporation and its suppliers using a survey research method. The buying company manufactures aircraft engines, avionics, and high-precision instruments. To ensure a co-opetitive relationship, the buying company's procurement managers were asked to name (1) two suppliers with similar production capability and (2) whether these two suppliers were currently supplying parts used for the same product. The first requirement was to ensure the two suppliers were competing, and the second was to allow cooperation between the suppliers. The survey data were collected from both the buyer and the pair of suppliers that met the two requirements. The supplier performance data and the buyer influence data were collected from the buying company, and the supplier-supplier co-opetition data were collected from the matching sets of two suppliers. After great difficulty, 43 matching sets of supplier-supplier data were compiled—the matching is first done at the buyer level and then at the supplier level (see Wu, Choi, and Rungtusanatham 2010 for more detail).

The first issue concerns the buying company's influence on the supplier-supplier relationship. The buyer has a visual of its relationship with the two suppliers, so it is not hard to ascertain that the buyer could influence the buyer-supplier relationship. However, the buyer does not have a direct visual of the supplier-supplier relationship because whatever relational dynamics the two suppliers may develop are entirely dependent on what unfolds there, that is, in the link once removed from the buyer (more on this in the next chapter on triads). Would two suppliers allow the buyer to influence how they work together? The results of the data analysis say yes. When the buyer directs the suppliers toward a co-opetitive relationship, the suppliers seem to oblige. However, supplier-supplier co-opetition is not associated with the supplier's performance. The data show a reasonable, although not very high, level of cooperation between competing suppliers but simply do not support the notion that supplier-supplier co-opetition is good for supplier performance. When the two competing suppliers are asked by the buyer to cooperate in a co-opetitive relationship, the two suppliers comply and make a concerted effort. However, it almost seems this extra effort they have to exert to cooperate with the other supplier may actually siphon resources to a point where it actually lowers their performance level. In support, the research, in fact, shows a negative relationship between co-opetitive relationships and supplier performance.

Alternatively, it may be that cooperation between competing suppliers occurs more on a case-by-case basis. Perhaps it is not something that can be generalized in the aggregate as the above survey research tries to do. To this end, Wu and Choi (2005) conducted a case study of eight supplier-supplier relationships and offered five archetypes of supplier-supplier relationships. Their case study captures the rich dynamics that take place between the suppliers when they are driven by the buying company to work together. There are performance implications for both the buyer and suppliers.

The supplier-supplier relationship archetype that Wu and Choi (2005) call "dog fighting" is closest to what we have referred to as the competitive supplier-supplier relationship. The suppliers have little to no interaction between them. They are not only intentionally kept away from each other but are also pitted against each other to compete on price and other terms. Another archetype called "networking" closely resembles the cooperative supplier-supplier relationship described above. In fact, this arrangement is used as an example when first introducing the concept of the cooperative supplier-supplier relationship in the preceding section. What is not mentioned, however, is that when the time comes to divide the job among the suppliers, they use the price as the decision criterion so that a sense of equity among the collaborating suppliers is perceived. The suppliers gathered once a month to share their experiences with the buying company and exchange industry information in terms of potential new job opportunities.

Table 3.2 offers an overview of performance implications for both the buyer and suppliers. In the left column, we have listed the archetypes progressing from the competitive supplier-supplier relationship of dog fighting to the cooperative supplier-supplier relationship of networking. The three archetypes in between are what we refer to as the co-opetitive supplier-supplier relationship. On the continuum going from competitive to cooperative, they are conflicting, contracting, and transacting archetypes.

Under the "conflicting" archetype, both suppliers are requested by the buyer to work together to share production capacity. However, one supplier

Table 3.2 Summary of Performance Implications

Archetype	Buyer Performance Implication	Supplier Performance Implication
Dog fighting	Lower purchasing price Lower supply risk	Reduced profit margins
Conflicting	Reduction in supply management costs	One supplier loses the buyer's goodwill, and the other gains its favor
Contracting	Integrated services from one supplier	One supplier learning from the other supplier
Transacting	Shorter product lead times Higher product quality New revenue sources	Attainment of market information One supplier gains knowledge about the buyer from the other supplier
Networking	Lower purchasing costs Better quality Flexible supplier capacity	Shared resources and learning More leverage toward the buyer

Source: Adapted from Wu and Choi 2005

is enthusiastic, while the other is cool to the idea. This supplier behaved hesitantly when the time came to share information. In contrast, the other supplier was much more accommodating to the buyer's requests and was ready to come forth with its internal operational information. The two suppliers had intermittent meetings, and their relationship seemed to be in a permanent state of unsettledness as if they were in limbo.

The "contracting" archetype involves two suppliers working for the same buyer, except one supplier is asked to send its products to the other supplier. Two suppliers were chosen for the job of supplying 10 workstations that would then be installed into an assembly line. One supplier was the incumbent supplier and was given the job for nine workstations, and a new supplier was chosen for one workstation. The new supplier was instructed to send its workstation to the incumbent supplier for further integration. This arrangement between the two suppliers seemed to work fine. The underlying discontent in the incumbent supplier was that by working with the new supplier, it feared that it was training a competitor that could potentially take over its business. Another example comes from how Apple manages its suppliers. We all have mobile phones and on the phone are camera lenses, which have become an important feature. In the Apple mobile phone supply network, Largan Precision in Taiwan supplies camera lenses to Foxconn in Shenzhen, China, which assembles Apple phones. Largan and Foxconn both have a contractual agreement with Apple, but Largan supplies the camera parts to Foxconn (more on Apple's supply chain management on extended supply chains when we discuss supply chain make vs. supply chain buy in Chapter 6).

The two suppliers in the "transacting" archetype regard each other as peers working together to meet the requirements of their buyer with an understanding that there will be equitable exchanges and the two companies will be given the same chance to win the contracts. In the case describing this relationship, the engineers from both suppliers frequently called each other and engaged in intense brainstorming. They were aware that by doing so they would gain additional market knowledge and a better understanding of the buyer. Then, when the buyer called for bids, they would respond independently to vie for the same contract. Both suppliers accepted this arrangement, knowing that they both would get the same opportunity and the winner would be chosen objectively.

The buyer has strategic intent on putting two suppliers into particular relational arrangements—competitive, cooperative, and various shades of co-opetitive. It appears the buying company is successful in gaining specific results. In Wu and Choi's (2005) study, they find that by engaging the suppliers to work together, one buyer was able to reduce supply lead time and improve product quality and cost. Another buyer was able to offload the task of new supplier onboarding to an incumbent supplier. Another buyer was able to tap into the engineering capability of both suppliers to develop a new product. However, there were also instances where one of the two suppliers chose to push back and hampered the buyer's plan to create a turnkey operation from a supplier. Different suppliers seemed to be motivated by different things (i.e., assembly work, new technology, etc.), and on occasion, the buyer missed such an underlying agenda at the supplier end.

The suppliers in various forms of supplier-supplier relationships seemed to gain knowledge about the buying company through the other supplier. One supplier learned about the business procedures and practices of the buyer by working with another supplier that worked for the same buyer. Working with another supplier in a supplier-supplier relationship was often an opportunity for development—one supplier learned how to behave more professionally by working with another supplier. When forced to work together, each supplier can also end up gaining more knowledge about industry trends or technology development. Without explicitly colluding, the suppliers shared knowledge about the size of the buyer's business and how each could grow with the buyer. Of course, there were negative consequences. For instance, by working with another supplier, one supplier became afraid it could lose its future business to this other supplier. The supplier also could potentially develop a negative relationship with the buyer if it were not to engage the other supplier in a collaborative project. This supplier then felt like it was caught between a rock and a hard place. Thus, a supplier-supplier relationship can create a dilemma for at least one of the two suppliers. The end game for some suppliers was not a desirable one because they knew in the end, if they were to cooperate, that would just lead to more competition and a reduction in their profit margins.

From the study by Wu, Choi, and Rungtusanatham (2010), it is clear that the buyer can influence the supplier-supplier relationship—the link once removed in the triad of buyer-supplier-supplier. What is puzzling is that cooperation between two competing suppliers does not increase their collective supplier performance. The answer to this puzzle is in part offered in the case study conducted by Wu and Choi (2005). The performance implications of the supplier-supplier relationship should occur more on a project level that has clear boundaries with respect to time and scope than on an overall supplier performance that is affected by a lot of other external factors.

We have discussed in this chapter the dynamics of buyer-supplier relationships and supplier-supplier relationships. Both of these business relationships take place at the dyadic level involving two nodes and one link. However, we also saw how the buyer-supplier relationship types might be updated if we were to consider how these nodes (i.e., suppliers) are embedded in their extended ties. In the same way, toward the end of the discussion involving the supplier-supplier relationship, it became apparent that considering the supplier-supplier relationship does not make sense unless it is in the context of the buying company. The supplier-supplier relationship makes sense only when we consider it as embedded in a common buyer. That brings us to the realm of triads which we will cover in the next chapter.

Key points

- The buyer-supplier relationship is typically categorized as cooperative and competitive, where a cooperative relationship is characterized by close communications and high trust, and a competitive relationship is characterized by unilateral cost concessions.
- Network scholars give us strong-tie and weak-tie relationships with network implications in that a node in the relationship (i.e., supplier) is considered embedded in its extended network ties.
- The dimension of strong-tie and weak-tie relationships is orthogonal to the dimension of competitive and cooperative business relationships. When we combine them, we get four new, practically relevant buyer-supplier relationship types—deep, sticky, transient, and gracious.
- When demanded, the supplier may conform to the buyer's requirements at the administrative level but shield its operations at the technical core from these requirements.
- Relationships between suppliers (i.e., supplier-supplier relationship) matter to the buying company because it wants them to cooperate sometimes, and other times it wants them to compete for business.
- Three types of supplier-supplier relationships have been proposed—cooperative, competitive, and co-opetitive. The co-opetitive relationship involves competing and cooperating simultaneously.
- A cooperative relationship between two competing suppliers does not increase the collective performance of the two suppliers. Instead, performance gains from supplier-supplier relationships happen in the project-based context with a bounded timeline and scope.

4

Triads in Supply Networks

A man and a woman meet and fall in love. When that happens, it is something special. Structurally, they become a dyad, and this dyad is identified by the link that represents a bond we call love. Soon, they have a baby, and the dyad becomes a triad (see the left-side diagram in Figure 4.1). This triad consists of three nodes and three links. As anyone that has had a baby would attest, things get much more complicated and interesting when the baby arrives. Complexity increases many folds. We add just one more node to a dyad to form a triad, but, in a triad, the complexity we have to contend with takes a quantum leap. With three nodes and three links, we have interactions between each node and all three links and between each of these three links and the other two links. In a dyad, a man and a woman have one link to contend with, like how much they love and care for each other. In a triad with the baby, all of a sudden, things get messy. Georg Simmel (1950), a German sociologist and philosopher, uses marriages as an illustrative context to explicate the intricacies of relational dynamics in a triad. We will discuss his work further throughout this chapter, especially when we get to the topic of balance theory.

I remember when we had our first son. Both my wife and I were very happy. Then, while we were still on emotional high, certain things began to happen. I noticed my wife was totally absorbed with taking care of the baby, and she paid a lot less attention to me. That was fine, except I could not help but remember how things were between us. Then, I realized this child was affecting the link between my wife and me. From the child's vantage point, this link was the *link once removed* because he did not have a direct visual of this link between me and his mother, my wife. Through his personality and his behaviors, he affected my wife and me as nodes, and he also affected the links between him and his father and him and his mother, as well as the link between me and my wife—the link once removed. In addition, maybe the link between my wife and the child was affecting the link between me and his mother, my wife. This was just from my perspective. I am sure there would be more stories to tell from my wife's perspective and the child's perspective.

The Nature of Supply Networks. Thomas Y. Choi, Oxford University Press. © Thomas Y. Choi 2023.
DOI: 10.1093/oso/9780197673249.003.0004

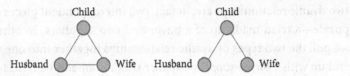

Figure 4.1 Family Triads

And it gets even more interesting. There was another fascinating network dynamic that we experienced. Like most young couples, we had quarrels, and sometimes we stopped talking to each other. That created a "structural hole" (Burt 1995, 2000a) between me and my wife. The structural hole refers to the blank space between the husband and wife, as shown on the right side in Figure 4.1. The concept of a structural hole is unique to networks, and it is related to power. Typically, we associate power with resources. When someone has the resources we need, that person has power over us. In networks, things are different. Certain structural features such as the structural hole offer power. The node sitting on a structural hole is called a bridge, or *tertius gaudens*—the third that profits (Burt 1995). When a husband and wife do not talk to each other but only talk through the child, who has power? Of course, the child. Why? Because he sits on the structural hole, and whether he likes it or not, he has power over his mom and dad so long as this structural hole persists. In networks, we come across such interesting phenomena, and the smallest unit of a network where we can observe such network dynamics is in a triad (Choi and Wu 2009b, 2009a). By the way, the triad on the left side in Figure 4.1 is called transitive (i.e., all nodes are connected), and the triad on the right side is called intransitive (i.e., there is a break in the triad). We will come back to this point again as we proceed with this chapter.

Smallest Unit of a Network

According to Choi and Wu (2009b), "to fully interpret the relational behavior of a firm, we need invariably to look beyond the dyad for answers. As the next logical step after having studied dyadic buyer-supplier relationships for several decades, a *triadic* relationship consideration becomes imperative to further understand the buyer-supplier dynamics in supply networks" (p. 264).

In the previous chapter, we discussed the buyer-supplier and supplier-supplier relationships in the dyad. In this chapter, it is posited that these two dyadic relationships are, in fact, two interdependent pieces of the same puzzle—a triad made up of a buyer and two suppliers. In other words, if we pull the two types of dyadic relationships together into one context, we end up with a *buyer-supplier-supplier* triad. Framed in a triad together, we suddenly realize that the supplier-supplier relationship makes sense only if we consider it with the buyer—because without the buyer, the supplier-supplier relationship would not make sense. And, in a network, we are able to study how a link affects another link and how a node affects a link once removed. The smallest unit where we are able to examine those issues is a triad. As such, we study how a buyer-supplier relationship may affect the supplier-supplier relationship and how the buyer may affect the supplier-supplier relationship.

As shown in Figure 4.2, we have a triad with three nodes and three links. In such a transitive triad, we can see how the interactions between nodes, between links, and between nodes and links get tangled. For instance, we see how a node may affect a link once removed (i.e., A affecting BC) and how a link may affect another link (i.e., AB affecting AC).

According to our research (Choi and Wu 2009c), Georg Simmel (1950) is the first to conceptualize such relational dynamics in a triad and differentiate the triads from dyads. Caplow (1956, 1959) has extended his work. In a book entitled *Two Against One: Coalitions in Triads*, Caplow (1968) uses the main characters in *Hamlet* to explain the dynamics in a triad involving Hamlet; Gertrude, his mother; and Claudius, his uncle and the murderer of his father. The following excerpt is uttered by Gertrude. Her words reflect intense pain and anguish.

> O Hamlet, speak no more:
> Thou turn'st mine eyes into my very soul;
> And there I see such black and grained spots
> As will not leave their tinct.

The tragedy of Hamlet unfolds when his uncle, Claudius, murders his father. Without knowing what happened, his mother, Gertrude, marries Claudius. The couple are now king and queen of Denmark. Hamlet knows the truth and feigns insanity. In network terms, this relational condition gives us a dyad and an isolate. Suppose, in Figure 4.2, Hamlet is A without AB and AC, as an isolate. B is Gertrude and C is Claudius. They make up the dyad with B and C as nodes and BC as the link called marriage.

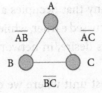

Figure 4.2 Nodes and Links in a Triad

On the surface, life appears simple—we have a king and a queen as a dyad ruling the land, and, off to the side, this person broken over the death of his father doing his crazy things as an isolate. Then, it gets messy when Hamlet confronts his mother, Gertrude, with the truth. The words in quotes above are then uttered. The plot thickens. A dyad and an isolate have now become a triad. Hamlet, Gertrude, and Claudius as nodes are now all connected. Each node is affecting the other two nodes, and each node affects all three links (i.e., A is affecting AB, AC, and BC). For Hamlet, the link between Gertrude and Claudius (i.e., BC) is the link once removed. He does not have a direct visual of the link between Gertrude and Claudius, but he has affected it profoundly. Claudius tries to kill Hamlet, Gertrude comes to Hamlet's aid, and Hamlet wants to avenge the murder of his father. Life would never be the same for all concerned. As we can see, in a triad, relationships get tangled, and we begin to deal with network dynamics of increasing complexity.

These dynamics have been applied beyond the interactions among individuals to the interplay between organizations and even among countries. Starting with Simmel (1950) and other scholars that wrote about Simmel and his work (Caplow 1959, 1968; Mills 1954, 1958), the triadic dynamics have been applied to large social entities such as countries. Political scientists have evaluated, for example, the U.S.-China relationship in the context of other third countries such as Singapore, South Korea, or Australia (Park and Tan 2018; Schreer 2019). For us, of course, the level of analysis we would be interested in is at the business-to-business level across the supply networks. In a *buyer-supplier-supplier* triad, two suppliers may operate in the same tier (e.g., the first tier to the buyer) or different tiers (e.g., one in the first tier and the other in the second tier). These different structural arrangements accompany different network dynamics. For instance, in the former, the buying company is the bridge between the two suppliers. In the latter, the supplier in the first tier operates as the bridge between the buyer and the supplier in the second tier. In networks, this bridge is the *tertius gaudens* (i.e., the third that profits). A company that occupies a bridge position garners leverage over the others. As discussed earlier, while power is typically associated with having resources others desire, in networks, power may be associated with the structural position.

A triad is also the smallest unit where we can examine how a network behaves as a complex adaptive system (Choi and Wu 2009a). As discussed in the previous chapter, a buyer-supplier relationship is established when a buying company commits to a buy decision and goes out to the market to seek available options. Upon finding a supplier, the two companies establish a contract that specifies the work expectations and payment terms. In this regard, the buyer-supplier business relationship is quite conducive to the concept of "control." Both parties are bound by the contractual terms, and, in that process, the buyer may conduct, for instance, a supplier performance evaluation and incoming shipment inspection. However, when we add one more node and turn this dyad into a triad (e.g., buyer-supplier-supplier), what happens in the link once removed entails an "emergent" process. While it is true the buying company can influence the relationship between the two suppliers in the triad (Wu, Choi, and Rungtusanatham 2010), it is also true, in many instances, the suppliers engage in behaviors contrary to the buyer's expectations. For example, the suppliers may refuse the buyer's request to work together (Wu and Choi 2005). Two third-party logistics (3PL) companies working for the same buyer refused to communicate with each other to do capacity sharing. In other words, triads are the smallest network structure where we can begin to observe how realities unfold in an emergent way—the hallmark of a complex adaptive system. We will discuss more on control and emergence in Chapter 8 on supply networks as a complex adaptive system.

As such, how a node affects a link once removed is an important network trait. In addition, how a link affects another link is also a quintessential network characteristic. In particular, triads offer an excellent context in which to study the effects one link has on another, not in how one link affects another link in an isolated way but how links in a triad affect one another in a system of relationships. Such dynamics are captured in balance theory (Caplow 1956, 1959, 1968; Mills 1954, 1958; Simmel 1950). Balance theory describes the balanced states and unbalanced states of relationships in triads. Its basic tenet is that unbalanced states tend to evolve toward a balanced state (Cartwright and Harary 1956; Heider 1958).

Balance Theory and the Buyer-Supplier-Supplier Triad

Two topics covered in the preceding chapter were the buyer-supplier relationship and the supplier-supplier relationship. If we pull them together, we have a *buyer-supplier-supplier* triad. Structurally, we have a triad as shown in Figure 4.2, with A as a buyer, B and C as suppliers, AB and AC as buyer-supplier relationships, and BC as the supplier-supplier relationship. This triad is a microcosm of the buying company and its supply base. We will discuss in-depth how a buying company manages its supply base in the next chapter, Chapter 5, on supply base management.

For now, suppose a corporate buyer is working with two suppliers from its supply base in a dual-sourcing arrangement or what Dubois and Fredriksson (2008) call "triadic sourcing." Instead of dealing with each supplier separately and pitting them against each other in competition as in a typical dual-sourcing situation, these authors promote the idea of closely intertwined business relationships among all three nodes, including the two suppliers. The authors highlight "a shift in the focal unit of analysis from two dyads handled separately to one triad consisting of three connected relationships" (p. 171). To illustrate, they present a triad involving Volvo, JCI, and Lear. Volvo is the auto manufacturer purchasing car seats from JCI and Lear. Volvo has orchestrated a highly dependent and intertwined relationship between its two car seat suppliers, JCI and Lear. From Volvo's perspective, these two suppliers are considered a package deal when discussing car seat sourcing. Both suppliers manufacture the car seats for two platforms that Volvo uses to build cars. JCI focuses on making the front seats while both suppliers make the rear seats. The two suppliers have a reciprocal relationship when it comes to assembling car seats—they assemble front and rear seats for each other. Such a triad would be considered in a balanced state, using the term from balance theory, with all three links in the triad reflecting a positive relationship. This balanced state is akin to a commonly known phrase, a friend of a friend is my friend.

Of course, then, there is another phrase, an enemy of an enemy is my friend. In this case, among the three, two links are negative, and one link is positive. This is also a balanced state. One example many of us are familiar with comes from the story of Harry Potter. Harry grew up living with his aunt and uncle. As a married couple, they share a positive link, while they have a common enemy in Harry. In this triad, we have one positive and two negative links. Unfortunately for poor Harry, this triad is balanced and stable. There are many other combinations of relationships in the triad in terms of positive and negative associations. We shall consider them and their implications for supply chain management.

Balance theory has its roots in Simmel (1950) and others that have followed his work (Cartwright and Harary 1956; Heider 1958; Hummon and Doreian 2003). The ideas were first applied in behavioral psychology to understand the triadic interpersonal relationships and social processes in groups (Alessio 1990; Curry and Emerson 1970; Gimeno 1999; Litwak and Meyer 1966; Madhavan and Gnyawali 2004; Newcomb 1961, 1981; Osgood and Tannenbaum 1955; Rodrigues 1967; Rodrigues and Coleta 1983).

To the best of our knowledge, Choi and Wu (2009c) are the first to apply it to supply chain management. By bringing the buyer-supplier relationship and supplier-supplier relationship into a triad and applying the balance theory, we attempt to take a step toward unearthing the internal relational dynamics of supply networks. We offer three observations that support adopting balance theory to study buyer-supplier-supplier triads. One, balance theory appears as the only theory available in an academic body of literature that explicitly addresses triads. Two, while it is true that the theory was originally developed for individual-level dynamics, management scholars have been applying it to collective social groups and organizations. Again, we are considering it at the company level. Three, balance theory describes the inter-company relationships similar to how the buyer-supplier relationship literature describes the relationship—competitive vs. cooperative or adversarial vs. collaborative. In both, the relationship is either a positive one or a negative one. And that is exactly how the balance theory describes the positive or negative relationship.

A plus (+) sign signifies a positive, voice-based relationship built on mutual trust and commitment. A minus (-) sign represents a negative, exit-based relationship coming from distrust and a sense of inequity between the buyer and supplier or between two suppliers. According to balance theory, a triad is balanced if all three links show a + sign, or one shows a + sign while the other two show a minus sign. In contrast, a triad is unbalanced if all three links show a - sign or one shows a - sign while the other two show a + sign. Given the transitive nature of the triad, if the product of all three signs comes out as a +, then the triad is balanced (i.e., $+ * + * + = +$ or $+ * - * - = +$). If the product of all three signs comes out as a -, then the triad is unbalanced (i.e., $+ * + * - = -$ or $- * - * - = -$).

An important tenet in the context of balance theory is that an unbalanced state tends to evolve toward a balanced state over time (Anderson 1975; Morrissette 1958; Newcomb 1961; Rodrigues 1967). Cartwright and Harary (1956) characterize this tenet in their discussion of the "structural theorem," which articulates that nodes in an unbalanced state would try to address the conditions that cause unbalance (i.e., inequity or mistrust) until the triad becomes balanced. In other words, nodes in an unbalanced triad can turn a + link into a − link to cause the triad to become balanced. Either way, a new relationship arrangement is created sequentially (Heider 1958), and we can use this theorem to predict potential arrangements that may come out of the particular state of an unbalanced triad. The underlying logic is akin to the cognitive dissonance theory (Festinger 2001; Scott 1963; Streufert and Streufert 1978) in that when a person sees themselves behaving inconsistently with their self-perception, that translates into cognitive dissonance. Then, that person will adjust either the behavior or self-perception to minimize the cognitive dissonance. The goal is to reach consonance or balance when the present state is in dissonance or unbalance.

Figure 4.3 lines up three balanced states in buyer-supplier-supplier relationships. A balanced state offers structurally stable relationships among the three companies in the triad. The state of relational balance is in equilibrium, regardless of how each organization may view the other businesses and its relationships with them. For instance, the buyer in the middle triad may not enjoy having adversarial relationships shown with a minus sign with both suppliers. However, those negative relationships have been established over the course of time, and unless something drastic happens, they are there to stay. Nonetheless, it is possible that the buyer may put in a concerted effort to improve its relationship with one of the two suppliers. If and when that happens, we end up with a triad with two pluses and one minus, which is an unbalanced state. At that point, unless the buyer diligently works to improve the relationship with the other supplier and change that into a plus relationship so that the triad becomes one on the left, the unbalanced state will want

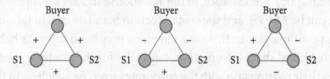

Figure 4.3 Balanced States in Buyer-Supplier-Supplier Relationships

to migrate toward one of the other two balanced states—the relationship the buyer has worked hard to improve may revert to a minus or the relationship between two suppliers may become one with a minus sign. We shall now review each balanced state and consider its managerial implications.

In the first balanced state with all plus links, the buyer has a cooperative relationship with both suppliers, and these two suppliers also share a cooperative relationship. This type of business relationship has been observed between Toyota and its suppliers. For example, in North America, Toyota leads a supplier association called Bluegrass Automotive Manufacturing Association (BAMA), through which Toyota suppliers meet to share information and learn from each other. Toyota leads by creating a culture of open communications while creating the norms to prevent opportunistic behaviors. As suppliers meet with each other over the course of multiple years, they develop trust between them (Provan 1993). It is also found in a practice called "parallel sourcing" (Richardson 1993; Richardson and Roumasset 1995), in which the corporate buyer divvies up the work among multiple suppliers with similar capabilities and asks them to share technical information. The buyer maintains a cooperative relationship with all suppliers, and these suppliers also have cooperative relationships with each other because they do not compete head-on for the same job. For instance, Toyota can use two tire companies to supply tires for different automobile models. In this arrangement, the two suppliers do not compete directly and would be more willing to share technical information that each can benefit from.

While in the first balanced state the buyer plays the role of a mediator (Simmel 1950) with the suppliers with whom it shares a positive relationship, the second balanced state in Figure 4.3 shows the buyer having adversarial relationships with both suppliers. The two suppliers, in essence, share a common enemy, which equilibrates into a cooperative business relationship between them. Such a relationship arrangement is often observed when the corporate buyer unilaterally initiates cost-reduction mandates on its suppliers that cut into what small profit margin there is for the suppliers (Stallkamp 2005). For instance, in the automotive industry, a supplier's profit margin can be 2 to 3%, and the cost reduction mandate can, in fact, be larger than its profit margin. In this case, suppliers may band together behind the buyer's back and share information, especially for those whose relationship predates their relationship with the corporate buyer. As suppliers in the same industry, they may have similar product lines and production technologies, and their business ties may have developed over the years through industry associations or personal networking. As such, they are aware their business relationship must tread carefully because any type of joint action can be construed as a collusion and may be interpreted as being unfair business practices against the corporate buyer (Baker and Faulkner 1993).

The third balanced state captures a buying company having a cooperative relationship with one supplier but an adversarial relationship with another. In a balanced state, such a bifurcated buyer's stance may cause the two suppliers to inevitably establish a hostile relationship. This relationship arrangement demonstrates the futility of a buying company having inconsistent relational postures with its suppliers and yet demanding that the two suppliers work together. Wu and Choi (2005) offer an example where the buying firm drives two suppliers to cooperate—an incumbent supplier and a new supplier the buying firm is trying to bring on board. In this delicate context, the buying firm unfortunately gives no heed to the fact that it is treating the two suppliers with partiality, and the incumbent supplier, receiving the brunt end of the stick, is harboring resentment toward both the buying firm and the other supplier. From the buying firm's perspective, it is merely trying to build a new relationship with the favored supplier, and it is within its right to ask the incumbent supplier to cooperate with the new supplier. However, from the incumbent supplier's perspective, the buying firm is partial and inequitable (Hatfield, Walster, and Berscheid 1978). It has been working for the buying firm faithfully, yet it realizes how a new supplier is being treated with a more favorable contract and is receiving expertise from the buying firm. If the buying firm asks the two suppliers to work together on a joint project, it is unlikely to see that request materialize. It may never know that lack of collaboration between the two suppliers originates from its varied treatment.

As discussed above, an unbalanced state tends to migrate toward one of the balanced states. Any one of the three links in an unbalanced triad can flip and become a balanced state. The first unbalanced state in Figure 4.4 shows the buying company having a positive relationship with both suppliers and the two suppliers maintaining an antagonistic stance toward each other. At a casual glance, this relational arrangement appears favorable to the buyer. Having a cooperative relationship with two competing suppliers with an adversarial relationship may bring obvious benefits to the buying company, especially during a competitive bidding situation. However, if the balance theory holds, this unbalanced state is transient and would not last long. If so,

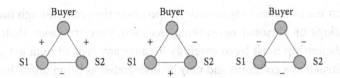

Figure 4.4 Unbalanced States in Buyer-Supplier-Supplier Relationships

the next favorable outcome may be for the buyer to work on improving the working relationship between the two suppliers so they can work together collaboratively. For example, the buyer could create a joint task program to bring the two suppliers together in collaboration (Ettlie and Pavlou 2006; Johnson et al. 1981). As long as the buyer treats both suppliers fairly and has good working relationships, it is in an excellent position to instill a positive business relationship between the suppliers. However, if the buyer fails to do so and the supplier's adversarial position between them prevails, then there is only one other balanced state that this unbalanced state could move toward. That is the third balanced state depicted in Figure 4.4. Unless the buying company succeeds in improving the relationship between the two suppliers, alas, one of the buyer's relationships with a supplier would deteriorate into a negative one.

The second unbalanced state describes a triad in which the two suppliers have a cooperative business relationship while one supplier (S1) maintains a cooperative relationship with the buying company and the other supplier (S2) does not. This supplier may have gone through a series of contractual disputes or performance problems that both the supplier and buyer argue were caused by the other. To resolve the tension with S2, the buying company may turn to S1 for mediation, given its cooperative relationship with S2. If so, that actually puts S1 in an advantageous position (Caplow 1956, 1959, 1968; Simmel 1950). If S1 is successful, then this unbalanced triad would become the first balanced triad depicted in Figure 4.3 with all plus signs. S2 may also recognize how S1 benefits from its cooperative relationship with the buyer and it is then motivated to improve the relationship with the buying company. In contrast, on the strength of the positive relationship it has with S2, S1 may conclude and side with S2 that the buying company has unfairly treated S2. Then, it is S1's relationship with the buyer that will deteriorate. If that happens, the current unbalanced triad will become the middle-balanced triad shown in Figure 4.3. It is not unusual for small suppliers to form a coalition against a powerful yet badly behaving buyer.

One remaining unbalanced state shows all links with a negative relationship. This relational arrangement is dysfunctional and transitory (Caplow 1968). The buying company can mistreat and mislead its suppliers with relentless cost-reduction mandates as happened in the aerospace industry. Rossetti and Choi (2005) describe the misapplication of strategic supply management in which some buying companies in the aerospace industry set up long-term contracts with their suppliers and then subjected them to unilateral cost-cutting initiatives. They liken this relational state to a bad marriage in which both parties are joined at the hip for the long haul, yet they maintain an adversarial posture toward each other. To survive, the suppliers moved into the lucrative after-sales market as a covert competitor to their customer—the buying company who owned the intellectual property on the parts they were manufacturing. The suppliers did not get along because they were all out there to fend for themselves. Of course, this unbalanced state may deteriorate to a point where the triad disintegrates. However, as long as all three companies need one another to stay in business, this unbalanced state will evolve into one of the balanced states. In the case of the aerospace industry, as recounted by Rossetti and Choi (2005), it is likely that suppliers may develop a cooperative business relationship between themselves, with the buying company continuing with its cost-reduction pressures. It would then turn into the balanced state shown in the middle triad in Figure 4.3. It would also be possible for the buyer to change its strategy and build a cooperative relationship with both suppliers, which would then be another unbalanced state. Depending on what occurs subsequently, one would observe various potential outcomes. Regardless, for the unbalanced triad with all negative signs, two suppliers coming together in a cooperative relationship seems to be the path of least resistance. Other combinations appear to require more corporate resources from the buying company and may take longer to unfold.

Bridge and Structural Hole

A bridge refers to the node that connects two otherwise isolated nodes. Such isolation can occur between two groups of nodes with one single node connecting the two groups. The node that connects the two groups is in the position of a bridge. The structural characteristic representing such isolation, either between two nodes or two groups of nodes, is called the structural hole.

Figure 4.5 Bridge and Structural Hole

As shown in Figure 4.5, a structural hole refers to the empty space between two disconnected nodes (Ahuja 2000; Burt 1995, 2000a, 2002; Gargiulo and Benassi 2000; Gulati, Nohria, and Zaheer 2000; Hansen 1999; Tsai 2002). A bridge is a node that sits on this structural hole—it acts as a bridge between two otherwise isolated nodes or groups of nodes. It acts as a go-between or information gatekeeper. As previously noted, this position gives bridge leverage over disconnected nodes. According to (Burt 1995), a structural hole "creates a competitive advantage for an individual whose relationships span the holes" (p. 6).

This particular triad with three nodes and two links is, therefore, considered a special type of triad—a triad with a structural hole. And it frequently happens in supply networks. In dual sourcing, for instance, the buyer works with two competing suppliers with no direct ties (Fujimoto 1999; Kamath and Liker 1994; McMillan 1990). The buyer keeps the two suppliers away from each other for competitive purposes, often by implementing a policy that prevents disclosing to the supplier the identity of its counterpart. Each supplier may be aware of the presence of another supplier, but the structural hole is maintained so that each supplier focuses on its own work without being able to communicate or coordinate directly with the other supplier (i.e., Burt 1995).

The buyer as a bridge adopts the role of a tertius—the third node that sits on the structural hole. This idea was first proposed by Simmel (1950) and was articulated into a theoretical concept in social networks much later by Burt (1995, 2000a, 2002). We need to note that the state of a structural hole is "neither balanced nor unbalanced" (Wasserman and Faust 1994, p. 227). It can perhaps best be described as an indeterminate state where two disconnected nodes (i.e., suppliers) are under pressure without a sense of stable equilibrium. Imagine a situation where two suppliers are participating in competitive bidding—there is a structural hole between them, and they are in limbo as to whether they might win the bid and get the contract from the buyer.

Simply, there is tension in the triad with a structural hole. According to Burt (1995), "no tension, no tertius" (p. 32).

The literature informs us that a bridge sitting on a structural hole can play the role of either a *tertius gaudens* or a *tertius iungens*. As a tertius gaudens, or the third that profits (Simmel 1950), the bridge can enjoy information arbitrage in the triad. The bridge may consciously exploit unfamiliarity or competition between the two disconnected nodes. As a tertius iungens, or the third that joins (Obstfeld 2005), the bridge focuses more on channeling information rather than leveraging information. The bridge, as a tertius iungens, actively engages in information transfer or facilitates coordination between the two disconnected entities (Obstfeld 2005; Obstfeld, Borgatti, and Davis 2014). The underlying motivation for the tertius gaudens is to leverage and profit, while the underlying motivation for the tertius iungens is to channel and coordinate.

Choi and Wu (2009c) offer three combinations of relational arrangements in the triads with a structural hole, as shown in Figure 4.6. In reality, the buying company as a bridge would likely be a bit of a tertius gaudens and a tertius iungens. However, there may be predominant behavioral tendencies depending on how business relationships are structured with the two suppliers in the triad. The one on the left with two plus signs would likely involve the buyer as a tertius iungens, whereas the one on the right with two minus signs would likely see the buyer predominantly behaving as a tertius gaudens. The middle one would have the buyer behaving in some combination of both tertius iungens and tertius gaudens.

The one on the left side shows the buyer as a bridge connected to two suppliers with whom it has a cooperative business relationship. The buyer is in a good position to coordinate activities between the two suppliers and harness ideas from the suppliers. Like an entrepreneur discovering a market niche, the buyer as a bridge may recognize the complementary capabilities (i.e., engineering expertise) the suppliers garner and move in to take advantage of that opportunity (Burt 1995; Simmel 1950). For instance, one supplier

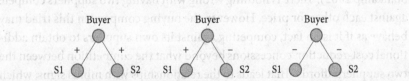

Figure 4.6 Triads with Structural Hole

may be good at value engineering that can help reduce costs while keeping the functionality of the product at the same level. The other supplier may be good at design engineering with lots of fresh ideas to improve the features of the product. In such a situation, the buying company may act as a knowledge broker (Burt 1995) to coordinate the new product development activities. Ultimately, the buyer would want to harness the engineering capabilities of both suppliers, picking and choosing what it wants to use and wants to discard. In that process, the buying company would likely have to selectively channel bits and pieces of the ideas from one supplier to the other to elevate the design activities toward the target.

The middle triad with a structural hole in Figure 4.6 shows the buyer's cooperative relationship with S1 while having an adversarial relationship with S2. Rossetti and Choi (2005) report a practice used by some buying firms where the buying firm takes the design blueprint done by one supplier (i.e., S2) as part of the bidding process and hands it to another supplier (S1) without the permission of that supplier (S2) because the other supplier (S1) can do the manufacturing more cheaply. This type of buyer practice would likely lead to an adversarial relationship with S2 because the supplier knows it is being exploited unfairly. Unlike the first triadic state with a structural hole where the buying firm has a positive relationship with both suppliers, here, the buying firm clearly favors one supplier over the other. The buying firm, on the one hand, is channeling information from S2 to S1. On the other hand, it is clearly taking advantage of its bridge position to profit, albeit unfairly. Even though it may have a sense of inequity, S2 may be stuck in this arrangement if it is dependent on the buying firm for business.

The triad with a structural hole where the buying company has adversarial relationships with both suppliers is shown on the right side in Figure 4.6. The buyer's relentless drive to cut costs from its suppliers often leads to antagonism from suppliers. The buyer plays one supplier against another, with the suppliers not even knowing who the other supplier it is competing against. The supplier often has no choice but to accept cost-reduction mandates when the buyer threatens it with contract termination (Rossetti and Choi 2005; Stallkamp 2005). There is nothing wrong with having two suppliers compete against each other for price. However, the buying company in this triad may behave as if it is, in fact, competing against its own suppliers to obtain additional cost-reduction concessions beyond what the competition between the two suppliers affords. That leads to the relationships with minus signs, which signifies the buying company behaving essentially as one that profits from one supplier not knowing the other across the structural hole.

Utility of Triads in Supply Networks

We now address how triads may manifest in actual supply networks. We will first discuss how a triadic consideration can offer additional ways to overcome the agency problem that is usually confined in a dyadic context. The buying company is the principal, and the supplier is its agent. Once we add the third node to a dyad, this new node can offer additional ways to overcome the agency problem. Building on the concepts of tertius gaudens and tertius iungens, I propose *tertius adiuvans* as a new concept to refer to the third that helps. One interesting aspect of tertius adiuvans is that this third does not have to be a fully willing partner. Its ability to help comes more from its structural position as the common third rather than its willingness. In other words, it can be a reluctant helper.

The concept of tertius adiuvans is then applied to how a weaker party in the buyer-supplier relationship may seek a coalition with the third that could help improve its leverage. Conceptually, the coalition is characterized as being temporal and context specific. For example, parts suppliers to large original equipment manufacturer (OEM) buyers have sought coalition with the customers of its OEM buyers. Structurally, what used to be an intransitive triad, with the buying company as the bridge between the parts suppliers and its customers, has turned into a transitive triad, with the disintermediation filling up the structural hole that had the OEM buyer as the bridge.

We then look at how a supplier is embedded in its extended ties with a third node, be it another supplier or buying company, and how such embeddedness could potentially affect the buyer. We will then consider services outsourcing—how a transitive triad is required to understand the underlying dynamics involved in services outsourcing. This is because the characteristics of services are different from manufacturing in that service work requires suppliers and customers to come in contact. In manufacturing, the buying company occupies the bridge position, but in services outsourcing, the buying company has to give up that bridge position by bringing its supplier and its customer together.

Agency Problems and Tertius Adiuvans—The Third That Helps

Buyer-supplier relationships occur in the principal-agent context. Problems exist in the buyer-supplier context because the two parties invariably suffer from goal incongruence and information asymmetry (Eisenhardt 1989a; Jensen 1983). Such dynamics between the principal and agent have been addressed by agency theory (Eisenhardt 1989a; Wiseman and Gomez-Mejia 1998; Rossetti and Choi 2008; Yang et al. 2022). The problems that may arise between the principal (i.e., buying company) and the agent (i.e., supplier company) have been called the agency problem. The buying company is the principal because it delegates work to the supplier. It establishes a contract with the supplier to carry out the work on its behalf, and the supplier becomes the agent of the buying company. According to Jensen and Meckling (1976), both the buyer and supplier are rational actors trying to maximize their own utility and, therefore, the agent is presumed to not always act in the principal's best interest. That causes agency problems. As discussed earlier (see Chapter 3 on dyads), every company is embedded in the supply network, and every business plays the role of a buyer and a supplier. Therefore, every company in the supply chain network experiences agency problems. They are ubiquitous and have relevance to all businesses.

As stated earlier, the problems are typically reduced to goal incongruence and information asymmetry (Eisenhardt 1989a; Jensen 1983). Goal incongruence is also called goal misalignment or goal incompatibility (Das and Rahman 2010; Handley and Benton 2012). Simply, the goals between the buyer and supplier can conflict, and their information-sharing process occurs imperfectly and selectively. The buying company and its supplier are utility maximizers (Jensen and Meckling 1976), so they operate under different set of factors and assign varying levels of importance to each factor. Therefore, goal incongruence between the buyer and supplier is inevitable. As for information asymmetry, it refers to the fact that "it is difficult or expensive for the principal to verify what the agent is actually doing" (Eisenhardt 1989a, p. 58). The condition of information asymmetry leads to the issues of adverse selection and moral hazard. For instance, when a supplier senses it has the trust of the buyer, that supplier may be more encouraged to act opportunistically, akin to what we refer to as the dark side of the deep buyer-supplier relationship (Villena, Revilla, and Choi 2011).

Agency theory offers two ways to address agency problems—by providing appropriate incentives and through monitoring (Demski and Feltham 1978; Eisenhardt 1989a). The use of incentives may help reduce goal incongruence. By adding incentives to the calculus the supplier has been operating with, the difference between what the buyer wants the supplier to do and what the supplier wants to do for its own end becomes reduced. Monitoring has been used to address agency problems as well. It refers to the "observation of agent efforts or outcomes that is accomplished through supervision, accounting control, and other devices" (Tosi, Katz, and Gomez-Mejia 1997, p. 588). The principal itself can monitor the agent, for example by hiring a third-party agency or by installing a monitoring device. One of the most famous ways of monitoring suppliers, as advocated by Toyota, is *Gemba*, which means to "go and see" what is happening in a supplier's plant.

Yang et al. (2022) observe that these solutions are confined to the dyadic context of the buyer and supplier. When we add a third node to the dyad, the tertius adiuvans (the third that helps), we begin to see additional ways to address the agency problem. As mentioned, the tertius adiuvans is different from the tertius gaudens or tertius iungens in the sense that it occurs in a transitive triad rather than in an intransitive triad with a structural hole. In the case of tertius adiuvans, the third is helping to overcome the problem in the dyad by virtue of being connected to both nodes.

There are four types of the tertius adiuvans that could help the buyer overcome its agency problem with the supplier—a supplier's supplier, buying firm's buying firm, another buying company of the supplier, and another supplier to the buying company. Beyond the two tiers in the supply network that the buying firm and supplying firm occupy, two of the tertius adiuvans come from different tiers—a supplier's supplier comes from next tier down from the supplier, and the buying firm's buying firm comes from next tier up from the buying firm. The other two tertius adiuvans come from the same two tiers—another buying company of the supplier comes from the same tier as the buying company, and another supplier of the buying company comes from the same tier as the incumbent supplier. These descriptions sound complicated because these four types exhaust all possible tertius adiuvans to the dyad of the buyer-supplier relationship. The diagrams shown in Table 4.1 should help visualize how they work. The structural arrangements should be straightforward.

At Arizona State University, we used to host supply managers from LG Electronics every year as part of our executive education program. LGE

Table 4.1 The Third That Helps

Triadic Structure	Tertius Adiuvans
Buyer ○ Supplier ○ ⋯ ● Tertius adiuvans	Supplier's supplier
● Tertius adiuvans Buyer ○ Supplier ○	Buying firm's buying firm
Buyer ○ ⋯ ● Tertius adiuvans Supplier ○	Supplier's other buying firm
Buyer ○ Supplier ○ ⋯ ● Tertius adiuvans	Buying firm's other supplier

Source: Adapted from Yang et al. 2022

sent 20 to 30 managers each year from South Korea, and these managers stayed with us for about a month in warm Tempe in the January–February timeframe when the weather is cold in South Korea. One of the training activities we conducted was to work on a live project that these managers would bring with them. There was one project that seemed to come up almost every year. That is what they used to call the Qualcomm dilemma. At the time, LGE procured about $1 billion worth of products from Qualcomm each year. LGE thought it was the big buying firm, and it should be able to take the lead role in managing its relationship with Qualcomm. However, whenever the time came for a new contract negotiation, it was not LGE but Qualcomm that drove the negotiation. The reason was mainly because Qualcomm owned the intellectual property of the CDMA chips it supplied to LGE (Choi and Linton 2011). When asked how they dealt with this problem, the managers seemed exasperated. After a pause, one manager replied, "Professor Choi, we plead with them." And he continued, "Professor Choi, there is more. If pleading doesn't work, we beg, and if begging doesn't work, we cry." LGE had an agency problem.

As it turns out, LGE tried all the usual tactics as prescribed by agency theory. It monitored Qualcomm's performance closely, and it tried to offer incentives by offering long-term contracts. It even attempted to build a deep buyer-supplier relationship. According to the LGE managers, none of these worked, and they grappled with this Qualcomm dilemma year after year. Then, at some point, they discovered Taiwan Semiconductor Manufacturing Company (TSMC) that was doing the manufacturing work for Qualcomm. Of course, LGE knew about TSMC, but it never consciously brought TSMC into the equation of the Qualcomm dilemma. We were now looking at a three-tier supply chain. LGE was the buying company, Qualcomm was the supplier, and TSMC was the supplier of Qualcomm, a second-tier supplier to LGE. Prior to that point, TSMC was a contract manufacturer that sat behind Qualcomm, and LGE did not have any formal relationship with TSMC. However, LGE approached TSMC and began establishing an informal relationship. That got Qualcomm's attention. It is hard to tell if the agency problem LGE faced was fixed, but the introduction of TSMC to the Qualcomm dilemma clearly changed the business relationship dynamics. There was subsequently a big meeting in LGE's headquarters in Seoul among the representatives from all three companies. This meeting marked the arrival of TSMC as a tertius adiuvans.

What was noteworthy is that TSMC, as a helper to LGE's agency problem, was not an active helper. We might say TSMC was a *reluctant helper*. Earlier, we discussed how a structural position in a network such as a structural hole is associated with power and leverage. The presence of tertius adiuvans is another interesting aspect of a network dynamic. Here, we see a situation where a structural position in the network can induce a helper regardless of the level of its willingness. Clearly, TSMC did not want to upset its customer, Qualcomm, but it had no choice when LGE came calling. It had to accept LGE's advances and take on the role of tertius adiuvans, albeit reluctantly. A few more examples of tertius adiuvans are offered in the following.

In addition to the role of the third that helps as the supplier's supplier, there are other types of tertius adiuvans. In the supply network study by Choi and Hong (2002), a buying firm called CVT (a fictitious name) operates as an assembler of Honda's center console module that goes into the Honda Accord (more on CVT in Chapter 7). CVT receives stamped parts such as metal brackets from a supplier called ATD. ATD is a family-owned stamping company that is well-established in the industry with a good reputation. At the time, CVT contributed to about 20% of ATD's sales but had a difficult time getting ATD to offer supplier flexibility (i.e., adjusting delivery dates), similar to how it was providing flexibility to its buying company, Honda. Clearly, goal incongruence and information asymmetry existed between CVT and ATD. CVT had an agency problem. Somewhere along the line, CVT got smart and decided to turn to its buying company, Honda, to help with its agency problem. Honda has a policy of informing all of its suppliers in its supply chain network that they are involved in making a Honda product—Honda's reasoning is that when a part breaks down after a consumer purchases a Honda, to the consumer, it is a Honda that breaks down. And 80% of ATD's sales in metal brackets went to Honda. Therefore, on behalf of CVT, Honda became involved as a tertius adiuvans and was able to help CVT address its agency problem. Again, Honda might have preferred not to become involved in disputes between its first-tier supplier and a second-tier supplier, but because it was in the position to help as the common, the company got involved and assisted CVT.

A few years after first noting the role of the tertius adiuvans from working with LGE, the researchers at Cranfield School of Management in the U.K. noted an agency problem a company called Doncasters was having with its supplier called Timet (Bastl, Johnson, and Choi 2013). This observation was made as part of another study on coalition-building behavior involving triads (more on this study in the next section). Doncasters is a U.K.-based company specializing in precision casting and alloy components manufacturing. Timet is a metal supplier specializing in titanium and other precious raw materials. At the time, Timet was certified by the U.S. Department of Defense, and, because of that, it became the sole source to Doncasters as the precious metal supplier. In the relationship between Lancaster as the buying company and Timet as the supplier, Timet dictated price and delivery, which was not acceptable to Doncasters. To overcome this agency problem, Doncasters formed a coalition with Rolls-Royce, another buying company for Timet. We did not have data on the details of the deal between Doncasters and Rolls-Royce, but it was clear Doncasters approached Rolls-Royce and, to that extent, Rolls-Royce fit the description of being a tertius adiuvans. By bringing this new buying company into the mix, Doncasters was able to get the price and delivery terms from Timet that it offered Rolls-Royce, which of course, were much more favorable.

Yang et al. (2022) offer an example of another supplier of the buying firm entering the mix as a tertius adiuvans. The example involves a buying firm in a relationship with an equipment supplier. This supplier dictated the pricing terms because it was the dominant player in the market. Additionally, the supplier also controlled the terms involving after-sales services and spare parts. Citing the intellectual property issues, the supplier did not allow the buying firm to work on maintenance and repair of the equipment, obligating it to the supplier's high prices of replacement parts and maintenance services. The buying firm had an agency problem. To overcome the problem, the buying firm made a strategic decision to approach another supplier to potentially develop a substitutable product. The first supplier monitored the business relationship between the buying firm and the new competing supplier for four years, and it eventually conceded that this new relationship was working out and a potential threat to its position in the market. So, the first supplier decided to work with the buying firm more closely to "regain the buyer's trust and business."

A similar example comes from a practice called reverse marketing (Leenders and Blenkhorn 1988; Choi 1999). A large bread manufacturer known as Malston Bakery had a difficult time working with its suppliers of hard flour, the main raw material for baking bread. To control their pricing, it tried to introduce competition among suppliers, but to no avail. With increasing hard flour costs and decreasing bread prices in the market, Malston was caught in a cost-price squeeze. The cost from the suppliers was going up, while the competition in the downstream market was driving down bread prices. The company desperately needed to do something. Malston finally convinced a soft flour manufacturer to move into the hard flour business—hard flour is used to take bread, a staple food, and soft flour is used to make cookies and cakes. Malston sold the idea of moving into a new business by developing a new capability for the supplier, and for this reason, this practice is called reverse marketing. Once this supplier successfully came onboard to produce hard flour, the other hard flour manufacturers became more cooperative. In these examples, a supplier, perhaps as a reluctant helper, had to be convinced to work with the buying company on a new business relationship. Once that business relationship became successful, the new supplier fulfilled the role of the tertius adiuvans.

Plight of a Weaker Player in the Buyer-Supplier Dyad

I propose that the concept of tertius adiuvan is applicable for whoever is a weaker player in the buyer-supplier dyad. In the preceding section, the agency theory took the perspective of the buyer as the principal. Adding the third node was applied to the benefit of the buyer. However, in the supply chain, the supplier is also in need of a tertius adiuvans. In fact, the supplier is usually the weaker of the two parties. An external node with whom a supplier could establish a coalition may help gain leverage to contend with the powerful buying company.

First conceived by Simmel (1950) and developed further by his followers (i.e., Caplow 1956; Wolff 1950), the theory of coalition focuses on power issues in the network. A weaker node in a dyad facing a more powerful node may seek a third node to attain leverage. As such, the theory of coalition explains the coalition-building behavior in the triad. The key point of departure is that it informs us about the necessary qualifications of the third node the weaker node should seek regarding the aggregate power level. It offers us more details on the qualifications for being a good tertius adiuvans. For the third that helps to be able to help, it has to bring a certain level of power to the mix. For instance, when a weaker node coalesces with a tertius adiuvans, the aggregate level of power would have to be greater than the power garnered by the other node; otherwise, the coalition would be for naught. In this regard, the coalition theory helps add more theoretical precision to the concept of tertius adiuvans.

Bastl, Johnson, and Choi (2013) explicate how a weaker player in a buyer-supplier relationship may set up a coalition with another company to help gain leverage against a more powerful player. The context begins in a dyad but grows into a triad when a coalition is formed. In the buyer-supplier dyad, the weaker player may be the supplier or buyer. We are more familiar with the supplier being in the weaker position because a corporate buyer, for example, has the contracting authority and is closer to the consumer market. In contrast, the examples offered above for the triadic relationships listed in Table 4.1 show that the buyer, too, may be in a position of want. Thus, either the buyer or the supplier can be the weaker player in the buyer-supplier context and may seek a tertius adiuvans.

Many scholars in supply chain management have studied power (e.g., Benton and Maloni 2005; Cox 2001; Zhao et al. 2008). In the supply chain context, they have investigated bargaining power (Crook and Combs 2007), trust and power (Ireland and Webb 2007), and power and commitment (Zhao et al. 2008). One common element in these studies is that they assume the buyer is the more powerful player. In contrast, we advance the possibility that the buyer can be the weaker player, just as a supplier can be the weaker player. A buyer can face a powerful supplier that is much larger and more resource rich (i.e., steel supplier) or holds an intellectual property the buyer depends on (i.e., LGE depending on Qualcomm for its CDMA chips). Of course, a supplier can face a powerful buyer that imposes unilateral cost-reduction targets and is threatening the supplier's profit margins. The supplier would need to find a way to fend off the threat. Rossetti and Choi (2005) recount how the smaller parts suppliers in the aerospace industry created a covert coalition with the buying company's customer (i.e., airliners) to combat the more powerful buyer as if in guerrilla warfare (more on this below when discussing supply chain disintermediation).

To understand the concept of a coalition, it might make sense to compare it to strategic alliances or partnerships. With power as the underlying mechanism, the concept of coalitions is applied to much broader contexts than the concept of strategic alliances. Coalitions are formed between individuals (Caplow 1956; 1959; Gamson 1961; Mills 1954; Stevenson, Pearce, and Porter 1985), groups (Gamson 1961; Stevenson, Pearce, and Porter 1985), organizations (Bastl, Johnson, and Choi 2013; Warren 1967), and nations (Caplow 1968), whereas strategic alliances happen almost exclusively between organizations (Parkhe 1991; Gulati 1995; 1998; Eisenhardt and Schoonhoven 1996; Dyer, Kale, and Singh 2001; Prashant and Harbir 2009).

Further, coalitions tend to be issue oriented, and the temporal context is short term. When a coalition is formed, the goal of that coalition exists external to each node involved in the coalition and is different from the goals of each node. In contrast, strategic alliances are expected to be longer lasting, and the goals of the alliance should align with the goals of the nodes (i.e., companies) that have come together. Coalitions entail informal relationships, and cooperation occurs as a means-oriented endeavour (Gamson 1961) and lasts only until the goal of that particular coalition has been met. For example, the coalition between LGE and TSMC, as described above, was temporary and informal, with TSMC as a reluctant participant. It was clearly different from a strategic alliance between businesses that tends to be formalized and long-term focused.

When the weaker player seeks a tertius adiuvans, the context becomes triadic, where a coalition of "two against one" happens (Caplow 1968). When a coalition is formed between two nodes, the coalition's goal is to counter the power of the node that has been singled out. According to Wolff (1950), Simmel contended: "No matter how close a triad may be, there is always the occasion on which two of the three players regard the third as an intruder" (p. 135). It is extremely unlikely all three would reach a state of "a really uniform mood" (Wolff 1950, p. 136), and small differentials in power among three nodes would significantly influence how coalitions form in a triad. Therefore, a triad where power is equally distributed across all three nodes would be highly unlikely in reality, it exists in theory only. Furthermore, we could also argue that two of the three nodes in a triad with a mathematically same level of power would also be highly unlikely. In the same way, the summation of the power levels of two nodes equaling the third node would also be highly unlikely.

Given these observations, Figure 4.7 shows two triads that have unequal levels of power across the three nodes. The figures come from Bastl, Johnson, and Choi (2013), who created them based on Caplow (1956, 1959, 1968). To note, Bastl, Johnson, and Choi (2013) actually show eight types of triads, but here is presented two of the eight that show unequal power distribution. These two triads are sufficient for discussing coalition building in supply networks and qualifications for choosing the tertius adiuvans. In this figure, the varied sizes of the circles reflect power differentials across the three nodes.

Under each type, power differential relationships are clarified in simple equations with the letters referring to the specific nodes. The solid lines represent the extant relationship, and double-headed arrows pointing at each other signify a potential coalition at that link.

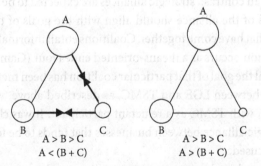

Figure 4.7 Power Differentials and Potential Coalitions
Source: Adapted from Bastl, Johnson, and Choi 2013

In the triad on the left side, we have a configuration that permits coalition building. Either B or C alone would have less power than A, but together their collective power is greater than A. Further, to prevent B and C from forming a coalition, A could be motivated to form a coalition with C. However, in the triad on the right side, the power differentials are such that even if B and C were to form a coalition, A would still be in the stronger position. A would not be motivated to join C.

Here is an example from the field when B and C formed a coalition to guard against the powerful A. In the automotive industry, Suzuki cooperated with Volkswagen for joint development projects and in particular, to learn more about its diesel technologies (Fuhrmans 2011). After a few years, it became clear that Volkswagen intentionally blocked Suzuki's advances from accessing its diesel technologies. Volkswagen was clearly in the dominant position. We might say Volkswagen is A and Suzuki is C in the diagram. Suzuki then reached out to Fiat, shown as B, and was able to establish a coalition. Whether B or C was more powerful between the two is inconsequential. Suzuki was able to gain the needed leverage against Volkswagen, the dominant player, through this move. After this coalition with Fiat, Volkswagen opened up to Suzuki more.

We can also consider the Doncasters-Timet-Rolls-Royce triad described earlier. Since Doncasters was the weak player among the three, let's call it C. Rolls-Royce was the dominant player, so call it A. Timet would then be B. Both Timet and Rolls Royce had more power than Doncasters. By establishing a coalition with Rolls-Royce, Doncasters gained the leverage it needed against Timet. This offers us a scenario where B was the common supplier to both C and A—two buying companies, one powerful and one not powerful—that formed a coalition against a moderately powerful supplier. Likewise, two suppliers can form a coalition to gain leverage against a dominant buying corporation. This type of coalition may represent the commonly seen relationship arrangement in supply networks. Two weaker suppliers can form a coalition to counterbalance the more powerful buyer (Jin and Wu 2006). For instance, in an online reverse auction situation, the buyer wields market power over its suppliers (Schiller and Gebhardt 2019). Suppliers may collaborate in an informal arrangement and share information to the extent allowed. It is quite conceivable that when the buying company considers which suppliers to invite to participate in an online auction, it might consider the supplier's size. It might avoid including large suppliers that by themselves may not have leverage over the buyer but may gain meaningful leverage if it coalesces with another supplier.

In the triad on the right side of Figure 4.7, neither B nor C can be the tertius adiuvans for the other. Going back to the online reverse auction example, this diagram helps us understand the buyer's logic in selecting which suppliers to invite to the online reverse auction. The buyer would look at the size and dependence of each supplier and invite only those suppliers whose power level is such that, even if two of them might coalesce, their combined power level would still be lower than the buying company. As such, there are no double-headed arrows to indicate a potential coalition in this triad. So, if B or C wanted to gain sufficient leverage against the buyer, it would need to go outside this particular triadic arrangement and look for another supplier that would offer a sufficiently high level of power so that, if combined, their collective power can be higher than the buyers.

Supply Chain Disintermediation

Not all coalition-building efforts occur openly. Coalition-building efforts often transpire covertly. It happened in the aerospace industry. Suppliers manufacturing parts for large OEMs in the lucrative after-sales market moved in to take away the business from OEMs, their customers. These parts suppliers, working for such OEMs as Boeing, Pratt-Whitney, GE, and Honeywell, established an alliance with the aircraft operators (i.e., American Airlines, FedEx, etc.)—the buyers' buyers (see the diagram for the buying firm's buying firm in Table 4.1). According to Rossetti and Choi (2005), "An important component of the PMA certification process is testing, and here the OEMs missed the emergence of important new *alliances* between aircraft operators and parts suppliers" (p. 6, italics added; PMA stands for parts manufacturing authority).

Rossetti and Choi (2005) call this phenomenon "supply chain disintermediation." Parts suppliers would bypass their customers (i.e., OEM buyers) and coalesce with their customer's customers (i.e., aircraft operators). The bypassing disintermediates the supply chain that used to have the OEM buyers as the bridge between their parts suppliers and aircraft operators. All this happened while the parts suppliers were trying to gain PMA from the Federal Aviation Administration (FAA). According to FAA regulations, to obtain PMA, a parts supplier would have to use its own blueprint, produce the parts using this blueprint, and test the parts in a test vehicle. To comply, a parts supplier would reverse engineer the component it manufactured based on the OEM's design and generate a blueprint. It would then use that blueprint to produce the parts. After that, it would need to find a test vehicle. For that, it would then simply reach out to an aircraft operator and ask for one. Because the replacement parts were usually marked up 100% or more and were expensive, an aircraft operator would become a willing partner and provide a vehicle to test the part. If the aircraft operator has a fleet of airplanes that use this part, it will stand to make considerable savings.

This type of behind-the-scenes operation initiated by the parts suppliers is likened to guerilla warfare by Rossetti and Choi (2005). So, why were the parts suppliers waging this fight against their own customers? The OEM buyers embraced the tenets of strategic sourcing by downsizing their supply base and consolidating their spending. To the remaining suppliers that survived the supply base downsizing, they gave larger and longer term contracts. However, when long-term promises came under the weight of short-term reality, the OEM buyers began subjecting their parts suppliers to relentless, year-over-year purchase price variance (PPV) targets. PPV looks at the price from the previous year and compares it against the current year's price, showing the differential. It refers to the hard savings that would show up on the company's balance sheet.

Further, to improve their cash flow, the OEM buyers unilaterally imposed 90-day or 120-day payment terms (more on payment terms and cash flow later when we discuss supply chain financing). It was like the OEM buyers were asking the parts suppliers that tended to be not as financially stable to be their bank. This process is depicted in Figure 4.8.

Rossetti and Choi (2005) compare these practices to a marriage gone bad. Long-term promises were made, but in the short term, the OEM buyers were punishing their suppliers. We quote from the movie *War of the Roses*, "A civilized divorce is a contradiction in terms. . . . There is no winning in this. It's only various degrees of losing" (Gavin D'Amato, played by Danny DeVito). To survive, many parts suppliers consciously chose to move into

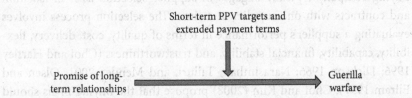

Figure 4.8 Misapplication of Strategic Sourcing

the lucrative after-sales market that had been off-limits and disintermediated the supply chain. In network terms, an intransitive triad had now become a transitive triad. Thus, business relationships in the triad became more complicated. There were disbeliefs, self-centered decisions at the cost of others, and lawsuits.

In a different study using survey and secondary data, Rossetti and Choi (2008) theorize this phenomenon using agency theory. They choose goal incongruence between the OEM buyer and parts suppliers as the driver for the supply chain disintermediation and empirically verified it. They frame supply chain disintermediation as the supplier's opportunistic behavior found in moral hazard (Jensen and Meckling 1976). Parts suppliers committed disintermediation when they perceived their opportunistic actions would not lead to a penalty, so the ultimate outcome would be positive, comparing the potential penalty versus improvements from their current situation. Violating the agreement with their OEM buyers, the parts suppliers sought a coalition with the aircraft operators as the tertius adiuvans. As discussed above, such coalitions would be temporal and based on focused goals, much as a husband or wife in a bad marriage might seek reprieve in the third that could help, even temporarily, while they are still bound by a long-term agreement.

Supplier Evaluation and Supplier's Embedded Performance

The triadic perspective urges managers to reconsider how they engage in supplier evaluation and selection (Choi and Kim 2008). In a typical supplier selection, the buyer evaluates the supplier's performance and decides whether to work with that company. However, the concept of triad informs us that this supplier is embedded in other third companies it does business with, either as a buyer or as a supplier, and the supplier's performance would be dependent on the performance of those third businesses linked to the supplier.

Regardless of the structural patterns of a supplier's extended ties, the buying company typically engages in supplier selection as if in isolation and contracts with one supplier at a time. The selection process involves evaluating a supplier's performance in terms of quality, cost, delivery, flexibility, capability, financial stability, and trustworthiness (Choi and Hartley 1996; Dickson 1966; Narasimhan, Talluri, and Mendez 2001; Olsen and Ellram 1997). Choi and Kim (2008) propose that the buying firms should also look at the performance of the supplier's other major suppliers and other major buying firms.

The following two stories come from Toyota during its visit to Arizona State University (ASU) with its representatives. We at ASU used to offer supply chain executive education to Toyota's North America operation. To design and execute the program, they visited us in Tempe many times. The two stories became known at different points in time. One story involved a second-tier supplier whose plant was operating in Phoenix, and the other involved a major U.S. automaker that competes against Toyota. In both stories, the same major first-tier supplier was involved.

Toyota had been building a close working relationship with a major U.S.-based first-tier supplier that provides powertrains, electronic parts and assemblies, and after-sales parts. There was one electronic assembly from this supplier that suffered from a quality problem. Toyota sent its engineers to this supplier and performed a root cause analysis. After considerable effort, they discovered an electronic parts supplier in Phoenix as the source of the problem—this supplier would be a second-tier supplier to Toyota. Therefore, during their visit to ASU, the Toyota delegates also paid a visit to this second-tier supplier to address the problem. In fact, they were practicing *Gemba* (go and see). Before this point, the first-tier supplier was the bridge between Toyota and this second-tier supplier. Now, Toyota was directly evaluating this second-tier supplier's performance.

The second story also involves the same first-tier supplier. This supplier had been spun off from a major U.S. automaker and was still doing a lot of work for them. However, the automaker, or we might say the mother company to this first-tier supplier, was not doing well in the market. It eventually declared bankruptcy. Eventually, this first-tier supplier started to suffer financially, and it began to fall behind in its work for Toyota. Initially, the whole situation did not make sense to Toyota. It had done its best to establish a fruitful long-term business relationship with this supplier. They did supplier development activities together, and the management teams from both sides met regularly to share information. Yet, Toyota realized its supplier's performance was lacking. Ironically, the fact that Toyota was doing well in the market became the cause of its competitor lagging behind and its major supplier falling behind in its performance. Choi and Kim (2008) offer a quote from a Toyota manager, "In the future, when we select a major supplier, we are going to review carefully who its key customers are" (p. 6).

Supplier evaluation and selection should be integrated with a triadic perspective. It would be prudent for a buying company to have a good understanding of which companies are doing business with its major suppliers, either as a supplier or as a buyer. The simple reason for this approach is the dependencies that come from being linked in a buyer-supplier relationship that is then connected to the supplier company's extended relationships. In particular, once a corporate buyer like Toyota evaluates a second-tier supplier, it may choose to select or deselect this supplier from its extended supply chain. If selected, Toyota may engage in a directed-sourcing arrangement in which Toyota establishes a contract with the second-tier supplier directly and then sells the parts to the first-tier supplier. Or, Toyota can direct the second-tier supplier to ship the parts to the first-tier supplier and ask the first-tier supplier to manage this second-tier supplier for quality and delivery since it is managing the second-tier supplier for the cost through contracting—more on this aspect of multi-tier supply chain management when we get to the chapter on extended supply chains.

Bridge Transfer in Services Outsourcing

Understanding how triads work is instrumental to understanding how services outsourcing works. This is because of the unique characteristic of service operations that requires customer participation. In other words, in delivering a service, the customer of services and the service supplier have to come in contact. In manufacturing outsourcing, the buying company (e.g., Dell) is almost always in the middle as a bridge between the suppliers (e.g., parts suppliers) and its customer (e.g., ASU). Of course, supply chain disintermediation can occur, as discussed above, but that happens more as an exception in unusual circumstances. When a buying company (e.g., Dell) outsources its service work, the supplier (e.g., a call center in India) always comes in contact with the buying company's customer (e.g., ASU) by design, given the nature of services work. We say "by design" because service work requires value co-creation involving the service supplier and the customer. Chase and Aquilano (1992) point out that "the main feature that sets a service system apart from a manufacturing system is the extent to which the customer must be in direct contact" (p. 17).

Building on Simmel (1950) and (Burt 1995), we have discussed the concepts of a bridge and a structural hole. Further, we have ascertained that the position of a bridge is not a permanent state and can undergo change. In fact, Burt (2000a, 2002) informs us how the bridge position may erode, which he calls "bridge decay." Bridge decay takes place when two nodes otherwise isolated come in contact and establish a direct link. When this happens, the path of connections that used to go through the bridge becomes redundant and is no longer of value (Johnson 2004). The bridge loses the leverage either as a tertius gaudens or tertius iungens. Burt (2001) confirms that the shifting of structural positions is dynamic, and, in social relationships, bridge decay happens quite frequently. Li and Choi (2009) extend this logic and propose that the structural shifting of relationships does not end with bridge decay. The structural shifting may continue to what we refer to as "bridge transfer." The bridge position first decays and then transfers to another node in the triad.

This concept of bridge transfer is critical to understanding services outsourcing. We have to understand how the buying company occupies the bridge position initially but then undergoes bridge decay and then bridge transfer (Li and Choi 2009). This process is captured in Table 4.2. It shows three stages of outsourcing—what happens prior to outsourcing and then during and post-outsourcing. Underpinning all three stages is the unique characteristic of service work that requires the service supplier and customer to come in contact, as noted above.

When a large manufacturer like Dell decides to outsource its call-center work, it first engages in search activities regarding potential suppliers that can perform it. Dell has done the make-or-buy analysis for the call-center

Table 4.2 Services Outsourcing and Bridge Transfer

Stages of Outsourcing	Buyer's Network State	Triadic Structures
Pre-outsourcing	Bridge	Buyer connected to Customer and Supplier
During outsourcing	Bridge decay	Buyer connected to Customer and Supplier
Post-outsourcing	Bridge transfer	Buyer connected to Customer and Supplier

Source: Adapted from Li and Choi 2009

work, and the decision is to buy, say, given the low cost of labor in India. We are now in the pre-outsourcing stage, and Dell occupies the bridge position between its customers and potential suppliers. As the search process proceeds to a negotiation phase and then to contracting, Dell is still in the bridge position. On one side, potential suppliers are in discussions with Dell. On the other side, the team of information technology services at Dell is still taking care of its customers through its internal after-sales support services. As a bridge, Dell would have full control of setting up the supplier for the upcoming services and how much information it wants to convey to its customers about the outsourcing project. For instance, the customers might be informed of the upcoming change but would have little influence on the capacity and capability of the future supplier.

Once a supplier is chosen, and the outsourcing of the call center is implemented, that would invariably bring the supplier and the customer together for value co-creation (Chase and Aquilano 1992; Kellogg and Chase 1995). Simply put, the customer begins to tell the supplier the nature and severity of the problems it is trying to solve. We are now in the phase of during outsourcing, and the bridge position is being decayed and weakened. By design, the buying company has no means of blocking this direct contact to the supplier by the customer and can still provide quality services. The leverage Dell has had as a bridge is eroded and is no more. The buyer can of course provide a script and recommended processes through which its customers should be cared for. However, it has no direct control over how the information flows between the supplier and the customer during the call.

During the transition phase, the supplier and customer are in contact. They begin to develop a working relationship. Li and Choi (2009) argue that the strength of this relationship is dependent on the strength of the past relationship between the buyer and supplier, including how the supplier selection process has been managed by the buyer. If the past relationship has been managed in an adversarial way, that relationship tone will spill over into how the supplier will engage the customer. If cooperative, that would also spill over to the new relationship between the supplier and customer. For instance, Balakrishnan, Mohan, and Seshadri (2008) report how Aviva, an insurance firm based in the U.K., successfully built a cooperative relationship with its service suppliers in India that did claims administration and software development. That cooperative business relationship between the buying firm and service suppliers spilled over, and the suppliers and customers were also able to develop a cooperative relationship.

Once the transition is complete, the buying company would cease to be involved in the service delivery activities. The buyer's intent has been to hand over the service work to the supplier and would expect its supplier as its agent to fully deliver the services to the customer without its direct involvement. The part of the equation that went into the make-buy decision has been to save on the administrative cost of delivering the service using its internal resources. Sanders et al. (2007) refer to this state of outsourcing as "total outsourcing." Therefore, by design, the buying company expects the supplier to fully care for its customers as it is being compensated for doing just that.

When all goes well with the outsourcing project by the buyer, a structural hole occurs between the buying firm and the customer firm, as shown in Table 4.2. The supplier is now the bridge sitting on top of a structural hole. The supplier becomes a tertius gaudens, with all the structural advantages that position brings. The bridge transfer has taken place—the buying firm used to be the bridge, but now the supplier is the bridge. The bridge position has now been transferred from the buyer to the supplier. In fact, many buyers seem to have missed this point when they first engaged in services outsourcing. Some buyers would do things to prolong this triadic structure with the supplier as the bridge—the position of power. For example, Lenox and King (2004) report how buying companies handed over critical knowledge to the supplier to help deliver better service to the customers. An unanticipated outcome was the buying companies becoming dependent on the supplier for updates on this critical information.

Li and Choi (2009) point out that so many service-outsourcing projects fail because the buying firms do not fully comprehend the implications of putting the supplier in the bridge position. We suggest the state of bridge decay would serve the buying company much better than the state of bridge transfer. We recommend the buyer keep a line of communication open with the customer. Also, we suggest the buyer monitor the link between the supplier and customer. These additional communications and monitoring would indeed increase the administrative cost for the buyer, but these costs should really be part of the calculus involved in the make-buy decision in the first place. One would think large buying companies should now have figured out the dynamics involved in services outsourcing, and they should have everything under control. Not exactly. One large personal computer manufacturer struggled with its call centers in India around 2017. After carefully re-evaluating the call-center operations in India, the firm finally considered re-shoring the call centers for its commercial accounts to the U.S. There were discussions of going back on its outsourcing decision and to insource all the call centers.

Key Points

- A triad is the smallest unit of a network. A triad can be transitive (three nodes and three links) or intransitive (three nodes and two links).
- In a network, one has to be able to consider how a link affects another link and a node affects a link once removed.
- A triad can be balanced or unbalanced. A triad in an unbalanced state will evolve toward a balanced state.
- A bridge sits on a structural hole, and it garners power that comes from that structural position.
- A bridge has two types—a *tertius gaudens* is the third that profits, and a *tertius iungens* is the third that channels.
- Additional ways to address the agency problem can be found when considered in the triadic context. The third node outside the principal-agent dyad is called the *tertius adiuvans*.
- A weaker player in a dyad can reach out to the third node (i.e., tertius adiuvans) to form a coalition to gain leverage. Unlike a partnership that tends to be long term and overarching, a coalition tends to be short term and specific issue oriented.
- When a buying company makes long-term promises but behaves in a short-term manner, suppliers may disintermediate the supply chain by establishing a coalition, albeit covertly, with the buyer's customer. When this happens, the supplier takes away the bridge position that buyer has enjoyed.
- A supplier's performance is embedded in its other business relationship ties—either its own supplier(s) or its other buying firm(s). When evaluating a supplier's performance, a buying company should evaluate the supplier's major suppliers and other buying firms.
- Services outsourcing entails a different dynamic from manufacturing outsourcing in that the service supplier and the end customer (i.e., buying company's customer) must come in contact. After service outsourcing, the bridge position, by design, transfers to the service supplier from the buying company.

5

Supply Base in Supply Networks

Human beings are social animals. We hang out together. We do things to-gether. Since the days of Aristotle, we have been aware of how we seek the companionship of others to sustain our well-being. For that, we have different groups of people with whom we socialize. We have our family members, per-sonal friends, work colleagues, and church brothers and sisters. We need them for love, friendship, professionalism, and spiritual fellowship. We are connected with these different groups for various needs. In the aggregate, we need all of them to attain a balance in life. Yet, some are more important than others. We speak of best friends and close colleagues. In this regard, there is an economic calculus in how we socialize—some are more important than others because such categorization helps create patterns in our behaviors and expectations to make things more efficient and effective.

In much the same way, companies can also be viewed as social animals. They have relationships, such as buyer-supplier relationships. They get entangled in triadic relationships as in buyer-supplier-supplier relationships (see Chapter 4). Businesses as buying companies are connected to suppliers with whom they engage in economic activities to fulfill their product and service needs. Various groups of suppliers provide maintenance, repair, and operations (MRO) items; capital goods such as equipment; chemicals; parts that come in contact with consumers; parts that go inside the product and are not visible to consumers; and different kinds of raw materials. Buying companies usually keep an active list of suppliers organized under different categories. They need all these suppliers in their supply base to manage a well-functioning organization. Yet, some suppliers are more important than others. They call their essential suppliers "core suppliers" or "strategic suppliers." Honda of America has thousands of suppliers in its supply base, but it maintains about 300 to 400 suppliers as its core suppliers. Just as we may have a large friendship base of individuals but keep a close relationship with only a handful, large corporations may have an extensive list of suppliers but maintain a close relationship with a smaller number of suppliers. A large

The Nature of Supply Networks. Thomas Y. Choi, Oxford University Press. © Thomas Y. Choi 2023.
DOI: 10.1093/oso/9780197673249.003.0005

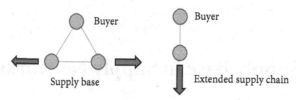

Figure 5.1 Horizontal and Vertical Expansions

aerospace and defense manufacturer may have 50,000 suppliers in its overall supply base but work with about 3,000 to 4,000 suppliers closely.

Through the previous two chapters, we have addressed dyads and triads in supply networks. Keeping our eyes on the upstream supply side, we now expand our coverage *horizontally* and vertically, as shown in Figure 5.1. A horizontal expansion is suggested by the two arrows on the left side of Figure 5.1. Here, we are expanding the number of suppliers a buyer works with beyond a simple buyer-supplier-supplier triad. By doing that, we get what is commonly referred to as a *supply base* (see Choi and Krause 2006). The focus of this chapter is this supply base and how a buying company would manage it.

On the right side of Figure 5.1, we expand the buyer-supplier relationship *vertically*. When we do that, we see a series of companies connected as buyers and suppliers. We call it an extended supply chain. That is the focus of the next chapter—Chapter 6 on the extended supply chains (see Choi et al. 2021). Once we consider both supply base and extended supply chains, we will be ready to discuss supply networks that propagate horizontally and vertically from the dyadic and triadic forms of relationships. The horizontal expansion of suppliers and the vertical extension of suppliers combined give us a company-to-company-level pattern of relationships we call a supply network. We discuss supply networks in Chapter 7.

In the rest of this chapter, we will consider how buying and supplying companies as social animals engage in various patterns of behaviors with economic calculus. A buying company typically works with multiple products, each of which would have a long list of parts and materials in its bill of materials (BOM) and a long list of suppliers of those parts and materials to which the buyer outsources. Therefore, the buyer must decide on the size of its supply base, which is often called supply base rationalization. For example, Ford Motor Company, at one point, reduced its supply base of 3,000 suppliers down to about 800. Volvo once reduced its supply base of 800 down to 40. Typically, companies tend to focus on the number of suppliers. However, if we adopt a network perspective, we begin to realize there is more to managing a supply base than just rationalizing the number of suppliers. We also have to consider the relationships between the suppliers. In this regard, we may think of the supply base as a complex system (Choi and Krause 2006). Per Stuart Kauffman's NK model, we consider the number of elements in the system (N), how they are connected (K), and how similar or differentiated they are in terms of work processes and culture (A). For instance, one of the reasons why Honda and Toyota consistently rate well on supplier surveys is because they put a conscious effort into promoting good relationships among suppliers (K) and ensuring they share common work processes and business norms (A) (see Liker and Choi 2004). Another hidden aspect of supply base management is that, while we tend to think of suppliers in a supply base as all first-tier suppliers, this is not the case for Honda and Toyota. Their supply bases have many second-tier and other tertiary-level suppliers they choose to manage directly.

Supply Base Rationalization

A supply base refers to a group of suppliers from whom a buying company procures goods and services. These procured items are necessary to engage in its transformation process (see Chapter 2). The buyer in this context is called a "focal company" in the sense that all goods and services must converge to this company. Figure 5.2 shows how the relationships between the focal company and its suppliers are arranged. The buyer, as the focal company, establishes a relationship with each supplier through selection, contracting, and performance evaluation. As there are buyer-supplier relationships, there are also supplier-supplier relationships. As such, some suppliers in the

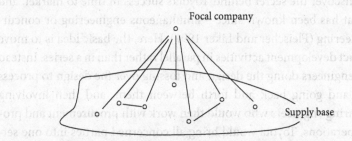

Figure 5.2 Supply Base and Relationships

supply base have relationships between them. They may buy and sell to each other or may have a joint venture project together. In this regard, the business relationships that exist between the focal company and its suppliers are a collection of overlapping transitive and intransitive triads. Transitive triads come from those suppliers with links between them (i.e., supplier-supplier relationships), while intransitive triads come from those without links (i.e., structural holes). The focal company monitors all the relationships as shown in Figure 5.2 and may intervene when necessary.

To manage their supply bases, the first thing corporate buyers usually focus on is maintaining the right number of suppliers. They have often used phrases like rightsizing, downsizing, or rationalizing their supply base. In practice, buying companies have primarily reduced the number of suppliers down to what they would consider an optimal size. There are multiple reasons for undertaking the downsizing of the supply base. However, three have been mentioned often—(1) reduce time to market, (2) lower administrative costs associated with managing many suppliers, and (3) consolidate orders for lower unit prices. We discuss these reasons in the following paragraphs.

Lexus, a luxury brand of Toyota, was first introduced in 1989. At the time, Toyota was known for its quality but inexpensive products, such as the Corolla. Many industry experts were skeptical that this new automobile brand could challenge the likes of Mercedes, BMW, and Cadillac. The gap between this new brand and the other established luxury brands seemed insurmountable. Well, we all know what happened. Lexus has now been fully entrenched as a leading luxury brand automobile. How did Toyota do it? Consider time to market. Around that period, there was a huge gap between Toyota and the other automobile manufacturers regarding how long it took them to bring a new model to the market. Toyota took about three years to introduce a new model, while it took other automakers over five years. We began to discover the secret behind Toyota's success in time to market, and it was what has been known since—simultaneous engineering or concurrent engineering (Fleischer and Liker 1997). Here, the basic idea is to move new product development activities in parallel rather than in a series. Instead of design engineers doing the design and tossing over the design to process engineers and going back and forth between them, and then involving manufacturing engineers who would then work with procurement and production operations, Toyota would bring all concerned parties into one setting and manage the work to progress in parallel.

An essential part of this approach was the involvement of suppliers in early design meetings, which we now call early supplier involvement (ESI). Toyota had suppliers with whom it had established long-term relationships. Here, a long-term relationship extends multiple decades, and they remain together as family members would stay together. This clan-like business-relationship structure (Ouchi 1980) has been called *keiretsu*. The suppliers in Toyota keiretsu understood Toyota's processes, and they had mutual trust established over the decades of working together. Perhaps it was not a coincidence that around this time the U.S. automakers and companies in other industries began downsizing their supply bases. The logic, of course, was that they would need a smaller number of suppliers to build deeper buyer-supplier relationships (Liker and Choi 2004).

By working with fewer suppliers, the buying companies discovered that they could more readily streamline the procurement processes (i.e., contracting with suppliers, certifying suppliers, making payments, etc.). That amounted to a reduction in internal administrative costs. For instance, the accounts payable process could more readily be streamlined when working with a smaller number of suppliers. In particular, Ford Motor was able to reduce the worker headcount of its accounts payable department from 400 to 125 (Hammer 1990). With a smaller number of suppliers, the buying companies also saved costs at the business-to-business level interface. They could reduce the frictional cost of doing business with suppliers (i.e., transaction costs). With a smaller number of suppliers on long-term contracts, they did not have to constantly haggle with multiple suppliers about price or deliveries.

With a smaller number of suppliers, the buyers could obtain favorable prices with consolidated purchase volumes. Many authors have reported on the state of supply base reductions (i.e., Handfield and Nichols 1999; Tully 1995). In particular, Trent and Monczka (1998) point out how aggressively some of the leading focal companies were downsizing their supply bases. General Motors and General Electric have been reported by various authors to have done just that (Ballew and Schnorbus 1994; Bamford 1994). Krause and Handfield (1999) discuss the outcome of supply base rationalization at a large buying company in the electronics industry. This focal company first downsized its business to be more agile in terms of responding to market changes. With a smaller size, it was forced to increase the level of outsourcing. At the same time, the company reduced the size of its supply base. The outcomes were staggering. Choi and Krause (2006) report that "the company reduced the supply base to such an extent that 97% of outsourcing expenditures were going to only about 40 suppliers, with the top 5% receiving 65% of the total spend" (p. 640).

There was a catch, though. With all the benefits of supply base reduction came an increased dependence on the remaining suppliers. A visitor came to Arizona State University from Volvo with this issue as a topic of discussion. He was a senior procurement executive with his office in Gothenburg, Sweden. His firm had made a bold move by downsizing its supply base from 800 suppliers to 40. It took a lot of effort, but implementing the change was successful. The suppliers took on more subsystem-level responsibility—they produced modules rather than individual parts. However, his firm also discovered that the dynamics of the supplier relationship management had changed as well. Sensing the buying firm's increased dependence on them, the suppliers became more assertive. His company was in unfamiliar territory with increased reliance on these 40 suppliers. At this point, to more effectively manage the new relationship dynamics, many leading companies took on a more hands-on approach and tried to learn about how suppliers operated to use that knowledge to manage the relationship (Liker and Choi 2004). By doing so, they would strengthen the buyer-supplier relationship, which is one of the best ways to manage dependency. For example, as children grow up, they gain their own voices and become more assertive in their relationship with their parents. The parents, in fact, become more dependent on their children. At this point, it would be wise for the parents to learn about their children as independent beings with their own personalities. That is why Toyota and other leading focal companies would send supply management representatives to supplier plants to learn about their internal operations. They would do things together. They would jointly work on problems on the supplier's shop floor. By getting their feet wet, the buying company categorically learns about the supplier's strengths and weaknesses. This practice initiated by the buying firm is often called supplier development (i.e., Hartley and Choi 1996; Krause, Handfield, and Scannell 1998). The important point here is that the improvement drive is initiated by the focal company, and as the customer company, it can play the role of the "catalyst of process changes" (Hartley and Choi 1996, p. 37). Just as parents would gain the respect of their children by doing things together, the buying firm gains the respect of the suppliers in this way.

There is also an economic calculus. One of the benefits of helping suppliers make improvements and gain additional efficiency is that doing so would lower their cost of goods sold (COGS). (See Chapter 3 for more on what constitutes COGS and how profit margin and return on investment are affected by COGS). That means the price per unit should go down next time the two firms negotiate a new contract. Further, getting to know the supplier's operations more closely is conducive to a practice called target pricing (Li et al. 2012). When there are many suppliers, the focal company may use competition to arrive at the best price. However, when there are fewer of them in a reduced supply base, the focal company can get to know the supplier more closely and its cost structure better. Therefore, instead of using large-scale competition to arrive at a price, the focal company can derive a target price to ensure the supplier covers its own manufacturing costs plus an agreed-upon margin. That way, the suppliers stay financially healthy, and the buying firm attains the best possible unit price.

Organizing Suppliers in a Supply Base

In more recent years, there have been efforts to integrate the company's rationalized supply base and the needs of their internal stakeholders (i.e., operations, engineering, human resources, etc.) (Hartley and Choi 2020a). The needed goods and services procured from the suppliers are categorized into groups with similar purchase characteristics. In this way, more coherent and consistent strategies can be applied to the suppliers to meet the focal company's needs. In this process, certain categories are considered more important than others in terms of the dollars spent, and suppliers are organized into A, B, or C groups, with A being the most important supplier. Using the logic of Pareto analysis, the A group would account for most of the dollars spent (i.e., 60% to 80%) but involve the least number of suppliers (i.e., 10% to 30%) in the supply base. However, when it comes to cyber threats, the suppliers in the C group become most vulnerable and require the most attention from the focal company (Rogers, Choi, and Jeong 2021). Further, with more focal firms competing on innovation, managing startup suppliers that can bring fresh ideas is emerging as a critical consideration beyond cost and delivery (Kurpjuweit, Wagner, and Choi 2021). In this section, we consider how suppliers are being organized in terms of category management, how ABC groupings take on a new meaning in cybersecurity, and how startup suppliers should be considered as a new category outside the traditional ABC groups.

Category Management

The practice of category management is still new to many companies. Many focal companies are starting to categorize their purchase requirements, but a few leading companies that are more mature in their use of category management have adopted it for all their purchases (Hartley and Choi 2020b). It is poised as a new way of organizing a company's strategic-sourcing initiatives and its supply base management. Once grouped into a category, the focal company could apply consistent policies and strategies to procuring specific groups of products and services. These policies and strategies would be applied to a group of qualified suppliers for that category. Generally, one supplier would belong in one category, but there could be instances where a supplier might be associated with multiple categories. As such, the concept of category management is intimately tied to the concept of supply base rationalization we discussed above.

In category management, the focal company organizes into a category a group of purchases that share similar characteristics. For instance, precious metals (i.e., platinum, palladium, gold, silver, etc.) share similar properties (i.e., how their prices fluctuate), and procuring them could be subject to the company's standard policies and strategies. Other examples of categories are chemicals, packaging, castings, logistics services, and so forth. Two important sources of information in creating categories are derived from spend analysis and market analysis. Spend analysis identifies how the money is being spent concerning various purchase items, and market analysis characterizes the external market pertaining to particular goods or services. Once a category is created, supply managers would then devise a strategic plan jointly with their internal stakeholders for procuring the listed items from a group of suppliers. A typical time horizon for such a plan is usually around three years (Hartley and Choi 2020b). A supply manager engaged in this type of category management activity has also been called a category manager. Category managers develop category-specific knowledge and experience with suppliers operating in that category and would be regarded as an expert in that category.

Pulling together similar purchases and coordinating their procurement would allow supply management to consolidate their supply base with fewer suppliers. With fewer suppliers, the conditions are more conducive for procurement processes to be standardized, and volume discounts and transportation economies are more easily realized. With fewer suppliers, the focal companies can receive goods and services of more consistent quality and with greater efficiency. For example, Honda of America limits its source of plastic resin to two or three suppliers for consistent quality (Choi and Hong 2002). In this regard, category management is also called commodity management. The goal of commodity management is to work with fewer suppliers with more consolidated purchases. Often, we see global commodity teams in large multinational corporations that come together to share information on the supply market of a particular commodity around the globe and to devise the best strategies to procure it in the global context.

For a very long time, focal companies have focused on cost-reduction efforts, which shows up on the company's balance sheet. As they increase their level of outsourcing, the impact of such savings on the bottom line becomes more significant. Some of these underlying dynamics are explained in Chapter 3. Consequently, supply management has worked with multiple suppliers to generate competitive pressures and then has searched for ways to optimize the size of the supply base, as discussed above. The emphasis has been on cost and efficiency. With category management, supply managers now add strategic orientation to their responsibility. Such responsibilities would rest within the context of identifiable categories of similar items that are distinguished by uniquely defined characteristics.

ABC Suppliers and Cybersecurity

The ABC grouping stems from the Pareto principle or more commonly known as the 80-20 rule. Vilfredo Pareto was an Italian economist who discovered how 80% of the land in Italy was owned by 20% of the population. This principle has been applied in the business context and observed how 80% of the revenue comes from 20% of products or how 80% of labor is spent on 20% of the stock keeping units (SKUs) in a warehouse (i.e., small items require more manual handling). The ABC grouping of purchase items works on the same logic—the A group contains the most important items but takes up the smallest number of items compared to the B and C groups. The C group contains the least important items but takes up the highest number of items compared to the A and B groups. Carter and Choi (2008) claim that grouping items into A, B, or C is "the single most important step in identifying savings opportunities within supply management" (p. 66). As a reminder, the A group represents items that are the most expensive or most

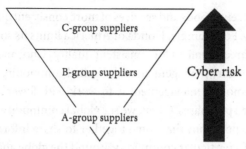

Figure 5.3 A-B-C Suppliers and Cyber Risk
Source: Adapted from Rogers, Choi, and Jeong 2021

critical, or both. We then recommend spending most of the supply management resources on these A items and suppliers that provide these items. The B and C items, while still required, do not warrant as much scrutiny.

Accordingly, focal companies have paid more attention to A-group suppliers as these A items offer the biggest bang for their buck. These suppliers handling A-group items receive the most attention while minimal resources and time are spent on C-group items. However, for cyber threats, C-group suppliers represent the most vulnerable points for the focal company. As shown in Figure 5.3, for cybersecurity, C-group suppliers demand more supply management attention as they represent the highest level of cyber risk (Rogers, Choi, and Jeong 2021).

This observation is in stark contrast to the conventional wisdom about how a focal company should manage A-group suppliers vs. B- or C-group suppliers. As previously noted, the conventional wisdom has the focal company spending more time and attention on A-group suppliers over B- or C-group suppliers. This is perfectly understandable. For instance, we would expect Walmart to spend significant resources on managing suppliers such as Proctor & Gamble or HP Inc. We would not expect Walmart to spend comparable resources on managing a regional supplier in the B- or C-group. However, cyber breaches are putting that calculus on its head, as shown in Figure 5-3. Once a cyber hacker breaks into a C-group supplier, the hacker would then steal the supplier's credentials and attack the larger and more resource-rich focal companies (Rogers and Choi 2018).

Therefore, the focal companies trying to manage their supply bases for potential cyber threats have a difficult task. There are a much larger number of suppliers in the B- and C-groups than in the A-group. The focal companies cannot possibly spend the level of time and attention on all B- and C-group suppliers that they spend on their A-group suppliers. Rogers, Choi, and Jeong (2021) make a few suggestions.

The key is controlling the supplier's access to digital information at the focal company. The situation the focal company wants to avoid is for a cyber attacker to hack into its information system and move about unhindered. For instance, if we hire a plumber to fix the drain under the kitchen sink, we would limit the plumber's access in our home to the kitchen. We would not allow the plumber to move freely around the whole house. It is the same concept. The focal companies should organize a cross-functional team comprised of supply management and information systems professionals. They should develop a cyber A-B-C grouping that would determine an appropriate level of access to their back-office information network. For instance, a C-group supplier providing simple brackets or copier maintenance services should not be allowed to access the focal company's point-of-sale data or customer records. A major A-group supplier may be allowed to access the focal company's inventory information, but a B- or C-group supplier that occasionally makes deliveries would not need the focal company's real-time inventory information. (More on cybersecurity in the next chapter on extended supply chains)

Startup Suppliers as a Category

Startup suppliers are an essential source of innovation for the focal company. They have to be considered as a new category of suppliers for the focal company to succeed in identifying these suppliers and establishing a working relationship with them (Kurpjuweit, Wagner, and Choi 2021). An important point is that if startup suppliers are subjected to the established and routine supplier selection process, they will not be able to offer their full potential to the focal company. They must be considered differently if the focal company is to reap the full benefit. In this regard, startup suppliers should occupy a distinct category within a focal company's supply base that is treated with special care.

The important characteristic the focal company needs to keep in mind is that, while startup suppliers offer the innovation potential, they lack financial stability and established operational processes. Therefore, if startup suppliers are subjected to typical supplier selection (i.e., quality, cost, delivery, flexibility, etc.), they are not likely to be competitive with other incumbent suppliers. Kurpjuweit, Wagner, and Choi (2021) offer an example of a focal company in construction equipment manufacturing. A startup supplier came up against other more established suppliers when bidding for a job of producing a new steering unit for construction machines. All established suppliers submitted a proposal that was clearly less innovative than the startup, but they scored better on key supplier selection criteria such as financial stability and various certificates. The startup supplier stood no chance of being selected. Ultimately, this startup was chosen because a senior R&D (research and development) manager championed this supplier and convinced the CEO of its unique technology. The only reason this startup supplier was selected was that it was pulled out of the routine supplier selection process and treated differently as if in a separate category.

According to Kurpjuweit, Wagner, and Choi (2021), there are three types of focal companies when it comes to how they manage startup suppliers—skeptical buyers, opportunistic adapters, and systematic selectors. Skeptical buyers would be steeped in the "not invented here" syndrome, and they would be skeptical toward startup suppliers. These focal companies do not trust startup suppliers. For these focal companies, the risk of working with unproven suppliers outweighs the potential benefits. They would not be willing to consider startup suppliers as a new category in their supply bases.

In contrast, opportunistic adapters and systematic buyers would be willing to consider startup suppliers as a new category and establish a separate track to qualify these suppliers. The difference between opportunistic adapters and systematic buyers is that the former would accommodate startup suppliers with a different selection process only partially, but the latter would fully accommodate startup suppliers. Opportunistic adapters would use an existing organizational structure (i.e., R&D department or a design engineer) to be responsible for working with startup suppliers. In contrast, systematic selectors create a dedicated group (i.e., department) to work with startup suppliers.

Opportunistic adapters and systematic selectors take an active approach to compiling a pool of startup suppliers in their supply base. The difference between the two is that systematic selectors cast their net much wider than opportunistic adapters when searching for potential startup suppliers in their supply bases. Opportunistic adapters would conduct more of a focused search depending on their needs, and because of that, their search goes through a hit-or-miss process. Sometimes, they get lucky and find a startup supplier they need, but other times they do not. Also, because they use an existing organizational structure to conduct the search, the entity that is doing the search has a more limited capacity since working with startup suppliers is an addition to their everyday work. In contrast, systematic selectors compile their supply base of startup suppliers and organize them systematically so that when the need arises, they can be much more efficient in locating the right startup supplier for their business requirements.

Managing Supply Base

Suppliers in a company's supply base may be organized in various ways, as we have discussed, and they are there for a purpose. With increasing levels of outsourcing, the focal company orchestrates various activities with suppliers in their supply base, from cost engineering to new product development, and this has become a key strategic issue for top management (Agrawal and Nahmias 1997; Dyer 1996; Fine 1998). As the focal company relies more on its supply base for a more significant share of the total input into its own transformation process, the percentage of purchased goods and services increases concerning its total COGS, as discussed in Chapter 3. Thus, the company's dependence on its supply base increases, and how it organizes its supply base becomes more critical to the company's success.

Organizing Supply Base as a System

As such, it is critical for the focal company to understand how its supply base is put together as a system. As shown earlier in Figure 5.2, in its supply base, some suppliers are connected, and some exist as isolates. Those that are connected have a supplier-supplier relationship from the focal company's perspective. Some may be working together on collaborative efforts at the behest of the focal company (i.e., to develop a new product, share capacity, etc.). Or, they may have their own buyer-supplier relationship arrangement or may be engaged in a partnership (i.e., to pool their resources to respond to a call for proposals from the focal company). How the ties once removed among suppliers (i.e., supplier-supplier relationship) are organized is important for the focal company as it manages the supply base as a system. Much of the triadic dynamics we discussed in Chapter 4 would be applicable here.

We now introduce an important term that we will come back to as we proceed in this book—*complexity*. This is because, to manage a system, understanding the complexity of that system is the critical first step (Gottinger 1983); otherwise, managerial intervention would lead to unanticipated outcomes that are less effective. For instance, the focal company may decide to bring two suppliers together to work on a joint project without knowing their history of animosity. This particular intervention would then face an uphill battle from the beginning. To execute the decision, the focal company may have to spend much more corporate resources than planned. Building on the work of Waldrop (1992), Kauffman (1996), and Dooley (2001), we state that complexity of a system is captured in three things (Choi and Krause 2006)— number of elements, level of connectivity among the elements, and how similar or different these elements are from one another.

Suppose we are managing a social club. The complexity will increase if we have more members to manage, more pre-existing ties among the members, and members' personalities are all unique and different. Managing a corporation as an executive works much the same way. The company's complexity would increase if there were many departments or divisions, if all of them had to coordinate with all the others, and if all departments or divisions had very different organizational cultures or work processes. Intuitively, complexity refers to the level of "load" the manager must take on to manage the system efficiently.

Applied to managing a supply base as a system, managers must know the number of suppliers in its supply base, the interrelationships among the suppliers, and how similar or different these suppliers are. In Choi and Krause (2006), we have discussed the number of suppliers in the context of supply base rationalization and interrelationships among suppliers in the context of the supplier-supplier relationship. The similarity or differences across suppliers in the supply base is perhaps one that is often overlooked but would be just as important for how we should manage the supply base. It refers to the degree to which suppliers are similar or differentiated in terms of their business processes, organizational culture, technology, size, and location. Toyota has in place Bluegrass Automotive Manufacturers Association (BAMA), where its suppliers come and share their experiences with Toyota in terms of work processes and technology. Once suppliers adopt common work processes as stipulated in Toyota's Production System, that would reduce complexity for Toyota when managing its supply base. Many focal companies may request the co-location of their suppliers to reduce complexity. Once co-located, the complexity that may arise from variations in transportation and deliveries in terms of the mode and geographical distances, for instance, can be minimized. As such, with a lower number of suppliers, interrelationships between suppliers, and differences across suppliers, the workload by the focal company in managing its supply base would be reduced.

Redefining Supply Base

A supply base is a portion of a larger supply network that is visible to the focal company. In this regard, we often say those would be the first-tier suppliers. That would be certainly correct, because all first-tier suppliers would necessarily be visible to the focal company. However, that would also be an insufficient statement. This is because the focal company may have a visual on a few key second- and third-tier suppliers. Honda, for example, has a visual on a few of its lower tier suppliers, and it actively manages them for quality and cost (Choi and Hong 2002). Actively managing means Honda has a contractual agreement with these lower tier suppliers and monitors them for performance. This practice is often called directed sourcing, meaning the focal company works directly with a lower tier supplier. (More on this when we get to the next chapter on extended supply chains.)

Therefore, in a supply network study by Choi and Hong (2002), Honda's supply base for its center console for the Honda Accord includes its first-tier suppliers (i.e., CVT and JFC). It also consists of a second-tier supplier, Emhart, a third-tier supplier, Garden State, and other third-tier suppliers, GE Plastics and C&C Tech. As first-tier suppliers, CVT assembles the center console module, except for the cupholders, and JFC supplies the cupholders. Interestingly, this division of work was induced mainly by the market research that, for American consumers, the cupholders represented one of the five most important features in an automobile that affected the purchase decision. JFC owned the intellectual property (IP) on the damping mechanism that controls the rate of release of the cupholder cover. At the time, Honda was trying to have the cupholders supplied to CVT so that CVT would become the one-stop shop for the complete cupholder assembly. CVT and Honda were in negotiations for this change, which would affect the relationship arrangement in the console supply base. If this change were to occur, JFC would then be a second-tier supplier, but it would still be part of Honda's supply base.

Emhart, in the second tier, manufactures fasteners (i.e., nuts and bolts). For the Accord center console, it was supplying metal clips. Honda had a direct contractual agreement with Emhart and directed it to provide the parts to CVT, a first-tier supplier. The reason why Honda engaged in directed sourcing for a metal clip supplier, which does not seem like an expensive part, was because Emhart supplied fasteners for many of the other Honda products. It was a common denominator supplier across all Honda products for fasteners. Garden State is the third-tier supplier that handles leather goods. Honda chose to engage in directed sourcing with Garden State because leather goods are expensive. That meant 1% cost savings would translate into more savings in dollars. Honda instructed Garden State to deliver parts to CVT and asked CVT to manage Garden State only for delivery since it manages Garden State for cost and quality. To this relationship structure, CVT inserted a fabrication supplier, Universal Trim, unbeknownst to Honda. This decision caused Garden State to become a third-tier supplier rather than a second-tier supplier. Lastly, Honda chose GE Plastics and C&C Tech as the only two qualified suppliers for plastic resin. This decision was primarily due to quality concerns, that is, if plastic resins come from multiple suppliers, that may cause more variation in the texture of finished plastic parts. As illustrated in this example of the Honda Accord center console, suppliers in Honda's supply base include not only the first-tier suppliers but also several second- and third-tier suppliers. Table 5.1 summarizes the definition of the key terms we have discussed. Conceptually, we have to think about the supply base as a portion of a larger supply network.

Table 5.1 Supply Base Management Key Terms

Terms	Definitions
Complexity	Number of elements, interrelatedness between elements, and variedness among elements in a system
Supply network	All interconnected companies that exist upstream of a focal company
Supply base	A portion of the supply network actively managed by the focal company
Supply base complexity	The overall number of suppliers, the level of supplier-supplier relationships, and the degree of differentiation among suppliers

Source: Adapted from Choi and Krause 2006

Choi and Krause (2006) define a supply base as "those suppliers (in the larger supply network) that are actively managed (by the focal company) through contracts and the purchase of parts, materials, and services" (p. 639). As illustrated in Figure 5.2 above, these suppliers may also have their own interrelationships. To manage these interrelationships, how similar or different they are would have significant implications. These observations again bring us back to the concept of complexity and how that might facilitate managing a supply base from the focal company's perspective.

Complexity and Supply Base Complexity

The concept of complexity has been addressed by scholars across different disciplines, from organizational design and social systems (Daft 2013; Dooley 2001; LaPorte 2015; Price and Mueller 1986) to computational physics and evolutionary biology (Holland 1995; Kauffman 1993; Waldrop 1992). In Daft (2013) and Price and Mueller (1986), complexity refers to the varied elements in organizations and how much structural differentiation exists. Blau and Schoenherr (1971) describe complexity as "the number of structural components that are formally distinguished" (p. 302) in a system. Price and Mueller (1986) say "complexity is the degree of formal structural differentiation within an organization" (p. 100).

There are many subsystems and varied goals of these subsystems that give rise to complexity. LaPorte (2015) contrasts a complex system that has many parts and a simple system that has only a few. According to Dooley (2001), how these subsystems are linked together also contributes to complexity. For instance, the degree of coupling (i.e., tight vs. loose) among elements in a system affects complexity. A tight coupling that requires lots of coordination would necessarily require more load on management in terms of their attention and resources. For instance, a *Kanban*-driven delivery system that arrives multiple times daily based on a precise timetable would represent a tight coupling. A more loosely coupled version of inventory delivery would be an agreement that assigns a six-hour window of time each month for the delivery arrival. As such, when the elements that are closely coupled together make choices, as two suppliers in the supply base, that would increase the management load for the focal company. Simply, a supply base with mostly non-transient triads would be less complex than a supply base with lots of transient triads that have suppliers interconnected between them.

Interestingly, all these researchers from organization design and social systems define complexity similar to researchers from science and engineering. The three dimensions of complexity (i.e., number of elements,
interconnectedness, and differentiated states) overlap perfectly with how
Kauffman (1993), a physician and computational biologist, defines complexity. He proposes three variables in his NK model of a complex system—N
is elements that reside in the system, A is alternate states these elements exist
in, and K is number of couplings among the elements. These dimensions map
one-to-one with how LaPorte (2015) captures a social system from a sociological perspective—number of individuals in a social system, social role differentiation of individuals, and degree of interdependence among the individuals.

Applied to a supply base, N refers to the number of suppliers in the supply
base that have enduring buyer-supplier relationships. When a focal company
says, it is rationalizing its supply base, that almost always means reducing the
number of suppliers in its supply base. Thus, the focal company is attempting
to reduce the complexity of its supply base. According to Handfield and
Nichols (1999), when a focal company uses multiple suppliers for a purchase
item, it incurs a higher level of coordination costs when compared to using
fewer suppliers. With a smaller number of suppliers (i.e., dual sourcing), the
focal company stands a better chance of implementing a more efficient supplier interface (i.e., inventory control).

The presence of A, alternate states, affects the level of complexity the
focal company has to manage in its supply base. Since it is easier for similar elements to connect with each other than with dissimilar elements, it
requires less effort to connect similar suppliers in the supply base than dissimilar suppliers. For example, one reason why Japanese automakers were
able to introduce new product lines quickly into the market was that their
supply base included many similar suppliers. Their clan-like structure, as
mentioned called keiretsu, had suppliers sharing common communication
styles and common business processes (Burt and Doyle 1993; Nishiguchi
1994; Womack, Jones, and Roos 2014). Typical sources of differentiation
among suppliers are operational practices, technical capabilities, organizational culture, and geographical dispersion. If suppliers share similar operational practices and technical capabilities, the focal company will find
it easier to have them work together. If the suppliers share similar cultural
norms and values, their communications and collaboration would be more
accessible. If the suppliers are not geographically dispersed, the complexity
of coordinating work would be less of a burden.

We discussed the pertinence of supplier-supplier relationships in Chapter 3. The K number of couplings among suppliers in a supply base builds on that discussion. In a supply base, for instance, we see many reciprocal business relationships between suppliers. A plastic-molding company that produces small molded parts in various shapes may supply to a metal parts manufacturer. Then, this metal parts manufacturer may provide metal parts (e.g., clips or brackets) to the plastic-molding company. This supplier-supplier example takes place in the dyadic context. As discussed in Chapter 4, business relationships among suppliers can become triadic. For instance, two suppliers that are competing against each other may supply to another supplier in the same supply base. All these crisscrossing interrelationships that may exist in a supply base add complexity to the focal company's management of its supply base.

Choi and Krause (2006) define supply base complexity as "the degree of differentiation of the focal firm's suppliers, their overall number, and the degree to which they interrelate" (p. 643). A supply base is more complex when there are lots of suppliers and lots of interrelationships of various types, but they do not share similar business processes or organizational cultures. With fewer suppliers and fewer interrelationships between suppliers and suppliers operating under shared business practices and norms, the load on the focal company from supply base complexity would be less.

Transaction Cost, Supply Risk, Supplier Responsiveness, and Supplier Innovation

When facing the complexity of a supply base, the four constructs arguably represent the most salient managerial concerns for the focal company— transaction costs, supply risk, supplier responsiveness, and supplier innovation. Transaction costs are incurred at the interface of the focal company and its suppliers. Based on Williamson (1981), we refer to it as the frictional cost of doing business with external companies. Supply risk (e.g., Schoenherr, Mena, and Choi 2019) addresses external disruptions that could get in the way of ensuring the continuity of supply from the supply base. Supplier responsiveness (e.g., Handfield and Nichols 1999) captures the timeliness of receiving goods and services from the supply base and the willingness and capability of suppliers to adjust to changing business conditions. Supplier innovation (e.g., Yan, Dooley, and Choi 2018) reflects how well a focal

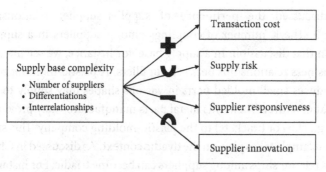

Figure 5.4 Supply Base Complexity and Its Effects
Source: Adapted from Choi and Krause 2006

company can harness the creativity of its suppliers in the supply base through new product development and process improvement.

Figure 5.4 shows the association between supply base complexity and each of the four constructs. A plus sign signifies a positive association, and a minus sign represents a negative association. A U-shaped sign signifies a positive quadratic association, and an inverse U-shaped sign means a negative quadratic association. In Euclidean coordinates, supply base complexity would represent the x axis, and the four constructs would represent the y axis. Supply base complexity on the x axis would be considered an independent variable that the focal company can manipulate depending on its strategic thrust to affect the four constructs as dependent variables on the y axis. The focal company can choose to emphasize any one or more of the three dimensions of supply base complexity; for instance, many focal companies have primarily emphasized the number of suppliers in their supply bases over differentiation and interrelationships between suppliers. The latter two dimensions may become more important as we consider supply bases as an ecosystem, which is the topic covered the following section.

The underlying premise of transaction cost theory (Williamson 1981) is that all industrial companies would behave in an opportunistic way that leads to goal incongruence, and they operate in a boundedly rational way that leads to information asymmetry. Therefore, suppliers will behave opportunistically, and the focal company will need to spend resources to monitor them. The frictional costs are incurred as the focal company engages in "developing and maintaining an exchange relationship, monitoring exchange behaviors, and guarding against opportunism in an exchange situation" (Pilling, Crosby, and Jackson 1994, p. 239).

Consequently, a focal company with a large number of suppliers in its supply base would necessarily incur higher transaction costs. When a supply base includes suppliers whose operating procedures are different from one another, transaction costs would be high for the focal company. For instance, two suppliers may have a different way of documenting their work processes, and that causes extra resources for the focal company. Of course, the focal company can impose a uniform way of processing documents, but that initiative in and of itself would incur additional costs.

Further, the suppliers may not comply to the focal company's satisfaction, and it may take some time to establish a uniform process, all of which would be an additional transaction cost. Further, as some suppliers begin to interact, the focal company has to monitor their activities lest they engage in opportunistic behaviors (i.e., potential collusion). All of these considerations suggest there is a positive association between supply base complexity and transaction costs.

The positive quadratic association between supply base complexity and supply risk means the supply risk is highest when the complexity of the supply base is really high or really low. It promotes the idea of finding a moderate level of supply base complexity for the best result in managing supply risk. This point is illustrated well by an example that involves a focal company that manufacturers electronics for consumer and industrial uses (Krause and Handfield 1999). This focal company first reduced its supply base to a minimum and then, realizing the risk of having too small of a supply base, increased the size back up to a moderate level.

This company had 84 cable suppliers and, with a desire to improve the continuity of supply, had a team of commodity managers responsible for cable supplies travel to these supplier's facilities around the globe to assess them. After analyzing the data they had compiled, the team reduced its supply base from 84 suppliers to four suppliers. They were attracted to all the benefits of the small supply base we discussed early in this chapter. The focal company could forge a deeper relationship with these four suppliers, and the four suppliers could develop a deeper relationship among themselves by meeting more frequently and sharing necessary information to ensure the needs of the focal companies are met. The focal company wanted to ensure it minimized the risk of being short on cable supplies and encouraged the four suppliers to support one another. It even implemented a risk-management plan for potential cable supply disruptions from possible man-made disasters (i.e., fire) and natural disasters (i.e., floods). This

focal company reduced the overall level of supply base complexity by reducing their supplier base to four suppliers from 84, lowering differences
among suppliers by having them meet to develop a common mode of communication and work processes, and encouraging them to work together
closely for risk-management plans. However, a few months later, the focal
company realized that having only four suppliers that worked closely together posed a risk over and above the risk associated with continuity of
supply. This focal company decided to increase the size of its supply base.
With its suppliers in the cable supply base between 10 and 15, the focal
company found a sweet spot—a moderate level of suppliers, supplier differentiation, and interrelationships.

Supplier responsiveness on the upstream side of its supply chain is critical
for the focal company to meet its customer expectations on the downstream
side. The focal company looks for promptness and accuracy from its suppliers
to new requirements (Goodman et al. 1995). At a casual glance, it may appear that a large number of suppliers might be good for supplier responsiveness because more suppliers would prompt more competition among them
and their willingness to comply with the focal company's emerging needs.
However, competitive pressure does not necessarily lead to supplier responsiveness (Celly, Spekman, and Kamauff 1999). What contributes to supplier responsiveness is open and trusting communication that comes from
a close buyer-supplier relationship (Handfield and Bechtel 2002; Liker and
Choi 2004).

A case in point is the buying company's use of "preferred" suppliers. Many
focal companies have a group of suppliers with this designation to indicate the suppliers with whom they maintain open communications. With a
smaller number of preferred suppliers, focal companies can more effectively
communicate their changing needs and prompt responsiveness. According
to a study by Treleven and Schweikhart (1988), single sourcing is better associated with supplier responsiveness. If a design change is required, working
with one supplier is more conducive to timely and accurate communication
than working with multiple suppliers. Larson and Kulchitsky (1998) concur
that single sourcing is associated with buyer-supplier cooperation that
induces supplier responsiveness. By the same token, a supply base with more
differentiated suppliers and more connected suppliers would make it more
difficult for the focal company to build close relationships for better supplier
responsiveness. Therefore, there would be a negative relationship between
supply base complexity and supplier responsiveness.

Initially, we might argue that more complex supply bases would lead to more supplier innovation. Having multiple suppliers (i.e., working with two to three suppliers versus one supplier) would offer more ideas for the focal company, and having them work together could provide synergy and integrated ideas. According to Ahuja (2000), "each additional node that a firm has access to can serve as an information-processing mechanism that goes well beyond the information-processing capabilities of a single firm" (p. 430). The suppliers can share their thoughts and commit more resources to joint activities such as new product development and participating in a learning network (Sobrero and Roberts 2002). Thus, collaboratively sharing ideas across multiple suppliers would lead to innovation. And when these suppliers have more differentiation (i.e., more heterogeneity), their ideas would tend to be more creative (i.e., innovative) (Choi and Krause 2006). Dooley and Van de Ven (1999) argue that a large number of suppliers with differentiated cultures and technical capabilities would lead to more innovation.

However, caution is issued against postulating a simple linear relationship between supply base complexity and supplier innovation (Bacon 1985; Dooley and Van de Ven 1999). Bacon (1985) suggests that highly differentiated and creative activities in a supply base would also increase the need to integrate them with existing products. At the extreme, they would lead to anarchy and act as an impediment to coherent activities. Dooley and Van de Ven (1999) also point out that without coordination, differentiated behaviors in a supply base would become unstructured and random. These effects would necessarily be accentuated when there are large numbers of suppliers and their dependencies are high. Therefore, there would likely be an inflection point in the positive association between supply complexity and supplier innovation beyond which the association actually becomes negative. That realization gives us an inverted U-shaped relationship between supply base complexity and supplier innovation.

Supplier Ecosystem

A supply base may be viewed as a supplier ecosystem. That might be the best way to manage complexity in the supply base (Wiengarten, Choi, and Fan 2020). In an ecosystem, every constituent (i.e., supplier) has a role to play and interacts with others for the functioning and well-being of the system (i.e., supply base). Then, one might wonder what might be the difference between a supply base and a supplier ecosystem. There are a few critical differences, and these differences are important as we anticipate continuing global disruptions and technological advancements (i.e., supply chain digitization) to cope with these disruptions.

First, a supplier ecosystem warrants more autonomy for supplier-supplier communication and coordination. Whereas we have thought of a supply base as a centrally managed system by the focal company, we are beginning to embrace a more decentrally managed system in a supplier ecosystem. For instance, a major aerospace manufacturer has a supplier room in the cloud through a software platform where suppliers work together on projects without the focal company's real-time presence. In a supply base, the focal company would typically have a presence in all projects involving suppliers to monitor their activities and steer them toward the target.

Second, in a supply base, the focal company would manage one supplier at a time, similar to how bilateral agreements occur in international trade. In contrast, a supplier ecosystem is like having a multilateral agreement among many countries. If the focal company wants to change its purchasing protocols and specifications, instead of updating the contract one supplier at a time, it can do that through an online platform instantly across the entire supplier interface. For example, a large information technology (IT) corporation has created a blockchain-based platform as a digital community. Through this platform, a group of suppliers can be onboarded for a group of focal companies.

Third, when moving from managing a supply base to a supplier ecosystem, the mode of a focal company's involvement migrates from buyer centric to "buyer led." In the buyer-centric mode, the focal company would manage the supply base. In contrast, as an ecosystem, the buyer would recruit members of an ecosystem, propose rules of engagement, and set goals. Then, it would allow the suppliers to converge and engage one another on their own.

CAPS Research recently published a report on supplier ecosystems (Wiengarten 2019). The study poses two questions—how could focal companies initiate and manage supplier ecosystems, and what value they should expect to get from it. A case study approach was used, and the data were collected from nine companies. Initially, the complexity issue had not been posed to the companies that participated in the study. Nonetheless, complexity kept coming up during the interviews and became a recurring theme when discussing the supplier ecosystem.

Globalization has increased the complexity of supply bases. Constantly looking for low-cost sources, focal companies have increased the geographical distance across their suppliers and have to cross multiple international borders. On the one hand, globalization has given focal companies greater opportunities for new technological capabilities and lower prices. On the other hand, it has exposed its supply base to higher levels of disruption risks and potential loss of overall efficiencies. One IT company in the CAPS report stated, "the traditional efficiency focused supply chain strategy is not working for our complex products and services anymore." In other words, increased complexity in its supply base requires a different approach beyond the buyer-centric, top-down approach. It needs a more decentralized collaborative approach that can offer a context in which a diverse group of suppliers could gather and be able to contribute to a common objective. In such an ecosystem approach, the focal company would operate as a facilitator that offers leadership but allows its members to operate with more autonomy.

One focal company in the consumer goods industry even brought the suppliers and its end customers together. It facilitated their interactions through which new customer requirements were identified by the suppliers. In a supplier ecosystem, suppliers are recognized as stakeholders and are offered a context through which to compete and cooperate at the same time, often not on the focal company's terms but their own terms. For instance, instead of worrying about the possibility of collusion when it brings suppliers together and instituting safeguarding measures, the focal company, in this case, leaves it to the suppliers to understand the risk of such potential collusion and lets them guard each other on their own.

A focal company in the fast-moving consumer goods industry is highlighted as exemplary. Benchmarking this focal company's practices reveals a few leading practices within the supplier ecosystem.

- The focal company offers an economic calculus to all suppliers. It makes sure everyone knows that, in its supplier ecosystem, there is "something in it" for everyone. For new products and services that come out of the ecosystem, rules and policies are explicitly stated for sharing gains.
- The concept of co-opetition among suppliers is openly embraced. The focal company poses competing and cooperating at the same time as an important aspect of the supplier ecosystem and value creation.
- Leadership exercised by the focal company is multidimensional. During the early phases of goal setting and value articulation, the focal company

behaves as a charismatic leader. However, once suppliers begin to act and move toward the goal, it practices more as a team-based leader focusing on solving problems and making progress.

- Socialization among suppliers and the focal company is valued. Much of the socialization occurs during supplier summits. Learning about the culture at each supplier's organization is deemed critical for selecting new suppliers for a specific ecosystem.
- Technologies are mainly used for two purposes. One is to facilitate connectivity and communication among ecosystem suppliers. The other maintains the database and analyzes data using AI over supplier capabilities and past performance. The focal company maintains transparency and shares relevant information with the rest of the ecosystem member companies. The intent is to maintain competitive pressure and promote creativity through collaboration.

This focal company is at the mature end of the ecosystem maturity levels. Other focal companies are less mature. All the participating focal companies operate their own respective supply bases, and more mature focal companies have shifted to managing their supply bases as ecosystems. One thing that stands out about less mature focal companies is that they tend to use supplier ecosystems as an ad-hoc approach on top of their supply bases. Thus, while the mature companies interface their supply bases as supplier ecosystems continually, the less mature companies manage their supply base as they have done before. Still, whenever a need arises to solve a particular problem or work on new product development, they resort to adopting a supplier ecosystem approach. These focal companies use a supplier ecosystem on a project-based approach.

We then ask, what kind of values do these focal companies attain? What other value attainment would more mature focal companies enjoy over those that are less mature? Value outcomes are grouped into two categories—operational and strategic. Operational value includes cost, quality, delivery, and flexibility. Strategic value addresses more long-term outcomes such as innovation, including activities such as new product development. As shown in Figure 5.5, more mature focal companies do attain more, and what they attain more is interesting. Without seeing the data, one may conjecture that less mature companies might gain operational benefits while more mature companies would gain operational and strategic values. In fact, what we see in the data is that more mature companies receive both the operational and strategic values,

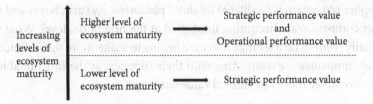

Figure 5.5 Ecosystem Maturity and Value Attainment
Source: Wiengarten, Choi, and Fan 2020

as expected. However, less mature companies receive the strategic values without the operational values. Less mature companies do not gain operational values at the functional level, while more mature companies do.

In supplier ecosystems, we find that strategic values are attained first and then operational values come. Strategic values are attained through new product or service development that represents a major departure from past offerings. Less mature ecosystems tend to focus on this type of radical innovation value. In contrast, mature ecosystems exhibit innovations that are radical as well incremental in nature. Less mature ecosystems seek low-hanging fruit that can be harvested quickly, which tend to be project based, whereas more mature ecosystems sustain themselves with many different types of ongoing activities. Another strategic value that may emerge as a byproduct is potential access to new markets. Some focal companies can take advantage of their suppliers' extended business ties that may bring them to sectors of the market they may not have been exposed to in the past. One participating focal company in the IT industry, in particular, has been able to take advantage of the new sources that came through its suppliers and associated new sales markets.

This focal company also discovered that it is gaining operational performance values as it attempts to attain strategic values in new sources, markets, and product ideas. As it tries to match supply with demand for the new products and services through its supplier ecosystem, it is repeating the operational benefits of shortened time to market, lower costs, and improved quality. Therefore, operational value performance emerges as a consequence of attaining strategic performance values. Only the more mature ecosystems may provide operational values to focal companies as their implementation of the supplier ecosystem is more comprehensive and continuous.

This is an interesting point we will come back to when we arrive at the last chapter that discusses emerging issues. With increased digitization, the supplier ecosystem is facilitated by cloud platforms. As such, buyer and supplier companies are becoming integrated at the functional level. What may initially seem to be a strange outcome begins to make more sense. Since the focal companies are connecting with their suppliers at the functional level, they would see more operational value outcomes.

Key Points

- If we extend the supplier-supplier relationship in the buyer-supplier-supplier triad horizontally, we get a supply base.
- Supply base rationalization has focused on maintaining the right number of suppliers, and a smaller number has, in general, been more conducive to building deeper buyer-supplier relationships.
- Suppliers in a company's supply base can be organized by different categories that share common product and market characteristics. We call this approach category management.
- In cybersecurity, C-group suppliers are the most vulnerable and represent the highest level of risk; therefore, they require more attention from the focal company compared to the A- or B-group suppliers.
- Startup suppliers as a source of innovation should be managed as a new category; for instance, its qualification should occur outside the routine supplier selection process.
- A company's supply base should be managed as a system, and for that, its complexity needs to be considered.
- A supply base is a portion of a more extensive supply network that is visible to the focal company. It consists of suppliers not only in the first tier but also in other upstream tiers.
- Supply base complexity can be captured per Kauffman's NK model—N suppliers that are in the supply base, A alternate states (i.e., organizational culture, work processes, norms, etc.) these suppliers operate in, and K number of interorganizational relationships among suppliers.
- The complexity of a supply base would have different effects on transaction costs, supply risk, supplier responsiveness, and supplier innovation.
- An ecosystem approach is a new way of managing complexity in a company's supply base.
- Mature ecosystems offer both operational and strategic values, while less mature ecosystems offer strategic values only.

6

Extended Supply Chains

The last time I went to the local bakery in search of my favorite Belgian chocolate cake only to find they were out, I was profoundly disappointed. I had tried very hard to eat fewer cakes during the past few weeks and succeeded to a certain extent. That day, however, I decided to treat myself and celebrate a small success. But, the cake was not available. I do not think my face was a happy face as I glanced at the baking staff in the back. I was indeed thinking to myself, "How could you run out of my favorite cake!"

Maybe I was blaming the bakery, and if I were, I would be behaving just like the buying companies that blame their suppliers when deliveries do not arrive on time or there is a quality problem. As a receiving node in the supply chain, we tend to blame the supplying node. Not just any arbitrary supplying node but typically one that is closest to us, one that is visible to us. As a consumer, I was upset at the bakery, a node immediately upstream to me, for lacking one Belgian chocolate cake. The bakery was in my visual, so it came naturally to assign blame there. In much the same way, the buying companies blame the suppliers they have in their visual range when things do not go right. We all tend to assign cause to a problem to what we see and look for solutions there. The following excerpt is taken from the editorial to a Special Topic Forum on extended supply chains in the *Journal of Business Logistics* (Choi et al. 2021).

> The sun has gone down the western skies. As the darkness descends, you decide to go for a walk. Street lamps have come on, and the air is cool. Soon, you run into an old man crouched down on the ground under a street lamp. He is looking for something. You ask, "Sir, may I help you find something?" He replies, "Yes, I dropped my key, and I do not seem to be able to find it." So, you crouch down next to him under the street lamp and try to look for it. After a while, you ask, "Sir, could you be more specific as to where you dropped the key?" The old man replies, "I dropped it over there, around the corner in that dark alley." A bit flustered, you reply back, "Sir, shouldn't

The Nature of Supply Networks. Thomas Y. Choi, Oxford University Press. © Thomas Y. Choi 2023.
DOI: 10.1093/oso/9780197673249.003.0006

you be looking over there where you dropped the key?" The old man coolly responds, "Ah, but this is where the light is."

It is obvious we should look for the key where it was lost. However, to this old man, it seemed like a no-brainer; we should look for things where we have light. In the dark, we stand a slim chance of finding the key. But, really, it is silly to search for the key a distance away from the place where we dropped it—that is the locus of the cause of our problem and where our efforts should be directed. However, this old man wanted to maximize his chances of finding the key by staying under the light. Yet, again, the fact that what this old man was doing almost seems reasonable, even for a fleeting moment, is a testament to how short-sided our behaviors may sometimes be.

I blame the bakery, and buying companies blame the immediate suppliers. This type of behavior happens even in cybersecurity. Suppose we purchase products from Target and their information system is hacked, and the company lost our credit card numbers. This happened. When the cyberattack descended on Target, it came through a little-known HVAC supplier called Fazio (https://krebsonsecurity.com/2014/02/target-hackers-broke-in-via-hvac-company/). The hackers broke into Fazio's system, stole its supplier credentials, and then slipped into Target's system. Yet, as consumers, we paid little attention to how it happened. We simply blamed Target because it was within our visual range. For consumers, the affected node in the supply chain, Target, as the consumer-facing node, became the immediate and obvious target of the blame.

It was possible the bakery did not receive a few critical ingredients from their suppliers, or another customer had come in earlier that day and purchased all the Belgian chocolate cakes. There could be many potential reasons that caused the shortage, but what did I do? I blamed the bakery. The buying companies would likely do the same in a similar situation. If a shipment arrives with a quality problem, the buying company would, of course, blame the supplier. The buying company would then go after this supplier to solve the problem. We tend to look for solutions where things are visible, where there is light. However, the cause of the problem may have come from outside our visual range, such as the supplier's supplier or the supplier's supplier's supplier (Choi and Hong 2002; Choi and Linton 2011).

When we realize there is a lot more to supply chain management than what meets the eye, causes to supply chain problems may lie in the depths of supply networks, and that is where we need to go to solve problems; we have entered the realm of extended supply chains (Choi et al. 2021). Extended supply chains lie beyond the immediate supply base that typically includes their first-tier suppliers. These suppliers have suppliers who provide them with goods (e.g., raw materials or sub-assemblies) or services (e.g., healthcare, logistics, or software). Once this realization sets in, the focus then shifts to strategies that buying companies may pursue to manage their lower tier suppliers that lie beyond their first-tier suppliers. Leading companies like Honda, Toyota, and Apple directly manage not just their first-tier suppliers but also second-, third-, and other tertiary-level suppliers. For example, Apple outsources its assembly work to Foxconn as its first-tier supplier. However, Apple does not outsource sourcing decisions to Foxconn (Chae et al. 2019). Apple reserves the right to make sourcing decisions for its products. It directly manages its second-, third- and tertiary-level suppliers for its touch-sensitive screens, camera lenses, semiconductor chips, microprocessors, and so forth.

Even so, there are decisions that happen across the supply network beyond the purview of the focal company. For example, even Apple does not know all the suppliers Foxconn uses to put together its products, such as chemicals, logistics services, and other maintenance, repair, and operations (MRO) items. Every focal company must decide how much of the supply network to control and how much to let emerge (Choi, Dooley, and Rungtusanatham 2001). Apple has chosen to control more of its extended supply chains. There are other companies that do not get involved in making sourcing decisions in their extended supply chains. For instance, Honda and Toyota make sourcing decisions for a few critical items in their second- and third-tier of the supply chain (Choi and Hong 2002). Outside these few suppliers, the rest of their extended supply chain would simply emerge for them. At the other extreme end, when Google outsources the manufacturing of its Chromecast to Flex, it sends the blueprint to Flex, its first-tier supplier, and entrusts Flex to make the sourcing decisions on its behalf. Google has chosen to delegate control of its extended supply chains to Flex.

As shown in Figure 6.1, at the center of extended supply chains is a concept called *multi-tier supply chain management*. This concept captures the need to consider not just the immediate supplier but also other suppliers across the supply chain when necessary. While the term, extended supply chain, provides the context, multi-tier supply chain management (SCM) reflects the management orientation. The practice of directed sourcing at the lowest level of abstraction shown in Figure 6.1 occurs more at the functional level (Chae et al. 2019). This practice addresses the decision to select which tertiary-level

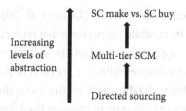

Figure 6.1 Key Constructs in Extended Supply Chains

suppliers the focal company would directly manage. When a focal company practices *directed sourcing*, it is engaged in multi-tier SCM. When we raise the level of abstraction a level above multi-tier SCM, we encounter how focal companies engage in make-buy decisions at the supply chain level. In other words, make-buy decisions occur at the supply chain level, just as at the organizational level (see Chapter 2). When Apple chooses to select all its parts suppliers scattered across the supply chain, Apple is *making* its supply chain. When Google delegates the sourcing decisions to Flex, Google, in fact, is *buying* Flex's supply chain. This is what we refer to as supply chain make and supply chain buy. In between these two extreme points, we have Honda and Toyota engaging in supply chain (SC) make decisions only for select parts in their supply networks.

In the remainder of this chapter, we will address multi-tier SCM first. Then, we discuss directed sourcing at the functional level and, after that, SC make vs. SC buy. Once we are done covering these three constructs, we return to the central construct of multi-tier SCM. We address multi-tier SCM in the triadic context (i.e., three nodes) and the tetradic context (i.e., four nodes). We will close with the emerging multi-tier concerns in cybersecurity. According to Rogers and Choi (2018), over 60% of all known cyberattacks on publicly traded companies in the U.S. have come through extended supply chains. In other words, cybersecurity is not just the problem of information systems, but it is also a supply chain problem.

Multi-Tier Supply Chain Management

One of the early references to multi-tier SCM occurs in the context of supplier selection (Choi and Hartley 1996). It investigates the supplier selection criteria at three different levels of the supply chain in the automotive industry—the focal-company level, first-tier supplier level, and lower tier supplier level. Focal companies are major automakers such as General Motors, Ford, Toyota, and so on. First-tier suppliers are those that supply products directly to the focal companies, while lower tier suppliers are those that supply products to other suppliers. The study reveals the selection criteria that occur differently across different tiers of the supply chain and those that occur commonly. Significant statistical differences appear between the focal companies and the lower tier suppliers in the areas of technological capability and financial concerns. The reason for this result is attributed to the fact that the focal companies would interface with much larger first-tier suppliers with more technological capability and financial emphasis in comparison to the lower tier suppliers. Further, contrary to the initial suspicion, companies across the supply chain all emphasize the value of good relationship management. Initially, the lower tier suppliers were thought be focused on transactional, short-term relationships, but the results indicate otherwise.

Choi and Rungtusanatham (1999) then look across the supply chain and across two different industries of automotive and electronics to investigate potential differences in quality management practices. As in Choi and Hartley (1996), the results do not support a difference in quality management practices across the supply chain. However, we find differences across the industries in the area of strategic quality planning, with the electronics industry lagging behind the automotive industry. This finding is attributed to the nature of these two industries in that the products in the automotive industry tend to have longer product life cycles than those in the electronics industry. With strategic quality planning dealing with more long-term quality issues, it would be expected for the automotive industry to develop advanced practices.

These early studies have taken steps toward looking across the supply chain from a multi-tier perspective. As academic studies, they are quite narrowly focused on specific topics—supplier selection and quality management practices. Choi and Linton (2011) subsequently discuss the broader managerial implications of multi-tier SCM. We make the case for multi-tier SCM by pointing out how solely relying on a first-tier supplier can hamper the focal company's ability to better manage its supply chains, especially in the areas of innovation, cost, and risk. The dangers of not doing multi-tier SCM are listed as less control over costs, less visibility into technology developments, less access to market information, and less control over sustainability. We urge focal companies to look beyond their first-tier suppliers and embrace the multi-tier practice. Only relying on first-tier suppliers is dangerous for focal companies. We argue that "(i)t weakens their control over costs, reduces their ability to stay on top of technology developments and shifts in demand, and makes it difficult to ensure that their suppliers are operating in a socially and environmentally sustainable fashion" (p. 3). This is because there is likely a major cost driver at the second- or third-tier level (i.e., precious metals, leather goods, etc.) or a critical technology development (i.e., filming technology that goes on plastic parts that come in contact with consumers).

Further, the supply chain activities on the upstream side are considered a leading economic indicator for the downstream market. The Purchasing Manager's Index (PMI) published by the Institute for Supply Management is a case in point (https://www.ismworld.org/supply-management-news-and-reports/reports/ism-report-on-business/). Regarding sustainability, much of the supply chain activities that hurt the environment happen on the upstream side of the supply chain, outside the visible range of the focal companies (Choi and Linton 2011). So, what should be done? To start, Choi and Linton recommend not giving up the sourcing decisions to first-tier suppliers completely. In other words, practice multi-tier SCM. The specifics of how to do this appear in the next section under directed sourcing. For now, we consider how multi-tier supply chains have been theorized.

A study by Carter, Rogers, and Choi (2015) theorizes the supply chain from a multi-tier perspective. We adopt the network language and use nodes to represent companies and links to describe the company-to-company relationships. We refer to companies as any node that can make decisions for themselves and offer examples, such as manufacturers, warehouses, transportation carriers, and financial services. We recognize supply chains as networks and networks as complex adaptive systems—in this book, supply networks are covered in Chapter 7 and complex adaptive systems in Chapter 8. As such, we emphasize the extended nature of supply chains. In particular, the relative nature of the extended supply chain is highlighted. Any node in an extended supply chain may look upstream and downstream across a supply chain. For instance, a plastic-molding company looks upstream to plastic resin suppliers and downstream to intermediate goods manufacturers in various industries, from furniture to automotives. One such intermediate goods manufacturer may be a sofa-frame maker, and this sofa-frame maker can also look upstream and downstream in the supply chain from its vantage point.

In this regard, Carter, Rogers, and Choi (2015) pose the relative nature of the extended supply chain. They highlight how every node in a supply chain is at the point of convergence of multiple supply chains at various tier levels. For example, the plastic-molding supplier may be at the convergence of a furniture supply chain at the second-tier level and an automotive supply chain at the third-tier level. Further, we emphasize the existence of a physical supply chain and a support supply chain. The nodes in a physical supply chain handle physical goods from fasteners to motors. The nodes in a support supply chain, in contrast, offer services such as transportation, warehouses, and supply chain financing. Again, there is no single entity that orchestrates all the activities in extended supply chains. Supply chains, juxtaposed across various industries, are then bounded by what we call a fuzzy horizon. As we extend out a supply chain that crisscrosses other supply chains at various tier levels, we would find it difficult to point to a clearly delineated boundary line. As researchers, the best we can do is to set purposefully defined boundaries in supply chains given our research questions.

Hakansson and Johanson (1990) articulate, "In principle . . . industrial networks are unbounded, but the observer (or a specific node in a supply chain) may, for analytical purposes, set suitable boundaries" (p. 460). As such, only a portion of multiple supply chains that are converging on a node (i.e., a supplier company) would be visible to that node in either direction, upstream or downstream in the supply chain. Many upstream suppliers that make small parts, such as plastic parts or semiconductor chips, would not necessarily know what type of final products their components will eventually end up in. This is why Honda has been making a conscious effort to inform its upstream suppliers that their products are ending up in a Honda. From the perspective of a parts supplier that obtains this information, it now gets some visibility to the downstream side of its extended supply chain—while it may know some of its parts are ending up in a Honda product, it may still not know where else its products may end up. From Honda's perspective, it wants all its parts suppliers to have this information, whether selected by Honda directly or indirectly by a supplier in Honda's supply chain, because if the part breaks down while being used by the consumer, it equates to a Honda malfunction.

As shown in Figure 6.2, Carter, Rogers, and Choi (2015) point out the need to do more research on the extended supply chains, especially the portion of the supply chain that is outside the visual range of the focal company. Some studies have been done on what happens outside the visual

	Within visibility	Outside visibility
Physical supply chains	Great deal	Very little
Support supply chains	Some	Almost none

Figure 6.2 Level of Research Focus
Source: Adapted from Carter, Rogers, and Choi 2015

range, primarily through computational simulations (Feizabadi, Gligor, and Choi 2021; Giannoccaro, Nair, and Choi 2018; Nair, Narasimhan, and Choi 2009). However, there have been virtually no studies on outside the visual range in the support supply chains. Choi et al. (2021) likewise offer a list of future research areas in extended supply chains. In reference to lower tier suppliers, we state that these suppliers "are much less visible and may not even be known to the focal company. Our intention is to bring awareness to the importance of these lower tier suppliers and capture possible strategies that buying companies may pursue to manage them" (p. 1). The lower tier suppliers refer to those that operate in the extended supply chains, often outside the purview of the focal company. They identify seven areas of future research, as shown in Table 6.1.

Every company in the extended supply chain needs to be able to plan and coordinate its activities to maximize its gains. To do that well, it needs some level of supply chain visibility from its vantage point. For example, companies need information on downstream and upstream market changes for better demand management and supply management. The element of the extended supply chain that provides this visibility is supply chain transparency. When a focal company like Honda decides to populate its upstream supply chain with information about how the parts manufactured by the suppliers end up in a Honda product, there would be more transparency for the Honda supply chain. However, if an upstream supplier decides not to share its own supply base information because such information is often considered proprietary,

Table 6.1 Future Research Topics in Extended Supply Chains

Relevant Areas	Topics
Planning and coordination	Visibility from a focal company
	Transparency across the supply chain
Resource endowments	Power differentials
	Supply chain financing
Globalization and localization	Long global supply chains
	Multiple local supply chains
Geography considerations	Physical geography
	Human geography
ESG imperative	Diversity, equity, and inclusion
	Consumer and societal awareness
Logistics and transportation	Reconfiguration of shipper-3PL relationships
	Evolving triadic relationship among shippers, 3PLs, and buyers
Supply chain risks	Increasing frequency of black-swan events
	Increasing threats of cyberattacks

Source: Adapted from Choi et al. 2021

then that part of the upstream supply chain would not be transparent. Moving forward, various technology platforms (i.e., a blockchain-based community of companies) are poised to offer more transparency.

In extended supply chains, the location of a company with respect to the downstream consumer market affects resource endowments. Generally, those closer to the consumer market tend to be more resource rich. On the physical supply chain side, these companies (e.g., GM, Apple, Unilever, etc.) drive new product developments and, thus, garner more power (Chae, Choi, and Hur 2017; Grimm, Hofstetter, and Sarkis 2016; Kembro, Näslund, and Olhager 2017; Benton and Maloni 2005). On the support supply chain side, these companies drive funding for other companies in the extended supply chain (Rogers, Leuschner, and Choi 2020). As an example, the payment terms they offer to their suppliers (i.e., first-tier suppliers) determine how quickly the funds are released into the upstream supply chain (i.e., 30-day net vs. 120-day net). Studies reveal how some of these more powerful companies routinely take advantage of those less powerful in the areas of minimum wages, safety requirements, and sustainability practices (Schleper, Blome, and Wuttke 2017; Sodhi 2015). During the COVID-19 pandemic, many companies abused their more powerful position by canceling projects or delaying or stopping payment to their suppliers (Hofmann et al. 2021). In contrast, a few of them (i.e., Walmart, Unilever, among others) have taken extra steps to offer additional funding to their suppliers. In particular, some of them are trying to offer funding to small-and-medium enterprise (SME) suppliers on the upstream side of the extended supply chain through the blockchain-based platform managed by Fintechs—more on this topic in Chapter 9 under supply chain financing and deep-tier financing.

Many corporations with global markets often manage one long, globally linked supply chain consisting of some of the best qualified suppliers from around the globe. That also means the movement of goods would cross many different time zones. Some companies have broken up the global time zones into three time zones to facilitate managing a large, global supply chain—Americas, Asia, and EMEA (Europe, Middle East, and Africa). At the same time, many companies have shown interest in reducing the span of their supply chains, favoring multiple regional supply chains. Feldmann and Olhager (2019) offer, as an example, a focal company that operates six regional supply chains, each of which sources, makes, and delivers to local markets. In the coming years, we should continue working on characterizing global supply chains and regional supply chains and how they can coexist in terms of integration and competition.

Geography should be considered in managing extended supply chains much more in future research. Novak and Choi (2015) bring to the fore the importance of physical geography and human geography in this regard. In physical geography, landforms come into play, such as mountains, oceans, rivers, and gullies. Climate conditions in terms of temperature, wind directions, and humidity are important considerations. Physical geography, in some sense, involves spatial characteristics and natural phenomena. In human geography, in contrast, we contend with national borders, cultural barriers, and differences in economic and political systems. With increasing transportation costs, barriers posed by physical geography should be considered more extensively, and with increasing political instability across the globe, human geography will come into play much more in coming years. Physical geography affects plant locations and modes of transportation. Human geography influences how companies in the extended supply chain that cuts across different national borders and different time zones maintain buyer-supplier relationships in terms of contracting and problem-solving.

In the spring of 2022, an executive from Citibank relayed in a private conversation how their investors are now big on environment, social, and governance (ESG) issues. Investors are increasingly placing value on diversity, equity, and inclusion in the extended supply chain (Kalkanci, Rahmani, and Toktay 2019; Narayanan and Terris 2020; Plambeck and Ramdas 2020). This reflects the changing consumer preferences on ESG issues and knowing where the parts in the products they use come from. Such emerging requirements are new to the focal companies that are used to dealing with only their first-tier suppliers. They are now being called on to gain more visibility across their extended supply chains. The case of Rana Plaza in Bangladesh, which collapsed and caused fatalities, makes this issue all too painfully clear. The garment products that Walmart sold came from this location, unbeknownst to Walmart, through its first-tier supplier Li and Fung in Hong Kong (https://www.wsj.com/articles/SB10001424405270230384810 4579310642770730778). The source of ESG problems often originates on the upstream side of the extended supply chains, such as unsafe working conditions, child labor, and ecologically harmful practices.

In the support supply chain, logistics services (i.e., third-party logistics, 3PL, companies) play a key role. They operate between a supplier and a buying company. Here, the supplier becomes the shipper, and a 3PL serves as a shipping company. In the past, the shipper as a customer of the 3PL had the leverage, but the COVID-19 pandemic changed this power dynamic. During the pandemic, the demand for 3PL services increased, and many shipping companies turned to reliable 3PL services as a strategic focus (Ashby 2016). In addition to the shipper-3PL dyad, the 3PL-buyer dyad was also important in the sense that the 3PL had to be in close communications with the buying company for order fulfillment and delivery requirements. Before the pandemic, these two dyadic relationships operated as two independent dyads. However, there is a movement toward a more integrated triadic relationship with the shipper (i.e., supplier), 3PL, and the buyer. For example, Microsoft, as the buyer, is taking the lead in bringing together its 3PL service company, C.H. Robinson, and several suppliers across the globe but mainly in China. Through this approach, all three companies communicate regularly, offering real-time shipment visibility and better coordination of activities (https:// news.microsoft.com/2020/07/14/c-h-robinson-announces-alliance-with-microsoft-to-digitally-transform-the-supply-chain-of-the-future/).   Such triadic relationships are prevalent across the extended supply chain post-pandemic and have become part of the new normal business operations.

As discussed in Chapter 1, many industry experts anticipate the continuation of black-swan events in the years to come. The implication is that a disruption at a supplier on the upstream of an extended supply chain can have a substantial impact on a focal company, depending on how long it takes for the disruption to propagate through the supply chain to reach it. One way companies attempt to mitigate disruption risks that may come through the extended supply chain is to engage in supply chain mapping. A recent *Harvard Business Review* article (Choi, Rogers, and Vakil 2020) describes how those focal companies that had done at least some mapping of their extended supply chains fared much better during the early months of COVID-19 in China. Those that had not were scurrying around to figure out which of their upstream suppliers were in the containment zone. In contrast, those that had done the mapping were drawing circles around Wuhan as the virus propagated outwardly, and they identified which of their suppliers were within the affected areas. They were then able to move in quickly to claim available inventory. Another major source of supply chain risk is cyber threats. With increased connectivity and computing power, companies across the extended supply chain are dependent on the internet for communications. They store software and data in the Cloud and use third-party software platforms. We will address cybersecurity issues more fully later in this chapter.

Directed Sourcing

Directed sourcing occurs when a focal company directs its first-tier supplier where to get certain parts at the second- or third-tier level. When Apple instructs its first-tier supplier, Foxconn, to receive camera lenses from Largan Precision in Taiwan, Apple is engaged in directed sourcing. When Honda tells its first-tier supplier, CVT, to get metal clips from Emhart, a second-tier supplier, Honda is engaged in directed sourcing (Choi and Hong 2002). In this case, Honda establishes a direct contractual agreement with Emhart, and Emhart as a second-tier supplier is part of Honda's supply base, as discussed in the preceding chapter. Honda manages this second-tier supplier for costs and asks its first-tier supplier, CVT, to manage this second-tier supplier for quality and delivery. Thus, Honda negotiates with Emhart in the area of cost management. As shipments arrive from Emhart to CVT, CVT should be in charge of making sure the deliveries arrive on time and products meet quality requirements before being released to the assembly time. CVT assembles center consoles for the Honda Accord. Please note that, as of 2018, CVT still worked with Honda in the same capacity. For the paper by Giannoccaro, Nair, and Choi (2018), we went back to Honda to verify the currency of the supply network data collected by Choi and Hong (2002), and it was confirmed that most of the same suppliers were still in place. CVT is a fictitious name used in Choi and Hong's study, but its real name of GTI was disclosed in the 2018 Giannoccaro, Nair, and Choi study. This 2018 study will be discussed more fully in Chapter 8 on supply networks as a complex adaptive system.

All four supply chains shown in Figure 6.3 offer a sample of how Honda reaches deeper into its supply chain beyond the first-tier supplier. The first-tier supplier, CVT, assembles the central console in the Accord model using the parts it manufactures and other parts it receives from other suppliers. In the first extended supply chain involving Emhart, Honda does directed sourcing because Emhart manufactures fasteners (i.e., nuts and bolts, metal clips, etc.) that go into other Honda products. This directed sourcing populates common parts across different product lines and controls costs through the consolidation of orders. The second extended supply chain offers more insight into how Honda manages potential gains in cost savings. Honda chooses to have a direct contractual agreement with Garden State because this supplier deals in leather goods. Leather parts are expensive, and 1% cost savings would translate into more dollars. Garden State appears as a third-tier supplier because Garden State on its own decided to contract a fabrication company called Universal Trim to prepare the leather parts for assembly. The third extended supply chain represents a plastic resin supply chain. Honda Trading deals in raw materials, and even though its name includes Honda,

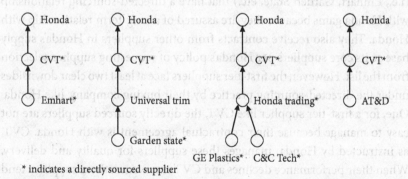

* indicates a directly sourced supplier

Figure 6.3 Honda's Directed Sourcing
Source: Adapted from Choi and Hong 2002

it operates as an independent company, a point Honda managers stressed. Honda limits the raw materials suppliers for plastic resin to only two (GE Plastics and C&C Tech) for consistency in the finished plastic parts. Honda Trading delivers plastic resin to CVT through a buy-sell arrangement.

The fourth and last extended supply chain shown in Figure 6.3 is a bit different from the other three. It reflects a clever way through which a focal company like Honda could take advantage of its core or approved suppliers to make more of the parts that go into its products. Honda makes great efforts to develop its core suppliers and stays on top of their performance through monthly report cards with detailed feedback. Therefore, in addition to using these suppliers in its directed-sourcing practice, Honda also releases the list of its core suppliers to the first-tier supplier (i.e., approved vendor list). In this case, that would be CVT. Honda instructs CVT to select its suppliers from the approved vendor list, ceteris paribus. AT&D is a small stamping company on that list that CVT chose to supply metal brackets. In sum, the first three directed-sourcing cases illustrate how Honda directly selects a lower tier supplier. The fourth case involving AT&D discloses how Honda indirectly engages in directed sourcing—it does not do that itself, but it creates a condition through which the first-tier supplier can choose from the list of Honda's approved suppliers.

What Honda gains from its directed-sourcing process have been enumerated in the two preceding paragraphs. What it gives up might be the high overhead costs. Honda has a huge supply management group— within the Honda organizational structure, the supply management group is called a division. It houses not just supply management professionals but also engineers and accounting professionals. The lower tier suppliers (i.e., Emhart, Garden State, etc.) that have a directed-sourcing relationship with Honda gains because they are assured of a long-term relationship with Honda. They also receive contracts from other suppliers in Honda's supply base as its core suppliers per Honda's policy of requesting supplier selection from the list. However, the first-tier suppliers face at least two clear downsides under the directed-sourcing practice by their buying company, like Honda. One, for a first-tier supplier like CVT, the directly sourced suppliers are not easy to manage because their contractual agreement is with Honda. CVT, as instructed by Honda, manages these suppliers for quality and delivery. When their performance declines and CVT intervenes, these suppliers tend to be unresponsive. Often, the first-tier supplier has to call on Honda to help resolve problems with these directly sourced suppliers, creating stress for

CVT. Two, the first-tier suppliers like CVT get cost-reduction pressures from Honda. When this happens, the first-tier supplier usually looks for second- or third-tier suppliers to relieve some of that pressure. However, its buying company, Honda, has already cherry-picked all the good second- and third-tier suppliers with potential such as Garden State, which handles high-cost parts. Therefore, first-tier suppliers working for the buying company that practices directed sourcing are forced to improve their efficiency to reduce costs and meet cost-reduction targets. Honda refers to this process as continuous improvement and offers supplier development opportunities to help first-tier suppliers gain additional efficiency.

Since the Choi and Hong study (2002), more scholars have shown interest in directed sourcing (e.g., Guo, Song, and Wang 2010; Yoo, Choi, and Kim 2021). The reports of their studies have been coming out steadily for the past 10 years or so. One thing common among these studies is that they all seem to investigate the three-tier supply chain context where we have the focal company (e.g., an original equipment manufacturer, OEM), a first-tier supplier (e.g., a contract manufacturer), and a second-tier supplier (e.g., a component manufacturer). The theoretical tension occurs between *directed sourcing*, where the focal company interfaces with both the first- and second-tier suppliers, and *sequential sourcing*, where the focal company interfaces only with the first-tier supplier and the first-tier supplier then interfaces with the second-tier supplier in sequence. It would be good to go over a few of them in chronological order.

Guo, Song, and Wang (2010) examine a three-tier supply chain consisting of an OEM, contract manufacturer (CM), and component supplier, where the OEM considers three outsourcing approaches. The first is a consignment approach, in which both the CM and supplier participate. The OEM maintains its inventories in-house that come from both the CM and supplier. The second approach is basically the sequential sourcing, which they refer to as a turnkey operation from the OEM's perspective—the OEM just interfaces with the CM, who would then interface with the component supplier from its end. The third approach reflects directed sourcing, which is called the integrated turnkey approach. The OEM establishes contractual agreements with both the CM and component supplier, and they work together in alliance.

A study by Deshpande et al. (2011) examines price-masking technology that can preserve private information regarding individual component prices. The context of their study is the determination of who, between the OEM and the CM, should procure the components from the second-tier supplier. If the choice is the OEM, that will translate into directed sourcing, but if the CM is selected, then that equates to sequential sourcing. The theme of control versus delegation of procuring components continues in a study by Chen, Shum, and Xiao (2012). A twist in this study is that the CM works for a smaller OEM in addition to the large OEM. The perspective is taken from the large OEM as to whether it should engage in directed sourcing through a buy-sell arrangement or in sequential sourcing. In a different study by Kayış, Erhun, and Plambeck (2013), the context is again given as the focal company trying to decide whether to control the component procurement from a second-tier supplier (i.e., directed sourcing) or to delegate it to a first-tier supplier (i.e., sequential sourcing). Recognizing how the focal company deals with information asymmetry from not knowing the cost at the first- and second-tier levels, the authors examine the effects of two different types of contracts (i.e., price only and quantity discount) and the profit implications of the focal company's sourcing decision (i.e., control vs. delegation).

Wang, Niu, and Guo (2014) continue to study directed sourcing (control) and sequential sourcing (delegation) in the three-tier supply chain—OEM, CM, and component supplier. They compare and contrast the effects of push vs. pull contracts. In a push contract, ordering occurs before the demand materializes, whereas, in a pull contract, ordering occurs after the demand becomes known. A new twist in the directed vs. sequential sourcing across the three tiers of a supply chain is offered in Bolandifar, Kouvelis, and Zhang's (2016) study. Their three-tier supply chain has two competing OEMs, one common CM, and a second-tier component supplier. Each OEM makes its own decisions about directed vs. sequential sourcing, and the CM may set its own pricing strategy. Their study offers guidelines for competing OEM's sourcing approaches. Lv (2019) continues with the same supply chain structure with two competing OEMs. Directed sourcing is called consignment (i.e., the OEM procures the components and assigns the CM only the production work), and sequential sourcing is called turnkey (i.e., the CM is tasked with procuring components and production). Their findings show the conditions that affect the equilibrium outcomes, such as the CM's procurement costs and the competition intensity between the two OEMs.

A study by Dong, Tang, and Zhou (2018) recognizes that the ability of the OEM and the CM would be different in getting discounts from the component supplier, given the different levels of economies of scale. Depending on whether the CM has its own brand products that would make it more competitive, the implications for the directed vs. sequential sourcing would be different for the OEM. Lastly, Yoo, Choi, and Kim (2021) consider the implications of directed vs. sequential sourcing on various supply chain financing strategies across the three-tier supply chain (i.e., commercial loans, factoring, reverse factoring with a payment term extension, and reverse factoring without the payment term extension). We will discuss this last article more when we get to the section below regarding financing across the multi-tier context.

Supply Chain Make Versus Supply Chain Buy

The initial idea that there might be a make-buy decision at the supply chain level just as at the company level appears in an unpublished doctoral dissertation by Chae (2017) at Arizona State University. In Chapter 2, we discussed how an individual company would engage in make-buy decisions by comparing its own governance costs against the transaction costs of going to the market. Building on the logic reflecting the company-level make-buy decisions, we propose make-buy decisions also occur at the supply chain level. These decisions can happen in a three-tier supply chain, as many authors have considered. They can also happen in the more extended supply chains beyond the three-tier supply chains, as shown in Figure 6.3.

While the empirical paper by Choi and Hong (2002) ascertain the importance of multi-tier SCM and delineated some of the ways Honda engages in directed sourcing, Choi and Linton (2011) highlight that a decision to outsource (i.e., a buy decision at the firm level) does not necessarily equate to the decision to *outsource sourcing*. A company can outsource production but still can hang on to decisions regarding sourcing. This realization marks an important point of departure from how we have looked at the make-buy decision as occurring only at the company level. The make-buy decision also happens at the supply chain level in that, on the one hand, if a focal company decides to outsource sourcing decisions, it is, in essence, *buying* its first-tier supplier's supply chain. On the other hand, if the focal company decides to maintain control of making sourcing decisions, that is equivalent to *making* its supply chain. Figure 6.4 illustrates this point.

We tend to think that if we decide on a buy decision and outsource production to a supplier, with that decision, we are outsourcing the company's sourcing decisions. In other words, we tend to view our supplier as offering a turnkey operation, and it will do all that is necessary to deliver us the product

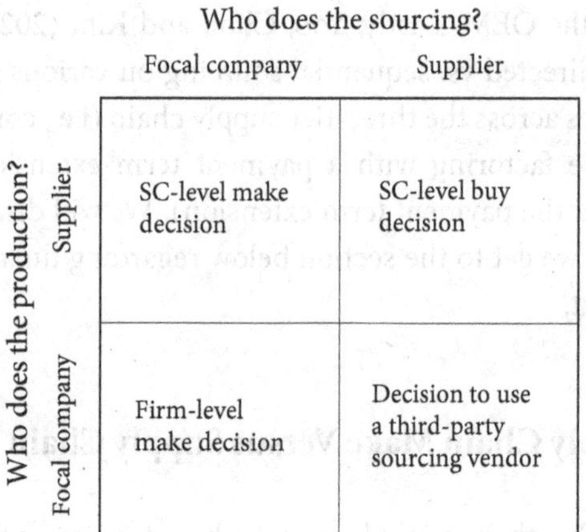

Who does the sourcing?

	Focal company	Supplier
Supplier	SC-level make decision	SC-level buy decision
Focal company	Firm-level make decision	Decision to use a third-party sourcing vendor

Who does the production?

Figure 6.4 Comparing Make-Buy Decisions at the Firm vs. Supply Chain Level
Source: Adapted from Chae 2017

we outsourced to it, including making decisions on sourcing required parts and materials. However, as we have been discussing, that is not necessarily the case. Focal companies like Honda and Apple reserve the right to do the sourcing themselves, even with the outsourcing decision.

The underlying decisions involved in these observations are captured in Figure 6.4. It is built on two questions—who takes on the sourcing responsibility (who does the sourcing) and who carries out the production activities (who does the production). If the focal company does the production and sources what it needs from its own end, that basically is the make decision at the company level. Given the make decision, the only way a supplier can do the sourcing is if the focal company decides to use a third-party sourcing service, for example, a broker or a group purchasing organization (GPO) in healthcare.

If the company-level decision is to buy, that presents a situation where the supplier (i.e., first-tier supplier to the focal company) does the production. The supply-chain level make-buy scenarios now happen. The two top quadrants in Figure 6.4 pertain to this situation. Given that the supplier is doing the production, if the focal company retains its sourcing authority, then that entails a supply chain make decision, as in the focal company chooses to *make* the supply chain (i.e., directed sourcing). However, if the focal company delegates the responsibility of sourcing to the supplier and the supplier takes on the sourcing work, that is a supply chain buy decision,

100%
SC-Make

100%
SC-Buy

Figure 6.5 Examples of Supply Chain Make-Buy

as in the focal company chooses to *buy* its supplier's supply chain. Staying with the examples we discussed earlier involving Google, Honda, and Apple, we would say Apple generally uses SC-make when working with its first-tier suppliers (e.g., Foxconn), and Google opts to use SC-buy when working with Flex for its Chromecast as shown in Figure 6.5. According to Apple Inc. (2012), it engaged in directed sourcing with 156 suppliers in its extended supply chain, which accounted for 97% of its total procurement expenditures. Foxconn, as a first-tier supplier, virtually does no sourcing for Apple iPhone or iPad. This is why Apple is listed close to 100% SC-make in Figure 6.5. At the other end of the continuum, we have Google Chrome. In my personal conversation with an executive at Flex, Google handed over the design of Chromecast to Flex and asked them to source the necessary parts and materials to produce it. That is why this product is listed as an example of 100% SC-buy. However, many companies, like Honda with its Accord center console or instrument panel and Microsoft working with Flex for its Xbox, operate somewhere in the middle on the continuum of 100% SC-make and 100% SC-buy. That simply means the focal company selectively practices directed sourcing.

It is here, in-between, where interesting implications for extended supply chains occur. As noted above, Honda selects key suppliers in its extended supply chain and allows the first-tier supplier to do its own sourcing for the rest. When Honda reserves the right to choose a few suppliers from its extended supply chain, that means Honda controls directed sourcing. That is a direct control exerted by Honda. Honda also uses an indirect approach to control its extended supply chain. It does this by imposing on its first-tier supplier to use Honda's approved vendor list when selecting suppliers at the second-tier level. With this approach, Honda gets to populate its extended supply chain with its own core suppliers.

In Chapter 5 on supply base management, we mentioned that Honda sends a monthly report card to these core suppliers, and their performance is closely monitored. Thus, it is to Honda's advantage, that many of these suppliers become part of its extended supply chain, even when its first-tier supplier is doing the supplier selection. Furthermore, CVT has learned from Honda, and it practices its own directed sourcing. In the supply network map for Honda Accord's center console (Choi and Hong 2002), CVT is shown as having done directed sourcing at its second-tier level and Honda's third-tier level. CVT shows up as having selected its first-tier supplier HFI for the armrest assembly and a second-tier supplier, Industry Products, for foam padding. It is clear that Honda's practices are being replicated across its supply chain to provide a stable extended supply chain. As a case in point, when we went back to Honda seeking an update on its supply network for the center console for the Accord for another study (Giannoccaro, Nair, and Choi 2018), it was found that most of the suppliers were still intact in Honda's extended supply chain.

Developments in Multi-Tier Supply Chain Management

Thus far, we have discussed multi-tier SCM, directed sourcing, and supply chain make and buy. To address extended supply chains, we began with multi-tier issues, considered more functional decisions through directed sourcing, and proceeded to the higher-level dynamic in SC-make vs. SC-buy. We now return to the overarching context of multi-tier SCM shown in the center of Figure 6.1.

First, we address how the three-tier, triadic context has been used to theorize the multi-tier dynamics. We draw from case studies in various industries, from food to healthcare. We look at supply chain financing and expand the consideration from a financial arrangement between a focal company and its first-tier supplier in the dyadic setting to the multi-tier, triadic setting that includes component suppliers. Taking things beyond the triadic context, we examine the tetradic context where there are four companies rather than three. Lastly, we consider the extended supply chain implications of cyber threats as an emerging multi-tier concern.

Theorizing Multi-Tier Supply Chain Management

Mena, Humphries, and Choi (2013) take a step toward developing a theory of multi-tier SCM. If the article in *Harvard Business Review* by Choi and Linton (2011) is written for the practitioners, the work by Mena, Humphries,

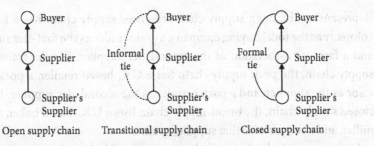

Figure 6.6 Three Prototypical Multi-Tier Supply Chains
Source: Adapted from Mena, Humphries, and Choi 2013

and Choi (2013) in the *Journal of Supply Chain Management* can be viewed as targeting the academic audience. It uses network terms to explain the dynamics across three tiers of a supply network. Taking a case study approach, we note that the simplest context within which to study multi-tier is the three-tier supply chain. As such, we adopt the network terms associated with triads.

As stipulated by the case study protocol, Mena, Humphries, and Choi (2013) use a purposeful sampling technique for three cases of a three-tier supply chain, each involving three companies. The three cases represent three prototypes of multi-tier supply chains, as shown in Figure 6.6. In this figure, the arrows represent the flow of goods moving from a second-tier supplier (i.e., supplier's supplier) to the first-tier and then to the buying company. The one labeled "Open Supply Chain" represents a typical sequential sourcing scenario where one company works with another company as a supplier in the next tier down. The middle labeled "Transitional Supply Chain" is where the buying company reaches out to the second-tier supplier for informal discussions. This scenario would be similar to the one we introduced earlier that involved LGE, Qualcomm, and TSMC, where LGE is the buyer. LGE reached out to TSMC, its supplier's supplier, to establish an informal relationship. In the process, LGE suggested to its supplier, Qualcomm, that it might consider establishing a formal contractual relationship with TSMC and having Qualcomm work off of that contract. This possibility was mentioned in passing, but that suggestion brings us to the third prototype labeled "Closed Supply Chain." This relationship arrangement represents the directed-sourcing approach we have been discussing.

Three supply chains are chosen to reflect these three prototypes of multi-tier SCM—beer supply chain, bread supply chain, and pork supply chain.

Representing the open supply chain, the beer supply chain has a brewing company as the focal buying company, a grain trader as the first-tier supplier, and a farmer's association as the second-tier supplier. For the transitional supply chain, the pork supply chain has a U.K.-based retailer, a pork processor as the supplier, and a pork breeder as the second-tier supplier. For the closed supply chain, the bread supply chain lists a U.K.-based baker, a grain miller, and a cooperative that supplies grains.

In the beer supply chain, the brewer is a multinational corporation that has malting and brewing facilities in the U.K. The grain trader supplies crops to the brewer, most notably barley to be malted and used in beer brewing. The grain trader does the marketing, testing, and transportation for the farmers that have organized themselves around a farmer's association. In the pork supply chain, a major retailer (i.e., a major supermarket in the U.K.) and a pork processor have worked together in a dyadic relationship, and the processor and breeder have worked together in a separate dyadic relationship. However, the state of the two dyads has started to change because the retailer is informally reaching out to the breeder to ensure its sustainability practices. Lastly, in the bread supply chain, the baker is a large U.K.-based, focal company engaged in baking bread and other baked goods with a well-known brand name. The miller operates one of the largest wheat mills in the U.K., and the cooperative is co-owned by the farmers that grow wheat and other types of grains. The cooperative has a formal and direct tie with the baker because it markets the arable crops to the baker. It has a direct contractual agreement with the baker and is responsible for delivering grains to the miller for processing.

Even though the analysis in Mena, Humphries, and Choi (2013) is based on a cross-sectional data set, we are able to draw implications to changes in multi-tier supply chains because the three cases we investigate exist in different phases of relationship development. Our assumption is that an open supply chain in which sourcing is done sequentially is what would typically happen first. Then, as the need arises, the multi-tier supply chain structure would evolve into the transitional and eventually into the closed supply chain. Using the mode of theory building based on case studies (i.e., Barratt, Choi, and Li 2011; Eisenhardt 1989b), we offer a proposition that associates changes in the structure of a multi-tier supply chain with changes in power balance. We make empirically grounded observations on how the company in the bridge position garners the power that comes with that structural position. As a corollary, we suggest another proposition that points out how the focal company would therefore need to disintermediate the company in the middle and reach out to the second-tier supplier that works with undifferentiated resources (i.e., raw materials) if the focal company is interested in making fundamental changes to its product characteristics. Simply, products cannot be improved unless quality is ensured at the raw materials level first. Working on such changes sequentially through a first-tier supplier would not guarantee the desired outcome.

A research finding illustrates how, as the multi-tier supply chain evolves from an open state into a transitional and a closed state, a sense of interdependence would grow among the companies. In other words, members of a multi-tier supply chain that exist as an intransitive triad would begin to sense a change in relational dynamics as their relationship evolves toward a transitive triad that accompanies much more complex relational dynamics. With this sense of interdependence also comes a sense of stability. Another finding we offer associates the closed multi-tier supply chain with a stronger perception of stability among the member companies. However, since the relationship structure is now more complex, members of the supply chain would have to spend more resources.

Institutional Dynamics Across a Multi-Tier Healthcare Supply Chain

This topic is an extension of Choi and Eboch's (1998) study, which was covered in Chapter 2, where we discussed the institutional dynamics in a dyadic context. The readers may recall how a supplier responds to institutional demands from the buying company by conforming to the demands at the administrative level, which leads to customer satisfaction, while shielding the operational activities at the technical core, which leads to a limited impact on operational performance through this institutional conformance. We extend this line of reasoning to a multi-tier or triadic context where we have three tiers of a healthcare supply chain—manufacturers, distributors, and hospitals (Bhakoo and Choi 2013).

What is unique about this context is that there are multiple companies within each tier of the three-tier supply chain. The assumption is that the institutional promotion of a technology (i.e., inter-organizational system) would come from the larger healthcare industry stakeholders such as government and professional associations. An inter-organizational system

(IOS) as a technology is designed to offer ways to facilitate transactions more efficiently, more readily enable information sharing with transacting partners, and coordinate activities between companies. Another assumption is that companies in the same tier would operate under commonly shared institutional norms. Bhakoo and Choi (2013), using the case study approach, examine how companies embedded in different tiers of a multi-tier supply chain would respond differently to the institutional pressures.

Figure 6.7 shows how institutional pressures impinge on an organization. When that happens, the organization conforms to the institutional pressure by making changes at the administrative level. If IOS is promoted by the institutional stakeholders, the organization complies with the institutional logic, such as attaining legitimacy or goodwill by investing in the technology and demonstrating that it has adopted it. This response, of course, does not mean the organization is actually using the technology because it would likely not see the full technical benefits of the technology and would not be fully integrated with the processes at the technical core where value-adding transformation activities take place. The organization would protect its technical core from institutional responses by decoupling it from what happens there. For instance, after adopting IOS, the management team may announce it and instruct the workers to start using it. However, the workers resisting changes

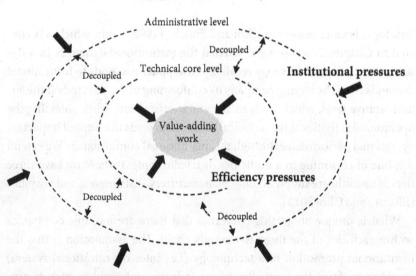

Figure 6.7 Institutional and Efficiency Pressures on a Company
Source: Adapted from Bhakoo and Choi 2013

may continue their routines without incorporating this new technology in their work process. As the workers engage in value-adding transformation processes at the technical core, there are efficiency pressures to manage the processes well with minimal input and maximum output. As discussed in Chapter 2, various companies learn to relax the state of decoupling and allow the technology to begin integrating with what goes on at the technical core. Therefore, Bhakoo and Choi (2013) also examine how exogenous institutional pressures might integrate with the endogenous, technical pressures across different tiers of an extended supply chain.

How would institutional dynamics play out in an extended supply chain? DiMaggio and Powell (1983) offer three types of institutional pressures on organizations—coercive, mimetic, and normative. Coercive pressures come from regulatory agencies, industrial customers, and parent corporations that the organization depends on for resources. Mimetic pressures cause the organization to model what others do in the institutional environment. When uncertainties are high, such pressures lead the organization to mimic what others do. They benchmark other more successful institutional constituents. Normative pressures generally come from professionalization that is represented by professional associations, trade organizations, and accreditation agencies. These organizations promote standards and common practices. Once companies decide to respond to these pressures, they make changes, but, at the same time, they protect their technical core from these exogenously derived, institutional responses. Meyer and Rowan (1977) articulate how organizations decouple what organizations create as a response to institutional pressures (i.e., safety department or sustainability department) from actual transformation processes at the technical core. What is being recognized here is a gap between institutionally rational behaviors at the administrative level and technically rational behaviors at the technical core. The question remains whether these two rationalities might integrate and if they do, how that may happen in organizations across an extended supply chain. That is central to the study by Bhakoo and Choi (2013).

The significant observation in our study at the supply chain level is that normative pressures are most acutely perceived by the organizations across the supply chain, while the salience of the mimetic and coercive pressures is more isolated in different parts of the supply chain. The mimetic pressures are more prominent in the downstream end at the hospitals, and the coercive pressures are more active at the upstream to the hospitals at the distribution and manufacturing tiers. At the technical core, four types of internally driven pressures are identified—efficiency improvement, patient safety, resource allocations, and internalization of the technology. The concerns for efficiency, resources, and internalization are observed across the supply chain. However, the resource pressures are observed mainly on the upstream side, and the safety concerns are more prevalent on the downstream side. Lastly, the institutional pressures focused on normative and mimetic combined with the internal efficiency pressure lead to the internalization that short-circuits the decoupled state between the administrative and technical core levels. Such a combination is instrumental in seeing the institutionally rational response and the technically rational routines converge to maximize the benefits of new technology (i.e., IOS) as intended.

Financing Across the Multi-Tier Supply Chain

Yoo, Choi, and Kim (2021) investigate how a focal company's sourcing strategies (i.e., sequential vs. directed) lead to the effectiveness of the financing strategies adopted across a multi-tier supply chain (i.e., commercial loan financing, factoring, reverse factoring with a payment term extension, and reverse factoring without a payment term extension). The multi-tier supply chain entails a three-tier supply chain with the focal company, a first-tier supplier, and a second-tier supplier. The goal of this study is to ascertain which combination of the sourcing and financing strategies leads to better operational performance for the individual companies and for the whole supply chain.

We recognize how focal companies have been using their supply chains to improve their return on investment (ROI) (see Chapter 3), and the cash conversion cycle (CCC). CCC looks at how quickly a company gets paid from its customers (days in receivables outstanding), how much they invest in assets (days in inventory outstanding), and how slowly they pay their suppliers (days in payables outstanding). Many companies have focused on cost reductions from their suppliers and have extended the payment terms. In the fall of 2019, just before the COVID-19 outbreak, we had a rather large gathering of procurement executives at Arizona State University. During my presentation, I happened to mention a 30-day payment term, and all the executives there told me that they had not heard of a 30-day term in a long time. Apparently, the focal companies represented there had increased the terms to 90 days and 120 days. For example, according to *Forbes* (https://

www.forbes.com/sites/greatspeculations/2018/08/30/how-has-apples-cash-conversion-cycle-changed-over-the-years/?sh=7111aae7cea3), Apple shows the days of payables outstanding in 2018 at 126.6 days.

When this happens, the suppliers have to find ways to overcome their cash flow problems, and if suppliers are cash strapped, that would invariably affect their performance, and the focal company would also suffer from underperforming suppliers. Therefore, focal companies have begun showing a keen interest in the negative impact of payment term extensions, and some of them have taken an active role in helping suppliers receive an early payment against their approved invoices through the focal company's bank or a financial technology (Fintech) company (i.e., reverse factoring). Of course, suppliers themselves can take initiatives from their end to receive funds earlier through commercial loan financing or factoring. Commercial loans would be made against the supplier's financial health and past performance. A loan would be issued typically by a bank and would involve interest payments to the lender during the credit period. For factoring, the supplier goes to its factor (i.e., bank) and sells its approved invoices from the buying company at a discount. In return, it receives funding immediately and does not have to worry about additional financial risks.

While commercial loan financing and factoring are initiated by the supplier, reverse factoring is initiated by the buying company. The financial penalty for the supplier for drawing out the money early is much more minor in this case because the interest rate is determined by the buyer's credit rating. Reverse factoring often occurs after a payment term extension to help alleviate the financial stress for the supplier. However, that is not always the case. A leading high-tech company in Korea is offering reverse factoring to its suppliers without the payment term extension as a way to improve the health of its supply chain.

A key point of departure in the study by Yoo, Choi, and Kim (2021) is that we bring the sourcing strategy and financing strategy together in the multi-tier context. As shown in Figure 6.8, in sequential sourcing, payments are made in sequence across the multiple tiers in a supply chain. In directed sourcing, payment is made directly to both the first- and second-tier suppliers by the focal company.

The results of our study offer counterintuitive observations regarding reverse factoring. The buyer-initiated reverse factoring should help suppliers in either sequential or directed sourcing. The suppliers are invited to get an early payment with an interest rate based on the financially more stable focal

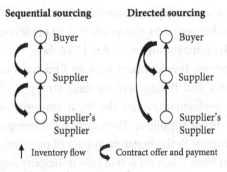

Figure 6.8 Inventory Flow and Payment Flow
Source: Adapted from Yoo, Choi, and Kim 2021

company's credit rating. However, when reverse factoring occurs with a payment term extension, the results inform us that only the buyer benefits from reverse factoring. Under reverse factoring with payment term extensions, the performance of both first- and second-tier suppliers suffer, regardless of sourcing strategies. One potential explanation is the ambivalence involved in this financing approach. The focal company is imposing an extended payment term to put stress on the suppliers on the one hand, but, on the other hand, the focal company is offering a lower interest rate for early payment. Indeed, the reverse-factoring approach without the payment term extension shows a positive impact on all companies in the supply chain and on the extended supply chain as a whole.

So, regardless of how much the focal company wants to help alleviate suppliers' financial stress through reverse factoring, our study suggests that the focal company's unilateral payment delay increases the suppliers' financial risks. And the payment term extension in the multi-tier supply chain operates differently than what we might observe in a dyadic buyer-supplier context. Thus, when the focal company extends the payment term to boost its earnings, that payment extension decision gets passed down to the next tier as the first-tier is also forced to extend the payment to the second-tier supplier.

The big message is that there is no "one-size-fits-all" financing approach in either sourcing strategy. For instance, there is an ambivalence about the efficacy of reverse factoring. Comparing commercial loans and factoring, factoring seems to do better at helping improve supplier performance because it hedges against the variability in the focal company's payment terms.

We argue that managers need to consider the importance of the component the second-tier supplier provides for the first-tier supplier and the focal company (i.e., impact on consumer demand). In other words, the focal company's financing approaches should consider how the second-tier supplier should invest in its operations, which should also affect whether to do sequential or directed sourcing. There are, of course, shortcomings in this study, some of which include focusing only on the second-tier supplier's production costs and not considering external financial institutions' call on interest rates, among others. We will discuss more on supply chain financing in the last chapter, Chapter 9, as part of emerging topics.

Tetrads and Multi-Tier

The financial performance of the focal companies is often affected by a disruptive event further upstream in a supply chain. Durach, Wiengarten, and Choi (2020) consider how two suppliers in a co-opetitive relationship (see Chapter 3) may act as a shield providing resilience for the focal company against a disruption that emanates from a second-tier supplier common to both first-tier suppliers. Figure 6.9 shows a tetradic supply chain structure with a common second-tier supplier as a source of disruption.

Durach, Wiengarten, and Choi (2020) use scenario-based survey research. To add realism, the scenario is written based on a real business disruption event that originated from a common second-tier supplier. The scenario posed to the focal company reads:

> It is 6:00 am on a Monday morning in late August when you receive mail from your two suppliers informing you that one of their common critical sub-suppliers was severely hit by a fire. The sub-supplier is a key

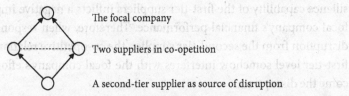

The focal company

Two suppliers in co-opetition

A second-tier supplier as source of disruption

Figure 6.9 Tetradic Context with a Second-Tier Disruption
Source: Adapted from Durach, Wiengarten, and Choi 2020

sub-supplier, as it delivers critical parts that go into the products that these suppliers supply to you. You are told that the sub-supplier will be down for at least five months.

The real names of two current suppliers are presented to the focal company, and the respondents at the focal company are then asked to rate the impact on various financial measures (i.e., ROI, net income before tax, etc.). The same scenario is then posed to both suppliers, again with the name of the other co-opetitive supplier specifically mentioned. A co-opetitive relationship refers to one that cooperates and competes at the same time (see Chapter 3). The respondents from both suppliers are asked how they would detect, respond, and recover from this disruption.

The data that is eventually compiled offers 33 complete buyer-supplier-supplier triads built based on responses from 99 companies and 132 survey responses. There were 66 co-opetitive suppliers and 33 focal companies, with two responses from each focal company, totaling 66 survey responses from focal companies. Two co-opetitive suppliers in each triad had similar production and technical capabilities and supplied non-overlapping components to the focal company. The real names of both suppliers were obtained from the focal company. The names of the companies were used in the survey for the purpose of data collection, but all respondents were assured that their real identities would not be disclosed in the report and that we would use the data only in the aggregate.

From the focal company's perspective, the source of disruption emanates from beyond its immediate suppliers. Yet, this disruption has the potential to affect its financial performance profoundly. This study begins with a theoretical premise that a buying company's resilience does not have to be confined to the four walls of its own company. Its capability to withstand an exogenous disruption may rest in its suppliers. The results corroborate this premise—a co-opetitive supplier-supplier relationship detects and responds positively to the disruption from the second-tier supplier. However, interestingly, the resilience capability of the first-tier suppliers inflicts a negative impact on the focal company's financial performance. Therefore, when responding to the disruption from the second-tier supplier, the co-opetitive relationship at the first-tier level somehow interferes with the focal company's efforts to overcome the disruption.

This counterintuitive result is eerily similar to the unexpected finding by Wu, Choi, and Rungtusanatham (2010), who studied the effects of the supplier-supplier relationship on buyer performance, as discussed in Chapter 3. Durach, Wiengarten, and Choi (2020) offer an explanation that the first-tier suppliers may be engaged in "bridging" rather than "buffering" the problem (Bode et al. 2011). In other words, suppliers may find it more expedient to just pass on the problem to the buying company. Given their co-opetitive relationship, both suppliers would likely behave this way in unison. Regardless, we have two independent studies (Durach, Wiengarten, and Choi 2020; Wu, Choi, and Rungtusanatham 2010) that examine the impact of the supplier-supplier relationship on buyer performance, offering corroborating, counterintuitive results. As a reference, Wu, Choi, and Rungtusanatham (2010) collected data from a major aerospace company in the U.S. and its suppliers, while Durach, Wiengarten, and Choi (2020) collected data 10 years later from companies in German-speaking countries in Europe. The negative effect of supplier-supplier relationship dynamics on the buying company's performance is definitely an area that needs further investigation.

Beyond the implications for supply chain resilience, the research context of a tetrad across four tiers of a supply chain provides additional implications for extended supply chains. Tetrads reflect many interesting and unique characteristics as applied to supply networks. Structurally, a tetrad involves four nodes and three to six links, as depicted in Figure 6.10. The linear tetrad has three links, while the saturated tetrad has all nodes connected with all other nodes with six links. There are, of course, two more tetrads between these two with four links and five links.

Many studies, as reported in this chapter and Chapter 4 on triads, conduct research in various triadic contexts (i.e., transitive vs. intransitive triads). We have noted that triads are the smallest unit of a network where we can

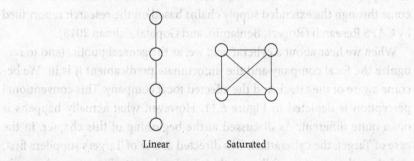

Linear   Saturated

Figure 6.10 Two Ends of the Tetrad Spectrum

observe network characteristics, and triads provide the context for studying extended supply chains. For consideration, if we stretch out the extended supply chain across four tiers, we have a tetrad with three links. This linear tetrad would be necessary if we wanted to study the extended supply chain from the first-tier supplier's perspective in conjunction with the presence of a downstream buyer.

There are more fundamental structural characteristics of a tetrad to SCM. A tetrad offers the smallest network context to study how two dyads are embedded in each other (i.e., how two buyer-supplier relationships are intertwined together). Similarly, it provides the smallest context to study multiple buyers and multiple suppliers. It gives us two overlapping triads. For instance, in the saturated tetrad in Figure 6.10, we see two triads with a shared dyad in between. In a triad, we can study only one structural hole. In a tetrad, we can examine multiple structural holes and how they might influence each other. As in Durach, Wiengarten, and Choi (2020), a tetrad offers a context where we can study multi-tiers (i.e., three) with multiple suppliers in one tier (i.e., two). Their tetrad has two suppliers at the first-tier level, but we can certainly have two suppliers in the second tier, which would reflect single sourcing by the focal company and dual sourcing by the first-tier supplier. More on tetrads in Chapter 9 where we discuss emerging topics.

Cyberattacks as a Multi-Tier Concern

Rogers and Choi (2018) claim, "According to our research, over 60% of reported attacks on publicly traded U.S. firms in 2017 were launched through the IT systems of suppliers or other third parties such as contractors, up from less than one-quarter of attacks in 2010." In other words, cybersecurity problems are supply chain problems. In this section, we consider how cyberattacks come through the extended supply chains based on the research report filed by CAPS Research (Rogers, Benjamin, and Gopalakrishnan 2018).

When we hear about a cyberattack, we, as the general public, tend to recognize the focal company and the unfortunate predicament it is in. We become aware of the attack and the affected focal company. This conventional perception is depicted in Figure 6.11. However, what actually happens is often quite different. As discussed at the beginning of this chapter, in the case of Target, the cyberattack was directed at one of Target's suppliers first, and then the attackers followed the supply chain to Target, as shown in

Figure 6.11 General Perception of Cyberattack
Source: Adapted from Rogers, Benjamin, and Gopalakrishnan 2018

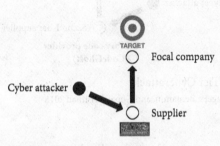

Figure 6.12 Path of Cyberattack on Target
Source: Adapted from Rogers, Benjamin, and Gopalakrishnan 2018

Figure 6.12. The cyber attackers tend to use a shotgun approach, in which they shoot at everyone in the supply chain and see which weak link breaks first. In this case, it was Fazio, a small family-owned HVAC supplier that was using a free version of an anti-virus software. Once the attackers obtained Fazio's supplier credentials, it was relatively easy for them to slip into Target's system and cause damage (i.e., lost records of 110 million customers and over $160M in financial losses).

The attack can happen at the second-tier supplier further upstream in the extended supply chain if that is where the point of vulnerability lies. Often, such a point of vulnerability operates outside the purview of the focal company, even for a well-known corporation for its multi-tier SCM. One such focal company, Apple, fell victim to a multi-tier cyberattack, as depicted in Figure 6.13 (see https://www.lookout.com/blog/xcodeghost).

In this case, the first-tier supplier were Apple's app developers (e.g., the Pokémon game app developer). These developers rely on a library of generic codes available from the second-tier suppliers. As such, almost all Apple smartphone apps share a common code drawn from the library code provider. Typically, 70 or 80% of the code that makes up an app is obtained from the second-tier provider, and the rest of the code is added by the first-tier developer. It is this latter development of proprietary code that differentiates one app (e.g., Pokémon) from another app (e.g., Angry Bird). From the

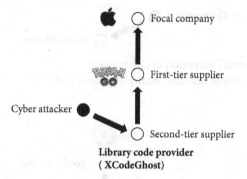

Figure 6.13 Multi-Tier Cyberattack
Source: Adapted from Rogers, Benjamin, and Gopalakrishnan 2018

cyber attackers' perspective, those that develop proprietary codes are not an attractive target because even if they succeed, they would be affecting only one particular app. Therefore, they go after the second-tier provider. If the attackers were to succeed there, they could infect many, many apps that would use that particular code. That is what happened to Apple in 2015. The cyber attackers had inserted into the library a malicious code called the XCodeGhost Code that looked like Apple's preferred XCode. In this case, the second-tier developers represented the path of least resistance, and the attackers began there.

We now close the discussion on the extended supply chain and are looking forward to the next chapter on supply networks. Visually, if we juxtapose the vertically expanded extended supply chain covered in this chapter and the supply base covered in the previous chapter that expands the supplier-supplier relationships horizontally, we have a supply network that stretches in both directions—vertically and horizontally. Of course, the topics covered in earlier chapters, such as dyads and triads, will still be relevant as the building blocks of a network.

Key Points

- We tend to assign blame to the most immediate supplier to us for a problem simply because they are within our visual range, but the cause of the problem may lie beyond that supplier in the extended supply chain.

- We need to adopt the multi-tier supply chain management (SCM) perspective and be cognizant of the areas of the supply chain not visible to us.
- Many leading focal companies (e.g., Honda, Apple, among others) reach deeper into their supply chain and engage in directed sourcing, through which they establish a contractual agreement with second-, third-, and other tertiary-level suppliers.
- Just like make-buy decisions happen at the organizational level, make-buy decisions occur at the supply chain level. If the focal company outsources everything to the first-tier supplier, including the sourcing work, then that focal company, in essence, is *buying* the first-tier supplier's supply chain. If the focal company outsources manufacturing work but reserves the right to do in-house sourcing of parts and components that go into its product, that would be equivalent to *making* a supply chain.
- As a supply chain migrates from sequential (i.e., supply chain buy) to directed (i.e., supply chain make), its member companies begin to sense interdependencies. Especially, the first-tier supplier that has now lost its bridge position would feel boxed in with fewer degrees of freedom (i.e., it would now be unable to transfer some of the cost-reduction pressure to its upstream suppliers).
- Institutional responses necessarily vary across a supply chain. For a healthcare supply chain, the mimetic and coercive pressures are perceived differently at different levels across the supply chain, whereas the normative pressures are perceived across the supply chain.
- When contemplating a supply chain financing approach (i.e., factoring or reverse factoring), different sourcing strategies (i.e., sequential vs. directed) should be considered together.
- Tetrads, where we have four nodes and three to six links, may provide a fruitful context to study supply network dynamics beyond triads where we have three nodes and two to three links.
- Most cyberattacks come through extended supply chains. Therefore, cybersecurity is a supply chain problem.

7

Supply Chains as Networks

He sat across the table and looked straight at me. I still remember his exact words, "Now, Thomas, what can I do you for?" I was in the office of David Nelson, executive vice president of Honda of America in Marysville, Ohio.

I was there to ask him to let me map the entire supply network of its flagship automobile, the Honda Accord. The supply network would encompass all the suppliers as far as raw materials. The suppliers in the supply network would be manufacturing parts and assembling them into different modules that make up a Honda Accord. When I made my request, that brought a smile to his face. He said, "Do you know how many parts there are in a car like the Accord?" Well, I was stumped. I think I said something like 5,000. He corrected me, "There are over 30,000 parts in it." Ah, now I realized why he asked me the question. He was implying that it would be impossible for a single researcher to take on the mapping of a whole vehicle. So, I did not get the answer right, but, at the same time, I became quite hopeful. At least he was not saying no to my request and seemed to be entertaining the idea.

I collected myself and tried again. I suggested then I could map a module that goes into the Honda Accord, whose procurement would be representative of Honda's overall supply management practices. Then, by mapping a smaller portion of the total supply network, I would learn how Honda manages its supply network. He liked that response much better. He proceeded to introduce me to a manager in supply management who would work with me to carry out the research. This manager's name was Jeff Thomko. From that point on, Jeff became my point of contact at Honda for about three years.

The first thing Jeff and I did was to decide on which module to focus on. In addition to the module offering general supply management practices, we agreed that it should also be a strategically important module for Honda, and it should be a module the general public could easily identify. After going back and forth several times, we decided on the center console module. This module sits between the driver seat and the passenger seat. It has a storage compartment, cup holder, and a few other things. The official description

The Nature of Supply Networks. Thomas Y. Choi, Oxford University Press. © Thomas Y. Choi 2023.
DOI: 10.1093/oso/9780197673249.003.0007

from Honda was the "center piece between seats [with] utility center for storage, space for gear shift, and power outlets." Jeff and other managers ensured me that the procurement of the center console would reflect their general supply management practices. They also assured me that this module was a strategically important unit for Honda. It contained the cupholder, which, according to the market research by JD Powers, was one of the five most important features in a passenger car that affected a consumer's purchase decision.

Jeff gave me a copy of the bill of materials for the Honda Accord's center console. It had about 50 parts listed, which was much more manageable than 30,000 parts. It was likely there would be suppliers that made more than one part from the list, which meant I would be dealing with less than 50 suppliers. Also, to contrast the supply network of the Honda Accord center console, I requested that I should be allowed to collect the same data from Acura. Jeff had informed me earlier they were manufacturing the Acura CL/TL in the Marysville location where they were manufacturing the Accord. From my perspective, that product was a luxury brand, and its data would complement data from the Honda Accord, a family sedan. They agreed, and I was off collecting data. It began with visiting the first-tier suppliers that assembled center consoles for the Honda Accord and Acura CL/TL.

Right about that time, I ran into an executive from Chrysler—at the time, they were DaimlerChrysler. His name was Jeff Trimmer. After exchanging niceties, he asked me if I was working on anything interesting. So, I told him about the supply network mapping project I was doing at Honda. He seemed very intrigued and asked me if I could share the results when available. As soon as he said that, I saw an opportunity to collect the data from DaimlerChrysler. I responded positively, but I also said we would need Honda's approval. Jeff, of course, said he understood. I had known that Honda and Chrysler had benchmarked each other before. Based on that knowledge, I thought Honda would agree but would also want something in return, such as the same type of supply network data from their side. And that was exactly what happened—when I posed the request from Jeff Trimmer to Jeff Thomko, that was the response I received. So, I went back to DaimlerChrysler and said, "Honda is fine with sharing the results of my research so long as they can get something similar from DaimlerChrysler." Jeff Trimmer was fine with that and asked me which vehicle I would want to focus on. Since I was engaged in doing a purposeful sampling as stipulated by the case studies research design protocol (e.g., Eisenhardt 1989; Barratt,

Choi, and Li 2011), I looked for a vehicle that would give me more variety beyond the Honda Accord, a family sedan, and Acura CL/TL, a luxury sedan. After some discussions, we decided on the Grand Cherokee, an SUV on a truck chassis. So, one thing led to another, and I was now working on three supply networks of the center console—Honda Accord, Acura CL/TL, and DaimlerChrysler Grand Cherokee.

This chapter begins by presenting that study and its outcomes (see Choi and Hong 2002). As shown in the first box in Figure 7.1, the center console supply networks of Honda Accord, Acura CL/TJ, and DaimlerChrysler Grand Cherokee are mapped and discussed individually, and the structure of each network is analyzed using the constructs of formalization, centralization, and complexity. After that, all three supply networks are compared and characterized in terms of how they are similar and dissimilar. The features of network structures are captured in a set of theoretical statements.

The second box in Figure 7.1 describes how a quantitative analysis, by means of social network analysis, is conducted on these three supply networks from the study by Choi and Hong (Kim et al. 2011). An overview of social network analysis is first offered in terms of what kind of network indices are used at the node level and at the network level. Then, based on Kim et al. (2011), we discuss the results of the social network analysis of the three supply networks that were mapped in the study by Choi and Hong (2002). Network structural characteristics are offered as numerical indices at the node level and the network level. We then consider how the results of the social network analyses converge and diverge from the earlier network mapping study done by Choi and Hong (2002). The quantitative analysis using the tools of social network analysis is possible because networks have been mapped and their structures have come into view. However, for typical focal companies, there are suppliers in the supply network visible to them and some are not visible to them. For instance, many of the second-tier suppliers selected by their first-tier supplier may not be visible to the focal company.

Choi and Dooley (2009) point to the need to consider the vast, invisible part of the supply network, as later echoed by Carter, Rogers, and Choi

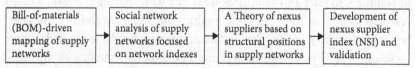

| Bill-of-materials (BOM)-driven mapping of supply networks | Social network analysis of supply networks focused on network indexes | A Theory of nexus suppliers based on structural positions in supply networks | Development of nexus supplier index (NSI) and validation |

Figure 7.1 Key Topic Areas in Chapter 7

(2015). In response, Yan et al. (2015) propose a theory of nexus suppliers—the suppliers that may be hidden from the purview of the focal company but are potentially critical given the structural positions they occupy in supply networks, as indicated in the third box in Figure 7.1. Choi, Shao, and Shi (2015) describe a study designed to ascertain whether it might be possible to identify such hidden, critical suppliers in the invisible part of the supply chain. As identified in the fourth box of Figure 7.1, Shao et al. (2018) subsequently offer a quantitative model of nexus suppliers using the aggregated network structural indices. We do the computations of what we call nexus supplier index (NSI) using the data collected from Bloomberg Terminal. (More on Bloomberg Terminal later in this chapter.)

This chapter concludes by looking to the future. We assess our current situation as operating far from equilibrium, where we begin to observe black-swan events more frequently, as discussed in Chapter 1. In this environment, as discussed in the previous chapter, having done multi-tier, supply network mapping versus not having done it makes a world of difference. What happened during the early months of COVID-19 in China is discussed (Choi, Rogers, and Vakil 2020). While most multinational corporations that had suppliers in the affected zone were still scurrying around to figure out which suppliers were there, a few leading companies that had done supply network mapping had more transparency into their supply networks. The discussion points out what needs to be done as we move forward.

Supply Network Maps

Presented in Figures 7.2, 7.3 and 7.4 are three supply network maps generated based on the bill of materials (BOM) obtained from the focal companies of Honda and DaimlerChrysler. They offer a cross-sectional view of what supply networks look like at one point in time. To the best of my knowledge, they represent one of the very first attempts at empirically mapping real-world supply networks. Also, as discussed in Chapter 6, most of the suppliers for the Honda Accord, as shown in Figure 7.2 are still intact, as indicated in a recent study by Giannoccaro, Nair, and Choi (2018).

All three supply network maps show the focal company at the top. Honda Accord shows two first-tier suppliers (CVT and JFC), whereas Acura CL/TL shows only one first-tier supplier (Intek). DaimlerChrysler Grand Cherokee also shows one first-tier supplier (Textron), but this is a qualified one because

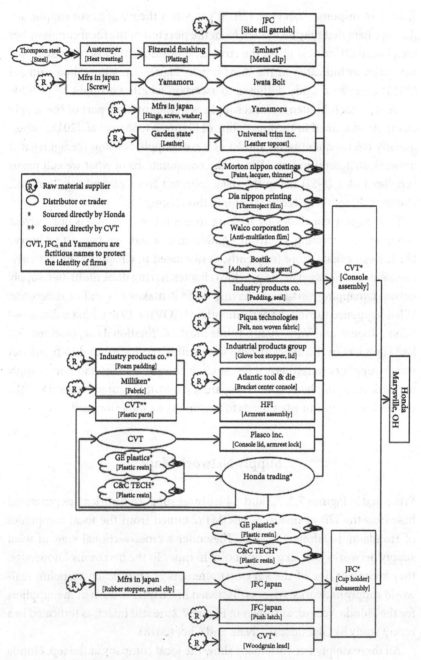

Figure 7.2 Accord Center Console Supply Network
Source: Adapted from Choi and Hong 2002

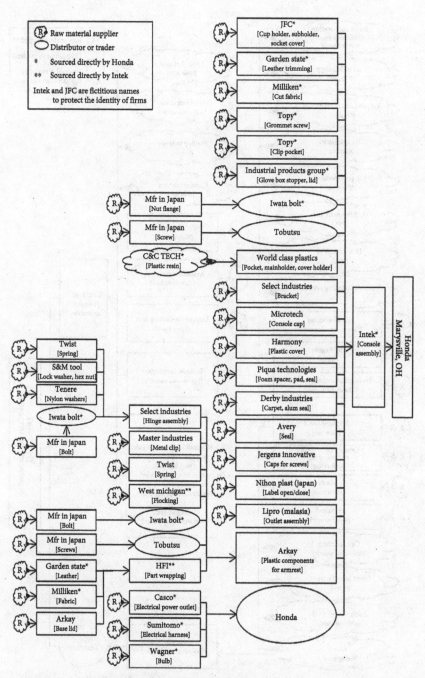

Figure 7.3 Acura CL/TL Center Console Supply Network
Source: Adapted from Choi and Hong 2002

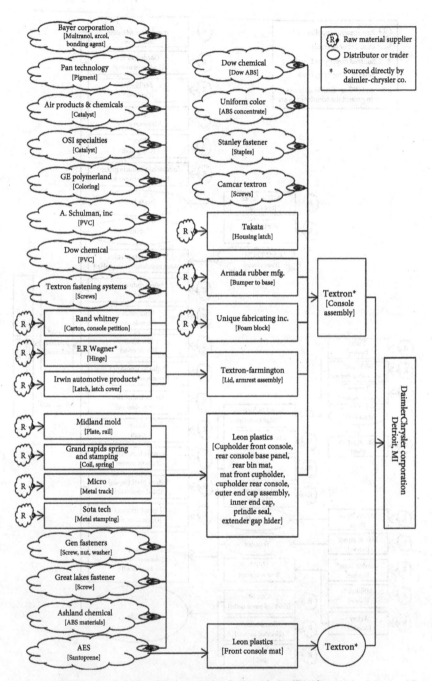

Figure 7.4 Grand Cherokee Center Console Supply Network
Source: Adapted from Choi and Hong 2002

a second-tier supplier (Leon Plastics) actually supplies the front console mat directly to DaimlerChrysler with the Textron label. All three maps show a large number of second-tier suppliers and a slightly fewer number of suppliers at the third-tier level. There are fourth-tier and fifth-tier suppliers that are mostly raw materials suppliers.

The suppliers shown in a rectangular box are parts manufacturers or assembly companies engaged in the physical transformation of a product. The suppliers in oval-shaped circles are brokers or traders engaged in buying and selling goods. Those in a cloud shape are raw materials suppliers (e.g., steel or plastic resin). Some of them are known, and their names are listed. Names of some raw materials suppliers were not disclosed, in which case they are listed simply with an R. In addition, there is an important notation included in these maps. The suppliers with an asterisk are those that have a direct, contractual relationship with the focal company (i.e., directed sourcing). For example, Garden State appears as a third-tier supplier on the Honda Accord map and as a second- and fourth-tier supplier on the Acura CL/TL map. Regardless of its position in the supply network, it shows up with an asterisk which means its contract is with Honda and not with its immediate downstream buyer. This phenomenon was explained in Chapter 6 as directed sourcing. Some show two asterisks—these suppliers appear in the Honda and Acura maps but not in the DaimlerChrysler map. These suppliers represent those that have been directly sourced by the first-tier supplier (i.e., CVT or Intek). For instance, Intek selects HFI to supply plastic wrapping to Arkay. Here, HFI would be Intek's second-tier and Honda's third-tier supplier. In this regard, each of the three supply network maps contains two types of information—material flows and contractual relationships. This becomes a critical distinction when we get to the social network analysis discussed later in this chapter.

As the first-tier supplier that assembles the center console, CVT can best be described as a Honda *keiretsu* company. A joint venture between Honda and Yamamoru that appears as a second-tier supplier in this supply network has become CVT. (Please note CVT and Yamamoru are fictitious names per their request at the time of data collection.) Yamamoru used to work for Honda in Japan as a plastic-molding company, and when it went to the U.S., the joint venture was formed. The other first-tier supplier, JFC, manufactures the cupholder—the cupholder is what makes the center console a strategically important module for Honda (as mentioned, it is one of the five most important features in a car that affects the consumer purchase decision). For this cupholder, Honda considers the rate of release of the cupholder cover as critical, and JFC owns the intellectual property on this mechanism that controls the rate of release—how quickly the cupholder cover opens when the release button is pressed by the user. Beyond these two first-tier suppliers, there are a few suppliers with one asterisk (i.e., Emhart, Garden State, and Milliken) and with two asterisks (i.e., Industry Products). Also, several second-tier suppliers are chosen by CVT but from Honda's approved vendor list (i.e., Piqua Technologies, Atlantic Tool & Die, and Industrial Products Group). As discussed in Chapter 6, Honda asks its first-tier suppliers to use its approved vendor list when selecting their suppliers, ceteris paribus. This is Honda's deliberate strategy to keep good suppliers in its supply networks to the extent possible, even in the portion of the supply network that might not be visible to them.

Whereas the Honda Accord supply network map shows two first-tier suppliers, the Acura CT/TL supply network map shows only one first-tier supplier. In fact, JFC, which appears as the first-tier supplier in the Accord map, comes up as a second-tier supplier in the Acura CL/TL map. JFC is supplying the same cupholder assembly in both instances. By digging into this difference further, I learned that Honda prefers the structure in the Acura CL/TL with JFC supplying Intek and Intek serving as a one-stop shop. Honda has been trying to convince CVT to take on this additional work and be a one-stop shop, but CVT has been pushing back on this request, arguing it should receive monetary credit for taking on this additional assembly work. Honda initially set up JFC as a first-tier supplier for the Honda Accord supply network because the cupholder assembly is such a critical item that requires close control on all dimensions of cost, quality, and delivery. However, now, CVT is resisting the change because its margins are so tight that it feels it simply cannot take on the work with no remuneration. For Acura CL/TL, Intek has been set up as its sole first-tier supplier from the beginning, and Honda has been able to set up the supply network with Intek as the integrator of the whole center console module. In fact, Intek has come on as the new first-tier supplier because the previous supplier could not meet the technology requirements Honda needed, such as laying down woodgrain on plastic parts. The woodgrain finish is considered critical for the Acura product line because it gives a more luxurious look and feel to the high-end product. For that matter, the Acura CL/TL center console shows a longer list of BOM with more parts, likely leading to more complicated supply network patterns with more nodes. For example, for the center console, Acura CL/TL has a total of 76 suppliers compared to Accord's 50. As is the case in the Accord map, many second-tier suppliers come from Honda's approved vendor list, such as Iwata Bolt, Piqua, Select Industries, and Topy. There are directly sourced Honda suppliers down to the fourth-tier level, such as Garden State, Iwata Bolt, and Milliken, demonstrating the deep reach of Honda into the extended supply chains.

The first-tier supplier, Textron, has enjoyed a good working relationship with Chrysler, now DaimlerChrysler, over multiple decades since the 1960s. According to the managers at DaimlerChrysler, Textron has an "evergreen contract" with DaimlerChrysler. That means, Textron is guaranteed to remain as the first-tier supplier for the center console module for the Grand Cherokee through model changes, as long as Textron does its job well and there is no major mishap. According to the managers at Textron, this type of evergreen contract comes at a cost. Textron engineers are invited to early design meetings at Chrysler and are asked to do the design of the center console as part of early supplier involvement (ESI). Unlike Honda, which prefers to do all the design work, DaimlerChrysler delegates the design work to Textron. According to Textron managers, all that simply means is that DaimlerChrysler is asking Textron to pay for expensive design work. Textron has even been asked to conduct market research of DaimlerChrysler customers and design in their requirements of the center console. At the second-tier level, Textron-Farmington and Leon Plastics appear as two major suppliers. Supplying to Textron-Farmington are two third-tier suppliers with an asterisk, E.R. Wagner and Irwin Automotive Products.

On the one hand, DaimlerChrysler has directed these suppliers to supply parts (i.e., hinge, latch, and latch cover) to its first-tier supplier, Textron. Textron then inserted its subsidiary Textron-Farmington to handle some assembly work as a second-tier supplier. On the other hand, while the arrangement may appear as directed sourcing, it really is not in the sense that these two parts suppliers at the third-tier level are being directed to supply the parts because of some legacy contractual issues and not due to conscious choices by DaimlerChrysler with strategic intent. Further, Leon Plastics, which appears as a major second-tier supplier, used to be a first-tier supplier to DaimlerChrysler. Through the downsizing effort of its supply base, DaimlerChrysler has now relegated Leon Plastics to the second-tier level. This is why, when the front console mat it produces is supplied to DaimlerChrysler, it does so by using the Textron's label.

Underlying Structures of Supply Networks

Given the three supply networks presented, we now investigate the under-lying structures therein. As a first step, we build on the organization design literature (i.e., Daft 2013; Gerwin 1984; Walsh and Dewar 1987) that offers key constructs (formalization, centralization, and complexity) to capture organization structure. According to Gerwin (1984), the structure of an organization is considered "the pattern of relationships among people" (p. 9). In the same way, the structure of a supply network is thought to emerge over time into a coherent form (Choi, Dooley, and Rungtusanatham 2001). It would reflect a pattern of relationships among companies, and three supply network maps offer those patterns.

Overview of Key Constructs

Three dimensions that capture the structure of an organization or a system are formalization, centralization, and complexity. *Formalization* in a system promotes standardization (Mintzberg 1979; Price and Mueller 1986; Walsh and Dewar 1987) facilitated by rules, procedures, and behavioral norms (Beyer 1984). Formalization ensures consistency of outputs and can be facilitated through written (document) or unwritten (work norms) forms. *Centralization* deals with how the level of control is concentrated or dispersed across a system (Price and Mueller 1986). If decision-making authority is concentrated in one part of an organization, that is a centralized organization, whereas if decision-making authority is dispersed across many parts, then that is a decentralized organization. *Complexity* refers to the degree to which differentiated elements operate in a system (Daft 2013; Price and Mueller 1986). As discussed in Chapter 5, complexity deals with the number of elements, how differentiated they are, and the degree to which they are connected. Overall, complexity can be viewed as the load required to coordinate activities in an organization or a system.

Applied to supply networks, *formalization* occurs at the dyadic, company-to-company level, either the buyer-supplier or supplier-supplier relationships. Toyota contracts with its suppliers and instills in them the principles of the Toyota Production System (TPS) (see Liker 2021). As the buyer and suppliers, they come to share a common language for efficient communication and work norms, such as keeping workplaces clean and organized (i.e., the 5S method) and getting at the root causes of problems (i.e., the 5 Whys technique). Then, Toyota brings suppliers together to share their learnings and ideas among themselves. The Bluegrass Automotive Manufacturing Association (BAMA) is one example. From these engagements, Toyota looks for standardized, efficient, and shared procedures and behavioral norms. *Centralization* in the supply network context would refer to the directed-sourcing practice by the focal company. The more the directed sourcing, the more centralized the supply network. As per our discussion in Chapter 6, Apple's supply network would exhibit high centralization since Apple makes all sourcing decisions for most of the parts on its BOM. What is interesting is that, while formalization occurs at the dyadic level, centralization seems to occur in the linear supply chain context. For example, in Figure 7.2, which shows the Accord supply network, we have Honda-CVT-Emhart going across three supply chain tiers as a case for centralization. We could also have centralization that begins with CVT as in the supply chain of CVT-HFI-Industry Products. Relevant to the structure of supply networks in the area of *complexity* is the organization design literature that offers three dimensions for structure in terms of horizontal, vertical, and spatial (Daft 2013; Gibson, Ivancevich, and Konopaske 2011). Once the mapping of a supply network is complete, we simply count the number of tiers as a measure of vertical complexity, the number of suppliers in each tier as a measure of horizontal complexity, and the geographical distances among suppliers engaged in transactions as a measure of spatial complexity.

In the following sections, we discuss the three dimensions of supply network structure (formalization, centralization, and complexity) for the Honda Accord, Acura CL/TL, and DaimlerChrysler Grand Cherokee. Formalization is discussed in the dyadic context, centralization is addressed in the extended supply chain context with directed sourcing, and complexity is considered in the broader network context.

Honda Accord

The hallmark of formalization between Honda and its core suppliers, including the two first-tier suppliers, CVT and JFC, begins with the signing of a document they call Purchasing Sales Agreement (PSA). This is an eight-page document that overviews basic activities that pertain to price, delivery, and warrantees. Honda managers consider it the formal contract between

Honda and its suppliers. Honda espouses a sense of reasonableness and open communication and promotes flexibility with its suppliers. From the supplier's perspective, such flexibility is viewed as "the cost of doing business with Honda." Before launching a new model, Honda intentionally keeps its quality expectations vague, for instance, by not explicitly articulating specific requirements, such as the drag coefficient of a hinge at opening and closing. Honda and the supplier talk things out through experiments to fine-tune the final product specification. This approach requires much effort from both Honda and the supplier, but how this process takes place is understood clearly by both parties. The suppliers overall agree that Honda operates under clear work norms that all suppliers understand and accept. Yet, both Honda and suppliers agree that when it comes to cost issues, Honda takes a stern and inflexible stance. A price negotiation takes place before the award letter and issuance of a purchase order (PO). A target price is typically put on the table by Honda, and even after an agreement from the supplier, Honda continues to monitor the supplier to ensure the target price is met.

The centralization of the Honda Accord supply network takes place in two ways. One is through directed sourcing by Honda and CVT, its first-tier supplier. The other represents a less direct approach in which Honda releases its approved vendor list to CVT and requests that they choose suppliers from that list. With Honda as the focal company, we have five linear, extended supply chains: Honda-CVT-Emhart; Honda-CVT-(Universal Trim)-Garden State; Honda-CVT-(HFI)-Milliken; Honda-CVT-Honda Trading-C&C Tech; and Honda-CVT-Honda Trading-GE Plastics. In these linear supply chains, suppliers shown in parenthesis are those chosen by CVT, not by Honda. CVT has learned from Honda and does its own directed sourcing. There are four linear, extended supply chains initiated by CVT: CVT-HFI-Industry Products; CVT-HFI-CVT; CVT-Plasco-CVT-Honda Trading-C&C Tech; and CVT-Plasco-CVT-Honda Trading-GE Plastics. CVT outsources some of its plastic-molding work to Plasco and channels plastic resin from C&C Tech and GE Plastics to Plasco.

The overall complexity of the Accord supply network appears to have been influenced by Honda's deliberate strategies to co-locate its suppliers and to keep using the same core suppliers across its supply network. Both practices reduce complexity. The average travel distance between Honda and its two first-tier suppliers is about 60 miles, and the average distance between these two first-tier suppliers and their suppliers at the second-tier level is about 90 miles. According to Honda managers, many core suppliers listed on the approved vendor list may supply only about 10% to 20% of its sales directly to Honda but may end up having 90% reliance on Honda work by receiving work from other core suppliers. The implication of this observation is that Honda gets to reduce the total number of suppliers in its supply network and enjoy lower complexity. In the Accord supply network, there are 50 suppliers altogether. Going from the first tier down to the fifth tier, the suppliers are distributed across as 2, 21, 18, 7, and 2. We will be able to compare these numbers against other supply networks when we get to the next section that discusses overall structural characteristics.

Acura CL/TL

The general formalization approach between Honda to produce this Acura model and its first-tier supplier, Intek, is very similar to what we discussed above for the Honda Accord. Intek and all other core suppliers have signed a PSA and receive a monthly performance report card. Price negotiations occur prior to launching a new model. Honda sometimes continues to tinker with the design even after Intek submits a quotation. After the design change, Intek is then burdened with justifying the price increase given the design changes. In addition, an annual cost-reduction target is usually set at 2% to 3%, but Honda suppliers know that Honda will be open to listening to their cases and might adjust the cost-reduction target. For instance, Honda might make the cost-reduction targets progressively higher across three years. One unique circumstance in the Acura CL/TL supply network is that the first-tier supplier, Intek, is relatively new, as discussed earlier. Honda usually has *jikon* meetings with its core suppliers in which they go over Honda's long-term plans and review the supplier's aspirations. In the case of Intek, Honda has asked them to submit its three-year investment plan for its capacity and capability expansions, and Honda shares how it projects sales revenues. The purpose of this exchange is explained as necessary to ensure Intek's long-term viability.

For centralization, Honda practices are similar to what we discussed above. It engages in directed sourcing, and it asks Intek to choose from the approved vendor list. We see a lot more Honda-controlled, linear supply chains in the Acura CL/TL supply network. There are 12 of them, compared to the five we see for the Accord supply network. They are Honda-Intek-JFC; Honda-Intek-Garden State; Honda-Intek-Milliken; Honda-Intek-Topy;

Honda-Intek-Iwata Bolt; Honda-Intek-(Arkay)-(Select Industries)-Iwata Bolt; Honda-Intek-(Arkay)-Iwata Bolt; Honda-Intek-(Arkay)-(HFI)-Garden State; Honda-Intek-(Arkay)-(HFI)-Milliken; Honda-Intek-Honda Trading-Casco; Honda-Intek-Honda Trading-Sumitomo; and Honda-Intek-Honda Trading-Wagner. Further, there are two extended supply chains direct sourced by Intek. They are Intek-Arkay-HFI and Intek-Arkay-West Michigan.

Likely because the Acura CL/TL is a higher end product than the Honda Accord, the complexity of the Acura CL/TL supply network appears higher compared to what we see for the Honda Accord. For one, there are more suppliers in the supply network. The Acura CL/TL supply network has 76 suppliers. The depth of the supply network goes further to the sixth-tier level. The distribution of their numbers going from the first tier to the sixth tier is 1, 20, 28, 17, 9, and 1. Further, the spatial distance among suppliers appears quite far. The physical distance between Honda and Intek is about 100 miles. Excluding overseas suppliers and brokers, the average distance between Intek and the second-tier suppliers is about 100 miles. If we were to include overseas suppliers, that average distance would grow by about 10 times.

DaimlerChrysler

For formalization, the Pre-Source Package (PSP) form is an important document that articulates the details of supplier requirements. DaimlerChrysler considers PSP as the contract, and the current PSP stipulates a five-year term. However, managers at DaimlerChrysler emphasize how Textron is on an evergreen contract, and the job would belong to Textron as long as there are no major problems. One manager said, "The job is Textron's to lose." Once Textron was chosen as the sole source for the center console, it was sent a PSP to formalize the understanding regarding delivery, materials, quality, target price, tooling, related investments, and after-market sales support. The selection of Textron was executed without a formal competitive bidding process. By then, the engineers from Textron had already been working with DaimlerChrysler engineers. In turn, Textron invited the engineers from Leon Plastics, the major second-tier supplier, to work with its engineers to further develop the design of the center console. Over the duration of a contract, Textron is subject to annual cost-reduction targets. DaimlerChrysler presently imposes annually a 3% hard savings (i.e., cost reduction that shows up on the profit and loss, P&L, statement) and 3% soft savings (i.e., cost avoidance that occurs through continuous improvements). Textron, in turn, imposes the same practice on its suppliers, such as Leon.

Whereas Honda centrally controls design work, DaimlerChrysler delegates the center console design to Textron. DaimlerChrysler takes a decentralized approach to design, and Textron is engaged in black-box sourcing. Textron does the design and makes all the sourcing decisions on behalf of DaimlerChrysler. Textron then transfers some of the design responsibility to Leon at the next tier down. There are relatively few direct-sourced supply chains compared to what we see from Honda supply networks. In fact, there are only two: DaimlerChrysler-Textron-(Textron Farmington)-Wagner; and DaimlerChrysler-Textron-(Textron Farmington)-Irwin. Wagner and Irwin are at the third-tier level and supply legacy parts that DaimlerChrysler has decided to buy from them to "maintain goodwill." The directed sourcing of these two third-tier suppliers is more of an exception. Overall, Textron is entrusted to make all sourcing decisions, and Textron also turns to Leon to make all its sourcing decisions at the next tier level.

To consider complexity, we look at the total number of suppliers in the supply network. There are 41 suppliers in total—a smaller number compared to 50 for the Honda Accord and 76 for the Acura CL/TL. The supply network goes down only to the fourth tier, shorter than what we see in Honda Accord at five tiers and in Acura CL/TL at seven tiers. The distribution of suppliers across the four tiers is 2, 10, 22, and 7. Two at the first tier really is one company, Textron. Given that Leon is a second-tier supplier, we count Textron as a broker between Leon and DaimlerChrysler, when it sends the front console mat to DaimlerChrysler with the Textron label. The distance between DaimlerChrysler and Textron is about 20 miles. This distance does not seem much; however, Textron is looking at about 400 miles of physical distance on average with the second-tier suppliers.

Integrating Structural Characteristics

In the preceding section, we introduced the structural characteristics of three supply networks separately (for more details, see Choi and Hong 2002). In this section, we dig deeper into their characteristics. We aim to integrate our observations of the three supply networks to ascertain the underlying structural characteristics and what drives these characteristics.

Formalization

A common formalization characteristic across all three supply networks is the coexistence of explicitness and implicitness. The literature attests to the presence of explicitness when considering the formalization aspect of system structures (i.e., Gerwin 1984), but in the context of supply networks, we also see the presence of implicitness. All first-tier suppliers have signed a document that explicitly states how they will work with the focal company. CVT, JFC, and Intek signed a PSA, and Textron signed a PSP. These first-tier suppliers replicate this same explicit practice with the second-tier suppliers. At the same time, Honda keeps certain expectations intentionally vague to allow for new ideas and adjustments to shape the product and related processes. DaimlerChrysler expects additional engineering work that may not have been explicitly called for. Much of the implicit nature of formalization seems to stem from how all first-tier suppliers are assumed to continue with new product lines unless they run into a major problem. For example, Honda began working with Intek when the former first-tier supplier was unable to acquire new technology Honda required (i.e., woodgrain on plastic). This implicit understanding appears to be what drives suppliers to offer flexibility to the focal company. For instance, Textron has been supplying the center console for the Grand Cherokee over several model changes, and it has been on what they call the evergreen contract. For such a long-term relationship to sustain, there has to be flexibility because, over time, both companies would need to make changes. DaimlerChrysler would likely need to make design changes, and Textron would need to respond and adjust its own design.

Clearly, cost concerns are ubiquitous across all three supply networks. All first-tier suppliers are under tremendous pressure from their focal companies (Honda and DaimlerChrysler) to lower their costs during price negotiations. Then, during mass production, they are under continuing pressure to reduce costs and meet annual cost reduction targets. A sense of suffocation and "cut-throat" demands prevail as a common behavioral sentiment. A derived behavioral norm is that the suppliers are responsible for justifying cost changes following specification changes from design updates made by the focal company. As discussed in Chapter 3, the upstream supply networks bear the tremendous burden of offering savings on the input side to improve the return on investment (ROI) that would contribute to the overall corporate performance goal of the focal company.

As such, from the focal company's perspective, all contracts are offered to one supplier at a time, and cost savings are achieved one supplier at a time. That is in the dyadic context. All formalization activities occur between two companies (i.e., between the focal company and the first-tier supplier, and between the first-tier and second-tier supplier). Documentations and procedures, the two most salient aspects of formalization, occur at the dyadic level (i.e., Honda and CVT at the first-tier level, and Textron and Leon at the second-tier level). This dyadic context gets elevated to the supply chain context when we consider centralization.

Centralization

As discussed earlier, centralization has to do with how extensively the visible hand of the focal company reaches into the supply chain. We refer to that practice as directed sourcing, meaning the focal company (Honda and DaimlerChrysler) directs the sourcing of parts and materials two or more tiers upstream in the supply chain. Of course, the first-tier suppliers (i.e., CVT and Intek) can also practice directed sourcing with suppliers upstream in their supply chains.

In the supply networks of Honda Accord, Acura CL/TL, and DaimlerChrysler Grand Cherokee, there are directly sourced supply chains. Honda Accord has nine directed supply chains; Acura CL/TL has 12, and DaimlerChrysler Grand Cherokee has two. The total possible supply chains contained in supply networks are 28, 32, and 27, respectively, for the Accord, CL/TL, and Grand Cherokee. With these numbers, we know that there are 32%, 38%, and 7% of directly sourced supply chains in the supply networks of the Accord, CL/TL, and Grand Cherokee, respectively.

These numbers are supported by the observation that, while Honda prefers to control key suppliers across the supply chain, DaimlerChrysler practices largely decentralized supply management. Once DaimlerChrysler selects its first-tier supplier, Textron, it delegates the responsibility of new product designs and second-tier supplier selection to Textron. Honda, in contrast, selects many key suppliers in the second-, third-, and fourth-tier levels. It also asks its first-tier suppliers, CVT, JFC, and Intek, to choose second-tier suppliers from the common approved vendor list provided by Honda. The reasons for engaging in directed sourcing are summarized in Table 7.1. The Accord and CL/TL show identical reasoning, given

Table 7.1 Reasons for Directed Sourcing

Reason	Honda Accord	Acura CL/TL	DaimlerChrysler Grand Cherokee
Commonize parts	✓	✓	✓
Attain additional expertise	✓	✓	
Take advantage of the high piece price	✓	✓	
Maintain goodwill			✓
Ensure consistent quality	✓	✓	

Source: Adapted from Choi and Hong, 2002

they are both made by Honda. Two rare instances of directed sourcing at DaimlerChrysler take on two reasons, but primarily it is for goodwill with the legacy suppliers.

Commonizing parts refers to efforts to populate the same parts across multiple products for standardization purposes. For example, Emhart as a second-tier supplier to Honda, makes metal clips and other fasteners. It makes sense to use their parts across other products so that Honda would gain economies of scale and save on tooling costs. Additional expertise points to capabilities that second-tier suppliers may have and the first-tier supply may lack. For instance, JFC has the expertise to manufacture the release mechanism on the cupholder that the first-tier supplier for the Acura CL/TL, Intek, does not have, so Honda arranges to have JFC as a second-tier supplier to deliver the cupholder to Intek. Parts with high piece prices are attractive targets for Honda to control directly because a 1% cost saving would translate to more savings in dollars. The leather parts from Garden State are a case in point. Maintaining goodwill with suppliers refers to honoring agreements on legacy parts that DaimlerChrysler inherited from past projects. Ensuring quality pertains primarily to limiting the raw materials suppliers to a few sources. Honda limits the sources of plastic resin to only two—GE Plastics and C&C Tech.

Looking across the table, it appears, overall, that between Honda and DaimlerChrysler, Honda takes a much more centralized approach to supply chain management. On the Honda side, its strategic intent is centralization to control activities across the supply chain. Honda wants to get involved in what happens at the lower tier suppliers as many of its core suppliers operate mainly as second- or third-tier suppliers. In contrast, DaimlerChrysler has a strong strategic orientation for decentralization. It wants to interface only with its first-tier supplier and entrust that supplier to manage the suppliers next tier(s) down. As has been alluded to before, the divergence between the two focal companies begins with their design approach. It is true both companies involve suppliers in the product design. However, Honda is quite adamant about controlling the design centrally from its own design group. For instance, even when a supplier owns intellectual property on a particular product (i.e., cupholder), Honda engineers would still monitor that supplier's design engineering and get involved in the design work there. Again, in contrast, DaimlerChrysler prefers to delegate the design responsibility to its first-tier supplier. It invites the engineers from its first-tier supplier to early design meetings and then releases them to do the design from its end.

Of course, both the centralized and decentralized approaches have cost implications. The decentralized approach provides tremendous cost advantages. DaimlerChrysler offloads the expenses associated with de-signing the center console onto Textron, its first-tier supplier. Textron then offloads some of that expense onto Leon, a second-tier supplier. Further, DaimlerChrysler considers Textron a turnkey operation for the center con-sole, and it avoids all the administrative costs associated with managing other parts suppliers as Honda does. Honda has a vast supply management group that houses accounting professionals and many different types of engineers (i.e., design engineer, cost engineer, etc.) in addition to buyers, contracting specialists, supplier managers, procurement managers, and so on. Honda carries a huge overhead cost to do all the design work, contract with key parts and raw materials suppliers further upstream in the supply chain, and monitor them closely with monthly performance report cards. However, as discussed above, Honda is in a much better position to commonize parts, take advantage of high-cost parts, and consolidate raw materials purchases. In fact, Honda's first-tier suppliers have expressed some level of resentment toward Honda, having cherry-picked all the good suppliers from the second- and third-tier levels. Honda's first-tier suppliers cannot transfer some of the cost-reduction pressures to the lower level suppliers, as the DaimlerChrysler supplier Textron has been able to. Yet, Honda's first-tier suppliers understand that they have to bring their cases to Honda to get relief from cost-reduction pressures. One manager from a Honda supplier said, "We may not make a lot of money, but we do not lose money."

Complexity

An overarching term that can be used to capture complexity from the management perspective is the "load" required to coordinate a system. In an organization, if there are a lot of separate divisions, then its complexity is high, thus the load required to coordinate activities in that organization would be high. We are not necessarily referring to the central corporate office trying to manage the whole organization. That, of course, would be part of it. Still, in each division, there would be a head and a top executive team that coordinates activities within that division. As a collective, the coordination cost of the entire organization would increase with more divisions.

In supply networks, we do not have divisions. However, we still have a span of control as organizations do. Each supplier as an independent entity has its own span of control within the network. For instance, CVT or Intek as a first-tier supplier would have a broader span of control compared to a single parts supplier at the second- or third-tier level. Because Textron does not practice directed sourcing as CVT and Intek do, Textron's span of control may not be as broad. And Leon, working with Textron, may have a relatively broader span of control as a second-tier supplier compared to other second-tier suppliers in Honda's supply networks. This is because DaimlerChrysler does not practice directed sourcing as Honda does, and Leon stands a better chance of transferring some of the workload and cost-reduction burdens to its suppliers. Ultimately, if a supply network has more suppliers, it likely requires more load to coordinate activities, whether centrally by a few key suppliers or decentrally with many suppliers sharing the load in a distributed way.

Table 7.2 lists basic measures of complexity. The horizontal measure reflects the average number of suppliers over all tiers in each supply network. The vertical measure captures the average number of suppliers across all possible supply chains in a network. The spatial measure gives us the average geographical distance between all suppliers in only the first two tiers of the supply network. Most activities that occur in the area of shipment deliveries are assumed to be contained in the first two tiers. Large spatial distance would equate to high complexity, and high numbers of horizontal, vertical, and total supplier measures would equate to high complexity.

Overall, the Acura supply network shows the highest level of complexity. It shows the highest numbers across all measures. This may be because Acura is a luxury automobile and, with more features, its center console BOM has a longer list of items. Overall, two Honda products show more complex supply networks compared to the supply network of DaimlerChrysler.

Table 7.2 Varied Elements in Supply Networks

	Honda Accord Supply Network	Acura CL/TL Supply Network	DaimlerChrysler Grand Cherokee Supply Network
Horizontal (average number of suppliers)	10	13	10
Vertical (average number of tiers)	4	5	4
Spatial (average distance in miles)	70	>1,000	200
Total number of suppliers	50	76	41

Source: Adapted from Choi and Hong 2002

On the one hand, Honda asks its first-tier suppliers to select from its approved vendor list, choosing to focus more on taking advantage of the approved capabilities of its core suppliers. On the other hand, DaimlerChrysler has given Textron explicit instructions to reduce the number of second-tier suppliers, with direct implications to complexity and showing a preference for a less complex supply network. As evidence, compare 20 second-tier suppliers of Acura CL/TL to 10 second-tier suppliers for the Grand Cherokee. Another example of Honda choosing design and quality at the risk of increasing complexity comes from the observation that the Accord supply network has two first-tier suppliers compared to one first-tier supplier in the Grand Cherokee's supply network. DaimlerChrysler made a conscious choice to keep one first-tier supplier for the center console from the beginning. However, Honda initially desired to manage JFC, which owns intellectual property on the release mechanism in the cupholder. Now, Honda wants to delegate managing JFC over to CVT and reduce the number of first-tier suppliers from two to one. However, in contention is whether Honda would pay extra for this additional assembly work that CVT has to take on.

Theorization of Supply Network Structures

We have drawn from the organization design literature the three constructs with which to study supply network structures—formalization, centralization, and complexity. These three constructs have worked well as we examine how supply network structures become operationalized. Conceptually, they are independent constructs, but as they become operationalized in the supply network context, they progressively affect each other. Formalization occurs at the dyad level between two companies (i.e., a buyer and a supplier). Then, as more companies are connected linearly (i.e., a supply chain), we begin to see how centralization can play out. Ultimately, as supply chains are connected and become a network, we see the effects of complexity. We make our first theoretical statement (TS).

TS1. Formalization, centralization, and complexity are operationalized progressively as the structure of a supply network expands from dyads to chains and to networks.

Connections are made between companies and become dyads that turn into chains and eventually into networks. Each company, as a node in the network, makes decisions on which other companies to connect with and in what capacity. In this regard, there are two primary decision drivers—cost concerns and technology potential. These two drivers are discussed further by Choi and Linton (2011) in terms of how focal companies should engage in multi-tier supply chain management. The focal company and other suppliers are engaged in constant tugs of war to find ways to do things more efficiently by connecting with other companies (i.e., see how Textron is working with Leon with the capability to do assembly work and design work) and to transfer work to another company (i.e., see how Honda is trying to offload cupholder assembly work to CVT so that it will work with one first-tier supplier). Another driver that is of interest, as shown in Table 7.1, is attaining additional expertise, which basically means each company looks for suppliers from whom they can learn about new technologies (e.g., woodgrain on a plastic part, release mechanism, etc.).

TS2. Cost concerns and technology potential are two primary drivers that shape the structure of a supply network.

In the organization design literature, organizations use formalization based on rules, procedures, and standardization to ensure consistency of outputs (Beyer 1984; Mintzberg 1979; Walsh and Dewar 1987). Formalization can take place either in written documents or unwritten forms such as tribal knowledge (Price and Mueller 1986). Whether written or unwritten, to work as behavioral guidelines, formalization needs to be explicit (Gerwin 1984). All such characterization of formalization applies to the context of supply networks. However, in supply networks, formalization also takes on an implicit nature. And implicit does not necessarily mean the rules and procedures are not clear. When Honda intentionally keeps things vague during the early stages of a new model launch, that does not mean the supplier lacks knowledge on what is going on. The supplier knows exactly what to expect in that process—they are expected to offer suggestions and remain flexible. In much the same way, DaimlerChrysler expects engineering input from its suppliers without being explicitly called for. The suppliers know they will eventually have to pay for the changes. What seems to fuel this type of implicitness operating in formalization is the context of a long-term relationship.

TS3. Formalization requires explicitness in rules and procedures, and, in supply networks where there are long-term relationships, formalization also takes on the characteristic of implicitness to offer new ideas and flexibility.

As discussed in Chapter 6, if the focal company and all suppliers were engaged in *supply chain buy* as opposed to *supply chain make*, then we would have a highly decentralized supply network. As we see more companies do supply chain make through directed sourcing, we would begin to see more centralized supply networks. For many focal companies like Honda and Apple, centralization makes a lot of sense. However, from the perspective of the suppliers that are told to receive parts from particular lower tier suppliers from the focal company that is practicing directed sourcing, this arrangement creates a difficult situation. For one, those suppliers that have been directly sourced by the focal company may not be as cooperative. These directly sourced suppliers have contracts with the focal company, and they do not regard the suppliers they are delivering to as full-blown customers. We have also noted that, just as Honda engages in directed sourcing, CVT also engages in directed sourcing. Therefore, the intermediate suppliers between the direct sourcing company and direct sourced suppliers would end up simply being a contract manufacturer (i.e., Foxconn).

TS4. The supply chain make through directed sourcing increases the centralization of a supply network.

TS5. The intermediate suppliers between the sourcing company and directly sourced suppliers operate as contracted manufacturers rather than full-blown buyers of goods and services of those suppliers from whom parts arrive.

We also observe an indirect means of affecting how the second-tier supply base would form. Honda gives its approved vendor list to its first-tier suppliers to choose from the list, and DaimlerChrysler instructs its first-tier supplier to reduce the size of their second-tier supply base. This approach can be practiced by the focal company and any other supplier in the supply base. In particular, adopting the approved vendor list by the first-tier suppliers would increase the reliance of the lower tier suppliers on the focal company business. This practice is advantageous for the first-tier supplier because they would be working with qualified suppliers that have already been onboarded by its focal company.

TS6. In addition to directed sourcing, a focal company can affect the structure of lower tier suppliers by giving them its approved vendor list or instructing its first-tier supplier about the size of the second-tier supply base.

TS7. The adoption of the focal company's approved vendor list tends to increase the reliance of suppliers on the focal company's business.

In essence, Honda's approach has more supply chain make, while DaimlerChrysler takes more of a supply chain buy approach. Beyond what was discussed in Chapter 6 about supply chain make vs. buy, we can now bring in additional context to taking these two approaches. In the case of DaimlerChrysler, the supply chain buy makes things more expedient for the focal company. It has in Textron a turnkey operation that will meet all its needs associated with procuring a center console from design to delivery. For its supply chain make approach, Honda pays for more overhead because it has to manage not just its first-tier supplier like CVT but also many lower tier suppliers. In return, Honda gains supply network stability. Suppose Textron decides to sever the business relationship with DaimlerChrysler. Since DaimlerChrysler has delegated the second-tier sourcing decisions to Textron, DaimlerChrysler would lose much of its supply network. If it selects a new first-tier supplier, then with that first-tier supplier, DaimlerChrysler would get a brand-new supply network with new parts suppliers. In contrast, in the same situation, Honda would still have all the key lower tier suppliers intact.

> TS8. The adoption of supply-chain make offers the focal company supply network stability, and the adoption of supply-chain buy makes sourcing more convenient and expedient for the focal company.

Risk management pertaining to supply chains has come to the fore as a significant issue among companies. To manage risk, an engineering approach would be to build in redundancy. An airplane, for instance, is designed that way—if one thing fails (e.g., an engine), it would still fly because there are redundant parts (i.e., the other engine). Increased redundancy means an increased number of elements in the system, which means increased complexity. However, in our supply networks, we see trends toward less complexity. All focal companies prefer to work with one first-tier supplier; even in the case of the Accord, Honda has been trying to have it reduced to one. DaimlerChrysler has instructed Textron to reduce the number of second-tier suppliers. Honda also recommends that its first-tier suppliers use its approved vendor list when selecting second-tier suppliers, which would reduce complexity. At the same time, it is clear that the Acura CL/TL, as a luxury brand, has the longest BOM and the most complex supply network (see Table 7.2). This may mean that the Acura CL/TL supply network has more elements that could go wrong and may be more vulnerable to manufacturing disruptions.

> TS9. The general trend in supply networks is to reduce the degree of complexity.

> TS10. More expensive product lines tend to require more complex supply networks.

Then, is complexity good or bad for risk management in supply networks? We have not settled this issue. On the one hand, if we build redundancy in our supply networks with many substitutable suppliers, that would make our supply networks more complex but would be good for risk management. On the other hand, more complexity means more elements that could go wrong and that would not be good for risk management. We will address more deeply the topic of complexity in Chapter 8, "Supply Networks as a Complex Adaptive System."

Quantitative Network Analysis

In this chapter, heretofore, we have tried to characterize the structure of supply networks based on the three supply network maps that were empirically compiled. The discussions have largely been based on qualitative observations of those three supply network maps that resemble a tree-like structure with the focal company at the top, first-tier suppliers at the next tier, and so on. We now take a more quantitative approach to analyzing these three supply network maps. The social network analysis approach (i.e., Carter, Ellram, and Tate 2007; Choi and Liker 1995; Harland et al. 2001) offers us a means to engage in quantitative analysis of the supply network maps.

To perform a social network analysis of the three supply network maps, Kim et al. (2011) first convert the information contained in each of the three supply network maps into a mathematical form called a matrix. Each of the three supply network maps gives us two types of information (i.e., material flows and contractual relationships), so each supply network map would give us two matrices. The materials flow matrix would contain information on which supplier supplies to which other suppliers and the contractual relationship matrix would contain information on which supplier the focal company has a contractual agreement with and which suppliers have contractual relationships between themselves. Material flows would have direction, while contractual agreements would not have direction since there is no directionality in a contractual relationship. Therefore, the materials flow matrix contains directional information (i.e., asymmetric matrix), and the contractual agreement matrix contains non-directional information (i.e., symmetric matrix). Once we build matrices, we can then perform mathematical operations on these matrices extracting quantitative measures to characterize the supply networks.

Social Network Analysis

Social network analysis originates from sociology to investigate the patterns of relationships among social actors (Burt 2000a; Carley 1991; Everett and Borgatti 1999; Freeman 1977; Krackhardt 1992; Marsden 2002). As described in the next paragraph, social actors may be engaged in friendship activities or interlocking business relationships. The computational foundation is built on graph theory, which studies mathematical structures involving vertices (nodes) and edges (links) (Carley 1991; Cook 1998; Kirchherr 1992). The mathematics used in social network analysis operates on the links that connect actors in social networks and identifies patterns therein.

This approach has been used to study friendship and community networks (Huckfeldt 1983; Antal, Krapivsky, and Redner 2006) and communication structures (Luo and Zhong 2015). For instance, a friend that everyone goes to talk to and another friend no one goes to talk to would have two entirely different patterns of social networks. The former is highly central in the social network, while the latter is isolated. We might call the former a star and the latter an isolate. We might also say the former is more "popular" than the latter. Social network analysis would allow quantification of differences in popularity between these two friends.

Further, social network analysis has been used to investigate how new technology may diffuse in a community (e.g., Abrahamson and Rosenkopf 1997; Valente 1996) and how the work orientation of continuous improvement, or *kaizen*, is affected by the communication patterns among workers in manufacturing plants (Choi and Liker 1995). Organization scholars have used social network analysis to explore interlocking corporate directorship (e.g., Robins and Alexander 2004; Scott 1986) and network effects on firm performance (e.g., Ahuja, Polidoro, and Mitchell 2009; Burkhardt and Brass 1990; Gulati 1999; Uzzi 1997).

Among the scholars of supply networks, the application of social network analysis has been gaining acceptance (Autry and Griffis 2008; Carter, Ellram, and Tate 2007; Grover and Malhotra 2003; Harland et al. 2001). In particular, Borgatti and Li (2009) have challenged supply chain scholars to start applying the techniques of social network analysis to study how patterns of firm-to-firm relationships in supply networks affect firm performance. They contend that the social network analysis approach would help us understand how supply networks operate and how different network patterns therein may affect individual firm performance and the performance of the network as a whole. A study by Kim et al. (2011) is a response to that challenge. We use the three supply network maps from Honda and DaimlerChrysler and compute social network metrics to characterize the behaviors of supply networks at the node and network levels. The outcome of this study is discussed in more detail below.

To explain how social network analysis works, let us consider a hypothetical supply network map, as shown in Figure 7.5. This tree-like supply network map should look similar to the ones we have seen in the previous section. We

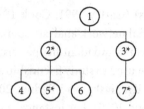

Figure 7.5 Hypothetical Supply Network

have the focal company on top as no. 1 (i.e., Honda or DaimlerChrysler). Then we have six suppliers scattered throughout the supply network. The first-tier suppliers are denoted as 2 and 3, while 4, 5, 6, and 7 are second-tier suppliers. The materials flow from the second tier to the first tier and then to the focal company. By virtue of being first-tier suppliers, 2 and 3 have an asterisk to signify they have a contractual agreement with the focal company. Numbers 5 and 7 also show an asterisk, which means they have been direct sourced by the focal company even though they are second-tier suppliers.

As discussed above, this supply network contains two types of information—material flows and contractual relationships. We now convert this information into two binary adjacency matrices (Wasserman and Faust 1994). That means we have a 1 in the cell (i, j) if company i and company j are connected and a 0 otherwise. There are seven companies shown in Figure 7.5, so we have 7x7 matrices. Both matrices in Figure 7.6 have all cells in a diagonal line filled with 1's, reflecting that each company works with itself. The matrix on the left side represents the materials flow. No. 2 supplies to 1, so the cell (2, 1) or c_{21} is ticked off as 1; no. 3 supplies to 1, so the cell (3, 1) or c_{31} is shown as 1; and so on. Only the top half above the diagonal line gets filled. With directionality, it is an asymmetric matrix, meaning the elements above the diagonal line and below are not symmetric. The matrix on the right side in Figure 7.6 contains the contractual agreement information with no directionality. Therefore, all the 1's above and below the diagonal line are mirror images. For instance, nos. 1 and 7 have a contractual relationship, so c_{17} and c_{71} are shown as 1 above and below the diagonal line.

These matrices can then be inputted into a network computation program such as UCINET 6 (Borgatti, Everett, and Freeman 2002). UCINET is the most widely adopted software program that performs social network analysis to get structural indices of interorganizational relationships (e.g., Gulati 1995; Human and Provan 1997; Ahuja, Polidoro, and Mitchell 2009). It is capable of computing various node-level and network-level metrics, identifying

	1	2	3	4	5	6	7			1	2	3	4	5	6	7
1	1	1	1	0	0	0	0		1	1	1	1	0	1	0	1
2	0	1	0	1	1	1	0		2	1	1	0	1	0	1	0
3	0	0	1	0	0	0	1		3	1	0	1	0	0	0	0
4	0	0	0	1	0	0	0		4	0	1	0	1	0	0	0
5	0	0	0	0	1	0	0		5	1	0	0	0	1	0	0
6	0	0	0	0	0	1	0		6	0	1	0	0	0	1	0
7	0	0	0	0	0	0	1		7	1	0	0	0	0	0	1

Figure 7.6 Hypothetical Supply Network in Matrix Forms

subgroups within the network, and providing drawings of sociograms that offer a visual representation of the relationship patterns.

Structural Indices

To introduce basic network structural indices, we consider three node-level metrics (degree, closeness, and betweenness centrality) and two network-level metrics (centralization and complexity). Node-level metrics capture the patterns with which a single node is embedded in its extended ties in the network. Through various centrality measures, we identify key suppliers occupying important structural positions in the network. Network-level metrics take a bird's eye view of the network and characterize the structural patterns of the whole network. They inform us whether the nodes are centralized or distributed across the network (centralization) and based on structural characteristics, how much load is required to operate the network by the members of the network at the collective level (complexity).

The node-level metrics focus on how central a node is. If a node is centrally positioned, it will affect the behavior and well-being of other nodes in the network (Mizruchi 1994). Centrality has been studied to reflect social status (Bonacich 1972; Freeman 1977), prestige (Burt 1982), and power and leverage over others (Coleman 2006). Three most commonly considered centrality metrics are degree centrality, closeness centrality, and betweenness centrality (Everett and Borgatti 1999; Krackhardt 1990; Marsden 2002).

The most prominent centrality among the three would be *degree centrality*. The basic idea is that the more ties the node has, the more central the node is. When there is a single individual in a social club to whom all the other members go to talk to, that individual is considered highly connected and highly central. A node with high degree centrality can be called popular and is visible in the network because connections converge to that point (Freeman 1977; Marsden 2002). *Closeness centrality* addresses how close a node is to all the other nodes in the network beyond the nodes it is immediately connected to. The closeness here reflects how many other nodes a node has to go through to reach others. Therefore, a node of high closeness centrality is relatively free from the influence of other nodes and, thus, is able to exercise independent actions (Freeman 1977; Marsden 2002). *Betweenness centrality* is a measure of how often a node sits on a geodesic (Marsden 2002)—the shortest path between all combinations of pairs of nodes in the network. If a node has a high betweenness centrality, that means other nodes depend on this node to access other nodes in the network. Thus, it would have a high capacity to control interactions between other nodes (Freeman 1977).

Table 7.3 summarizes how these centrality metrics can be applied to supply networks of two types—materials flow network (directional) and contractual relations (non-directional). As discussed in Wasserman and Galaskiewicz (1994), nodes with high degree centrality are "where the action is" (p. 179). In a directional network like the materials flow supply network, the action divides into two types—one that points in and one that points out, called *indegree* and *outdegree*, respectively. Using a popular friend with high degree centrality as an example, one type of high-degree centrality might refer to a friend who other friends go to talk to (i.e., high indegree) and another friend who talks to lots of other friends (i.e., high outdegree).

In a supply network, a supplier that receives a lot of materials from upstream suppliers would show high *indegree* centrality (i.e., it has to handle a high supply load), and another supplier that supplies to a lot of downstream companies would show high *outdegree* centrality (i.e., it has to handle a high demand load). In this regard, a supplier with a high supply load would be like an integrator that has to integrate different materials and parts from lots of upstream suppliers, and a supplier with a high demand load would be an allocator that has to deliver goods to many downstream companies. The nodes with high betweenness centrality are those that do "gatekeeping" for other nodes (Everett and Borgatti 1999; Spencer 2003). In a materials flow network with directionality, a supplier with high betweenness centrality would be those that are more critical to other companies (i.e., high operational criticality) and would affect the daily operations of other companies operating on

Table 7.3 Centrality Metrics and Roles in Supply Networks

Network Type	Centrality Metrics	Supply Network Constructs	Node Role	Role Description
Materials flow	Indegree centrality	Supply load	Integrator	To put together or transform different parts into a value-added product and ensure it functions well
	Outdegree centrality	Demand load	Allocator	To distribute limited resources across multiple customers, focusing on scale economies
	Betweenness centrality	Operational criticality	Pivot	To facilitate or control the flows of supply across the supply network
Contractual relationship	Degree centrality	Influential scope	Coordinator	To reconcile differences of network members and align their opinions with the greater network goals
	Closeness centrality	Informational independence	Navigator	To explore, access, and collect various information with greater autonomy in the supply network
	Betweenness centrality	Relational mediation	Broker	To mediate dealings between network members and turn them into its own advantage

Source: Adapted from Kim et al. 2011

the downstream, including the focal company (i.e., by controlling resources or lead times). In essence, it acts as a hub or pivot in the supply network.

For the contractual agreement supply network with no directionality, a supplier with high degree centrality means that the supplier influences other suppliers in terms of their operations or decisions (i.e., high influential scope) as it is connected with numerous other suppliers (e.g., Cachon and Lariviere 2005; Ferguson, Paulin, and Bergeron 2005). By virtue of having extensive connections through contractual agreements, either as a buying company or a supplying company, this supplier would need to coordinate or allocate resources for other members of the supply network. Nodes with high closeness centrality would not depend much on other nodes for information transfer or communications (Bavelas 1950; Beauchamp 1965). They can reach others more readily and enjoy relatively high autonomy.

In supply networks, those suppliers with high closeness centrality would be able to act more autonomously (i.e., information independence) and freely navigate across the supply network in search of resources. High betweenness centrality means being frequently on a geodesic or shortest path between two other nodes. In the contractual agreement supply network, those suppliers with high betweenness centrality are in a position to affect the interactions of other companies in the same supply network. The fact that they are central in many shortest paths means they are in a good position to mediate the information exchanges between other suppliers (i.e., relational mediators). Structurally, a node that serves as a bridge between two otherwise disconnected groups of nodes would have high betweenness centrality (Burt 1995, 2000b). This node would be the broker of information serving as a gatekeeper, as discussed above.

Network-level metrics are concerned with characterizing the overall network structure. The *network centralization* metric gives us a measure of how the whole network is connected around a few select nodes within the network (Provan and Milward 1995). A network with the highest possible centralization is one that has all connections go through one node, whereas a network with the lowest possible centralization is one that has all nodes connected with all other nodes. Conceptually, it reflects how power or control is distributed across the network (Scott 2000). The *network complexity* metric refers to "the number of dependency relations within a network" (Frenken 2000, p. 260). In other words, it is concerned with both the number of nodes and the degree to which the nodes are connected (Frenken 2000; Kauffman 1993). As discussed before, it can be viewed as the total load required to operate the network, and the load is born by the nodes in the network. If there are a lot of nodes, the collective load would increase, and if there are lots of connections, the collective load would also increase in the form of coordination costs (Kim, Oh, and Swaminathan 2006; Provan 1983). In addition to centralization and complexity, there are a few other concepts we need to touch on. There are network density and core versus periphery subgroups in a network. *Network density* refers to the ratio of actual links to possible links. High density means a high percentage of connections regarding all possible connections in the network. Core and periphery subgroups appear when we partition a network into two groups based on their interconnectivity. A *core subgroup* emerges among the nodes that share high network density, and a *periphery subgroup* appears among the nodes that are more densely connected to the core nodes than to each other (Borgatti and Everett 2000; Luce and Perry 1949).

Table 7.4 presents a summary of the network-level metrics organized around the two types of supply networks—material flows and contractual relationships. Honda's materials flow supply networks reflect much of the directed-sourcing decisions done by Honda as the focal company and its first-tier suppliers, CVT and Intek. In contrast, DaimlerChrysler delegates sourcing decisions to its first-tier supplier, who would then delegate it to its second-tier suppliers. Therefore, we surmise that Honda's supply networks would reflect higher centralization at the network level; however, as we will find out, this is *not* entirely the case based on social network analysis. Complexity of the materials flow network will be high if there are lots of suppliers in the network and lots of connections among them. Network size

Table 7.4 Network-Level Metrics and Implications

Network Type	Network-Level Metrics	Conceptual Definitions	Implications for Network Structure
Materials flow	Centralization	The extent to which select companies control and manage the movement of materials in a supply network	Operational authority and decision-making concentrated in a few companies (e.g., power to make decisions on materials flow)
	Complexity	The amount of collective operational burden born by the member companies in a supply network	More companies engaged in delivering and receiving materials, and more steps required to move the materials along
Contractual relationship	Centralization	The extent to which select companies control relationship management over other companies in a supply network	Interactions concentrated in a few central companies, and lack of interactions between central and peripheral companies in a supply network
	Complexity	The amount of load on the supply network as a whole that requires relationship coordination	More companies involved in transferring information, and slow relaying of communications from downstream to the focal company

Source: Adapted from Kim et al. 2011

may be attained by simply counting the number of members in the network, but it may also be gauged by the average path length among the members as well (Ebel, Davidsen, and Bornholdt 2002). More suppliers and a higher number of steps required to complete tasks in a supply network would require more resources and effort at the network level, reflecting high complexity. Again, as we will discover later, the results of social network analysis portray a more complicated picture.

As far as centralization goes for the contractual relationship supply networks, given no directionality, the connectivity gap between the central versus peripheral members of the network becomes more salient (Borgatti and Everett 2000; Luce and Perry 1949). If a network is partitioned into two groups of central and peripheral, where the central group is densely connected, and the peripheral group may be more sparsely connected through contractual relationships, this network would reflect high centralization. For Honda, given its history of operating in a keiretsu-like structure, this type of separation among suppliers may be more feasible.

Further, we would see more overlapping relationships with many reciprocal and interlocking relationships in Honda supply networks, which would translate to high complexity. For instance, as discussed before, Honda asks its core suppliers to buy from each other, and if so, it is not hard to visualize how such a practice would lead to a high score in core density. Therefore, a supply network with high complexity would, in general, show high scores on network size, network density, core size, core density, periphery density, core-to-periphery (CTP) density, and periphery-to-core (PTC) density. In the contractual relationship supply network, CTP and PTC would be the same because there is no directionality. All these listed metrics would increase the load the network members would have to exert to maintain activities in the network.

Analyzing the Three Supply Networks

We are now ready to quantitatively analyze three center console supply networks for the Honda Accord, Acura CL/TL, and DaimlerChrysler's Grand Cherokee shown in Choi and Hong (2002). These three supply networks have been mapped based on the bill of materials, and each supply network contains materials flow information and contractual relationship information. Given the two types of network data, each supply network map generates two NxN adjacency matrices, where N is the number of companies in the supply network. We end up with six matrices (i.e., three material flows and three contractual relationships). These matrices are generated through the same conversion process, shown in Figures 7.5 and 7.6, which illustrates how a tree-like structure of a network map (i.e., Figures 7.2, 7.3, and 7.4) can be turned into matrices as a mathematical form.

These matrices are then inputted into a social network analysis software; in our case, we use UCINET 6 (see Kim et al. 2011 for details). The software contains the capability to analyze a host of different network metrics such as various types of centrality, network density, and subgroup or clique identification, among others. It can also generate sociograms of networks that offer a pictorial rendition of how members (i.e., nodes) are interconnected (i.e., edges) in the network.

We begin by showing the six sociograms that UCINET 6 produced. The first three sociograms (Figures 7.7, 7.8, and 7.9) show the materials flow supply networks. The links on these sociograms are represented by arrows because they are directional. The second three sociograms (Figures 7.10, 7.11, and 7.12) show how companies are connected through contractual relationships. Their links do not show arrows because there is no directionality in contractual relationships. Both sets of sociograms contain identical information we have in our tree-line supply network maps. What is different is how the network information is presented. The structures of the networks are presented much more visually—we can visualize the underlying structures immediately and attain various metric values in numbers.

In our Honda Accord supply network map, we show Honda at the top and two first-tier suppliers underneath, followed by multiple second-tier suppliers. In our sociogram, we can see immediately that CVT as a first-tier supplier, not Honda, is at the center of the materials flow supply network. Further, there are key suppliers that we do not notice in the supply network map that emerge as being central. Obviously, we have noted the importance of JCF as a first-tier supplier and Honda Trading as one that handles plastic resin. However, we do not notice the importance of Yamamoru just by looking at the supply network map of Honda Accord (see Figure 7.2). In this sociogram as shown in Figure 7.7, however, this company visually stands out as being important with more connections compared to other suppliers.

In much the same way, the materials flow supply network sociogram of the Acura CL/TL also shows the first-tier supplier, Intek, at the center (see Figure 7.8). Honda appears off to the side. Notably, a few key second-tier suppliers

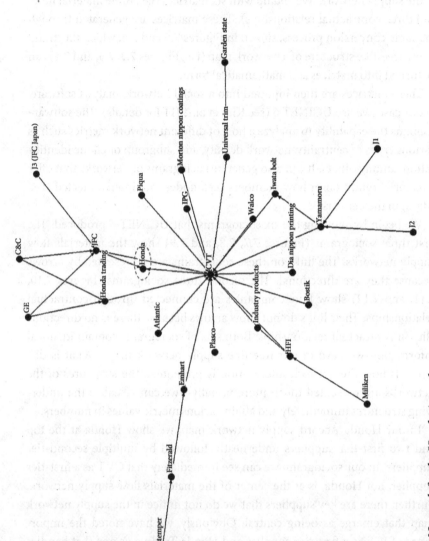

Figure 7.7 Materials Flow Network for the Honda Accord

Source: Kim et al. 2011

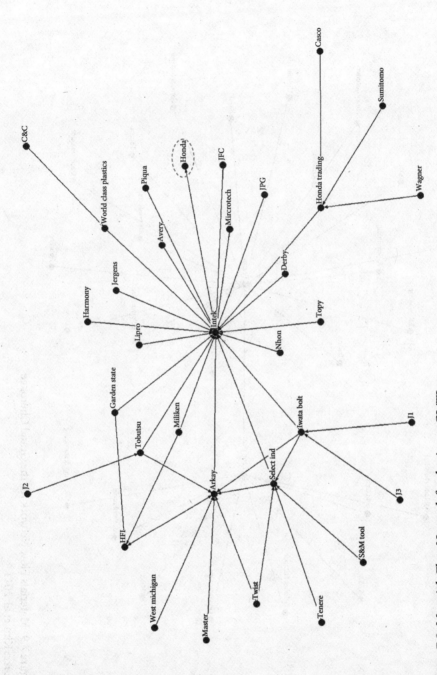

Figure 7.8 Materials Flow Network for the Acura CL/TL
Source: Kim et al. 2011

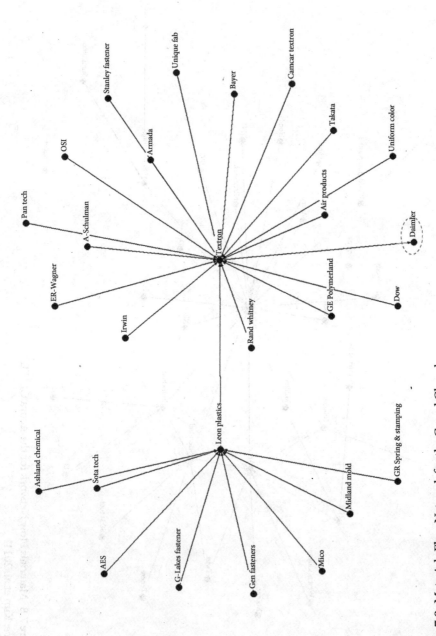

Figure 7.9 Materials Flow Network for the Grand Cherokee
Source: Kim et al. 2011

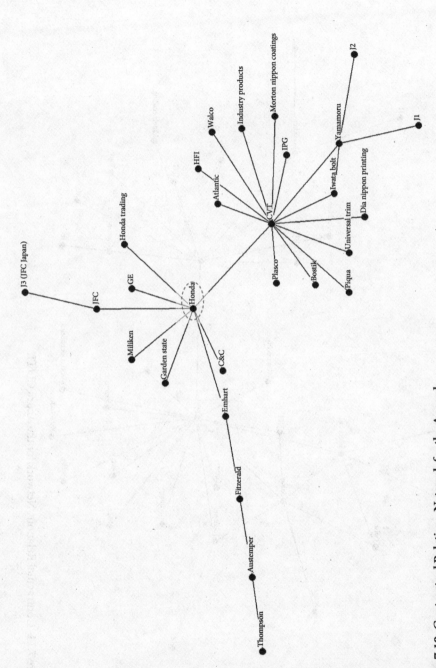

Figure 7.10 Contractual Relations Network for the Accord
Source: Kim et al. 2011

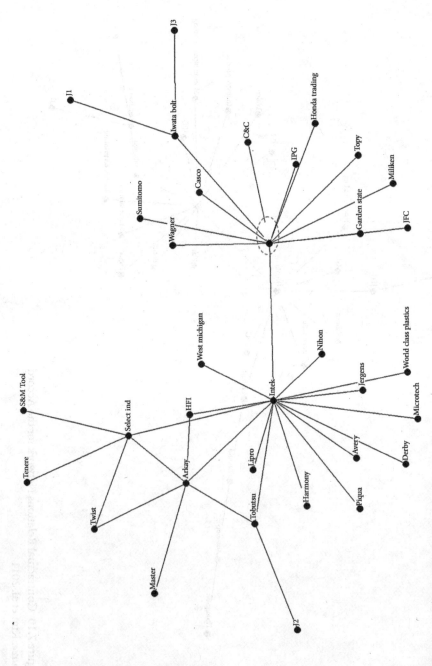

Figure 7.11 Contractual Relations Network for the Acura CL/TL

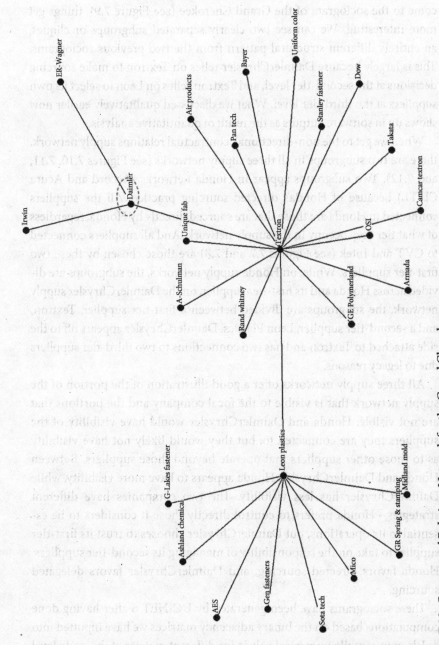

Figure 7.12 Contractual Relations Network for the Grand Cherokee
Source: Kim et al. 2011

stand out immediately in a very visual way—Tobutsu, Arkay, Slect Ind., and Iwata Bolt. And HFT shows up as a key third-tier supplier. Now, when we come to the sociogram of the Grand Cherokee (see Figure 7.9), things get more interesting. We can see two clearly separated subgroups or cliques, an entirely different structural pattern from the two previous sociograms. This is largely because DaimlerChrysler relies on Textron to make sourcing decisions at the second-tier level, and Textron relies on Leon to select its own suppliers at the third-tier level. What we discussed qualitatively earlier now shows up in software outputs as the result of quantitative analysis.

When we get to the non-directional, contractual relations supply network, there are two subgroups in all three supply networks (see Figures 7.10, 7.11, and 7.12). Two subgroups appear in Honda networks (Accord and Acura CL/TL) because of Honda's directed-sourcing practice. All the suppliers connected to Honda are those that are sourced directly by Honda, regardless of what tier they occupy in the supply network. And all suppliers connected to CVT and Intek (see Figures 7.7 and 7.8) are those chosen by these two first-tier suppliers. While, on Honda supply networks, the subgroups are divided across Honda and its first-tier supplier, on the DaimlerChrysler supply network, the subgroups are divided between a first-tier supplier, Textron, and a second-tier supplier, Leon Plastics. DaimlerChrysler appears off to the side attached to Textron and has two connections to two third-tier suppliers due to legacy reasons.

All three supply networks offer a good illustration of the portion of the supply network that is visible to the focal company and the portions that are not visible. Honda and DaimlerChrysler would have visibility of the suppliers they are connected to, but they would likely not have visibility as to those other suppliers that operate beyond those suppliers. Between Honda and DaimlerChrysler, Honda appears to have more visibility, while DaimlerChrysler has less visibility. The two companies have different strategies—Honda prefers to control directly those it considers to be essential to its operations, but DaimlerChrysler chooses to trust its first-tier supplier to take on the responsibility of managing its second-tier suppliers. Honda favors directed sourcing, and DaimlerChrysler favors delegated sourcing.

These sociograms have been generated by UCINET 6 after having done computations based on the binary adjacency matrices we have inputted into it. We now compile numerical values for different metrics at the node level and network level. Table 7.5 identifies companies in the supply network with

Table 7.5 Identification of Key Suppliers from Node-Level Analysis

Network Type	Supply Network Constructs	Honda Accord	Acura CL/TL	DaimlerChrysler Grand Cherokee
Materials flow	Supply load[a]	CVT (59[g]), JFC (15), HFI (11)	Intek (58), Arkay (21), Select Ind. (12)	Textron (65), Leon Plastics (31)
	Demand load[b]	CVT (15), C&C (7.4), JFC (7.4), Yamamoru (7.4), Industry Products (7.4)	Iwata Bolt (9.1), Tobutsu (6.1), Arkay (6.1), Twist (8.1), Milliken (6.1), Garden State (6.1), Select Ind. (6.1)	None
Contractual relationship	Operational criticality[c]	CVT (13), Emhart (2), Yamamoru (1.7), Fitzerald (1.7), JFC (1.7)	Intek (3), Arkay (1.7)	Textron (3.8), Leon Plastics (2.5)
	Influential scope[d]	CVT (52), Honda (30), Yamamoru (15)	Intek (45), Honda (36), Arkay (18), Select Ind. (15)	Textron (62), Leon Plastics (35)
	Informational independence[e]	CVT (57), Honda (53), Yamamoru (40)	Intek (62), Honda (56), Arkay (44), Select Ind. (43), Tobutsu (41), HFI (40)	Textron (72), Leon Plastics (58), DaimlerChrysler (46)
	Relational mediation[f]	CVT (79), Honda (64), Emhart (21), Yamamoru (15), Fitzerald (14)	Intek (77), Honda (63), Select Ind. (14), Iwata Bolt (12), Arkay (10)	Textron (88), Leon Plastics (53), DaimlerChrysler (15)

[a] Firms with indegree > 10
[b] Firms with outdegree > 6
[c] Firms with betweenness > 1.0
[d] Firms with degree > 15
[e] Firms with closeness > 40
[f] Firms with betweenness > 10
[g] Centrality score

Source: Adapted from Kim et al. 2011

high centrality scores, building on the node-level supply network constructs shown in Table 7.3.

As indicated in the legend below the table, centrality scores shown in Table 7.5 next to the company names are those above a cut-off point. As in a typical scree plot, there would be scores bunched up together before a significant inflection point. The last of the bunched-up scores would be used as the threshold for cut-off. There is only one case where the threshold could not be ascertained. That is the demand load for the Grand Cherokee. Demand load is measured by the outdegree centrality, and, in this case, it lists none. This is because every supplier trying to meet the demand has only one customer, which means every node in this network has the same value for outdegree centrality and, thus, no threshold value.

In Table 7.5, CVT, as the first-tier supplier for the Accord, appears as highly central on all accounts. For the materials flow supply network, CVT assumes a lot of responsibilities on both the supply and demand sides and is an operationally critical company that controls the movement of materials. In contrast, another first-tier supplier for the Accord, JFC, does not appear as central. For demand load, there is C&C, and for operational criticality, there are Emhart and Yamamoru that show high centrality scores. JFC's centrality scores are much lower than those of CVT. This is because the lower tier suppliers supplying to JFC also supply to CVT, but those that supply to CVT mostly do not supply to JFC (see Figure 7.2).

For the Acura CL/TL materials flow supply network, its first-tier supplier, Intek, appears most central in Table 7.5 but not to the extent that CVT does in the Accord supply network. Intek is most central for the supply load and operational criticality, as much of the materials flow in and out of this company. However, for demand load, there are many other suppliers but not Intek. This observation simply means that Intek does not supply to other companies in the Acura CL/TL supply network, as CVT does in the Accord supply network. Another interesting observation is that Arkay is the only supplier that appears important in all three centrality metrics. This is an important observation that may be overlooked just by qualitatively reviewing the tree-like supply network map.

There are noticeably fewer numbers of central companies in the Grand Cherokee materials flow supply network in Table 7.5. It implies that its supply network structure is much simpler (see Figure 7.9) compared to that of the Accord or Acura CL/TL. As discussed above, there is no company listed for demand load because every supplier in this supply network has only one customer, including Textron and Leon Plastics, suppliers at the first tier and second tier. In fact, these two suppliers appear as central to supply load and operational criticality. They both take an active role in pulling together supplies and integrating them. They also facilitate the flow—the material flows in this supply network are facilitated primarily by these two suppliers.

We now turn to the non-directional, contractual relations supply network. In Table 7.5, for the Accord supply network, CVT again appears most central in all three areas—influential scope, informational independence, and relational mediation. When compared to the materials flow network, however, there are a couple of notable differences. In the contractual relations supply network, Honda appears as the second most central company in all three areas, and the other first-tier supplier, JFC, does not appear in any of the three areas. In the materials flow supply network, it is just the opposite— Honda does not appear at all, and JFC appears in all three areas. This is because both CVT and Honda practice lots of directed sourcing, while JFC does not. Compared to the materials flow supply network, JFC is less central in the contractual relations supply network.

In the Acura CL/TL supply network, Intek again appears as the most central, with Honda a close second. As shown in Figure 7–11, about two-thirds of the suppliers must go through Intek to get to Honda, and this structural position allows Intek control over information flows. HFI is one supplier that does not appear under the materials flow supply network but appears central for informational independence under contractual relations. This is because HFI is connected to other central suppliers such as Intek and Arkay. HFI is another supplier we would have overlooked unless we had done the network analysis.

In the Grand Cherokee supply network, Textron and Leon Plastics again emerge as being central. Both suppliers contract with lots of upstream suppliers—Textron with second-tier suppliers and Leon Plastics with third-tier suppliers. The only exception under the contractual relations supply network is the appearance of DaimlerChrysler. This is because DaimlerChrysler does directed sourcing with two third-tier suppliers, Irwin and E.R. Wagner (see Figure 7.4). Since the products of these two suppliers channel into Textron, DaimlerChrysler might have to mediate the relationship between these two suppliers, and Textron and would not be dependent on Textron as much for information regarding these two suppliers.

From discussing the node-level metrics, we now consider the network-level metrics, as listed in Tables 7.6 and 7.7. We note first that the network size

Table 7.6 Network-Level Analysis Results

Network Type	Network Measures	Honda Accord	Acura CL/TL	DaimlerChrysler Grand Cherokee
	Network size (companies)	28	34	27
Materials flow	Network density	0.046	0.037	0.037
	Indegree centralization	0.567	0.556	0.641
	Outdegree centralization	0.106	0.056	0.001
	Betweenness centralization	0.128	0.029	0.038
Contractual relationship	Network density	0.074	0.066	0.074
	Degree centralization	0.479	0.413	0.585
	Closeness centralization	0.459	0.513	0.641
	Betweenness centralization	0.748	0.738	0.854

Source: Adapted from Kim et al. 2011

in terms of the total number of companies is different from what we counted in the supply network maps (see Table 7.2). This is because, for social network analysis, we have chosen not to count those raw materials suppliers with no names. This decision not to include raw material suppliers has no significant effect on the relative positions of the other companies in the networks.

Comparing the three materials flow supply networks in Table 7.6, the Accord supply network exhibits a higher score for network density than the Acura CL/TL and Grand Cherokee supply networks. That just means the Accord supply network is more densely connected, most likely due to the same suppliers being used for more than one part. Looking at the centralization scores, the Grand Cherokee supply network shows the highest degree of centralization. This is mainly because most materials flow through two suppliers—Textron and Leon Plastics. For the outdegree centralization, the opposite happens—the Grand Cherokee supply network shows the lowest score. Again, this is due to the fact that all suppliers have one downstream customer. The Accord supply network has the highest betweenness centralization score, which dovetails into our earlier observation about the same suppliers being used for multiple products.

Table 7.7 Key Indicators of Network Complexity

Network Type	Network Measures	Honda Accord	Acura CL/TL	DaimlerChrysler Grand Cherokee
	Network size (companies)	28	34	27
Materials flow	Network density	0.046	0.037	0.037
	Core size	19	23	4
	Core density	0.067	0.059	0.250
	CTP density	0.006	0.000	0.000
	PTC density	0.064	0.043	0.250
Contractual relationship	Network density	0.074	0.066	0.074
	Core size	17	6	3
	Core density	0.125	0.467	0.667
	Periphery density	0.036	0.000	0.000
	CTP/PTC density	0.048	0.179	0.333

Source: Adapted from Kim et al. 2011

For the contractual relationship supply networks, as shown in Table 7.6, the network density scores are all much higher compared to the network density scores for the materials flow. This is because contractual relationships can leapfrog over several tiers as in the directed-sourcing practice. Looking across the centralization scores, it is noteworthy that the DaimlerChrysler Grand Cherokee supply network shows consistently higher scores on all three types of network centralization. In this regard, the Grand Cherokee supply network is structurally more centralized than the Honda Accord and Acura CL/TL supply networks. This is in contrast to our earlier observation that the supply networks on the Honda side would be more centralized because of the more prevalent directed-sourcing practice. This structural characteristic of the centralization in DaimlerChrysler's Grand Cherokee comes from the fact that most of the connections pertaining to contractual relations in the supply network go through two suppliers—Textron and Leon Plastics.

Key metrics associated with network complexity are listed in Table 7.7. The network size and network density scores are listed to provide the network-level metrics. We also offer scores at the group level that can be used to gauge network complexity. The table lists the size of the core group and its density and the density of the links between the core and periphery subgroups (i.e., CTP density or PTC density).

Just by looking at the network size, the Acura CL/TL supply network shows the highest number of companies, suggesting high network complexity. However, the scores on network density for the materials flow supply network suggest that the Honda Accord supply network has much higher connectivity among the companies, indicating high network complexity.

When we look at the group-level metrics, core sizes are higher for the Accord and Acura CL/TL supply networks compared to the Grand Cherokee supply network. For the Accord supply network, the discrepancy between the CTP density and PTC density is high. That just means the materials flow generally goes from peripheral to the core but not the other way around. For the Acura CL/TL supply network, the core size is high, but the core density is lower than the others. That likely means that the materials flow activities are more spread across the suppliers. This pattern of a high discrepancy between the CTP density and PTC density continues for the Grand Cherokee supply network. This network has a small size for the core subgroup and relatively high core density. That would likely suggest the majority of materials flow in this network would go through a small number of suppliers.

For contractual relations, the Honda Accord supply network has a high core size and relatively high network density. However, its core density is lower than the other two. High scores for the network density and core size suggest complexity, but the low core density score does not. Yet, the Accord supply network is the only one among the three that shows some periphery density, which means there are connections among the peripheral companies. That might add to the complexity. Interestingly, the CTP/PTC density is highest for the Grand Cherokee supply network. While there is no interaction among the peripheral companies, these companies do connect with other companies in the core. Overall, it seems it is largely inconclusive as to which of the three supply networks might be labeled the most complex. It appears that there is a lot more going on in the area of complexity than simple metrics used to portray complexity.

Integrating the Two Studies

Choi and Hong (2002) and Kim et al. (2011) conduct different analyses on the same three supply networks. Choi and Hong (2002) map three supply networks of center consoles for the Honda Accord, Acura CL/ TL, and DaimlerChrysler Grand Cherokee. That study captures the structural patterns of supply networks based on qualitative (i.e., buyer-supplier relationships) and quantitative (i.e., number of tiers) observations. Kim et al. (2011) then covert the same supply network maps into binary adjacency matrices and subject them to mathematical operations using a social network analysis software called UCINET 6. We now integrate the findings of these two studies that operate on the same network data using different analysis methods.

The Choi and Hong study discloses how the three focal companies use varying degrees of directed sourcing and delegated sourcing. The Kim et al. study confirms that—the contractual relations supply networks that reflect directed sourcing show clearly higher centrality scores and network density compared to the materials flow supply networks, especially for Honda and its first-tier supplier, CVT, which practices lots of directed sourcing as indicated by Choi and Hong. As expected, based on the Choi and Hong study, some of these directly sourced suppliers (i.e., HFI for Accord and Arkay for Acura CL/TL) appear to be highly central, showing high centrality scores (see Table 7.5).

The two studies show divergent results also. The differences mainly pertain to network-level centralization and complexity. The Choi and Hong study, in general, frames the supply networks for the Accord and Acura CL/TL by Honda to be more central and more complex. The Kim et al. study offers evidence to the contrary. Choi and Hong pose Honda and Acura supply networks to be more centralized with their prevalent directed-sourcing practices and how Honda's reach goes much deeper into its supply networks than that of DaimlerChrysler. However, as shown in Table 7.7, it is not so clear-cut that the Accord and Acura CL/TL would necessarily be more centralized.

For the materials flow network, the different types of centralization metrics seem a bit mixed. Based on the indegree centralization, the DaimlerChrysler supply network comes out most centralized. Based on the outdegree and betweenness centralization, the Honda Accord supply network comes out most centralized. Then, we get to the centralization scores for the contractual relations supply network. There, all three centralization measures (degree, closeness, and betweenness) are dominated by the DaimlerChrysler supply network as being more centralized. This is because, in the Choi and Hong study, the observations regarding network centralization are made from the individual node's perspective, particularly that of the focal company and the first-tier supplier. These two companies reach deep into the supply network, and we do not see this in the DaimlerChrysler supply network. Therefore, the conclusion is that Honda's supply networks must be more centralized. In the Kim et al. study, however, the measurements are taken at the network level to see how central all companies are at the network level and evaluate the relative centrality scores of all companies to ascertain the overall centralization of the network.

Furthermore, the Choi and Hong study suggests that the Acura CL/TL supply network is the most complex (see Table 7.2). It has the highest number of companies, long physical distances between companies, and the most number of vertical tiers. However, according to the Kim et al. study, the Accord supply network seems to show the most complex supply network, and the Grand Cherokee supply network also shows strong evidence of being complex (see Table 7.6). As discussed above, the Kim et al. study shows much more nuanced results about complexity through the various network-level measures such as network density, core density, and CTP and PTC densities. There may be opportunities for future studies to theoretically integrate these network-level measures with the more qualitatively ascertained measures in the Choi and Hong study.

One thing that the Kim et al. study offers beyond Choi and Hong's study is the identification of potentially hidden critical suppliers. Take Yamamoru, for example. In the supply network map of Choi and Hong, this supplier appears as one of the many suppliers in the Honda Accord supply network. However, in the Kim et al. study, this supplier shows up as a central supplier in the sociogram and in various centrality measures. We propose that hidden critical suppliers occupy important structural positions in the supply network. We have come to call these structurally important suppliers "the nexus suppliers" (Yan et al. 2015). The implication is that a disruption at a nexus supplier would have a significant impact on other companies in the same supply network because of its structurally central position.

A Theory of the Nexus Supplier

In April 2012, there was an explosion at an Evonik Industries plant in Germany. Consequently, the production line was halted, and all outbound deliveries were delayed (https://www.wsj.com/articles/BL-DSB-8739). Until then, major automakers like GM and Toyota would not have paid attention to

Evonik Industries. This raw materials supplier at the third- or fourth-tier in the automotive supply chain was likely hidden from major focal companies' view. As it turns out, this supplier made a particular type of nylon resin called PA-12, which is widely used in fuel lines, brake lines, and many other parts that go into an automobile (https://www.huffpost.com/entry/pa-12-resin-shortages-evonik-industries_n_1432386). Ultimately, the shutdown of Evonik Industries' production line brought the world's automotive supply chains to a halt. This supplier was at the base of all automotive supply chains. One might call it a common denominator supplier in that from that supplier, many supply chains would extend, one to GM, another to Toyota, and so on. In other words, structurally, Evonik occupied a central position in the automotive supply network. Evonik would be considered a nexus supplier as discussed next.

Nexus Suppliers and Strategic Suppliers

Nexus suppliers are those in a focal company's supply network whose importance comes from occupying a particular structural position in the network. This concept is new to many of us. Another type of important supplier we are more familiar with is strategic suppliers. We propose that nexus suppliers and strategic suppliers are both essential to the focal companies; yet, they are different in terms of how they become important and how they should be managed. For instance, a strategic supplier would typically be a first-tier supplier, whereas a nexus supplier could occupy any tier in the supply network. Strategic suppliers would be a subset of the supply base, as discussed in Chapter 5. Nexus suppliers could come from some of the directly sourced suppliers in the lower tiers, as discussed in Chapter 6. Some of those suppliers may be in the visual range of the buying company, but many of them may operate outside the visual range of the focal company.

Table 7.8 presents some of the key characteristics of nexus suppliers compared to strategic suppliers. Strategic suppliers would necessarily be included in the supply base of a buying company, as many of them would be first-tier suppliers. For instance, Foxconn would be a strategic supplier to Apple, and Denso would be a strategic supplier to Toyota. Nexus suppliers could be part of the supply base, but they could also operate from beyond the supply base, outside the visual portion of the supply network to the focal

Table 7.8 Comparing Nexus Suppliers to Strategic Suppliers

	Strategic Suppliers	Nexus Suppliers
Location in the supply network	Typically first tier	Any tier
Visibility to the focal company	Visible	Not necessarily visible
Profit impact	Direct and high	Indirect and potentially high
Mutual dependence	Direct and high	Indirect and potentially high
Relationship with the focal company	Close	Not necessarily close
Sources of value	Internal capabilities and resources	Structural position in the network

Source: Adapted from Yan et al. 2015

company. They could come from any tier level in the multi-tiered supply network. For example, as discussed above, Evonik Industries would be a nexus supplier to GM and Toyota. Therefore, strategic suppliers are necessarily visible to the buying company, but nexus suppliers are not always visible. Strategic suppliers are visible because the buying company wants to keep them close, and depending on how well they do could have a direct and high-profit impact on the focal company.

In contrast, the profit impact and mutual dependence of a nexus supplier is indirect but potentially high. As demonstrated by what happened with Evonik Industries, even if GM and Toyota are now aware of the importance of Evonik Industries and closely monitor this supplier in the periphery of their supply networks, they would not necessarily have a direct tie to this supplier. This supplier would still be a nexus supplier, and its profit and mutual dependence would be indirect and potentially high. Just because it is being monitored, that does not mean Evonik Industry now has a close relationship with GM or Toyota. Ultimately, strategic suppliers are important to the buying company because they have certain capabilities and technological resources (e.g., Foxconn and Denso). In contrast, nexus suppliers are important because they occupy a central, structural position in the supply network, and other companies in the supply network become reliant on that supplier to ensure continuity of products or for new information about the market or new technology.

Typologies of the Nexus Supplier

We develop a theory of the nexus supplier in the form of typologies. According to Doty and Glick (1994), typologies represent ideal types with implications for performance. As ideal types, they may not actually be observable in their pure form, but they provide a referent point toward which real-world events would gravitate toward. For example, participative management and authoritative management are typologies in that, as ideal types, we may not be able to observe them in their pure, theoretical forms. However, they provide the referent points toward which managerial practices would tend to move toward depending on the circumstances that companies face. Typologies provide constructs with a set of attributes that can be measured and tested with respect to performance outcomes in the expected direction (Bacharach 1989). In this regard, typologies provide theories that can be empirically tested (Doty and Glick 1994).

We propose three typologies of nexus suppliers—operational nexus suppliers, monopolistic nexus suppliers, and informational nexus suppliers. *Operational nexus suppliers* reside in the core subgroup of a focal company's supply network. Many of them would be visible to the focal company but not necessarily so. They would be critical to the focal company in terms of their structural positions to integrate and allocate the flow of materials. They would necessarily have high centrality measures. *Monopolistic nexus suppliers* operate in the extended supply network in the peripheral subgroup of the supply network. They likely reside in the invisible part of the supply network. These suppliers become embedded in many other parts in the downstream from their structural position, and they would be difficult to be substituted. *Informational nexus suppliers* refer to the suppliers that do business with companies in many industries. They can reside either in the core or peripheral subgroups. They would have high diversity in the type of companies they are connected to in their extended ties. In network terms, their ego network would have lots of other nodes or alters that comes from diverse backgrounds.

Operational Nexus Suppliers
An operational nexus supplier receives lots of parts and materials from other upstream suppliers and integrates them for the focal company (i.e., high indegree centrality). It also allocates its products to many other downstream

suppliers working for the focal company (i.e., high outdegree centrality). It might also take up a critical position in the network in facilitating the flow of materials across the supply network (i.e., high betweenness centrality). In this regard, the chances are that they would be part of the core subgroup in the focal company's supply network. All suppliers listed in Table 7.5 would be potential candidates for being an operational nexus supplier for the focal company. For instance, Emhart in the Accord network comes up high on betweenness centrality, which implies that Emhart's structural importance comes from its control of the materials flow. Combine that with the observation that Emhart provides parts to other downstream suppliers as a common denominator supplier, and it is a good candidate for an operational nexus supplier. Consequently, an operational nexus supplier would play a critical role in the performance of the focal company by ensuring the continuity of supply. Further, because it supplies to many other downstream suppliers in the focal company's supply network, it would affect the overall supply cost for the focal company as well as supply risk and responsiveness.

Monopolistic Nexus Suppliers

A monopolistic nexus supplier would be one that likely resides in the periphery of the focal company's supply network but is difficult to be substituted. In this regard, other suppliers depend on this monopolistic supplier, and many of them need parts and materials that would have passed through this supplier. It would, therefore, garner a high betweenness centrality score. For instance, Evonik Industries operates in the extended automotive supply network and takes up over 50% of PA-12 global production. For a focal company in the automotive supply network like GM or Toyota, it would be difficult to locate a substitute. That means Evonik Industries plays a pivotal role in bridging the suppliers of the chemicals even further upstream in the extended supply network and many other automotive suppliers and focal companies that operate downstream. Evonik Industries, as a supplier in the extended automotive supply networks, would show a high betweenness centrality.

In this regard, given it resides in the extended supply network, a monopolistic nexus supplier would likely be non-substitutable for the downstream companies. It would affect a relatively high percentage of the components that go into the products of the focal company. Compared to an operational nexus supplier, a monopolistic supplier would more likely be on the periphery of the supply network. That means a monopolistic supplier would have many downstream companies as customers, and any one focal company in one particular industry, such as automotive, would not account for a significant portion of its business. At the same time, the products the monopolistic suppliers provide may not account for much of the spending from the focal company's perspective. Therefore, it is highly likely the focal companies may not be aware of these monopolistic suppliers until a disruption occurs. In that sense, it would be prudent for the focal companies to actively search for these monopolistic nexus suppliers and monitor them for any potential disruptions even if they do not have direct business relationships together.

Informational Nexus Suppliers

An informational nexus supplier conducts business with a diverse set of companies in its extended ties. In network terms, this supplier has many alternates with a diverse background in its ego network. That simply means this nexus supplier is exposed to diverse demands from its customers and the non-redundant ideas that they bring. So, this nexus supplier occupies a unique position in the network to potentially bring fresh perspectives and new information to the focal company. In particular, an informational nexus supplier can bring to the focal company early market trends or early responses to how various industries are responding to new government regulations. Such information would be instrumental to how the focal company adapts to significant environmental changes. An informational supplier can also be exposed to leading technologies and advances in science that the focal company may find useful in its strategic planning.

Similar to a monopolistic supplier, an informational supplier is likely difficult to identify. One measure might be to look for those suppliers that have ties to multiple industries. One example of an informational supplier is TSMC to LGE. We discussed the informal relationship between these two companies in Chapter 4, where we saw how LGE informally approached TSMC to address what LGE called the Qualcomm dilemma. In this scenario, Qualcomm is a supplier to LGE, and TSMC is a supplier to Qualcomm. We might call Qualcomm a first-tier supplier to LGE and TSMC a second-tier supplier to LGE. Beyond what is discussed in Chapter 4, we know from the accounts published in Choi and Linton (2011) that LGE gained early market information from visiting TSMC purely by accident. In early 2009, the world was still struggling with a major recession, and leading companies were looking for early signs of the economy shifting, mainly by monitoring the downstream consumer market. However, LGE received an early sign by going upstream to TSMC. During the first quarter of that year, Tom Linton, then the chief procurement officer of LGE, went to TSMC and saw how the company was ramping up. Orders from a large number of customers from diverse industries converged on this point in supply network, TSMC, and became a discernable demand increase. LGE took that as a sign and went all out to renegotiate with its suppliers and locked in prices and delivery dates.

Table 7.9 summarizes our descriptions heretofore of the three types of nexus suppliers. We organize their characteristics on multiple dimensions, from network types to performance implications.

Understanding nexus suppliers is a critical step toward engaging in multi-tier supply network management. It will help managers to look beyond their strategic suppliers and begin paying attention to some of the other critical suppliers, such as nexus suppliers, whose importance comes from occupying a particular structural position in the supply network. To that end, the next section addresses how to assign a nexus supplier index to each supplier to provide a first cut at which suppliers to consider as nexus suppliers among myriad suppliers in the supply network.

Table 7.9 Typologies of Nexus Suppliers

	Operational Nexus Supplier	Monopolistic Nexus Supplier	Informational Nexus Supplier
Network type	Core subgroup of the supply network	Extended, peripheral supply network	Ego network in the core or peripheral subgroup
Structural characteristics	High degree and betweenness centrality	High betweenness centrality	High diversity in its extended ties
Industry examples	Emhart	Evonik	TSMC
Criticality	Significant impact on the operational performance of the end product	Significant impact on supply continuity due to low substitutability	Sources of early market and technological information
Performance implications	Cost, risk, and responsiveness	Responsiveness and risk	Risk and innovation

Source: Adapted from Yan et al. 2015

Nexus Supplier Index

We investigate the feasibility of creating the nexus supplier index (NSI), building on existing centrality metrics and using a large-scale database. It is first discussed by Choi, Shao, and Shi in 2015. Appearing in the *Harvard Business Review*'s Future of Operations forum, we report the basic premise of our NSI research, funded by CAPS Research (see www.capsresearch.org). We define NSI in that online article as "an aggregate measure of criticality of a supplier in a buying firm's supply network."

The details of our NSI formulation are then laid out in Shao et al. (2018). We present a mathematical model based on data envelopment analysis (DEA) that incorporates various centrality measures, in particular, degree, betweenness, eigenvector, and closeness centralities. The proposed NSI aggregates these centrality measures because no single centrality measure is deemed comprehensive enough to capture the overall structural criticality of a supplier. The intent is to help focal companies make the first cut at identifying structurally important suppliers in their networks as nexus suppliers to investigate their potential impact, monitor them for risk management, and evaluate them for possible supplier development opportunities.

We collect data from the Bloomberg Supply Chain Database (SPLC) that maintains buyer-supplier relationships of about 28,000 publicly traded companies worldwide. Using SPLC, we compile a network of buyer-supplier relationships with Honda Motor as the focal company. The data compilation takes the network down to the fourth-tier level. Then, this network data is applied to the NSI model that has been developed. The NSI scores are computed for all suppliers in the network. The results are then shared with the top supply management team at Honda of America and reviewed by them for validation purposes.

Degree, betweenness, and closeness centralities were discussed earlier in this chapter under the section "Structural Indices." Intuitively, degree centrality is a measure of popularity, betweenness centrality is a measure of gatekeeping, and closeness centrality is a measure of how quickly a node can reach the other nodes. Eigenvector centrality is the only new metric among the four different centrality measures used in the NSI model. It can be viewed as a measure of prestige. It measures how well a node is connected to other important nodes (i.e., high centrality measures). By virtue of being connected to other important nodes, that node itself then carries prestige and influence.

It is, of course, possible to use these centrality measures separately to evaluate a supplier's structural position. For example, degree centrality by itself can be used as a measure of NSI; looking at the number of ties would be a good first step to gauge the structural importance of a node. However, a single centrality measure might miss the other structural characteristics and importance as stipulated in other centrality measures. To attain comprehensiveness, we use degree, eigenvector, and betweenness centralities in the numerator of the NSI equation and distance farness measure (i.e., inverse of closeness centrality) in the denominator. Theoretically, degree centrality is a node-level construct, eigenvector centrality measures what is happening in the neighborhood, and betweenness centrality captures the network-level characteristic. We maximize these three centrality measures (a combination of degree, eigenvector, and betweenness centralities) and minimize the distance farness in the NSI equation (see below). As an inverse measure of closeness, distance farness reflects the average distance of a node to all other nodes. If a node is far from the other nodes, that node would be considered less important.

Our NSI model uses the framework of data envelopment analysis (DEA). Initially developed to measure a production frontier, DEA can be used for benchmarking purposes—it offers a differential score between an entity and best practices to gauge its overall performance with respect to the others (Cook, Tone, and Zhu 2014). Applied to our research, the overall performance as measured by DEA can be captured in a composite measure that reflects the aggregation of various indicators. In other words, we can use DEA to aggregate different centrality measures to offer a single composite score for NSI for the suppliers in a supply network. We are not the first to use DEA to develop performance-related measures. DEA has been used for quality management (Chin et al. 2009), strategic sourcing (Talluri, DeCampos, and Hult 2013), and to compare production output across firms, industries, and economies as per the Malmquist Index (Chou and Shao 2014; Fare et al. 1994).

The DEA-based NSI model is summarized here. NSI of the node as a supplier p in a supply network is computed by the equation as shown.

$$\text{Maximize NSI}p = \frac{\alpha Dp + \beta Bp + \gamma Vp}{\sigma Fp} \tag{1}$$

$$\text{subject to } \frac{\alpha Di + \beta Bi + \gamma Vi}{\sigma Fi} (i = 1, \dots, N) \tag{2}$$

$$\alpha, \beta, \gamma, \sigma \geq 0 \tag{3}$$

where D is degree centrality, B is betweenness centrality, V is eigenvector centrality, and F is distance farness measure. For a more detailed discussion of each measure and development of the model, see Shao et al. (2018).

As stated earlier, Bloomberg SPLC maintains approximately 28,000 publicly traded companies worldwide. In the United States, the Securities and Exchange Commission (SEC) requires a publicly traded company (i.e., a buying company) to report other companies it does business with (i.e., suppliers) if 10% or more of their revenue comes from sales to that company. In this regard, the data from Bloomberg SPLC is at the company level and does not offer product-level information. The supply network we compile from Bloomberg SPLC reflects a network of company-level buyer-supplier relationships. Bloomberg does not allow automation of data collection from the user end, so the data collection was done through a painstaking manual process.

Starting with Honda, we identify the names of its suppliers and then their suppliers, and so on. As a decision rule for which tier a supplier operates in, we use the length of the shortest path to Honda. For instance, Bridgestone shows up as a first-tier supplier, and it can have a direct sales flow into another first-tier supplier. In this case, Bridgestone would then be labelled as a first-tier supplier. All buyer-supplier relationships captured in the supply network are unidirectional—if two companies have a reciprocal buyer-supplier relationship, we capture their relationships as two separate relationships in our data. To manage the network data, we use a dedicated graph database. This database captures network data as nodes, edges, and properties rather than in a tabular format. The advantage of a graph database is that it is easily scalable and can handle substantial network data (see Shao et al. 2018 for more details). In the end, our supply network contains 10,833 companies and 47,183 buyer-supplier relationships. Excluding Honda, 10,833 companies constitute 245 first-tier suppliers, 1,643 second-tier suppliers, 4,605 third-tier suppliers, and 4,339 fourth-tier suppliers.

Intuitively, one can think of this data-collection process and analysis as similar to what we have done with the Honda and DaimlerChrysler supply network map data for the center console. We need the network data in a form we can do mathematical operations on, and then we can do computations and create visual representations of all companies at the individual-node level and the network level. The visual representations are done easily in the case of center console supply networks because the number of companies is much less, around 50. However, with over 10,000 companies, the new buyer-supplier network data from SPLC surrounding Honda is not conducive to visual representation at the network level because it would just show up as one big blob. Instead, we can list numerical values in tabular forms. For instance, we can present the top-50 suppliers ranked by NSI scores at the second-tier level and third-tier levels (see Shao et al. 2018). We do not present suppliers at the first-tier level because they are already known by the focal company and would already be deemed important. We also organize the company names in the second- and third-tier levels around the three typologies of operational, monopolistic, and informational nexus suppliers.

During an in-person visit, all these outputs of the data analyses were presented to Tom Lake, the chief procurement officer of Honda of America at the time, and his top managers. Based on a day-long visit to Tom Lake's office in Marysville, Ohio, we report here a few key observations and comments from the managers at Honda. At the beginning of the meeting an explanation was offered to Honda. First, what we did was not high-precision research. Rather, it was an exercise intended to offer a general direction for where to look in terms of potential sources of supply network risk. The research provides a general list of supplier names whose importance comes from their structural positions in the supply network. By reviewing the list, Honda can then make a decision whether to further investigate any of the listed suppliers. Toward the end of the meeting, Tom Lake made an overarching comment, "If we can glean one or two or ten key hints on the list, these might be suppliers we need to dig into more, partner with, mitigate risk with; there is huge value to that." More specifically, when the managers looked at various NSI-ranked supplier lists, they first noticed supplier names they did not recognize. Clearly, these were the blind spots from their perspective that they needed to look further into. They said for these suppliers, Honda could start with a small contract to begin the relationship-building process or to introduce them to other suppliers.

Furthermore, seeing that Volkswagen was listed as a supplier with the highest NSI score at the second-tier level and Volkswagen at the time was having difficulty with various scandals about its emissions testing, the managers pointed out how they could take more proactive measures to mitigate any potential negative impact for the other companies doing business with Volkswagen in Honda's supply network. Lastly and perhaps more interestingly, the managers saw Apple listed with the highest NSI score at the third-tier level. They noted that Apple offers three things to the market—hardware, software, and service. It is possible that Apple came out on top at the third-tier level because other downstream companies buy Apple products such as smartphones and tablets. It might also be possible that the software Apple produces could end up in a product that would eventually become part of Honda's products. It was noted as an area that they needed to investigate further. Ultimately, the NSI scores could help Honda decide which suppliers and extended business relationships to monitor more closely when making policy or investment decisions. Our lists offered the first cut.

Extreme Events and Supply Network Mapping

As discussed in Chapter 1, we are observing more extreme events captured in the term "regression to the tail" (Flyvbjerg 2020). We anticipate this trend to continue into the foreseeable future, fueled by global phenomenon such as COVID-19 and its episodic recurrences; unusual weather patterns such as heat waves, earthquakes, and tsunamis; trade wars; and real, boots-on-ground wars involving combat and destruction. When these extreme events occur, regardless of their reasons, supply chains are disrupted in unanticipated ways. For example, only after war broke out in Ukraine, we have learned how the semiconductor industry relies on neon gases from there and how the world relies on Ukraine for food. We all know we cannot wholly anticipate everything, so the best we can do is to prepare ourselves to respond and adapt more quickly when these extreme events hit our supply chains.

Choi, Rogers, and Vakil (2020) make a strong recommendation to engage in supply network mapping as a strategic thrust for companies to be able to rapidly detect which of their suppliers are affected and how to reserve available capacities. We note what happened during the early months of COVID-19 to illustrate our point.

Immediately following the coronavirus outbreak, all multinational companies that had a presence in China were struggling to figure out how to respond to the spread of the virus. They needed to find out which of their suppliers and their suppliers were in the infected zone to secure their supply line. In late January and early February of 2020, right after the outbreak of COVID in China, most companies were still in data-collection mode, according to a survey done by Resilinc (see www.resilinc.com). However, there were a few leading companies that had done supply network mapping in the affected area. These companies had information on which of their suppliers and their suppliers had manufacturing plants in the affected areas. They were drawing expanding concentric circles around Wuhan as the virus propagated outward, identified which of their suppliers were inside these circles, and moved in quickly to secure inventory and associated production capacity. The companies that were still collecting data were left to scurry for whatever else was available a few months later when they came to realize what was happening.

Without having done supply network mapping, we believe it would take about two to three months on average for a focal company to triangulate a disruption that has hit its supply chain and identify exactly which of its suppliers might be impacted. Imagine a second-tier supplier that runs into a disruption. That supplier takes a few days or weeks to assess the situation and develop a plan before it notifies its buying companies. It would rely on inventory in the meantime to continue making deliveries. Say, after about two weeks, it has figured out a few things (e.g., inventory allocation) and alerts its buying companies that it has a problem and will have to delay some shipments. A typical buying company might not react immediately because it believes it has sufficient inventory in its warehouse to take care of the issue. However, the effect of the disruption is much broader, and the situation escalates. This buying company, a first-tier supplier to the focal company, takes a few weeks to assess the situation before it notifies the focal company. It takes four weeks or more before the focal company is notified of the disruption at the second-tier level, and by then, other first-tier suppliers that use the same second-tier supplier inform the focal company of the shipment delays. Another few weeks have gone by. If the disruption involves a third-tier supplier, it will take longer for the news to reach the focal company. We witnessed this type of disruption escalation in the supply chain after other disasters—the Fukushima disaster, Thailand floods in 2011, the 2012 explosion at Evonik in Germany, and after Hurricane Maria in 2017.

So, supply network mapping seems inevitable. However, doing so is not easy. The supply network mapping projects that have been described in this chapter are confined to a limited scale—a center console in an automobile with about 50 parts and the firm-to-firm level network of buyer-supplier relationships from SPLC in the Bloomberg Terminal. Large corporations have many products with many BOMs with a long list of parts and materials. Here are two examples of large corporations that discovered how difficult it is to take on supply network mapping. One Japanese semiconductor manufacturing company decided to map its supply networks after the 2011 Fukushima incident as part of its overall risk-mitigation strategy. According to the executives at this company, it took a team of 100 people over one year to map its entire supply networks down to the sub-tier suppliers. More recently, a major Korean consumer goods company expressed the need to map its supply networks but acknowledged that had not done so because of the difficulties involved. Necessary data were scattered across the organization, and its supplier base changed at different rates depending on the type of parts involved.

The thing about supply network mapping is that having done some is better than not having done it at all. In other words, having some visibility into the supply network is better than having no visibility. Many leading focal companies mentioned above that were able to take proactive measures during the early months of COVID-19 had done mapping only down to their second-tier level. The mapping effort typically begins with a BOM, similar to how the supply networks for the Honda, Acura, and DaimlerChrysler center consoles have been mapped. However, it is challenging to map the suppliers for all the products, so the mapping could start with the top-five products by revenue. It would include information about what activities supplier plants perform, what alternative plant locations the supplier may have available, and how long it might take for the supplier to make the shift to alternative manufacturing locations. The mapping effort could also include investigating more deeply into the supply network where unexpected dependencies may exist. For instance, some second- or third-tier suppliers may use the same semiconductor suppliers, such as TSMC (tsmc.com), ASE (ase.aseglobal.com), or UMC (umc.com) in Taiwan or AMKOR (amkor.com) in the United States. Depending on the type and details of the supply network analysis, these companies may appear as hidden checkpoint suppliers with high centrality scores.

Some leading companies have supply network visibility and mapping worked into their supplier contracts and service-level agreements. They require their suppliers to stipulate recovery time objectives during force majeure events and recovery plans to ensure continuity of supply. Another benefit of engaging in supply network mapping is that information is no longer in the heads of a few procurement employees (i.e., institutional knowledge) that may be lost if they decide to leave the company. A supply network map can be leveraged across the company and protect the company from the loss of institutional knowledge contained by a few employees. It provides information anyone in the organization can tap into for daily activities, not just for extreme events. Companies can do supply network mapping themselves, but there are also technology and data service companies that can help in this regard. A few of the companies that operate in this space are Elementum (elementum.com), Coupa (coupa.com), and Resilinc (resilinc.com). The expense associated with working with these solution providers and others like them would be a fraction of the cost of insurance premiums and easily recouped in a single extreme event. The hidden costs that arise from supply network disruptions are expedited shipments, premiums on raw materials, shortages, and allocations and decommits to customers.

Choi, Rogers, and Vakil (2020) look ahead to what may happen as the disruptive effects of an extreme event like COVID-19 subside. We may see companies settle into one of two modes. One mode is to move on to other problems as the disruptions of the recent extreme event fade from the collective memory. These companies might celebrate since they survived the ordeal—they were hurt, but they are still in operation. Yet, they should know they are gambling with their shareholder value. The other mode involves learning from this event, investing in mapping their supply networks at some level, and analyzing their supply networks. These companies do not want to be blind during the next extreme events that are expected to happen more frequently in the coming years. They do not forget the painful lessons they learned from dealing with the crisis. They can remedy that by working to anticipate future problems (e.g., nexus suppliers) while making sure they understand the shape and structures of their supply networks.

Key Points

- To create supply network maps, the BOM is used for the center console, whose procurement represents the general supply management practices of Honda of America.
- Formalization, centralization, and complexity affect each other in a progressive way as the structures of a supply network are operationalized.

- Formalization occurs in a dyadic context, centralization in a supply chain context, and complexity in a network context.
- The adoption of supply chain make would offer the focal company supply network stability, and the adoption of supply chain buy would make sourcing more convenient and expedient for the focal company.
- Once an NxN matrix can be generated, we can do mathematical operations on it using social network analysis software such as UCINET and generate node-level and network-level indices.
- The outputs of such analysis can more readily identify some of the hidden critical suppliers the focal company would need to monitor more closely.
- The qualitative analysis of supply network maps and the quantitative analysis of the same supply network using social network analysis complement each other and point to a more complete picture of how the structure of a supply network is operationalized.
- The suppliers whose importance to the focal company comes from occupying a particular structural position in the supply network are called "nexus suppliers."
- The nexus supplier index (NSI) is developed as an aggregate measure of existing centrality metrics.
- As we anticipate more extreme events and supply network disruptions, the supply network mapping and associated analytic approaches will prove to be indispensable.

8

Supply Networks as a Complex Adaptive System

We see migrating birds in the sky. It is an amazing sight to behold, especially if they are flying against a sunset. When we see that, we can't help but notice how they fly in formation, typically in a V-shaped one. To a casual observer, it may look like there is a designated leader at the head of the formation, and then other birds fall in depending on their packing order; after all, we hear how some birds have a social system. However, in flight, this is not what really happens. There is no designated lead bird, and their packing order lacks the precision to determine exactly which bird should go ahead of which other birds. So, how do they fly in a formation? This is what actually happens. While in flight, different birds take turns leading. Their flight formation lacks intentionality. In fact, the birds themselves do not know they fly in a formation. Then, how? The individual birds fly, obeying a few local rules, and the V-shaped pattern emerges at the collective level. The local rules, in this case, include flying most comfortably (i.e., flying in the most energy-efficient way) and all birds sharing the burden of flying at the head of the formation (i.e., withstanding the most air resistance at the apex of the V-shaped formation). Air vortices created during flight have a direct influence on flying efficiently. When a bird flaps its wings, that movement creates a vortex at each end of the tips. This vortex first pushes down the air (downwash), but then it rotates to create an upward draft behind it (upwash). All birds behind the lead bird take advantage of this upward airflow created by the bird in front of it. To maintain their flight together, they take turns flying at the head of the formation where the most energy consumption takes place. When the bird at the apex of the formation gets tired, it falls back, and another moves up to take its place.

In essence, a flock of migrating birds is a complex adaptive system (CAS). The formation appears as birds fly following simple local rules. The birds do not know they have created a formation, but from a distance, we can observe the pattern at the collective. It is a *complex* system with individual birds as

The Nature of Supply Networks. Thomas Y. Choi, Oxford University Press. © Thomas Y. Choi 2023.
DOI: 10.1093/oso/9780197673249.003.0008

the constituting elements with shared flight behaviors linking them together. It is *adaptive* because, as a collective, they respond to changing conditions. As one bird gets tired, another bird responds by making an adjustment; it moves up in the formation. Birds also respond to changing weather patterns, such as shifting wind directions. It is a *system* bound by a common goal of migrating together to reach their destination. As a CAS, its pattern emerges and evolves, adapting to environmental changes. As such, it is more than a complex system. It is a complex adaptive system, with adaptivity as the hallmark characteristic of a CAS.

Not all complex systems are complex adaptive systems. A water molecule is a complex system. It consists of two oxygen atoms and one hydrogen atom. However, it is not a complex adaptive system because oxygen and hydrogen atoms lack agency. They cannot make decisions like migrating birds do. This is an important distinction. Across the preceding chapters, we have alluded to the concept of complexity in various places. We have implied companies as constituent elements with agency in a system (i.e., supply base or supply network). However, we have primarily considered the complex nature rather than the complex adaptive nature of such systems. In Chapter 5, we framed the supply base as a complex adaptive system by noting how suppliers can make their own decisions to engage with other suppliers. However, for theorization, we focused on the complexity of supply bases. Referring to Kauffman's NK model, we focused on how many suppliers there are (N), how many of them are interconnected (K), and how different they are (A). In Chapter 7, we considered the complexity of supply networks by counting the number of suppliers vertically and horizontally and looking at spatial distances in supply networks. However, we did not consider the adaptive or evolutionary nature of a supply base or supply network. We also computed patterns in network connectivity using social network analysis. Missing there again is the consideration of adaptivity and the evolutionary nature of supply networks. In this chapter, we offer a more explicit consideration of supply networks as complex adaptive systems.

We do that by first theoretically framing the supply networks as a CAS (Choi, Dooley, and Rungtusanatham 2001). That paper was referenced in the Preface of this book as to how it was first conceptualized. In this chapter, we consider how framing supply networks as a CAS has led to additional theoretical work. It has helped in developing a theory of supply chains (Carter, Rogers, and Choi 2015) and a conceptualization of supply chain adaptation through jury-rigging (Kauffman et al. 2018). After that, three simulation-based studies to investigate the evolutionary, adaptive nature of supply networks are introduced—how buyer-supplier relationships as an interplay of voice and exit decisions evolve over time in supply networks (Nair, Narasimhan, and Choi 2009), how much control a focal company should exercise on supply networks behaving as a CAS (Giannoccaro, Nair, and Choi 2018), and how adaptive responses through jury-rigging methods may help create intertwined supply networks when faced with unknown-unknowns, such as the COVID-19 pandemic (Feizabadi, Gligor, and Choi 2021).

Framing Supply Networks as Complex Adaptive Systems

Recognizing supply networks as a system is a good start, and considering the complexity of supply networks is helpful. However, Choi, Dooley, and Rungtusanatham (2001) argue that we need to do more—we need to recognize and consider supply networks as a complex adaptive system. We offer a quotation from a manager at a leading U.S.-based automobile company (Choi, Dooley, and Rungtusanatham 2001, p. 352). This company attempted to map a supply network of an engine assembly to manage it as a system but soon realized the futility of their effort.

> A few years ago, our engineers mapped a supply chain of a small as-sembly [by] tracing it all the way back to the mine. From that exercise, we demonstrated the benefits of supply chain management, and we set out to manage the supply chain as a system. Frankly, we have not been able to do it. The problem was, as soon as we came up with a strategy for managing the chain, the chain changed on us—we got new suppliers and new relationship configurations. It took a lot of effort to map one supply chain, and we could not possibly map it every time something changed.

This company clearly had good intentions. What it missed was the dynamic and evolutionary nature of supply networks. It missed viewing supply networks as a CAS. Citing Holland (1995), we define CAS as "a system that emerges over time into a coherent form, and adapts and organizes itself without any singular entity deliberately managing or controlling it" (Choi, Dooley, and Rungtusanatham 2001, p. 352). If so, what should this leading automobile company have done? From a focal company's perspective, it needs to decide how much of a supply network it should control and how much of the supply network it should let emerge.

Practically, given the current state of data-collection technology, it would be impossible to map a supply network in real-time as changes occur dynamically in various parts of the network. Someday, it may be possible as technologies advance, where different databases are able to talk to each other (i.e., shipping data talking to financial transactions data) under smart contracts and artificial intelligence (AI) automating the integration of unstructured data and structured data (Rogers et al. 2018; Handfield et al. 2017). Someday, we may be able to follow the movement of every single part and piece of material at the stock-keeping unit (SKU) level across the supply network. Even then, I think there will be uncertainty associated with time lags and opportunistic behaviors of companies. In any case, for now, we are unable to map the supply networks in their entirety in real-time. So, what are we to do? I think we first need to recognize supply networks as CASs. Then, we should do what is practically possible. Chapter 7 provided a few hints. The leading companies that had done mapping and reaped many benefits during the early months of the COVID-19 pandemic, as referenced at the end of that chapter. They had done mapping down to only the second-tier level. This is an important observation. I believe, practically, most of the suppliers in the core subgroup (see Chapter 7) of a supply network would be captured within the first two tiers of a supply network. Also, this subgroup of a supply network would be more stable compared to the peripheral subgroups in a supply network operating beyond the second tier. To manage the peripheral region of a supply network, focal companies should focus on identifying nexus suppliers (see Chapter 7) and try to monitor them. In sum, once we recognize supply networks as a complex adaptive system, we are faced with a strategic decision as to how much of the supply network we should apply control and how much we should let emerge.

Overview of Complex Adaptive Systems

The literature on theories and models of CAS (e.g., Cheng and Van de Ven 1996; Dooley 1997; Goldstein 1994; Kauffman 1996; McKelvey 1997) focuses on the interactions across complex adaptive systems, their environment, and their co-evolution. The CAS for us is a supply network made up of companies with agency operating in the supply network. As shown in Figure 8.1, the

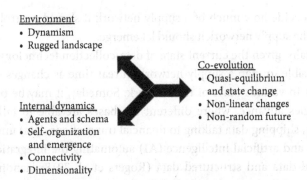

Environment
• Dynamism
• Rugged landscape

Co-evolution
• Quasi-equilibrium
  and state change
• Non-linear changes
• Non-random future

Internal dynamics
• Agents and schema
• Self-organization
  and emergence
• Connectivity
• Dimensionality

Figure 8.1 Underlying Framework of the Complex Adaptive System
Source: Adapted from Choi et al. 2001

various aspects of *internal dynamics* are listed that characterize the operation of a CAS. The *environment* refers to the consumer market that puts demand on the supply network, general economic conditions (i.e., recession, inflation, etc.), and governmental and institutional players that affect how the agents in the system interpret reality and make responses. The environment and the system, together, *co-evolve*, undergoing changes.

Internal to a supply network, a CAS can be defined at different levels. A triad involving a focal company and two dual-sourced suppliers can be a CAS (Choi and Wu 2009a), and a supply base can be a CAS (Choi and Krause 2006). The CAS of a triad involving a focal company and two suppliers would consider the rest of the supply base as an environment, and the supply base as a CAS may consider the larger supply network to a focal company as the environment. The interactions between the environment and the CAS lead to co-evolution, and what comes out of the co-evolution can affect what happens in the environment and the CAS as depicted in Figure 8.1.

Internal Dynamics

Internal to a CAS are agents that make up the system. They connect at various levels—at the individual level, project level, divisional level, organizational level, or inter-organizational level. They share common rules of behavior governed by norms, beliefs, and assumptions, which reflect their mental models or schema. Of course, there can be many rules, but when behaviors are enacted, only a few rules usually affect most of the behaviors in the system (Eoyang 1997; Zimmerman, Lindberg, and Plsek 1998). Using a few shared rules, the agents meaningfully intervene to manage the system through a desired course of action. They do that to increase the fitness of the system to which they are a member. For instance, to improve the performance of the supply management department in a company, the agents that work there may try to work with suppliers to meet their performance targets in the areas of cost, quality, and delivery. These agents would also try to meet their individual-level key performance indicators (KPIs), such as year-over-year cost savings. In this regard, with the supply management department as a system, fitness refers to performance both at the local level (i.e., individual KPIs) and at the global level (i.e., department-level performance involving suppliers).

Agents working together at various levels operate simultaneously and in parallel. Some of them may be aware of what the others are doing, but many of them may not. A migrating bird, as described above, may be aware of what its immediate neighbor is doing but may not be aware of what the other birds are doing. In fact, they are all flying under the same conditions simultaneously and in parallel using the same set of local rules. In other words, all behaviors being enacted are distributed across the system by individual agents, which as a collective leads to the organization of the system. With no single entity orchestrating the activities of the entire organization, we call that self-organization. According to Goldstein, as quoted in Zimmerman, Lindberg, and Plsek (1998), self-organization reflects a condition where "new emergent structures, patterns, and properties arise without being externally imposed on the system" (p. 270). In this regard, emergence is "the arising of new, unexpected structures, patterns, properties, or processes in a self-organizing system. . . . Emergent phenomena seem to have a life of their own with their own rules, laws and possibilities" (Goldstein cited in Zimmerman, Lindberg, and Plsek 1998, p. 265).

Connections among agents give rise to the complexity of a system. If there are no connections, then the collective system behavior would be random and unstructured since all agents would behave independently (Dooley and Van de Ven 1999). Therefore, some level of connectivity is a condition for a system to be complex. Even at low levels of connectivity, it is possible for unrelated industries to be connected. For example, during the COVID-19 pandemic, it became clear how seemingly distant industries were competing for the same resource in semiconductors. Generally, the impact of connectivity on interrelationships happens non-linearly (Kauffman 1996). The number of new relationships increases slowly with increasing connectivity at low and high levels of connectivity, while it changes dramatically at a critical value. For instance, cars on a freeway can travel independently with light traffic (i.e., low levels of traffic density). However, there is a critical level at 18–20% of traffic density, at which point the sensitivity of the traffic to a small increase of cars increases dramatically (Nagel and Paczuski 1995).

Agents in a CAS have certain degrees of freedom to enact their behaviors. Dimensionality refers to the degrees of freedom or autonomy given to the agents (Dooley and Van de Ven 1999). Two forms of feedback are at play here— negative feedback and positive feedback. Negative feedback is associated with control and low dimensionality. Control operates on deviation-correcting feedback, and this approach is critical to managing consistency and reliability in a system. In a supply network, suppliers are given performance report cards regularly to ensure quality products and on-time delivery. In contrast, positive feedback is associated with autonomy and high dimensionality. It operates on deviation-amplifying feedback and is critical to innovation and creativity. According to the documentation reported by Nishiguchi (1994), suppliers do much better in coming up with new product configurations with more creative features when given autonomy to think freely.

Table 8.1 summarizes our description of how a CAS operates. We will continue discussing the concepts under environment and co-evolution, as shown in Figure 8.1. The environment exists external to a given CAS. In the environment, there are also agents and their interrelationships. There would be connectivity between the agents in a CAS and the agents in the environment. Through such connectivity, they would affect each other and co-evolve.

Environment

The environment of a CAS changes all the time. When there is no change, that could signify death for CASs that operates in that environment (Dooley 1997). These changes are interdependent, as the environment of a given CAS would also have many other CASs that depend on one another. In this context, when CASs populate the environment are independent, global optimization is simple. Each CAS needs to focus on its own performance. In contrast, when they are dependent and closely coupled together, then global optimization is not possible, as their performance becomes interdependent. The landscape of the environment becomes rugged (Kauffman 1996).

Table 8.1 Illustrating CASs as Supply Networks

	CAS Descriptions	Supply Network Illustrations
Internal dynamics		
Agents and schema	Agents make choices and share local rules and fitness criteria	Suppliers work together to solve a common problem or to engage in new product development
Self-organization and emergence	Patterns are created by simultaneous actions of agents	When a product hits the market, we know by implication a coherent form of supply network had to have been in operation
Connectivity	Extended interrelationships are possible even at low levels of connectivity	Companies in seemingly unrelated industries (e.g., auto vs. toy) may be connected and compete for the same resources (e.g., semiconductors)
Dimensionality	Control reduces dimensionality, while autonomy increases it	Control through standardization (i.e., QS or ISO) reduces variation in supply network, while autonomy and decentralization increase creativity and adaptation in supply network
Environment		
Dynamism	Changes are constant and they are interdependent	Suppliers are constantly being selected and de-selected based on their performance and the supply market changes
Rugged landscape	When CASs are independent, global optimization is simple, but when they are dependent, it is not possible	Modular design is to create independence among modules and to provide autonomy for the suppliers to optimize locally
Co-evolution		
Quasi-equilibrium and state change	Attractors are sensitive to change as they are pulled away from quasi-equilibrium toward a far-from-equilibrium state	The Japanese *keiretsu* as an attractor has undergone a state change when the globalization pressures pulled them away from its quasi-equilibrium state
Non-linear changes	Causes and effects do not follow linear correlations	Massive, unilaterally imposed cost-reduction initiatives by the focal companies have led to random results
Non-random future	Common patterns of behavior are observable in CAS	A small change at the downstream of a supply chain can cause amplification and oscillation with phase lag moving up the chain

Source: Adapted from Choi, Dooley, and Rungtusanatham 2001

One most obvious way changes occur in CASs is by connecting with new agents in the environment or by disconnecting with existing agents in the system. The outcome is equivalent to altering the boundaries of the system. For instance, for a very long time, buyers and suppliers communicated through fax machines, so the suppliers associated with the faxing technology was part of the extended supply network. However, that soon changed to other communication technologies such as Adobe Acrobat PDF files as attachments to emails or through emerging service suppliers like DocuSign (see www.docusign.com). Further, the environment can bring out new rules and norms. For instance, buying companies that used to pay their suppliers in 30 days have now shifted to 90 or 120 days (Rogers, Leuschner, and Choi 2020). With these changes in rules and norms comes new fitness measures and how they are measured. For example, many companies are now looking to supply management to take more responsibility in working capital management. These changes affect other changes in other CASs operating in the same environment. For instance, as payment terms to suppliers are extended, we have seen the emergence of supply chain financing activities and associated service suppliers such as financial technology (Fintech) companies (Rogers, Leuschner, and Choi 2020).

There are many CASs in the environment, and they change constantly, including how they measure their fitness. A system operating in the environment has to navigate the landscape of many interdependent CASs and their dynamic fitness criteria. As discussed above, if all systems were hypothetically operating independently, finding a single peak in this landscape would be simple. However, that is not the case in reality. In supply networks, all companies depend on one another; shared parts, materials, and services make them interdependent (see Chapters 1 and 2). Each company has its own fitness measures based on the mandates of its internal stakeholders. At the same time, companies have to contend with the fitness measures promoted by their buying companies (e.g., industrial customers) (see the section "Performance Implications of Buyer-Supplier Relationships" in Chapter 3). When systems work in a closely coupled way, the landscape becomes rugged. The more tightly coupled they are, the more rugged the landscape becomes. According to Kauffman (1996), the rugged landscape appears for a system whose fitness criteria are highly dependent on others. Therefore, to search for optimization of their fitness, companies look for ways to decouple the problems they face. For example, focal companies have tried to modularize their products into independent pieces. As discussed earlier, I once had a visit from a senior executive at Volvo, who shared how his company downsized its supply base from 800 suppliers to 40 suppliers, each of which now supplies a module. From Volvo's perspective, coordinating the parts and materials from 800 suppliers involved handling many closely coupled problems. Currently, the company modularizes tasks both in design and manufacturing. The landscape has become less rugged, and, at least in theory, finding global optimality has become more attainable.

Co-Evolution

Among scholars that study organizations, the environment has been viewed as something that organizations as systems need to cybernetically react to (Simon 1976) and as something that organizations enact or create (Weick 2006). In the context of CASs, organizations do both—they react to and create their environment. In a business environment, there are many niches that companies can fill as well as create in response. It allows the cohabitation of many companies from disparate industries such as high-tech, automotive, chemical, and so on. Waldrop (1992) quotes Holland, "The rain forest has a place for tree sloths and butterflies. Moreover, the very act of filling one niche opens up more niches for new parasites, for new predators and prey, for new symbiotic partners" (p. 147). From this description, we begin to get a sense of the co-evolution of CASs and their environments that is not in static equilibrium but rather in dynamic disequilibrium.

Being in dynamic disequilibrium, however, does not mean being in disorder. In fact, a CAS maintains a state between complete order and incomplete disorder (Goldstein 1994). We, therefore, use the term *quasi-equilibrium* to capture how a CAS interacts with the environment. A CAS needs to keep order and, at the same time, contend with major changes in the environment that may press it further away from quasi-equilibrium. In response to such pressures, a CAS may undergo a state change. When this happens, the system jumps from one state to another. When there are small perturbations in the environment, a system in quasi-equilibrium would make adjustments but revert to or be attracted to its original state. However, with a state change, it jumps from one attractor to another (Goldstein 1994). For example, Japanese corporations operated under the system of *keiretsu* for decades. Nipondenso (now called Denso), a major supplier in the Toyota keiretsu, used to supply only to Toyota. However, global competition caused a state change in that system of a clan-like supply chain structure, and Denso now supplies to many other focal companies, including American companies such as GM. At the same time, seeing how the Japanese focal companies can introduce new products so quickly by working closely with their suppliers, the focal companies in the U.S. have made state changes by downsizing their supply base and introducing a tiered supply chain structure (see Chapters 3 and 5). These state changes occurring on both sides are evidence of how CASs and their environment influence one another and how their responses are interdependent.

One point we have stressed is that a CAS has many interdependent parts that are loosely coupled together. When they interact, outcomes will emerge idiosyncratically. In other words, changes in CASs happen in a non-linear way. According to Guastello (2016), in a non-linear system, a small change on the input side may lead to a large change on the output side, and a large change on the input side may lead to a small change on the output side. For instance, a large-scale organizational restructuring initiative may involve breaking apart divisions and departments and merging them in different ways. In the end, though, a job at the individual level may change very little. Similarly, a small change in a policy statement or worker training can lead to an unexpected major response that may permeate through the whole organization. For example, a short training course in worker health and safety may lead to a sudden increase in healthcare or worker compensation claims throughout the organization. Therefore, trying to predict the future becomes an exercise in futility. The only sure way to predict the future is to wait for the future to unfold. The managerial implication of this realization is to create a capacity in an organization to respond and adapt to changes after the future happens. Kauffman et al. (2018) use the term "jury-rigging" to refer to this strategic response, building on the ideas of evolutionary tinkering by Francois Jacob (1977)—more on jury-rigging in the next section.

Still, just because the future is unpredictable, that does not mean the future is random. This statement may sound paradoxical, but there is no contradiction in saying unpredictability does not equate to randomness. In how CASs and their environment co-evolve, we can observe common patterns. While small changes can take individual organizations to entirely different future paths (i.e., path dependence), the emergent state for these organizations would exhibit common patterns. In system dynamics, as captured in the beer game (see Chapter 2), interdependent human behaviors make predictions difficult in terms of how each node in the supply chain would respond to changes in demand. However, we see patterns in how different systems of a four-tier beer supply chain respond as more games are played— amplifications, oscillations, and phase lag (Lee, Padmanabhan, and Whang 1997). On the one hand, predictions are difficult in a CAS. On the other hand, overarching patterns can be observed. For instance, we see how focal companies have downsized their supply bases and moved toward a more tiered structure for their supply networks (see Chapters 5 and 6).

Theoretical Extensions

Since the publication that framed supply networks as CASs (Choi, Dooley, and Rungtusanatham 2001), I have been involved in extending that work theoretically through two additional papers (Carter, Rogers, and Choi 2015; Kauffman et al. 2018). In Carter, Rogers, and Choi (2015), we theorize the behaviors of supply chains as networks and CAS plays an integral role in this effort. The basic premise of Kauffman et al. (2018) was first presented as a keynote speech by Stuart Kauffman at the 2012 Decision Sciences Annual Meeting when I was serving as the program chair for the institute. With Kauffman's help, we theorize how supply networks as a CAS can best respond to unknown-unknowns (Unk-Unks) that suddenly descend on them. The COVID-19 pandemic is an Unk-Unk.

CAS and a Theory of the Supply Chain

Early in this book, we framed supply chains as networks (see Chapter 2). That is consistent with the observation made by Borgatti and Li (2009). They state, "SCM has not been just dyadic . . . but has—through the notion of chains— implicitly considered paths through a network of firms" (p. 6). As such, we bring to the fore the presence of networks. That observation is further echoed by Choi and Dooley (2009), who argue that supply chain research "strives to examine the network beyond the dyad, from triads to the extended networks" (p. 25). This important realization is designated as a foundational premise 1 (FP 1) in Carter, Rogers, and Choi (2015), and additional observations are made, as shown in Table 8.2.

Once the supply chain is framed as a network, we make the next big observation on how a supply network operates as a CAS (FP 2). Individual

Table 8.2 Foundational Premises for Supply Chains

	Foundational Premises
FP 1	The supply chain is a network
FP 2	The supply chain as a network operates as a complex adaptive system
FP 3	The supply chain is relative to a particular product and agent
FP 4	The supply chain consists of both a physical supply chain and a support supply chain
FP 5	The supply chain is bounded by the visible horizon of the focal agent
FP 6	The visible horizon of the focal agent is subject to attenuation, where distance is based on factors including physical distance and cultural distance

Source: Adapted from Carter, Rogers, and Choi 2015

companies that populate a supply network have their own set of stakeholders whose requirements they attempt to satisfy. They make their own decisions to maximize the outcome to meet the performance goals. In this regard, they have agency and do their best to control other companies working with them to their ends. For that, they try to gain visibility across the supply network. However, their visibility is invariably limited, as would their ability to control. Beyond the realm of control and visibility, things simply emerge for the companies in a supply network. They have no choice but to accept and adapt to what happens there.

In this regard, every company, as an agent, sees different things as it surveys upstream and downstream across its supply chain (FP 3). For instance, Honda would see its first-tier suppliers and a select group of second-tier and higher tier suppliers on the upstream side (see Chapter 7). On the downstream side, it would see its dealer network clearly but might not see the consumers as clearly as its dealers would. CVT, Honda's first-tier supplier for the Honda Accord, would have a clear view of all of Honda's second-tier suppliers and some higher tier suppliers that Honda might not have a clear visual on. Yet, on the downstream, CVT would likely not have a visual of what happens at the dealership level. Therefore, we acknowledge the relative nature of the supply chain with respect to the particular company and its product lines.

We then differentiate the physical supply chain and support supply chain (FP 4) (see Chapter 6). Of course, the physical supply chain would include all direct items on the bill of materials and indirect items such as maintenance, repair, and operations (MRO) items. The support supply chain would primarily include logistics and financial services. Logistics involves warehousing and transportation. They help overcome time and space. Warehouses help overcome time by storing goods until needed, and transportation helps overcome space by transferring goods from one location to another. The financial services move capital across the supply network. Without financial services, transactions across the supply network would not happen. According to a senior executive at Citi Bank, Citi alone handles $2.5 trillion per day to help facilitate commercial transactions in supply networks (Rogers, Leuschner, and Choi 2020). This executive also noted other competing banks, such as HSBC and Deutsche Bank, would also transact at about the same level. Needless to say, supply networks such as CASs on the support side are important and would need to be investigated further.

As we have theorized earlier in this chapter, supply networks as CASs and their interactions with their environments create dynamic and non-linear phenomena. They create rugged landscapes that would stretch out from their structural position to peripheral regions of the supply network. We have also discussed how each company as a node is at an intersection of many different supply networks involving diverse products and industries. When a company looks outwardly toward the horizon of a particular supply network (e.g., automotive), the outer edges of a supply network are fuzzy and not easily defined (FP 5). For instance, there could be a chemical company connected to many other industries, and for a company in an automotive supply network, for example, it would not be clear how much of this chemical company's extended supply networks would be relevant to its existence. Any focal company may have some visibility; they may monitor a nexus supplier that operates there (i.e., raw materials supplier of a critical mineral). However, the supply network can best be described as being bounded by a fuzzy horizon. It can only make conjectures and draw implications about what happens there in the invisible portion of the supply network. A more strategically meaningful way to consider supply networks is to focus on the visible portion of the supply network from a focal company's perspective. Therefore, we posit that, from a focal company's vantage point, the supply network is bounded by its visible horizon.

Within the visible horizon is where a focal company can use controls to ensure consistent performance. Take the case of Honda (see Chapter 7). This focal company controls its first-tier suppliers and parts of second- and tertiary-level suppliers within its visual range. It does so through monthly report cards, by providing deviation-correcting feedback, and via meetings at the management level (i.e., *jikon* meetings). Its first-tier suppliers replicate much of what Honda does, and they comply with Honda's request to use its approved vendor list when selecting their suppliers. However, as we move further away from Honda as the focal company, the influence of Honda is attenuated (FP 6). Such attenuation is akin to the skin-depth concept in physics, where electromagnetic waves enter a conductor, and its energy gets dissipated with respect to various frequencies in the electromagnetic waves. In supply networks, the influence and control of the focal company may dissipate in terms of the physical and cultural distances (Novak and Choi 2015). Here, the physical distance refers to the number of tiers in the supply network (i.e., multiple tiers would represent long distance), and the cultural distance refers to how much alignment of cultural artifacts (i.e., norms, values, etc.) there may be between the focal company and its suppliers.

Jury-Rigging and Supply Networks' Adaptive Behaviors

A major theoretical question remains: How do supply networks (SNs) as CASs respond to major unknown-unknowns (Unk-Unk) like the COVID-19 pandemic? Throughout the pandemic, many scholars and industry experts voiced concerns about the fragility of supply networks (i.e., https://www. visionofhumanity.org/fragility-of-global-supply-chains/). Even the U.S. government called for more research to help supply networks become less fragile and more resilient (https://www.whitehouse.gov/wp-content/uploads/2022/ 04/Chapter6.pdf). In Kauffman et al. (2018), we address this issue. Given SNs as CASs, what can we do *ex ante* and *ex post* an Unk-Unk to help supply networks behave more adaptively and with more flexibility so they become more resilient?

We introduce the idea of "jury-rigging," building on the work of Francois Jacob, a molecular biologist, and Nobel Prize recipient. In his seminal article in *Science*, "Evolution and Tinkering," Jacob (1977) offers us a concept of evolutionary "tinkering." It describes a process of complex adaptation through which a cell or an organism is co-opted to behave in a way it was not intended to at the functional level. When facing an Unk-Unk from the environment, a biological entity can utilize its heretofore unseen capability to adapt and thrive. He characterizes a living being as a CAS that "persists only by a constant flux of matter, energy, and information" (p. 1163). In much the same way, supply networks as CASs can be co-opted through jury-rigging to be used for functional purposes different from what they were intended when facing Unk-Unks. As a living system with the flow of matter, energy, and information is a CAS (Jacob 1977), a supply network is a CAS with the flow of matter, energy, and information.

Companies in supply networks face much uncertainty. At least some of such uncertainty involving demand fluctuations (see Chapter 2) are known-unknowns (K-Unks). For instance, we know our forecast is going to be off but not by how much and in which direction (i.e., over-forecast vs. under-forecast). To deal with K-Unks, companies use standardized parts, delay differentiation through modular manufacturing, and adopt multiple sourcing strategies (Gualandris and Kalchschmidt 2014, 2015; Kim, Chen, and Linderman 2015). These strategies are helpful to a certain extent. However, they have proven inadequate when facing disruptions from unexpected risk events (Talluri, DeCampos, and Hult 2013; Tomlin 2006). These strategies require ex post responses and time to figure out how to adapt to a disruption. Flynn, Koufteros, and Lu (2016) offer three types of K-Unks across micro, meso, and macro levels, with micro dealing with technical inputs, meso with lack of information, and macro with environmental factors. Tactical preparations, built-in design features (e.g., redundant parts), and other anticipatory mitigation strategies may be adopted ex ante to allow companies to adapt to disruptions (e.g., Ellis, Shockley, and Henry 2011). In general, the literature has focused on the mitigation strategies for K-Unks through known probability distributions.

Scholars have addressed Unk-Unks. Some work has been done in project management. Pich, Loch, and Meyer (2002) tackle unknown events that are outside the predefined strategy of a project manager. Ramasesh and Browning (2014) extend their work by posing two categories of Unk-Unks. One is *knowable* Unk-Unks, representing knowable events that were left out during planning, which is not the same as a K-Unk. The other is *unknowable* Unk-Unks that appear as a complete surprise. Beyond project management, much work still needs to be done in supply networks and how companies embedded in supply networks deal with Unk-Unks. One exception is Kauffman et al. (2018) where the concept of Unk-Unk is applied to supply networks.

In Kauffman et al. (2018), we describe Unk-Unks as "events that have no prior and are evident only in their realizations" (p. 53). The COVID-19 pandemic has been an Unk-Unk for many companies, including medical equipment and pharmaceutical industries, and for those who supply consumer goods such as laptops and automobiles. Such an event offers no known probability distribution, and the only thing companies can do is engage in ex post responses. Yet, as episodic recurrences of COVID-19 and its variants continue to press us, some of what has been an Unk-Unk might become more of a K-Unk. For example, logistics services were hit hard at first, but then the companies figured out how to deal with the problems through digitization and other technological means. The automobile companies figured out how to deal with semiconductor shortages by learning to repurpose existing inventories of semiconductors and by focusing on high-end products. These are encouraging signs, yet, the big question remains, what happens the next time we are hit with an Unk-Unk?

To answer this question, we note Jacob's (1977) observation that a CAS has to deal with more variety of environmental demands when facing Unk-Unks. We couple that with Ashby's (2015) statement about the requisite variety in that the level of variety of a system must match the variety of the environmental demand placed on it. The left side of Figure 8.2 illustrates how efficient design exists when the response matches the stimuli (Boisot and Mckelvey 2010). The x axis reflects the design choices of companies in supply networks. For example, such choices would range from supplier contracting to supply base rationalization. The y axis contains environmental stimuli and the uncertainty they pose on companies. Theoretically, efficient design exists when company responses match the environmental stimuli, which is captured in the diagonal line that goes up at a 45-degree angle.

Companies can take one of two paths as a design choice in anticipation of Unk-Unks, which are depicted on the right side of Figure 8.2. We have two diagrams where there is a mismatch between the environmental stimuli and design responses. The upper diagram reflects the ex post strategy. Companies face a predicament where the environmental stimuli overwhelm the design responses (i.e., the black dot moving up vertically), most likely after the manifestation of an Unk-Unk event. When this happens, the best that companies can do is to respond by instituting ex post changes to bring their current state back to the line that represents the efficient design (i.e., the black dot moving right to get back on the diagonal line representing the efficient design). This is what occurred during the onset of the COVID-19 pandemic. Many companies were scurrying around by making ex post changes to get back on the efficient design line (see Chapter 7). As we have witnessed, these changes are very expensive and usually incur high opportunity costs (i.e., consumer dissatisfaction and loss of reputation).

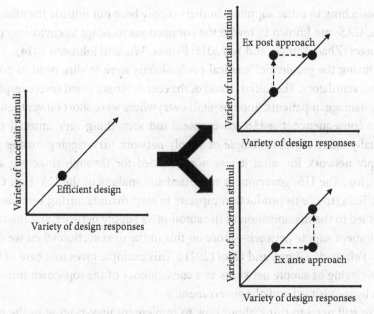

Figure 8.2 Response Approaches in Ashby's Space
Source: Adapted from Kauffman et al. 2018

As an alternative, to help increase more adaptive capability and flexibility in supply networks, we promote the ex ante strategy when facing an Unk-Unk event. This idea is shown in the lower diagram on the right side of Figure 8.2. Here, companies intentionally get off the diagonal line before an Unk-Unk happens (i.e., the black dot moving right horizontally). They develop ex ante capabilities to adapt quickly to the disruption, and their response time would be much shorter and more economical. For example, going back to what happened in China during the early months of the COVID-19 pandemic, leading companies had done multi-tier supply network mapping (see Chapter 7). Before this particular Unk-Unk event struck them, they had increased their response variety by investing in supply network mapping. While those companies that chose the ex post approach (upper diagram on the right side in Figure 8.2) were running around like a chicken with its head cut off, trying to get back on the diagonal line, companies that had taken the ex ante approach were much more systematic and efficient in how they handled the emerging disruption. As the virus propagated outwardly from Wuhan, they were able to identify the affected suppliers and rapidly locate alternate sources. Further, they could have "re-wired" the supply network by switching to other suppliers in their supply base but outside the affected area. CASs are known to rewire the connections to adapt to environmental changes (Zhao, Kumar, and Yen 2011; Pathak, Wu, and Johnston 2014).

During the pandemic, medical professionals were in dire need of additional ventilators. The initial strand of the coronavirus caused severe respiratory damage in patients, and hospitals everywhere were short on ventilators. As a consequence, the U.S. government did something very unusual that actually offers a great example of supply network jury-rigging—using the supply network for what it was not intended for through tinkering and rewiring. The U.S. government requested automakers in the U.S. (i.e., GM and Tesla) to use its production capacity to start manufacturing ventilators. That led to the juxtaposition of the automotive supply network and medical equipment supply network—more on this in the next section when we discuss Feizabadi, Gligor, and Choi (2021). This example gives us a case of the jury-rigging of supply networks as a consequence of the top-down imposition by the visible hand, the government.

We still need to think about how to implement jury-rigging in the private sector operating under the invisible hand. This is a difficult quest given that we are talking about designing a supply network ex ante in anticipation of Unk-Unks where we would be unable to pre-state all jury-rigged uses of objects and processes. What can a focal company do to facilitate jury-rigging in its supply networks? There is no clear answer to this question. However, we can begin to consider a few conditions that must be present to encourage jury-rigging when the next Unk-Unk strikes the supply networks. We believe the first thing that needs to happen is for the focal company to decide ex ante which suppliers would work on developing jury-rigging capability. The idea is for them to lead spontaneously, repurposing the portion of a supply network they can influence for the emerging needs if and when an Unk-Unk event occurs. In this regard, the role of core suppliers may take on added meaning. The core suppliers should provide the first cut for considering such rainy-day suppliers. These suppliers may be called "integrative" and should receive additional supplier development and cross-functional training. These suppliers would be tasked with integrating activities and facilitating distributed learning and knowledge sharing (Brusoni 2005; Brusoni, Jacobides, and Prencipe 2009). In particular, Brusoni (2005) points out the importance of sanctioned autonomy (i.e., delegated authority) so these suppliers are able to "identify, propose, and implement solutions to complex problems."

These integrative suppliers should be closely embedded with the focal company (Uzzi 1997) so that their success is closely tied to the success of the focal company. Other suppliers that this integrative supplier works closely with should also be embedded with one another. Such deep relationships (Liker and Choi 2004) would allow them to avoid overly complicated, explicit contracts and help save on monitoring costs (Asanuma 1985; Dore 1983; Gerlach 1992). For jury-rigging to take place in a supply network, high trust and deep relationships among the companies must exist. Uzzi (1997), however, warns against overly embedded supply networks that would pose the risk of "deviance-amplifying effects." A system whose elements are overly embedded with one another faces a risk in which the failure of one node can cause the entire system to fail. Therefore, the focal company needs to choose its integrative suppliers from those whose extended ties are not overly embedded. Theoretically, a desirable supply network would show a modularized supply network where each module is controlled by a few integrative suppliers, and the network landscape within the module's supply network would not be overly rugged.

The integrative suppliers should understand that they would be expected to exercise delegated authority from the focal company in times of potential disruptions. We call these "unspecified decision rights." This understanding is critical to facilitate self-organization during jury-rigging without the direct involvement of the focal company. It can be supported by using incomplete contracts (Cummins, Kauffman, and Choi 2021), which focus more on getting the job done rather than meeting the letter of the contract. (We will discuss incomplete contracts more in Chapter 9.) In sum, to implement a jury-rigged supply network, we need the following four conditions—integrative suppliers, an optimal level of embedded ties, ex ante sharing of unspecified decision rights, and incomplete contracts.

Computational Studies Through Simulations

Three simulation studies are introduced in this section. All three studies build on the premise that supply networks are complex adaptive systems (Choi, Dooley, and Rungtusanatham 2001). Because the network-level data are extremely difficult to obtain, especially considering the dynamic nature of the networks as a CAS, we resort to computer simulations to study the complex adaptive behaviors of supply networks. My role in these three papers focuses primarily on conceptual framing, and all computations have been done by my co-authors (Feizabadi, Gligor, and Choi 2021; Giannoccaro, Nair, and Choi 2018; Nair, Narasimhan, and Choi 2009).

Decision-Making in Supply Networks

In our study (Nair, Narasimhan, and Choi 2009), decision-making pertains to cooperation (voice decision) and defection (exit decision) in supply networks. In Chapter 3, we discussed how buyer-supplier relationships have primarily been considered in the voice-exist dichotomy (Helper 1990; 1993; Helper and Sako 1995). We look at the evolutionary process of this binary decision-making by the companies that populate the supply network. How supply networks operate as a complex adaptive system is studied by adopting cellular automata (CA) (Wolfram 1986) that simulate self-organization to emerge. How decisions are made is grounded in the incentive schemes based on the payoff matrix from game theory.

To add a bit more context, there are many interdependencies and indeterminacy in supply networks as discussed in Chapter 7. A company can be a supplier in one supply network, and a buyer in another supply network. Such overlapping roles can span across several different industries. When two companies come together and form a buyer-supplier relationship, the predominant taxonomy in the literature has been voice (e.g., cooperative, collaborative) and exit (e.g., competitive, adversarial) (see Chapter 3). We use this voice-exit dichotomy as the decision-making context at the company level when facing other companies, either as a buyer or a supplier. To investigate the evolutionary behavior of supply networks and companies therein, we inquire how a decision by a single company (i.e., an exit decision) affects the decision-making in the aggregate, how the size of a supply network influences the evolution of decision-making behaviors, and how an increase in the payoff from opportunism affects the evolution of decision-making, especially the voice decision. In this context, evolution means "that a global order is formed through bidirectional dynamic processes where local interactions between elements reveal a global behavior, and a global behavior results in new constraints to the behavior of the elements" (Nair, Narasimhan, and Choi 2009, p. 786).

In this regard, CA, based on the game-theoretic arguments (Nowak and May 1992), is used in our study because it allows the investigation of complex behaviors of supply networks by considering how individual companies interact at the local level (Davis, Eisenhardt, and Bingham 2007; Pathak et al. 2007). According to Davis, Eisenhardt, and Bingham (2007), the adoption of CA is appropriate when studying the "emergence of macro patterns from micro-interactions via spatial processes (e.g., competition, diffusion) in a population of agents" (p. 486). CA-based studies can capture how the interactions of agents at the local level lead to complex dynamics at the more global level (Lomi and Larsen 1996). The details of how interactions occur in the local neighborhood are described in Nair, Narasimhan, and Choi (2009). Ultimately, CA simulates a CAS in which complex behaviors emerge from the interactions of agents following simple local rules, and the payoff for each agent is determined based on the prisoner's dilemma payoff matrix as each agent interacts with its neighbors iteratively over time.

In our study, interactions among agents are determined by the Moore neighborhood, as shown on the left side of Figure 8.3. At every step, each cell interacts with the other cells in its neighborhood, so the cell labeled B (i.e., buying company) would interact with the other eight cells labeled S (i.e., supplier company) by deciding whether to cooperate or defect. We can view the center cell as the buyer and the other eight cells as suppliers in a supply base. Each of the nine agents in the Moore neighborhood observes the payoff for itself from the eight interactions based on the payoff matrix, as shown in Figure 8.4. Then, in the next step, each agent adjusts its decision to cooperate or defect based on what happened in the previous step—it knows which agent got the best payoff and which decision it selected. Thus, there is learning among the agents. The model is an iterated prisoner's dilemma game across time steps.

As happens in real-world supply networks, over time, a supplier can be a buyer, and a buyer can be a supplier. The CA mimics this, as illustrated by the cells on the right side of Figure 8.3. As the Moore neighborhood at the center of the lattice moves to the northwest of the lattice center, buyer B becomes supplier s6', and supplier s1 becomes the buyer B'. The suppliers s2 and s4 remain suppliers.

In our computer simulation, we use a CA made up of a 51x51 lattice. The size of the lattice is arbitrary and is similar to the one in Nowak and May (1992). The lattice contains 2,601 agents, and each supply network consists of nine agents in the Moore neighborhood, as shown in Figure 8.3. At the beginning of the simulation, the initial condition is set up in such a way that the buyer at the center defects while the suppliers in the Moore neighborhood

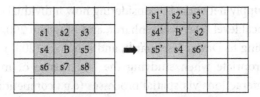

Figure 8.3 The Moore Neighborhood and Changing Role of Buyer and Supplier
Source: Adapted from Nair, Narasimhan, and Choi 2009

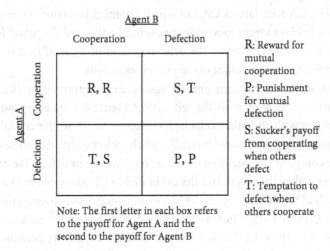

Note: The first letter in each box refers to the payoff for Agent A and the second to the payoff for Agent B

Figure 8.4 Payoff Matrix for the Prisoner's Dilemma Game
Source: Adapted from Nair, Narasimhan, and Choi 2009

cooperate. This condition resembles what typically happens in a real supply network wherein the buyer, as the contacting principal, agrees to work with a supplier when it deems the supplier is fully cooperative. Once the relationship is set up, the buyer is in the best position to behave opportunistically and defect; for example, a buyer could unilaterally impose a new cost-reduction target. As the simulation ensues, all agents learn and make decisions to maximize their own payoffs, and many of them would undoubtedly choose defection along the way. For example, in response to the buyer's cost-reduction mandate, a supplier may choose to use materials of lesser grade without informing the buyer.

We consider eight cases based on varied payoff configurations. We do so by choosing appropriate values for payoffs involving cooperation or

Table 8.3 Payoff Structure and Parameter Values

	Possible Scenarios	Parameter Values
Case 1	R=T>P=S	R=3; T=3; P=0; S=0
Case 2	R>T>P=S	R=5; T=3; P=0; S=0
Case 3	R=T>P>S	R=3; T=3; P=1; S=0
Case 4	R>T>P>S	R=5; T=3; P=1; S=0
Case 5	T>R>P=S and R≥(S+T)/2	T varied from 0 to 5.99; R=3; P=0; S=0
Case 6	T>R>P=S and R<(S+T)/2	T=5; R=2; P=0; S=0
Case 7	T>R>P>S and R≥(S+T)/2	T=5; R=3; P=1; S=0
Case 8	T>R>P>S and R<(S+T)/2	T=5; R=2; P=1; S=0

Source: Adapted from Nair, Narasimhan, and Choi 2009

defection. Varied configurations depend on the relative payoffs based on R, P, S, and T, as shown in Figure 8.4. Cases 1–4 consider the payoff matrix where R ≥ T. The payoff from mutual cooperation leads to a payoff higher than or equal to the payoff from opportunism. All possible scenarios are listed in Table 8.3 for these four cases. Cases 1–4 should theoretically lead to all agents cooperating. The results of these four cases should give us the obvious, which would offer validation of our simulation setup. The parameter values that conform to our scenarios are provided in Table 8.3.

Cases 5–8 consider the payoff matrix where T>R. Opportunism leads to a higher payoff than mutual cooperation. Possible scenarios for Cases 5–8 are listed in Table 8.3. In particular, Cases 5 and 7 show R ≥ (S+T)/2, similar to Axelrod (1984), and Cases 6 and 8 show R < (S+T)/2 to gauge further into low incentive for cooperation. The parameter values are provided in Table 8.3. For Cases 5 and 6, S and P are set to 0 to model the situation where the payoff would be nil with a defecting agent. For Cases 7 and 8, P = 1 and S = 0 reflect "moderate envy" (Lahno 2000) that tries to avoid being taken advantage of by other defecting agents. The results of all cases except Case 5 are not influenced by the parameter values chosen as long as they meet the conditions shown under the scenarios. The result of Case 5, however, comes up with a complex outcome, so the initial parameter values were adjusted as shown.

The simulation has been done in Mathematica 6.0 with a modified program from Gaylord and Nishidate (1996) to model the evolutionary game based on the spatial prisoner's dilemma. Figure 8.5 display the outputs of the

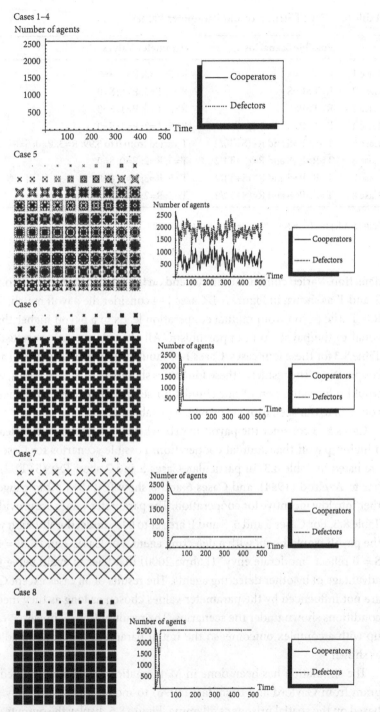

Figure 8.5 Lattice Patterns and Number of Cooperators and Defectors in the Lattice

Source: Adapted from Nair, Narasimhan, and Choi 2009

simulation. As expected, Cases 1–4 show only cooperation, which offers support for our model setup. In Case 5, defection dominates but a complex pattern of cooperating and defecting prevails. In Case 6, defection dominates, and a small number of cooperating agents remain in some organized form. In Case 7, cooperation dominates, and a small number of defecting agents remain in some organized form. Case 8 shows only defection.

There are additional outputs, and the interested reader may find more details in Nair, Narasimhan, and Choi (2009). We now turn to how we came up with our findings in the form of propositions. All propositions are compiled and shown in Table 8.4. Overall, there are no surprises in the results from Cases 1–4. Cases 6 and 8 also give us relatively straightforward results. In contrast, the results of Cases 5 and 7 are surprising in an interesting way.

From Cases 1–4, we learn that, with the incentives that encourage cooperation (i.e., $R \geq T$), companies cooperate. As $R \geq T$ attests, companies seem to still favor cooperation even under the possibility that the payoff from defection may equal the payoff from cooperation. However, Cases 6 and 8 tell us that if the reward from cooperation is below a certain point as per $R < (S+T)/2$, they might choose defection over cooperation. This observation adds more nuance to the simple notion that a reward for cooperating would lead to cooperation. Thus, a long-term contract may not necessarily always lead to cooperation. Refer to Table 8.4 for P1.

Member company satisfaction is a key determinant of cooperation among those in a supply network (Phillips, Lin, and Costello 1998). Hunt and Nevin (1974) agree that satisfied member companies are more likely to cooperate than to exit a company-level relationship. Of course, satisfaction is strongly affected by the incentive structures under which companies in the supply network operate. In our study, Case 7 informs us about an incentive structure that promotes cooperation with a safeguard by which potential defections are kept under control. Case 7 poses a potentially high payoff by defecting, yet the cooperation strategy remains dominant. This is interesting and counterintuitive. Perhaps, this is what we have been observing in the supply networks of Honda and Toyota (Liker and Choi 2004). See Table 8.4 for P2 and its corollary.

Case 5 gives us a complex pattern of cooperation and defection, with defection as the dominant strategy. In this case, we observe the quasi-equilibrium state (see Figure 8.1) in supply networks that is between complete order and incomplete disorder (Goldstein 1994). In Case 5, even with defection as the dominant strategy, not all companies get locked into opportunistic behavior.

Table 8.4 Overview of Propositions

	Relevant Case(s)	Stated Propositions
P 1	Cases 1–4 and Cases 6 and 8	In supply networks, companies may not necessarily cooperate even in the presence of repeated interactions; there is a threshold of reward below which they will not cooperate
P 2	Case 7	When both buyer and supplier trust each other for mutual cooperation, they will continue to do so even at the risk of extreme loss from cooperation Corollary: When there is trust for mutual cooperation, buyer and supplier tend to behave in a risk-prone way
P 3	Case 5	Even with defection as the dominant strategy in the supply network, companies can continue to exhibit cooperative behaviors
P 4	Case 5	Reaction to a supply network partner's opportunism follows a complex, non-linear pattern

With continuous feedback facilitating the co-evolution of company strategies and environment, we end up observing cooperative behaviors sustained over time. See Table 8.4 for P3.

It is fascinating to observe that beginning with a single buyer defecting, the entire network of supply networks ends up exhibiting complexity and being dominated by the strategy of defection. Still, some companies resist defection and persist in cooperative strategy, as evidenced by the spikes in Figure 8.5 for Case 5. The pattern is not gradual—it comes across as a struggle between cooperation and defection. Clearly, the pattern is not linear but non-linear. We would not know the exact time lag between a reaction to others' defection decisions, but this time lag would follow a complex adaptive process. See Table 8.4 for P4.

One big observation is that if the incentive structure is set up so that the payoff from cooperation is lower than a threshold value, with a single company behaving opportunistically, the whole supply network can be dominated by noncooperative, exit behaviors. This observation points to the importance of choosing the right incentive structure to promote cooperation for the whole supply network. That does not, of course, mean we should simply focus on the payoffs from cooperation; rather, it means we need to weigh the relative payoff carefully from cooperating versus the payoff a company may get by not cooperating. In particular, a buying company should consider carefully before unilaterally imposing a cost-reduction target on the suppliers or dumping off the inventory management cost to the suppliers. The potential payoff from cooperating has to be greater than one from defecting.

Control and Complexity of Supply Network Performance

For every focal company, how much of the supply network to control is a critical strategic decision (see Chapter 7). In the current chapter, we have raised the level of this strategic question by applying the observation that supply networks are complex adaptive systems. If we know supply networks behave as a CAS, then how should we manage it in terms of how much of it to control (i.e., scope of control)? To answer this question, we use the NK model (Kauffman 1993) and conduct an empirically informed, agent-based simulation model (Giannoccaro, Nair, and Choi 2018). The focus is on how the extent of the focal company's control affects supply network performance.

Initially, we began the study by using the Honda supply network data, as shown in Choi and Hong (2002), and submitted it to a journal subjecting it to a peer-review process. However, during the revision process, the journal reviewers instructed us to collect updated data on the Honda Accord's supply network on its center console. We complied and returned to Honda, who graciously offered us its current supply network information, shown in Figure 8.6. What we see immediately is that many of the same suppliers still appear in the updated supply network—some have different names because in the Choi and Hong study we were asked not to disclose the names of certain suppliers. In the updated supply network, their real names are disclosed. For example, GTI, NIFCO, and Moriroku in Figure 8.6 are CVT, JFC, and Yamamoru in Figure 7.2. We should, however, clarify two key differences between the new supply network and what was shown in Choi and Hong (2002). First, in the updated supply network, we see only one first-tier supplier rather than two. That just means Honda has succeeded in getting its first-tier supplier (GTI in Figure 8.6) to work as a one-stop shop for the whole assembly (for more details, see Chapter 7). Second, the new information does not give us as many vertical tiers in the supply network simply because the new data from Honda includes only the visible portion of the supply network from Honda's perspective.

As discussed in Chapter 7, we convert the tree-like structure in Figure 8.6 into a matrix form. The directional materials flow supply network is shown

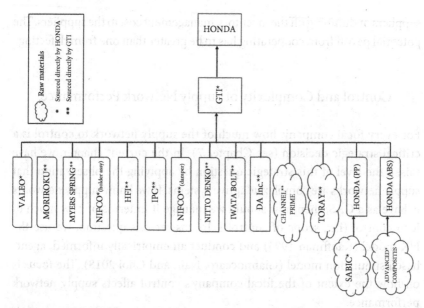

Figure 8.6 The Honda Accord Center Console Supply Network
Source: Giannoccaro et al. 2018

in Figure 8.7 in a matrix form. The non-directional, contractual relationship network is shown in Figure 8.8 as a sociogram.

We note, as discussed in Choi and Hong's (2002) study, the focal company controls its supply network in two ways—it does so directly through directed sourcing and indirectly through its first-tier supplier. To develop the baseline model, we design the scope of control with this information and use the updated Honda network data to calibrate the NK model parameters. We formulate nine experimental scenarios by varying the scope of control by the focal company, directly and indirectly, as discussed, the number of companies (N), and the level of interactions (K) in the supply network. Our goal is to clarify how the scope of control affects the supply network (SN) performance. We also study how SN complexity influences the network-level performance and the moderating effects played by the scope of control.

In this study, we have ascertained that the focal company's control decision clearly affects SN performance. Thus, how much of the supply network to control should be a carefully weighed decision by the focal company. The study informs us that a moderate level of control scope should be favored over controlling too much (i.e., all of the supply network) or too little of the supply network (i.e., just the first-tier supplier). Controlling too much constrains the ability of the supply network to adapt to changes as a CAS,

	HONDA	GTI	MS	HFI	IPC	ND	NFD	IB	DA	MO	VA	NFH	SA	AC	CP	TO
HONDA	1	1											1	1		
GREENVILLE TECNOLOGY INC.		1	1	1	1	1	1	1	1	1	1	1			1	1
MYERS SPRING			1													
HFI				1												
IPC					1											
NITTO DENKO						1										
NIFCO (DAMPER)							1									
IWATA BOLT								1								
DA Inc									1							
MORIROKU										1						
VALEO											1					
NIFCO (HOLDER ASSY)												1				
SABIC													1			
ADVANCED COMPOSITES														1		
CHANNEL PRIME															1	
TORAY																1

Figure 8.7 Materials Flow Network Matrix
Source: Adapted from Giannoccaro, Nair, and Choi 2018

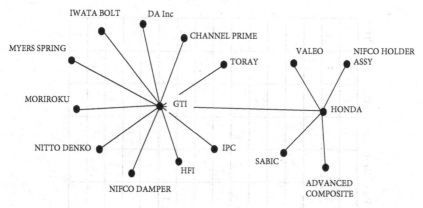

Figure 8.8 Contractual Relationship Network
Source: Adapted from Giannoccaro, Nair, and Choi 2018

while controlling too little leads to a lack of coordination for SN performance. Therefore, when controlling, the focal company should be mindful of the fact that SNs are CASs, and it should allow SNs some level of autonomy to adapt and evolve.

Furthermore, the SN complexity (i.e., the level of interactions in the supply network and the size of the supply network) should be considered when applying control. As in related studies found in the literature (i.e., Bode and Wagner 2015; Bozarth et al. 2009), we too find that these two dimensions of complexity affect negatively on performance. Our study extends their findings by identifying how the scope of control affects the negative influence of complexity on performance. When there is a high level of interaction in the supply network, a high scope of control helps alleviate its negative effect on supply network performance, and a low scope of control worsens the negative effect. That means the focal company should try to coordinate the activities of its suppliers, if and when in a highly interconnected supply network. Regarding the negative effect of the number of suppliers in a supply network, a high scope of control seems to worsen the negative effect. In other words, when the complexity of a supply network is heavily influenced by a large number of suppliers, less control is better. In sum, we offer two suggestions for managing complexity in supply networks. If the complexity of a supply network stems largely from the interactions of suppliers, a higher scope of control should be considered. If the complexity of a supply network stems mainly from a large number of suppliers, a lower scope of control should be considered.

To develop our conceptual model, we first begin by noting the evolving literature emphasizing the importance of managerial control in supply chains (Lee and Billington 1992; Huang and Iravani 2005; Stouthuysen, Slabbinck, and Roodhooft 2012). Control is required for coordination and alignment in supply chains and can have a positive impact on performance, such as cost, quality, and delivery (Carr and Ng 1995; Chen 2003; Narasimhan and Jayaram 1998). A big part of control is managing interdependencies among the suppliers and helping coordinate activities there by overcoming conflicting goals among them (Lee, Padmanabhan, and Whang 1997). Otherwise, suppliers might accomplish their own local goals but at the sacrifice of the larger network-level performance (Simchi-Levi, Kaminsky, and Simchi-Levi 2000; Vickery et al. 2003). As discussed in Chapter 2, localized forecasting and ordering policies can lead to harmful effects on the supply chain, called the bull-whip effect (Lee and Billington 1992; Lee, Padmanabhan, and Whang 1997). At the same time, centralized controls of a system tend to lead to tall hierarchies that would be slow in decision-making (Carzo and Yanouzas 1969) and reduce requisite heterogeneity to respond to dynamic market demands (Jones 2013; Morgan 2006). A centrally controlled supply network tends to constrain the autonomy of suppliers and get in the way of suppliers trying to respond quickly and adapt to environmental changes (Langfred and Moye 2004). Therefore, the scope of control by the focal company may be good at some level, but too much of it may hurt the supply network's adaptive performance. As shown in Figure 8.9, we propose a negative quadratic relationship between scope of control and SN adaptive performance.

In the existing literature, complexity has been shown to have a negative effect on performance (i.e., Bozarth et al. 2009; Larsen, Manning, and Pedersen 2013). For example, it affects negatively on organizational performance (Bozarth et al. 2009), supply chain disruptions (Bode and Wagner 2015; Brandon-Jones, Squire, and Van Rossenberg 2015), responsiveness (Choi and Krause 2006), and delivery speed (Vachon and Klassen 2002). In particular, Brandon-Jones, Squire, and Van Rossenberg (2015) point out how the number of companies may influence the frequency of disruptions, and Bozarth et al. (2009) show how complexity negatively affects plant performance. In this chapter and preceding chapters (Chapters 5 and 7), we have considered supply network complexity in terms of the level of interactions and number of companies in the supply network. In Figure 8.9, therefore, we propose a negative relationship between SN complexity in terms of the level of interactions and number of companies and SN adaptive performance.

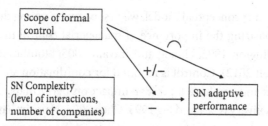

Figure 8.9 Conceptual Framework
Source: Giannoccaro, Nair, and Choi 2018

Accordingly, SN performance would decrease as the level of interactions in supply networks increases. The total cost of localized coordination and resolving conflicting objectives among the suppliers would increase. Therefore, the involvement of the focal company in terms of a high scope of control would be beneficial to help manage interactions. The focal company may offer common processes to exchange goods and provide relevant information (Dyer and Nobeoka 2000) to keep the suppliers working toward a common goal. For example, Honda and Toyota inform their suppliers about the consumer market (see Chapter 7). In addition, a high level of control is counterproductive when a supply network under consideration has a high number of suppliers (Flamholtz, Das, and Tsui 1985; Snell 1992). As discussed in Chapter 7, controlling a high number of suppliers requires a lot of resources in terms of required staff and information processing. Such an attempt may even lead to information overload and cause detrimental outcomes for the focal company. Attempting to process centralized decision-making when there are many suppliers would then have a negative effect on supply network performance. Therefore, the scope of formal control would moderate the relationship between SN complexity and SN adaptive performance in a +/- way, as shown in Figure 8.6. High scope of control would help alleviate the negative effect between SN complexity and SN adaptive performance coming from a high level of supplier interaction, while it would intensify the negative effect coming from a large number of suppliers.

Figure 8.10 illustrates the simulation process through which the conceptual model, shown in Figure 8.9, is tested. From the materials flow network, we can identify the number of companies (N) and the level of interactions among the companies (K). We also build a materials flow matrix, which is commonly referred to as the influence matrix in the NK fitness landscape methodology—it shows whether the decision of one company is influenced

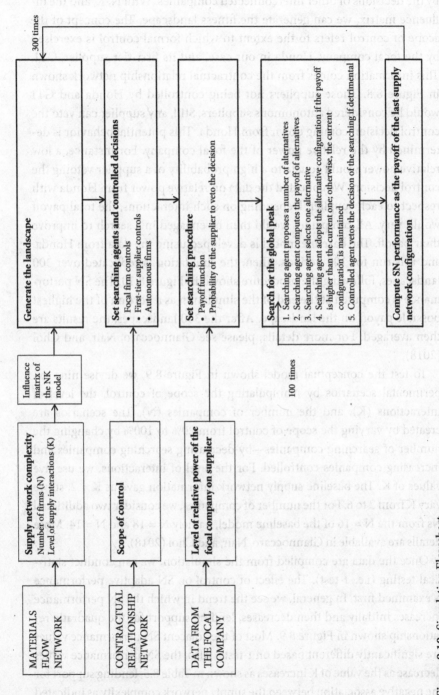

Figure 8.10 Simulation Flowchart

Source: Adapted from Giannoccaro, Nair, and Choi 2018

by the decisions of other interconnected companies. With N, K, and the influence matrix, we can generate the fitness landscape. The concept of the scope of control refers to the extent to which formal control is exercised by the focal company, Honda in our case, and its first-tier supplier, GTI. This information comes from the contractual relationship network shown in Figure 8.8. Those suppliers not being controlled by Honda and GTI would be considered autonomous suppliers. Still, any supplier can veto the control decision coming down from Honda. This potential behavior is determined by the relative power of the focal company. For instance, a low relative power would equate to a high probability of a supplier vetoing the control decision. We collected the data on relative power from Honda with respect to each supplier. Depending on such interactions, the total payoff would vary. All companies would then be engaged in a search to improve their payoff. The baseline model is developed using the data from Honda, and it is run for 100 periods. Then, the simulation is replicated over 300 landscapes, following the procedure shown in Figure 8.10. The SN performance is computed at the end of the simulation as a portion of the highest possible payoff on the landscape. After the 300 landscapes, the results are then averaged. For more details, please see Giannoccaro, Nair, and Choi (2018).

To test the conceptual model shown in Figure 8.9, we devise nine experimental scenarios by manipulating the scope of control, the level of interactions (K), and the number of companies (N). The scenarios are created by varying the scope of control from 20% to 100% by changing the number of searching companies—by decreasing searching companies and increasing companies controlled. For the level of interactions, we use five values of K. The baseline supply network information gave us K = 2, so we vary K from 2 to 6. For the number of companies, we consider two additional Ns from the N = 16 of the baseline model, namely N = 18 and N = 14. More details are available in Giannoccaro, Nair, and Choi (2018).

Once the data are compiled from the simulation, we can conduct statistical testing (i.e., *t*-test). The effect of control on SN adaptive performance is examined first. In general, we see the trend in which the SN performance increases initially and then decreases, lending support for the quadratic relationship shown in Figure 8.9. Most of the adjacent SN performance values are significantly different based on *t*-tests. Also, the SN performance values decrease as the value of K increases as shown in Table 8.5, lending support for the negative association between the supply network complexity as indicated

Table 8.5 Supply Network Performance and Scope of Control and K (N = 16)

	Scope of Control								
	20%	33%	47%	60%	73%	80%	86%	93%	100%
K=2	0.9508	0.9751	0.9769	0.9769	0.9778	0.9777	0.9823	0.9768	0.9628
K=3	0.8943	0.9029	0.9049	0.9218	0.9254	0.9274	0.9259	0.9258	0.9156
K=4	0.8435	0.8684	0.8830	0.8847	0.8967	0.9063	0.8961	0.8962	0.8592
K=5	0.7777	0.8068	0.8116	0.8121	0.8292	0.8398	0.8565	0.8321	0.8379
K=6	0.7034	0.7555	0.7698	0.7717	0.7991	0.8249	0.8202	0.8077	0.8021

Source: Adapted from Giannoccaro, Nair, and Choi 2018

Table 8.6 Supply Network Performance and Scope of Control and K (N = 14 and N = 18)

	Scope of Control								
	23%	31%	46%	62%	77%	85%	92%	100%	*Mean*
	N=14								
K=2									
K=3	0.9178	0.9178	0.9178	0.9232	0.9207	0.9250	0.9316	0.9252	*0.92239*
K=4	0.8437	0.8491	0.8510	0.8605	0.8951	0.8855	0.9016	0.8936	*0.87251*
K=5	0.7715	0.7662	0.7991	0.8212	0.8520	0.8449	0.8577	0.8514	*0.82050*
K=6	0.6947	0.7218	0.7438	0.767	0.8155	0.8230	0.8336	0.8308	*0.77878*
	N=18								
K=2	0.9219	0.9256	0.9270	0.9280	0.9326	0.9226	0.9033	0.8864	*0.91843*
K=3	0.8733	0.8749	0.8758	0.8643	0.8950	0.898	0.8656	0.8494	*0.87454*
K=4	0.8070	0.8019	0.8062	0.8295	0.8787	0.8603	0.846	0.8255	*0.83189*
K=5	0.7547	0.7954	0.7979	0.7995	0.8530	0.8321	0.8217	0.8231	*0.80968*
K=6	0.6929	0.7181	0.7266	0.7659	0.8374	0.8286	0.8208	0.8149	*0.77565*

Source: Adapted from Giannoccaro et al. 2018

by supplier interactions and SN performance. Further analysis is done with N = 14 and N = 16, and the results are shown in Table 8.6. This is to investigate the effect of SN complexity as indicated by the size of the supply network on the SN performance. As N goes from 14 to 18, SN performance tends to decrease. This analysis confirms the negative relationship between the size of supply networks and the SN performance.

Table 8.7   Supply Network Performance Difference Between K = 2 and K = 6

	Scope of Control								
	20%	33%	47%	60%	73%	80%	86%	93%	100%
Performance difference	24.74%	21.96%	20.71%	20.52%	17.87%	15.28%	16.21%	16.91%	16.07%

Source: Adapted from Giannoccaro, Nair, and Choi 2018

In Figure 8.9, the moderating effect of control on the association between complexity and performance is shown with +/-, which implies (1) the scope of control would help reduce the negative effect of complexity coming from interrelationships among companies (K) on performance, and (2) the scope of control would intensify the negative effect of complexity coming from the size of the network (N) on performance. Table 8.7 displays the differences in performance between K = 2 and K = 6 across the varying scope of control. We can clearly observe that the difference is affected by the scope of control. The difference of 15.28% as the lowest value appears at 80% of control, a moderately high scope of control. The difference of 24.74% as the highest value appears at 20%, a very low scope of control. In other words, when complexity is high due to high-level interrelationships, the moderately high scope of control helps reduce the negative effect of complexity on performance and leads to better performance results.

In Table 8.8, we show the differences in performance between N = 14 and N = 18 across varying levels of control at different values of interrelatedness and across four different levels of control. The negative impact of complexity clearly intensifies with the increasing scope of control at all values of K. The mean performance difference goes from, on average, 2.96% to 3.12%, 3.31%, and 5.65%, progressively.

With globalization, our supply networks have been increasing in complexity. More suppliers in distant parts of the world become dependent, which would have increased both K and N. Our study suggests, in this type of situation, a higher scope of control is more beneficial to supply network performance. With high K and N, the landscape becomes more rugged with multiple peaks. Therefore, it becomes necessary, at least in theory, for the focal company to expand its scope of control to help overcome the local peaks. However, it would also be necessary to modularize the supply networks so that the scope of control does not become excessive and remain

Table 8.8 Supply Network Performance Difference
Between N = 14 and N = 18

	Level of Control			
	23%	46%	62%	100%
K=2	4.84%	4.70%	5.29%	9.44%
K=3	4.45%	4.60%	5.89%	7.58%
K=4	3.67%	4.48%	3.10%	6.81%
K=5	1.68%	0.12%	2.17%	2.83%
K=6	0.18%	1.72%	0.11%	1.59%
Mean	*2.96%*	*3.12%*	*3.31%*	*5.65%*

Source: Adapted from Giannoccaro, Nair, and Choi 2018

at the moderate level. We will consider modularizing supply network in the next section where we consider jury-rigging of supply networks.

Jury-Rigging and Intertwined Supply Networks

The COVID-19 pandemic imposed tremendous pressure on supply networks. People now commonly talk about how fragile our supply chains are. As discussed in Chapter 1, recent events have placed pressure on our supply networks in ways we did not anticipated. Clearly, supply networks have been operating far from equilibrium. We have learned how the responses of supply networks can be mismatched to external stimuli.

On the bright side, we have seen evidence of how supply networks can be adaptive and remain resilient. During the COVID-19 outbreak, we witnessed jury-rigging (Kauffman et al. 2018) in supply networks to cope with the descending Unk-Unk. When hospitals ran out of ventilators, the automotive supply network was rewired to produce ventilators. In essence, the automotive supply network was used for a different purpose than the one it was designed for. It was jury-rigged to become intertwined (Ivanov and Dolgui 2020) with the medical supply network. The intertwining of the two otherwise disparate supply networks showed how our supply networks could adapt to changing conditions brought on by an unexpected event.

Such jury-rigging did not happen naturally. It happened at the behest of the U.S. government, putting pressure on three U.S.-based automakers to start making ventilators and Hanes Inc. to tweak its supply network and make face masks. There have been other governmental interventions in different parts of the world. When COVID-19 caused big buying companies to hold on to their cash by stretching out the payment terms to their suppliers, the Australian government pressed these big companies to pay suppliers more quickly, ultimately helping its supply networks to remain viable (Hofmann et al. 2021). When its automakers struggled to acquire needed semiconductor parts, the German government contacted the Taiwanese government to strike a bartering deal—semiconductors for vaccines. Taiwan needed more vaccines, and Germany needed more semiconductors. Both governments subsequently tried to capitalize on their assets for their own interest—Taiwan with TSMC and Germany with BioNTech. It appears that when Unk-Unks happen, the role of government becomes significant.

Therefore, it would make sense to study more deeply the role of jury-rigging and its impact on supply network adaptivity. Potentially, it can help policymakers consider jury-rigging as a way to prepare their supply networks for Unk-Unks. Researchers have pointed to the possibility of building ex ante adaptive features into the system (Ivanov and Dolgui 2020; S. Kauffman et al. 2018; Zhao, Zuo, and Blackhurst 2019). The idea is to build jury-rigging capability in supply networks, so they can behave more adaptively when an Unk-Unk occurs. One way jury-rigging can be utilized during an Unk-Unk is to rewire different supply networks for purposes they were not intended for. Such rewiring would often lead to what Ivanov and Dolgui (2020) call the intertwining of supply networks. In this chapter, we investigate the adaptivity of intertwined supply networks from the perspective of jury-rigging.

To do that, we adopt a computer simulation approach using a modified Kauffman's (1993) NKC computational model. N, K, and C denote, respectively, how many decisions an agent makes, how dense interactions are among the decision choices, and how intense interdependencies are among the agents. The NKC model is an extended version of the NK model. It has been adopted by Ganco and Agarwal (2007) to investigate competitive relationships of companies at the industry level, by Ganco, Kapoor, and Lee (2020) to analyze innovative processes of firms by developing a rugged ecosystem, and by McKelvey (1999) to model the co-evolution of firms. The NK simulation itself has been instrumental in investigating how the complexity of strategies affects imitation behaviors of firms (Rivkin 2000), how the turbulence and complexity of the business environment influence the design of organizations (Siggelkow and Rivkin 2005), and whether embedded buyer-supplier relationships are advantageous or disadvantageous (Sting, Stevens, and Tarakci 2019). For a thorough review of the application of NK models, please see Baumann, Schmidt, and Stieglitz (2019). Building on these studies, our modified NKC model is designed to analyze how companies as buyers and suppliers work together in a supply network. We modify the NKC model to study how different supply networks work across each other and create a rugged supply network landscape.

Figure 8.11 illustrates one example in regards to how two supply networks may be jury-rigged together into an intertwined supply network. As mentioned earlier, automotive and medical equipment supply networks came together during the pandemic to produce increasing demands for ventilators (https://techcrunch.com/2020/04/05/tesla-shows-how-its-build ing-ventilators-with-car-parts/; https://www.testandmeasurementtips.com/ can-you-really-make-a-respiratory-ventilator-in-a-car-factory/; https:// www.theverge.com/2020/4/15/21222219/general-motors-ventec-ventilat ors-ford-tesla-coronavirus-covid-19). In Figure 8.11, we can see how the two

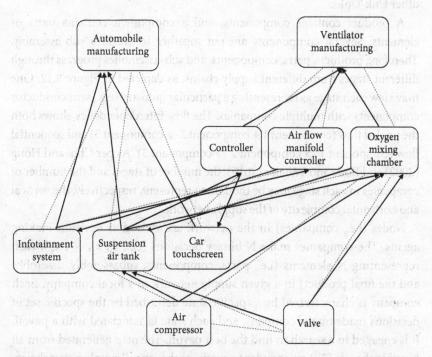

Figure 8.11 Jury-Rigged Ventilator Supply Network
Source: Adapted from Feizabadi, Gligor, and Choi 2021

networks were intertwined. On the right side of the figure, we see the ventilator supply network and how the critical components from that supply network are being fed into the automotive supply network. The arrows signify
the flow of materials, and the broken lines represent technology relations. The
two supply networks have shared mechanical and electronic technologies.
The automotive manufacturers (i.e., Ford, GM, and Tesla) found ways to integrate their supply networks with ventilator supply networks and produced
additional ventilators for the welfare of society under duress.

In this example, we see both pooled flow and sequential flow. The pooled
flow is shown by the air compressor and valve flowing into the suspension air
tank and oxygen mixing chamber. The sequential flow is shown by the suspension air tank into the oxygen mixing chamber and then to the ventilator
manufacturing. They show how two supply networks can be jury-rigged to
create a symbiotic outcome in a way they were not originally intended. It was
an ex post response to the impending supply network disruption due to an
Unk-Unk (i.e., onslaught of the pandemic). Our study builds on this example
to consider what ex ante capability may be developed in supply networks for
other Unk-Unks.

A product contains components, and a component contains parts or
elements. Several components are put together to create a sub-assembly.
Therefore, products, parts, components, and sub-assemblies progress through
different stages from different supply chains, as depicted in Figure 8.12. One
may view each stage as representing a particular industry (e.g., semiconductor
component) with multiple companies. The flow interdependency shows both
the pooled flow (component 1 + component 2 -> component 3) and sequential
flow (component 1 -> component 2 -> component 3). As per Choi and Hong
(2002) and Bode and Wagner (2015), the number of stages and the number of
companies in each stage may be thought to represent, respectively, the vertical
and horizontal complexity of the supply network.

Nodes (i.e., companies) in the network are viewed as decision-making
agents. The companies make N binary decisions (i.e., x_1, x_2, . . . x_N), each
representing N elements (i.e., parts, components, subassembly, assembly,
and the final product) in a given supply network of a focal company. Each
company is characterized by a specific state described by the specific set of
decisions made by the company, and each state is associated with a payoff.
It is engaged in a search to find the best payoff. The map generated from all
possible choices (2^N) on attendant payoffs, or the overall supply network performance, is called the fitness landscape. Each choice interacts with K other

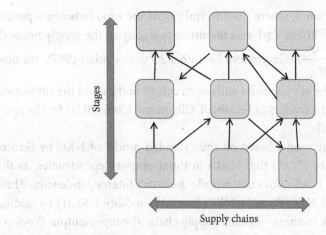

Figure 8.12 Basic Supply Network Model
Source: Adapted from Feizabadi, Gligor, and Choi 2021

choices; in other words, K reflects how each decision affects the performance change given its interaction with another decision. Representing how dense interactions are among the decision choices, K controls the complexity a company faces in its decision-making process.

In regards to stages and supply chains, C refers to the density of interactions across stages, and Cs refers to the density of interactions across supply chains. As noted earlier, K reflects the performance change (i.e., marginal benefit or cost) of a decision element in a company given changes in K elements in a component. In the same way, C and Cs also reflect the performance changes of a decision element across the components in multiple stages and across the supply chains, respectively. C captures the interdependencies of components within a supply chain across multiple stages, and Cs capture the technological interdependencies across multiple supply chains. One may view C to occur in the buyer-supplier relationship context and Cs to occur in the supplier-supplier relationship context. The fundamental difference between K and C and Cs is that while K is something that a company can control (i.e., K elements in a component), C and Cs span across components and entail interdependencies that undergo co-evolution beyond the control of a company.

The adaptiveness of the companies and supply chains in a supply network is captured by the height of the peak in the fitness landscape. The average mortality probability is used as a measure of the viability of companies and supply chains. The mortality probability is computed by subtracting the

survival rate from 1, where the survival rate is the ratio between a particular company's fitness (ψ) and the fittest company in the supply network
(ψ_{max})(*i.e.*, $1-\dfrac{\psi}{\psi_{max}}$) (Gavetti and Levinthal 2000; Levinthal 1997). We now
have covered the key variables and constructs to understand the simulation
results. I refer the readers to Feizabadi, Gligor, and Choi (2021) for the computational details.

We build our model based on the extended model of NKC by Ganco,
Kapoor, and Lee (2020) that works in input-output dependencies, as the
standard NKC model does not include the flow's interdependencies. Their
model is called NKC(f), as in NKC(flow). We modify NKC(f) by adding
supply network features—in each supply chain, the input-output flows are
modeled as being pooled where stage1 + stage2 -> stage3. This information
is important to understand the simulation experiments described in the
next paragraph. In our model, adaptations by companies occur either locally as a within-component search or more globally within and across their
supply chains. The former is equivalent to refining the knowledge within
the component, and the latter resonates with recombining the knowledge through replacing the components (Lee and Alnahedh 2016). In this
sense, the cross-component adaptation may be referred to as the distance
chunky search and recombination (Baumann and Siggelkow 2013; Ethiraj
and Levinthal 2004), and it can occur within a supply chain or across the
supply chains. In particular, the adaptation across the supply chains closely
corresponds to jury-rigging through which companies collaborate to respond to an Unk-Unk by rewiring the components of diverse companies in
the supply network.

The simulation model has two experiments, each of which entails two
supply chains and three stages. The two experiments entail one without jury-
rigging (Experiment I) and another with jury-rigging (Experiment II). Each
experiment considers two supply chains to see how different supply chains
can be integrated and three stages to reflect the progression of the product
formation. The simulation is run for 200 time periods and goes through 300
runs. The adaptiveness of companies in each stage and each supply chain is
averaged over all companies in the network first, and then they are averaged
over all time periods, which are then averaged over simulation runs.

Table 8.9 offers results that compare the adaptiveness of a supply network
without jury-rigging (Experiment I) and one with jury-rigging (Experiment
II) across three stages. As the level of interdependencies increases (i.e.,

Table 8.9 Average of Company's Adaptiveness

		$C_s=0$	$C_s=1$	$C_s=2$	$C_s=3$	$C_s=4$
Experiment I	Stage 1	0.0815	0.1114	0.1358	0.1493	0.1563
	Stage 2	0.0630	0.0850	0.1067	0.1176	0.1229
	Stage 3	0.0552	0.0735	0.0920	0.1004	0.1042
Experiment II	Stage 1	0.0795	0.1118	0.1354	0.1490	0.1561
	Stage 2	0.0604	0.0846	0.1054	0.1165	0.1228
	Stage 3	0.0522*	0.0727*	0.0912*	0.0996*	0.1036*

* Two-sample mean difference t-tests at Stage 3 are significant at $p<0.05$
Source: Adapted from Feizabadi, Gligor, and Choi 2021

increasing Cs levels), adaptiveness decreases in both supply networks, confirming our earlier reasoning. Increasing Cs means the state of increasing intertwining between two supply networks. The fitness landscape has become more rugged, and the height of the peaks get lowered. Comparing the two experiments, the fitness scores are higher and more significant for the jury-rigged supply network compared to the one without jury-rigging. As suspected, the collective adaptiveness is higher for the jury-rigged supply network compared to the baseline supply network without jury-rigging. In a jury-rigged network, there would be a higher number of companies that can respond to an Unk-Unk event in the environment.

Table 8.10 compares the mortality rates between the two experiments. The clear pattern between the two networks is that the supply network with jury-rigging shows significantly lower mortality rates across different levels of Cs. This observation aligns with the adaptiveness pattern we see in Table 8.9. However, at a high level of Cs, the difference in the mortality rates seems to diminish between the two networks (i.e., 0.0006 difference at Cs = 4). It suggests that as complexity increases, the positive effects of jury-rigging may be reduced. One possible explanation is that complexity and environmental turbulence may shift the adaptive space into a chaotic range (Boisot and Mckelvey 2010).

In Tables 8.9 and 8.10, Cs = 0 and Cs = 1 show the best performance. Since Cs = 0 is unrealistic, we observe that Cs = 1 is best, and the following levels of Cs show diminishing performance outcomes. This observation aligns with modularity principles (Baldwin and Clark 2000; Ethiraj and Levinthal 2004) in that, given the inevitability of interdependencies across supply chains, containing them in modularized supply networks would yield better performance. As

Table 8.10 Average of Company's Mortality Rate

		$C_s=0$	$C_s=1$	$C_s=2$	$C_s=3$	$C_s=4$
Experiment I	Stage 1	0.7298	0.7108	0.6735	0.6413	0.6227
	Stage 2	0.7179	0.6995	0.6625	0.6305	0.6106
	Stage 3	0.7040	0.6874	0.6532	0.6231	0.6074
Experiment II	Stage 1	0.7304	0.7115	0.6729	0.6413	0.6229
	Stage 2	0.7200	0.7009	0.6628	0.6302	0.6105
	Stage 3	0.7069*	0.6898*	0.6552*	0.6248*	0.6083*

* Two-sample mean difference t-tests at Stage 3 are significant at $p<0.05$
Source: Adapted from Feizabadi, Gligor, and Choi 2021

Table 8.11 List of Key Lessons

Key Lessons
1   A supply network with jury-rigging capability has a higher ex ante adaptiveness at the collective level
2   At the organizational level, a company in a jury-rigged supply network would ex ante garner more adaptiveness.
3   A supply network with jury-rigged capability would show a comparatively lower mortality rate
4   As the level of connectivity increases among companies, the adaptive effect of jury-rigging would diminish
5   The interdependencies in intertwined supply networks should be designed modularly and follow the concept of nearly decomposable system

attested by Choi, Dooley, and Rungtusanatham (2001), modularization helps reduce interdependencies among companies in a supply network. It combines many small peaks in the rugged landscape into a few large peaks, which leads to increased fitness performance. Here, the concept of "near-decomposability" (Simon 1962) may be applicable. One example of near decomposability comes from a modularized product, where the interactions within each module are more significant than those across the modules. The interdependencies should be reduced when considering C and Cs. Naturally, one should favor placing interactions within the control of a company (i.e., K), following the concept of modularity and near decomposability. That means the density of interdependencies within a subsystem (e.g., component or sub-assembly) should be much higher than the density across subsystems (e.g., supply chains), consistent with the concept of near decomposability. This observation has an important implication to re-optimize the just-in-time (JIT) supply chains post-pandemic in contrast to the growing tendency to practice just-in-case (JIC) inventory (Sodhi and Choi 2022), and we will address this issue in the next chapter. Table 8.11 presents a summary of the key lessons from Feizabadi, Gligor, and Choi (2021).

Key Points

- A supply network is a complex adaptive system (CAS) that emerges over time with no single entity (i.e., a focal company) orchestrating its entire activities.
- How much of that supply network to control should be a strategic decision made by a focal company.
- A supply network as a CAS, its environment, and the co-evolution of the supply network and its environment form a tripartite relationship in which all three are interdependent.
- Events happen in a supply network that are beyond the control and visibility of the actors involved.
- The supply chain as a network is relative to a particular product and agent and is bound by the visible portion of the network.
- Jury-rigging is instrumental in reducing fragility and increasing resilience in supply networks when facing an unknown-unknown (Unk-Unk) event like the COVID-19 pandemic.
- A computer simulation using cellular automata (CA) informs us how persistent cooperative behaviors can happen even in a supply network dominated by defection behaviors.
- An empirically informed, agent-based simulation using Kauffman's NK fitness landscape framework informs us that a moderate level of control scope should be favored over controlling too much (i.e., all of the supply network) or too little (i.e., just the first-tier supplier).
- A modified Kauffman's NKC simulation informs us that a supply network with jury-rigging capability has higher ex ante adaptiveness at the collective level.

9

Emerging Topics

The goal of this chapter is to introduce a few emerging topics related to supply networks. These topics come purely from my perspective and some current and recent projects I have been working on. They are not meant to be an exhaustive list. Some of them may have been mentioned in preceding chapters, but many are new topics that have not yet been covered in this book. Even for those topics that may have been previously discussed, we will pay closer attention to their implications for future research. As we consider each topic, I will note which of the preceding chapters might be relevant and how some concepts covered in earlier chapters may be expanded further.

Most of the topics included in this chapter derive from my experience working for CAPS Research (https://www.capsresearch.org/). CAPS Research is a joint venture research organization of the W. P. Carey School of Business at Arizona State University (https://wpcarey.asu.edu/) and the Institute for Supply Management (https://www.ismworld.org/). It is a nonprofit research organization catering to the chief procurement officers (CPOs) of Fortune 500–type companies (i.e., organizations of $2 billion or above in annual revenue). CAPS Research was established in 1986, and I served as executive director for five years, from 2014 to 2019.

My primary job was to interact with the CPOs of these major organizations and crystallize the most pressing issues they faced. The CPOs that served as chair of the Advisory Board during my service were Christie Breves of U.S. Steel, David Hammerle of Bechtel, and Dan Carrell of IBM. The total membership was about 115 companies, and the board had about 25 members. We would often talk about the issues that kept them awake at night. I would then help turn those issues into research questions and sought out the most qualified researchers from across the world to work on them. Once the research is done, we would then file a research report and invite the researchers to present the findings at various meetings we offered (e.g., CPO Roundtable). Many of the most pressing issues have emerged from this process, such as supply chain financing, cybersecurity, supply chain data analytics, and so forth.

The Nature of Supply Networks. Thomas Y. Choi, Oxford University Press. © Thomas Y. Choi 2023.
DOI: 10.1093/oso/9780197673249.003.0009

A few other topics have come from my part-time affiliation with the Department of Industrial Economics and Technology Management at the Norwegian University of Science and Technology (NTNU) (https://www.ntnu.edu/iot). As an affiliate faculty member since 2016, I spent time with colleagues there discussing research ideas. Additional topics have come from my personal association with other researchers, and references are made as we cover each topic.

We begin by discussing incomplete contracts and how they can contribute to supply chain resilience. The discussion takes place in the dyadic context. We then reframe dyadic buyer-supplier relationships by looking inside the buyer as a node and the supplier as a node. The discussion remains in the dyadic context, except we look at what is happening inside each of the two nodes and the role of the individual level social networks in the buyer-supplier relationship. We also examine the impact of digitization on buyer-supplier relationships and the role of the supplier ecosystem. We then expand this discussion into supply chain digitization and digital supply chains and consider their differences and future research implications. Turning to fundamental structural issues in supply networks, we consider tetrads that consist of four nodes and their relationships. We point out unique network characteristics that exist in tetrads but not in triads. Then, recognizing the flow of capital as a critical area of supply chain management (SCM), we discuss supply chain financing (SCF) and how SCF can help small suppliers in the long tail of the supply chain. We continue our discussion on cybersecurity and the role of SCM in mitigating this burgeoning threat to organizations. We anticipate innovation to remain a critical topic in SCM. Therefore, we discuss how focal companies can find innovation in their supply chains. We refer to Austrian economics, which promotes entrepreneurialism and innovation. Lastly, we present modularization of supply networks as a way to instill more resilience in global supply chains. We refer back to the complex adaptive systems (CAS) theory (Choi, Dooley, and Rungtusanatham 2001; Kauffman 1996) and the idea of near decomposability in the context of complexity (Simon 1962).

Incomplete Contracts and Supply Chain Resilience

During the COVID-19 pandemic, we witnessed how supply chains worldwide shut down without warning. Supply chains appeared fragile, and many of us have been thinking about whether anything can be done to make them less fragile and more resilient. A common understanding underlying supply chain resilience is that the more efficient the supply chains are, the more fragile they are. We witnessed this during the early days of COVID-19 when companies operating on just-in-time (JIT) with minimal inventory started to shut down first—more on JIT later in this chapter.

Many of these companies grappled with rigidly worded contracts and faced limited options. In Cummins, Kauffman, and Choi's (2021) study, we promote the adoption of incomplete contracts to help companies gain more flexibility and resilience. The term "incomplete contracts" was first used in the Nobel Prize–winning work by Oliver Hart (see Hart and Moore 1988). The big point of departure is that, in practice, no matter how hard one tries, contracts are always incomplete. They cannot specify all eventualities. Therefore, we should try to accept incompleteness rather than avoid it. This point is in stark contrast to the current contracting paradigm that strives to make all contracts as air-tight as possible or, put differently, as complete as possible. So, we set forth two points to keep in mind—all contracts are incomplete, and we should embrace incompleteness.

Stuart Kauffman and I began discussing the implications of incomplete contracts while working on a paper that promotes jury-rigging for more adaptive supply networks (Kauffman et al. 2018) and how incomplete contracts could support jury-rigging activities (see Chapter 9). When the COVID-19 pandemic struck in early 2020, we began thinking more seriously about how incomplete contracts could potentially improve supply chain resilience. Then, we invited Tim Cummins, president of the World Commerce and Contracting Association (https://www.worldcc.com/), who is well acquainted with the work of Oliver Hart, to join us to provide his expertise in contracting.

Our initial thoughts were that if we could successfully implement incomplete contracts, companies at the buyer-supplier interface might be able to operate with more flexibility and reduce local failures, which would make the entire supply network more resilient. Here is one example that demonstrates how exact specifications, promoted in complete contracts, could lead to the fragility of supply chains. Many of us recall the significant toilet paper shortage during the early days of the coronavirus outbreak. What we did not know is that, at the time, toilet paper for industrial use was in abundant supply, which would make sense because companies were shutting down and people stopped going to work. In the consumer's mind, toilet paper had to be in certain dimensions and materials, as would be dictated by the complete contract paradigm. However, if consumers would relax their requirements for dimensions and materials and focus more on functionality, we might not have experienced the breakdown in the toilet paper supply chain.

In the same way, if a contract specifies an exact number of laptops with a particular type of CPUs, the supply chain has to comply with those specifications. If the supplier runs into a problem getting the required CPUs, then the supply chain will be broken. In contrast, if the contract specifies broadly how the laptop should work, then the supplier has more leeway regarding how it might put together laptops for its customer. Of course, for this type of arrangement to work, the buyer and supplier must have mutual trust and share a common value system.

Two examples are shown in Table 9.1 as to how incomplete contracts could work. Over the years, we have observed how Japanese automobile manufacturers appear to use what we would call incomplete contracts. During one of my visits to Honda, a manager showed me what he called an overall contractual agreement with their strategic suppliers. It was basically a one-paragraph statement that said, "We will work together." That kind of verbiage offered Honda and its suppliers more flexibility as they worked together (see Chapter 3). When I shared what I saw at Honda with my contacts at Toyota, they told me Toyota uses similar types of contracts. As evidence, when a fire broke out at a Toyota's supplier plant called Aisin Seiki and its manufacturing line went down, that supplier and other suppliers voluntarily came together to address the problem (Nishiguchi and Beaudet 1998). These suppliers made decisions and took action without worrying about the exact contractual terms about what could be done and what could not. They were not concerned about the compensation for their effort. Their focus was on ensuring the continuity of supply to Toyota and, thereby, keeping their supply chain resilient.

Table 9.1 Examples of Incomplete Contracts

Types	Characteristics
Buyer-supplier work agreement	• A short, signed document that says "We will work together" • Voluntary mobilization of suppliers during a crisis
Community-supported agriculture (CSA) agreement	• Early commitment of consumers • Consumers remain open to types of vegetables • Local farmers gauge the needs of consumers • Local farmers deliver freshest vegetables available

Another example comes from closer to home. Some of us sign up for a community-supported agriculture (CSA) agreement (see www.localharvest. org/csa/). When we go to a grocery store, we typically know what kind of vegetables we want. Depending on what dish we want to prepare, we might require a certain amount of cabbage, broccoli, brussels sprouts, and so on. However, if the store is out of brussels sprouts, we would not be able to prepare the dish we wanted, and the brussels sprouts supply chain would appear broken to us. However, if we are open to trying other types of dishes, then we could buy other vegetables that are available. A CSA agreement would ask the consumers to be flexible on what they get. It calls for a high-level agreement that says the consumers would take whatever fresh vegetables the local farmers could deliver, and they would commit to that agreement by making payment upfront. Therefore, when consumers agree to a CSA, the farmers receive an early inflow of cash and learn about the consumer preferences without exact specifications as to what and how much. Consumers get fresh vegetables on a regular basis in return for being flexible on the type and quantity of vegetables available. For CSA to work, of course, the consumers and farmers have to share a common value system.

I believe this is an important area to consider if we are interested in looking into what practices might create more supply chain resilience. How can incomplete contracts be implemented in supply chains? Oliver Hart speaks of residual rights, addressing the issue of disputes that might occur even among those that share a common value system. With incomplete contracts, the current legal system might not be appropriate. Could we set up ex ante a third-party organization that could mitigate disputes? What would this look like in supply chains? We anticipate that more functional activities in supply chains might be getting on smart contracts that require exact terms and conditions. How can we integrate the concept of incomplete contracts into the implementation of smart contracts?

Roots of Buyer-Supplier Relationships

To establish a working buyer-supplier relationship, a buying company has to make a buy decision, and a qualified supplier has to be willing to provide what the buying company requires (see Chapter 3). Once a contract is established, the work begins. The supplier does its part, and the buyer receives the shipment and should pay the supplier on time. In that process, the buyer and supplier would communicate how the work is progressing, solve problems together, and may implement technologies at the interface, such as electronic data interchange (EDI). A relationship develops over time. In this context, the buyer-supplier relationship is portrayed as something that exists between two organizations.

We pose the question of whether buyer-supplier relationships are actually defined more by what is within each organization rather than in between. In an article by Andersen, de Boer, and Choi (2022), we propose that we need to understand the person-to-person network (i.e., social network) within the organizations of the buyer and supplier to really gauge how strong the relationship is between the two organizations. We refer to the social networks of individual workers internal to each organization as *the roots of buyer-supplier relationships*. Such intra-organizational network would feed the relationship between two companies and help stabilize the company-level, buyer-supplier relationship.

We begin with a simple observation. Suppose there is a strong personal connection between a procurement manager at the buying company and a sales manager at the supplier company. They communicate closely and trust each other regarding the details of transactions that occur between their two companies. On the surface, there appears to be a close buyer-supplier relationship. However, if one of the two managers were to leave the company and another person stepped into the position, then the personal rapport is gone, and the close buyer-supplier relationship no longer exists. We hear about situations like this from our contacts in the industry. The two individuals had a certain level of understanding, were enthusiastic about the working relationship, and looked forward to a long-term engagement. However, when one of the two leaves the company, the other person is left holding the bag. With the new person as a replacement, the enthusiasm wanes, and many verbal agreements about the working relationship need to be revisited.

Unless there is an underlying network internal to the company at multiple levels that supports the relationship, the close buyer-supplier relationship at the company level would be tenuous. In this regard, the social network that exists *within* the organizations needs to be considered carefully to establish the relationship that exists *between* the two organizations. If the two companies in a buyer-supplier arrangement want to make their relationship less dependent on individual-level relationships, for example, between a procurement manager and a sale manager, they would need a supportive

Table 9.2 Managing the Roots of Buyer-Supplier Relationship

Areas of Focus	Descriptions
Constituent elements	• Coherent, evolving, and semi-permanent network of individuals • Documents and other supporting data
Structural factors	• How deep in the organization • How wide in the organization
Supporting functions at the Interface	• Continuity of buyer-supplier relationships • Conflict resolution • Communications ensures future co-prosperity
Management tools	• Interview workers to identify key actors • Social network analysis to identify quantitatively the stars, peripherals, and cliques

Source: Adapted from Andersen, de Boer, and Choi 2022

network inside each company and multiple connections (i.e., multiplexity) between the two companies. Table 9.2 offers an overview.

A Korean supplier attempts to ensure its relationship with its buying company in Italy will not be dependent on a single sales manager from its side. The supplier is a brand mobile phone manufacturer, and the buying company is a telecommunications company. This supplier notes that there is high turnover among the sales staff, and, therefore, it needs to involve other managers when interfacing with its Italian customer. These other managers may come from marketing, operations, and even engineering. When the meetings are arranged, either in person or online, the supplier makes sure multiple people from its side are present so the two companies can work across multiple levels. The supplier notes that they involve their top executives when the situation calls for it. Therefore, the extent to which the roots might grow entail how deep and wide they go within the organization.

Such roots would ensure the relationship is not dependent on one or a few individuals. Many joint meetings at various levels would be held to resolve conflicts and to communicate how the two companies could grow together. As discussed earlier, Honda holds buyer-supplier meetings at different levels—functional level and executive level (see Chapter 3). Managers from both sides discuss some of the common transactional problems they face at the functional level and the future strategic directions and requisite technologies at the executive level.

In this regard, it is helpful to study intra-organizational social networks and their structural patterns and how they support the buyer-supplier relationship. Different network topologies and the types and levels of multiplexity affect what happens between two organizations over time. The data on intra-organizational social networks can be collected through interviews to identify central individuals. A social network analysis at the company level can be conducted to engage in more quantitative analyses to identify central and peripheral individuals and whether there might be any cliques within the company. Chapter 7 introduced conducting a social network analysis with the organizations as nodes, but the analysis can also be done with individuals as nodes.

Future studies can take on such research to examine the conceptual and empirical connections between the social network characteristics within organizations and how they support buyer-supplier relationships at the company interface. Further, there are implications to transaction cost economics (TCE) (see Chapter 2). TCE looks at the governance costs and transaction costs. Comparing these two types of costs allows organizations to decide whether to make or buy. However, as far as the maintenance and operation of the roots are concerned, there is an extended transaction cost associated with the buy decision. A buying firm would incur costs to ensure the continuity of a buyer-supplier relationship by building the roots within its organization. A future study may look at this overlooked issue by considering the roots of buyer-supplier relationships and the associated transaction cost over time.

Digitization and Supplier Ecosystem

Earlier in Chapter 5, we discussed the supplier ecosystem. Building on research done at CAPS Research (Wiengarten 2019), we made a counterintuitive observation. Companies with *less* mature supplier ecosystems see benefits mainly in the strategic areas, whereas companies with *more* mature supplier ecosystems see benefits in both the operational and strategic areas. Traditional thinking would have us believe operational benefits come first and then strategic benefits. What we saw was just the opposite—strategic benefits (i.e., innovation) came first, and then operational benefits (i.e., quality and cost improvement) followed, and only the mature companies reaped the operational benefits.

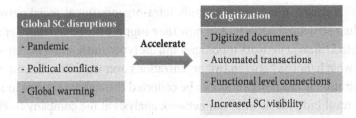

Figure 9.1 Accelerated Digitization
Source: Adapted from Choi et al., forthcoming

We now have a potential explanation for that counterintuitive observation. As noted previously, advancements in supply chain digitization and technology allow connectivity and improvements at the functional level. Such functional-level advancements would offer operational benefits. It is more likely that companies with more mature supplier ecosystems would be associated with more advanced supply chain digitization. Clearly, supply chain digitization is afoot, and its implementation has accelerated during the pandemic and because of global warming and political conflicts. In Chapter 1, we articulated these macro-level issues and how supply chain disruptions have become more frequent. In Figure 9.1, adapted from Choi, de Boer, and Andersen (forthcoming), we list pandemics, political conflicts, and global warming as drivers of accelerated supply chain digitization.

During the pandemic, there was an urgency to digitize documents for fear of spreading the virus. In some countries like Japan, where seal stamps are still being widely used on documents, there was a push toward digitizing documents and the approval process, so people did not have to meet physically. In particular, for shipping companies and freight forwarders, workers were reluctant to handle physical documents, so the pressure to digitize was immense. Of course, in general, employees began to work remotely from home, so the overall work environment became more digital. For example, rather than meeting in person, workers began meeting on virtual platforms. Further, the contents of these virtual meetings (i.e., Zoom meetings) would be digitized for subsequent access rather than printed on paper for distribution.

To minimize physical handling and traveling in person, many processes are being automated between the buyer and its suppliers. Many companies started to look into implementing a robotic process automation (RPA) that digitizes and automates the transactional work in the procure-to-pay (P2P) cycle. Further, looming supply chain disruptions are accelerating the pace of implementation. A Japanese bank operating in the U.S. adopted smart contracts with a U.S.-based cloud service provider. When the performance of its cloud service goes below a certain level, the service provider is automatically alerted. If the warranty agreement allows some compensation back to the bank per the terms of the smart contract, that is done automatically using the company tokens. Also, we see increasing use of digital twins, which is a virtual model of a unique physical object, such as a container with a cooling unit. It simulates the physical state of the container by tracking its location, temperature, and humidity. If the container is carrying fresh strawberries, such digitized information would be critical in pricing the value of the strawberries.

Notice that much of these automation processes occur at the functional level. In a CAPS Research report on emerging technologies for supply management, Gray, Prud'homme, and Barley (2019) highlight key technologies such as cloud computing, big data analytics, artificial intelligence (AI), RPA, conversational things, blockchain, additive manufacturing, internet of things (IoT), social media, and immersive technologies that are poised to make an impact on what we do in supply chain management. They also articulate how increasing functional-level connectivity would migrate supply management professionals away from transactional work and toward more strategic work. This would allow them to focus less on transactional work such as issuing purchase orders and reconciling numbers on invoices and receiving documents and more on strategic work such as managing emerging technology interfaces with suppliers and exercising leadership in supplier ecosystems (see Chapter 5). In this digitized environment, a major aerospace company is taking a supplier ecosystem approach and has instituted a supplier room in a virtual platform. Suppliers meet in this virtual room to engage in specific activities with their sales and pricing teams.

A supply management professional working with suppliers in supplier ecosystems would have to show different types of leadership, depending on where they were on the maturity curve. For instance, early on, a more charismatic leadership might be appropriate to rally the suppliers to collaborate toward a common goal. Later on, as suppliers become more used to exercising their autonomy, the leadership style might shift toward a distributed or team-based leadership, as discussed in Chapter 5. In other words, a major rescoping of the tasks performed by supply management professionals may be on the horizon, from interacting with suppliers for transactional activities to exercising leadership and engaging in strategic work. As such, moving forward, how digitization is changing the work performed by the supply management professional will need to be investigated further. For instance, one might investigate the behavioral and cognitive complexity required of supply management professionals by engaging in more technical and strategic work in the digitized environment. As shown herein, there is an association between leadership style and how an ecosystem should be managed. A new taxonomy of leadership may be developed, perhaps one that focuses on the evolving nature of leadership, as supply management professionals oversee the operation of supply ecosystems through the maturity curve (Wiengarten 2019).

Moreover, a supplier ecosystem can be used to reduce the overall complexity of global supply networks (Wiengarten, Choi, and Fan 2020). This aspect also requires further research—how the transfer of autonomy to suppliers might work out and how that would eventually reshape the global supply networks (see Chapters 7 and 8). Of particular interest might be the association between digitization and the complexity of supply networks (see Chapter 8). One potential area pertains to how digitization could help usher in the migration of supply networks toward nearly decomposable (Simon 1962) supply networks where we have densely connected clusters of companies linked by sparse connectivity. This could provide more supply network resilience in the digital space. This point is discussed in more detail later in this chapter under the section "Modularizing Global Supply Networks."

Supply Chain Digitization and Digital Supply Chains

Much of what we discussed in the preceding section on digitization is about *supply chain digitization*. Documents are digitized, and processes of transactions are digitized and automated. Materials and services that flow through the supply chain may be better tracked and monitored. In contrast, *digital supply chains* mean something entirely different. The product or service is configured digitally, and customer needs are fulfilled through digital means (Jeong, Oke, and Choi 2022). Examples are online artwork and online games. Non-fungible token (NFT) artworks are being traded digitally on blockchain platforms, and online games are being played among many users across the globe. The case of digital twins introduced in the previous section might be considered something in-between supply chain digitization and digital supply chain. The physical flow in a supply chain is digitized (i.e., movement of a shipment), and then necessary information is processed digitally (i.e., information is provided to the user in a digital form).

In supply chain digitization, supply chain activities are digitized into data, and decisions are made based on analyzing the data for better coordination (Handfield et al. 2017). Such data encompasses both structured and unstructured types. The structured data are those that reside in enterprise resource planning (ERP) systems, the kind that we can capture in a spreadsheet. The unstructured data take the form of text or pictures. They may be digitized, but they cannot be integrated with structured data and analyzed quantitatively. Examples are emails, social media postings, newsfeeds, company reports, and so on. As one might imagine, there are large amounts of unstructured data in supply chains. A general rule of thumb is that 80% of all data are in unstructured form. In this regard, future studies could examine how to bring structure to unstructured data in supply chain management. For example, what type of taxonomies would be most appropriate for spend analysis or risk management to organize unstructured data so they can be integrated with structured data, so both types of data can contribute to the overall data analysis?

Whether structured or unstructured, data are ubiquitous. Not too long ago, I visited a U.S.-based, major high-tech company and learned that people there thought 90% of the data the world has ever known was generated in the last two years, and they anticipated the amount of data to double every two years. Handfield et al. (2017) compile a number of claims that give us some idea about the enormity of the data that comes from the digital world. For instance, Facebook generates about 5 billion pieces of shared content daily, and Twitter posts about 6,000 tweets every second, which means 500 million tweets per day. The number of connected devices may amount to about 200 billion, and about 12 billion connections occur at the machine-to-machine level. Facing such large amounts of data with no limits, we find ourselves in the realm of big data in a digitized space.

The big question is how we can take advantage of all these data to help make better decisions. In Handfield, Jeong, and Choi's (2019) study, we point out that much of the analytic work is done through software platforms. A few leading vendors are Ariba, Coupa, Emptoris, Oracle, Watson, Zycus, and others (for more discussion on available software platform services on a timeline, see Handfield et al. 2017). Key areas of applications in these platforms include spend analysis, inventory, and supply chain risk. We also report the executive survey responses in terms of where they think they most need data analytics. These are spend analysis, price benchmarking, supplier performance management, and risk alerts. These could be considered key areas of executive decision-making.

One of my recent doctoral students, SK Jeong, introduced me to the idea of digital supply chains. As discussed above, the offerings are digitally configured, and the customer needs are met digitally. Online games are one context where a digital supply chain is in operation. Gone are the days when a few students would gather in the basement of a dormitory to play Galaga, an early video game, or when parents kept their children away from online games because they were considered a fringe activity. According to recent statistics (see https://www.cloudwards.net/online-gaming-statistics/), in 2021, the total revenue in the online game industry globally was $178.2 billion, and this number is expected to grow to close to $200 billion. Given the increases in connectivity and speed, this total revenue at the industry level is expected to grow continuously. In the U.S., 67% of adults play games, which is higher for younger players under 18 at 76%. In particular, 77% of millennials and 81% of Gen Z play games. They spend time playing, on average, about seven to eight hours a week. To support these consumers, the online gaming companies segment the consumers by genres, and the digital services are provided by digital supply chains, as depicted in Figure 9.2.

Jeong, Oke, and Choi (2022) describe a three-tier supply chain in the online gaming industry. Figure 9.2 shows, on the left side, how the service flow goes from service developer to service provider and to consumers (Tschang 2007). The service provider does the directing, financing, and distribution of games, and the service developer does the designing and production of the digital content of the game. For example, TERA: Fate of Arun is a highly successful

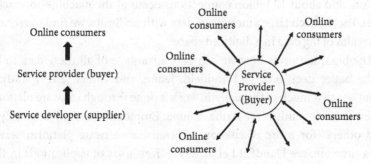

Figure 9.2 Digital Gaming Supply Network

online role-playing game that allows a massively large number of consumers to connect virtually and play together. As shown on the right side of Figure 9.2, the online consumers are connected through a hub-and-spoke structure with the service provider at the center. Individual consumers may play using their PlayStation or Xbox, but many use PC-service stores in places like South Korea where a local store owner provides the computer hardware. The service provider is a company called Nexon that published the game and operates it, and the service developer is Bluehole Inc., currently a subsidiary of Krafton. The buyer-supplier relationship management in this context is done through a profit-sharing arrangement between the service provider and the service developer. This type of arrangement may potentially offer a very interesting context to study a new form of buyer-supplier relationship (see Chapter 3).

A unique characteristic of digital supply chains is that any change in a competitor's service offering would be known to other competitors instantly (Jeong, Oke, and Choi 2022). Through the internet, they are all digitally connected. For example, if a service failure were to occur, all the other competitors in the same market would learn about that failure instantaneously. Consequently, they have a small window of time to respond and attempt to take away the consumers displaced by the failed offering. It is conceivable that we would also see a similar characteristic in the NFT industry, where sales are known instantly by others. Operating within blockchain technology, all transactions are immutable, and the trust among the suppliers and buyers (i.e., consumers) is built into the system. Therefore, how digital assets are created and traded as an NFT may be an interesting area of future studies in digital supply chains.

It remains to be seen how the *digitized* supply chains and *digital* supply chains might integrate, if at all. The idea of a digital twin offers some possibility, as it is a virtual capture of a physical supply chain for the purposes of testing, simulation, and monitoring. Perhaps, we may end up with digital twins that connect the real-world supply chains that have been digitized and the digital supply chains in the world of, shall we say, Metaverse, where the features of the real world are virtually represented.

Tetrads in Supply Networks

Shifting gear in this section, we turn to more fundamental structural issues in supply networks. A tetrad is created by adding one more node to a triad.

The importance of tetrads builds on the importance of triads. Choi and Wu (2009a) pose triads as the smallest unit of a network and argue if we accept that supply chains are networks, then we have to study triads (see Chapter 4). It was the first of three debate articles published in the *Journal of Purchasing and Supply Management*, and since that debate, there has been increased interest in studying triads in supply networks (Vedel, Holma, and Havila 2016). For example, the *Journal of Operations Management* dedicated a special issue on service triads (see Wynstra, Spring, and Schoenherr 2015). More recently, we see researchers using triadic configurations to study innovative projects (Patrucco et al. 2022), and a doctoral student just completed his dissertation on transportation triads (Eriksson 2021). At the very end of his dissertation, after having studied a triad including a wholesaler, construction company, and transportation company, Eriksson (2021) concludes, "no triad is an island" (p. 152), and I could not agree more. He is pointing squarely at the need to investigate tetrads.

As discussed earlier in Chapter 6, a tetrad becomes relevant when studying a network disturbed by an external source. That can be modeled as a triad (i.e., the smallest unit of the network) being intruded on by a disruptor (i.e., a new node). Durach, Wiengarten, and Choi (2020) consider how a buyer-supplier-supplier triad responds to a disruption from a second-tier supplier shared by first-tier suppliers. We observe that the supply chain resilience can operate in relation to its suppliers in the network. From a focal company's perspective, the capability for resilience may come from the suppliers and how they work together. Therefore, as shown in Figure 9.3 on the left side, we model the network as a buyer-supplier-supplier triad and the shared second-tier supplier as the source of disruption. In our study, the fourth that disrupts (i.e., a shared second-tier supplier) is not connected to the focal company.

It is still entirely possible that the disruptor can also be connected to the focal company. Consider, for instance, the context where the focal company is engaged in directed sourcing, as shown in Figure 9.3 on the right side (for a discussion on directed sourcing see Chapter 6). Beyond the study by Durach, Wiengarten, and Choi (2020), one potential research question is, what would happen if the focal company is engaged in directed sourcing in the relationship arrangement shown in Figure 9.3? We would then have a saturated tetrad, and the question becomes, how would the disruption at this directed sourced, second-tier supplier affect the triad under investigation? Future studies can consider many different configurations of how an external disruptor may impinge on a triad.

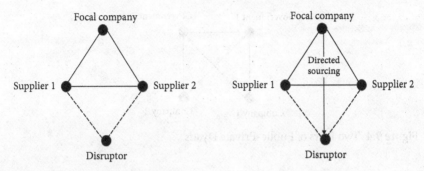

Figure 9.3 Triad with a Disruptor
Source: Adapted from Durach, Wiengarten, and Choi 2020

One important configuration that a tetrad can help us model is the *two-against-two* condition. In networks, subgroups or factions happen, and tetrad is the smallest network context that would allow us to study subgroups or factions. While triads can allow us to study two against one (Caplow 1968), tetrads can help us study two against two. For example, an ongoing research I am collaborating with the colleagues at National Taiwan University, Jiuh-Biing Sheu and Jason Choi, examines two pairs of public-private dyads in a tetradic context, where each pair contains a government and a private company. As discussed in Chapter 8, during the COVID-19 pandemic, Germany needed semiconductors, and Taiwan needed vaccines. As so happens, in Germany, there is BioNTech that can supply vaccines, and in Taiwan, there is TSMC that can supply semiconductors. One thing led to another, and the two governments got together and engaged in a bartering deal. We model this tetradic context in Figure 9.4. The two pairs face off each other while the deal is made at the governmental level. Once the deal is struck, the deliveries would be made as the arrows indicate. Our study focuses on optimizing conditions from TSMC's perspective. However, we could be looking at different types of tetradic contexts where relationships across the two pairs of subgroups are configured differently. For instance, all possible connections might be present as in a saturated tetrad (i.e., BioNTech and TSMC begin communicating directly), or only one connection may exist between the two pairs (i.e., both governments inform their own private company to deliver to them). Various scenarios can address different research questions.

Choi and Holmen (2023) make a case for tetrads. We first point out a fundamental issue regarding triads as conceived by Simmel (1950) in his balance theory (see Chapter 4 for an overview of balance theory). While useful in

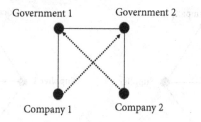

Figure 9.4 Two Pairs of Public-Private Dyads

explaining the underlying dynamics within triads, balance theory seems to assume there is equilibrium in triads. It theorizes how unbalanced triads are in disequilibrium and tend to migrate toward a balanced state in equilibrium (Choi and Wu 2009c).

However, networks are always in flux, and they are never in equilibrium. If triads are the smallest unit representing a network, then they need to go beyond a balanced state framed as an end state. In other words, a balanced triad would be disturbed if a fourth intruder is introduced, as modeled in Figure 9.3. Of course, a node in a balanced state can change its position in regards to how it views other nodes, and that could create disturbance even to a triad in a balanced state. However, we have learned how difficult it is to change an individual's personality or organization's culture. Choi and Holmen (2023) point out that a balanced triad would more likely get shaken up by the introduction of a fourth node as an intruder than by the changing of an inherent position by a node in a triad. If we accept this notion, then we have entered the territory of a tetrad.

A tetrad gives us the context where a network (triad) within a network (tetrad) happens. Additionally, in a tetrad, we can also study how factions or subgroups are formed in a network. Instead of two against one, we can study two against two. Two pairs may align themselves in a strong tie, with weak ties going across these two pairs. For example, in Figure 9.4, each government and its domestic company would be connected by a strong tie. If the governments run into problems during the bartering deal, the chances are they would more closely align with the company in their own country. That is how relationship arrangements will shake out in a two-against-two fashion. And there would be weak ties going across the two pairs of strong-tie relationships. Therefore, we submit that, just as triads offer the smallest unit to study networks, tetrads offer a context through which we could study network within a network, subgroups or factions as strong and weak ties play out in two against two, and other dynamic nature of networks in disequilibrium.

Supply Chain Financing and Deep-Tier Financing

Supply chain management is ultimately about sourcing, making, and delivering (see Chapter 2). To facilitate these activities, companies in the supply chain require capital. As such, Rogers, Leuschner, and Choi (2020) add one more to the three as a fourth leg—to fund. We argue, therefore, supply chain management should really be about to source, to make, to deliver, and to fund. We refer to funding in the supply chain as supply chain financing (SCF) as an area of study that investigates the movement of capital through supply networks. I think SCF holds much promise as a new research area that requires a multi-tier or supply network perspective (i.e., Yoo, Choi, and Kim 2021).

The supply chain capital or operating capital is different from other types of capital (i.e., debt or equity) in that a company does not have to gain approval from banks or a board of directors. It can be obtained by reducing costs in supply chains (see Chapter 3) or increasing revenue through supply chain innovation—more on this later in this chapter. Compared to debt or equity capital, it is less expensive and easier to obtain (Rogers, Leuschner, and Choi 2016a). SCF that focuses on supply chain capital is typically divided into two areas—pre-shipment (i.e., work-in-process inventory financing or purchase order financing) and post-shipment (i.e., dynamic discounting or reverse factoring). Some of these concepts were discussed in Chapter 6.

A new breed of companies that have emerged to facilitate SCF activities are called financial technology (fintech) companies (Rogers, Leuschner, and Choi 2016b). Large buying companies such as Apple, Colgate, Dell, Kellogg's, P&G, and Siemens are working with fintechs to help facilitate funding for their suppliers at these buying companies' lower cost of capital. A few of these fintech companies are C2FO, Orbian, PrimeRevenue, SAP Ariba, and Taulia. Fintechs are internet companies that act as a broker between buying companies, suppliers, and lending agencies with money (i.e., banks). An expanding role for these fintechs could offer a fruitful area of future research. For one, fintechs help reach small suppliers in the long-tail of the supply chain that are often overlooked in funding opportunities through SCF. They are engaged in what is commonly called the deep-tier financing

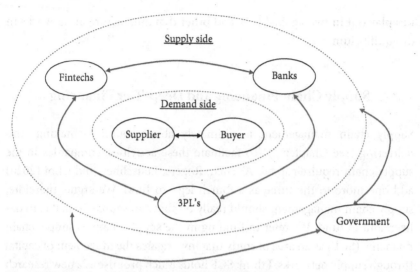

Figure 9.5 Key Supply Chain Financing Roles and Ties
Source: Adapted from Templar, Hofmann, and Findlay 2020

(DTF). I have been working on a research with my colleagues at University of St. Gallen in Switzerland, Erik Hofmann and Calvin Klein, on developing taxonomies of DTF.

As shown in Figure 9.5, the demand for SCF services is created by the transactions between the buyer and supplier. Both the buyer and its suppliers require funding to transact goods and services. That demand is met by fintechs, banks, and third-party logistics (3PLs) working together. Fintechs facilitate the flow of money, banks provide the capital, and 3PLs move goods. Governments, particularly through their central banks, monitor all their activities and set appropriate monetary policies.

At the core, buying companies are mainly interested in managing their cash flow and improving their cash conversion cycle (CCC). They extend payment terms to their suppliers, which helps improve their CCC. Of course, they are interested in keeping their suppliers financially healthy, and some may offer fintech-driven solutions to their suppliers (see Chapter 6). One such solution is dynamic discounting, which helps suppliers receive early payments from the buyer by offering a discount. At a glance, there may be nothing wrong with this arrangement. Suppliers were always willing to offer additional discounts for early payment from the buyer (i.e., 2/10 net 30), and the buyer is just scaling this process by working through a fintech (i.e., PrimeRevenue) that has a software platform through which discounting could occur dynamically given the needs of the supplier. However, there is a huge difference between a supplier voluntarily offering a discount to motivate the buyer to make a payment sooner than 30 days and a buyer unilaterally extending the payment terms to, say, 90 days and trying to get the supplier to offer discounts for early payment.

Now, let us look at this from the supplier's perspective. A supplier works hard to get a purchase contract from a buyer. It would require a series of meetings with the buying company and responding to a request for quotation (RFQ) or proposal (RFP). Once the supplier finally gets the contract, as the less resource endowed of the two parties engage in a transaction, it generally starts to fund the buyer by procuring necessary parts and raw materials and reserving capacity. It finishes the job and delivers the goods as agreed. It would also send an invoice. Often the invoice approval takes time, but once it is approved by the buyer, the supplier would then have to wait for the payment as per the agreed-upon payment term (i.e., net 60, 90, or 120 days). We say agreed payment terms, but often they are imposed by the buyer. As the supplier waits for the extended payment term, the buyer might offer an opportunity to participate in reverse factoring (see Chapter 6) or dynamic discounting. In dynamic discounting, the buyer is often the funder, meaning the buyer has cash to pay. This approach would improve the buyer's CCC, but it would likely create difficulties on the supplier's financial accounting.

At this point, we should ask a few simple questions. Is it fair for someone not to pay when the goods are delivered? I mean, when we purchase a cup of coffee or get a haircut, we pay at the point of service. It seems like a fair thing for the buyer to pay the supplier at the time of delivery. A 30-day net is understandable since the buying company has its own payment cycle, and it needs some time to facilitate the payment to the supplier. However, 60 days? 90 and 120?

Another question we might ask: Is it fair for someone to not pay when, in fact, they have the money to pay? This is what happens when the buying company extends the payment terms and asks the supplier to offer a discount to get paid, when it offers its suppliers dynamic discounting. More simple questions: Is it fair for someone to try to pay less than what was first agreed upon? Is it fair for less financially endowed suppliers to finance the more financially rich buyers? Many of these suppliers are small-to-medium enterprise (SME) suppliers that are essential to our economies. According to the U.S. Small Business Administration (https://www.sba.gov/), in 2019, SMEs represented 99.9% of all companies and employ 47.3% of the private sector workforce. In the European Union, SMEs with less than 250 employees represent 99.8% of all enterprises (https://ec.europa.eu/eurostat/de/web/produ cts-eurostat-news/-/EDN-20191125-1.%2009.09.2021). I believe we should raise these questions above in future studies, perhaps by taking the perspective of social justice. *Inequality* may be unavoidable in a capitalistic society, but we should be able to ensure *equity*.

During the pandemic, buyers delayed payments or stopped payments to conserve their own cash (Hofmann et al. 2021). The number of days in payment outstanding (DPO) expanded during the pandemic. Many of these suppliers turned to the fintechs. Demand for fintech services increased, and more banks got into the fintech business as they saw their cash management revenues were down and noticed an increased demand for their SCF services. Clearly, there is an asymmetric distribution of working capital across the supply chain, with SME's operating on the long tail of the supply chain (i.e., upstream side) being short-changed. They often struggle with insufficient working capital compared to those companies downstream closer to the consumer market. For example, SCF tools and techniques have mainly focused on first-tier suppliers and their buying companies.

Deep-tier financing is designed to help these SME suppliers several tiers removed from large buying companies. These large buying companies are often called "anchor companies" because they are known in the consumer market and are in a better position in terms of working capital. Also, their cost of capital is lower than that of SME suppliers. In collaboration with these anchor companies, fintechs leverage blockchain-based software platforms through which approved invoices are tokenized based on the anchor company's creditworthiness and placed on the platform. Participating SME suppliers can then be paid early from the tokenized, approved invoice. Alternatively, SME suppliers submit their accounts receivables to a fintech platform which would then create an electronic voucher. The voucher can flexibly be transferred within the platform, and those SME suppliers can acquire financing from funders. Some of the major fintech companies that operate in deep-tier financing are Centrifuge, Tallyx, Skuchain, Tradeshift, and Rootant.

Re-assessing the SCF practices from the supplier's perspective would be a fruitful area of future research. An executive at Citi Bank reminded me in a recent conversation that environment, social, and governance (ESG) issues are huge among investors now. Perhaps, the time is ripe for us to consider the effects of SCF practices on SME suppliers on the long tail of the supply chain.

We might even take the social justice perspective that compares equality and equity. Future research should address the dynamics involved in DTF and the role of technology and fintechs.

Cyber Threats Through Supply Networks

We have noted that cybersecurity problems are supply chain problems, with over 60% of all known cyber breach cases coming through the supply chain (Rogers and Choi 2018). In Chapter 5, we pointed out how C-level suppliers are more vulnerable to cyber threats compared to A-level or B-level suppliers in the supply base. Then, in Chapter 6, we delved deeper into cybersecurity issues and observed how the attacks come through weaker points (i.e., C-level suppliers) across the extended supply chain. We discussed a few prominent breach cases and how best to mitigate the cyber threats from a multi-tier perspective.

To wage a war against an enemy, the *Art of War* by Sun Tzu tells us to get to know the enemy first. Likewise, to wage war against cyber attackers, a CAPS Research report on cybersecurity poses that it is important to know who these cyber attackers are and what motivates them (Rogers, Benjamin, and Gopalakrishnan 2018). The report identifies three types of cyber attackers— financially driven attackers, ideologically driven attackers, and advanced persistent attackers. The financially driven attackers are most common. These attackers are not selective in terms of who they attack. They are indiscriminate. They look for low-hanging fruit and attack any company that is vulnerable. Once they are in, they steal its credentials and infiltrate, using the credentials of that company, other partnering companies that may be more resource rich. The ideologically driven attackers usually place little value on monetary returns from their attacks. Instead, they would put a premium on some ideological or political issues. For example, there are hacker activists, called hacktivists, who are motivated to protect the natural environment. One such group is Operation Green Rights, which engaged in various cyber-criminal operations. The advanced, persistent attackers are typically supported by a nation-state, often have access to military personnel, and have ample resources to carry out their attacks. This type of attacker potentially can pose a greater threat compared to the other two types. Detection is challenging for this type of attacker because, with deep-pocket resources, they can wage a long-term, clandestine campaign and even lay dormant for extended periods.

In a future study, it would be interesting to correlate different types of attackers and their behaviors regarding how they attack the supply chain. We have stated that cyber attackers generally look for weak links in the supply chain. Would all three types of attackers use this strategy? One type may prefer directly attacking a large focal company to obtain publicity. Also, it is conceivable that the attackers would prefer to stay close to the focal company they would eventually infiltrate. In other words, to minimize their risk of getting caught, they may not go too deep into the supply chain because it would take longer to reach the focal company. It would be interesting to conduct an empirical study to verify these potential tendencies.

Clearly, with the lasting effects of the pandemic and increased digitization, these attackers are expected to be more active. Cyber threats are going to be increasingly more severe with more grave consequences. In an on-going study I am currently involved in with SK Jeong at University of Tennessee and Zac Rogers at Colorado State University, cyberattacks increased by 40% immediately after the COVID-19 pandemic, which also drove increased digitization as discussed earlier in this chapter. The attacks first targeted individual employees working remotely from home. When companies implemented added security measures, such as two-factor log-in and the use of local area networks, the attacks shifted to the suppliers providing these services. So, it is not surprising that in a recent Dun & Bradstreet report (https://www. dnb.com/perspectives/supply-chain/resilient-supply-chain-infographic. html), supply chain executives ranked the complexity of globalization and cybersecurity risks as their top-of-mind concerns. Nearly all executives who responded said they have some cybersecurity measures in their supplier evaluation.

Still, many focal companies are learning to cope with these threats. How Maersk dealt with a cyberattack offers a good illustration of the company's jury-rigging capability. In Chapter 8, we discussed how technologies and other means of combatting disruptions could be jury-rigged to address emerging needs as the situation calls for. Maersk overcame a cyberattack by jury-rigging its IT-communication infrastructure. In 2017, Maersk fell victim to the NotPetya attack at the cost of $300M in damages (https://www. wired.com/story/notpetya-cyberattack-ukraine-russia-code-crashed-the-world/). The whole system at the company level went down, and a ransom was demanded. The company decided not to give in to the cyber attackers; instead, they jury-rigged the resources they had without their normal IT infrastructure. Maersk resorted to an offline server with shipping information and utilized text messaging on the workers' individual smartphones as the mode of communication operating across different nodes in its supply network. The company bought enough time to reboot its system, and it eventually succeeded in fending off the threat. So, with digitization, there will be an additional risk of cyberattacks, but, at the same time, there may be additional ways to jury-rig as potential disruptions materialize. This would be an interesting avenue to study in future research.

Finding Innovation in the Supply Chain

When we discussed the embedded nature of buyer-supplier relationships in Chapter 3, we singled out the gracious relationship as the most suited buyer-supplier relationship for innovation. In a gracious relationship, the buyer and supplier have a weak yet cooperative relationship. The weak relationship allows the supplier to venture out and explore, searching for more innovative ideas, while the cooperative relationship would facilitate the supplier to share these innovative ideas with the buyer. For example, the data collected from a leading Japanese automaker in North America showed about 20% of its suppliers fall into the gracious relationship category—the others were also more or less evenly distributed across the deep, sticky, and transient relationships (see Figure 3.5).

One example of a gracious relationship involves a supplier in the second tier that has a particular filming technology that is important for finishing a part that physically comes in contact with a consumer. This supplier has a weak relationship with this Japanese automaker, so it is not beholden to this focal company and has a cooperative relationship that keeps the line of communication open and is willing to share new ideas. The Japanese automaker treats this supplier with respect and looks for opportunities to stay up to date on filming technology. Choi and Linton (2011) urge focal companies to identify this type of innovative suppliers in their extended supply chains. When they find innovative suppliers at the lower tier, the focal companies should monitor them closely and might even want to establish direct contact.

To identify those suppliers with innovation potential, Yan, Dooley, and Choi (2018) report a study that proposes ways to measure supplier innovation. One of the leading indicators to measure future innovation potential is how well a supplier is connected through its extended ties. This indicator is, in fact, considering the embeddedness of a supplier as the gracious relationship does. The verbiage used to measure it is stated as follows: "compared to its competitors, this supplier is actively involved in collaborating with a wider variety of external partners, such as customers, suppliers, universities, consulting firms, and government, for innovations." In a sense, this is how contract manufacturers such as Flex and Foxconn can stay ahead on innovation and how consulting companies as service suppliers accumulate new knowledge and innovative ideas.

Yan, Dooley, and Choi (2018) describe how some focal companies acquire innovation in their suppliers. When General Motors received Motor Trend's Car of the Year recognition in 2016 for its electric vehicle, Chevrolet Bolt, GM credited the propulsion technology from its supplier, LG Electronics. Beyond the automotive industry, focal companies in the pharmaceutical industry rely on innovation from their analytical software suppliers to develop new molecular designs. Farmers can irrigate their fields with more precision because of the suppliers that can model soil conditions. Furthermore, Google and Microsoft also search across their supply networks to look for startup suppliers that can provide innovation. We stated in Chapter 5 how important it is to consider startup suppliers as a new category because of their innovation potential and how important it is to take a more active approach when evaluating startup suppliers (Kurpjuweit, Wagner, and Choi 2021).

To measure supplier innovation, Yan, Dooley, and Choi (2018) present three sets of measurements—past innovation performance, future innovation potential, and buyer readiness (see Table 9.3). It is important to measure a supplier's past innovation performance because, to a large extent, its past behavior would be the best predictor of its future behavior. At the same time, innovation can happen as a black-swan event in a non-path-dependent way. Therefore, we need to gauge a supplier's future innovation potential separately. Lastly, we need to ask whether the buyer is ready for supplier innovation. Many focal companies suffer from the "not invented here" syndrome. Therefore, we need to be able to measure buyer readiness. The study by Kurpjuweit, Wagner, and Choi (2021) introduced in Chapter 5 addresses how to work with startup suppliers from the focal company's perspective.

Supplier innovation is driven by the entrepreneurialism that exists in supply networks. In this regard, the basic tenets of Austrian economics become relevant—see Chiles and Choi (2000) for an overview. In Austrian economics, the focus is on human actions (i.e., entrepreneurial actions) and unintended consequences (i.e., failures and qualified successes). As such, the market operates away from equilibrium, and market niches are created

Table 9.3 Measuring Supplier Innovation

Measurement Areas	Specific Indicators
Supplier's past innovation performance	• The supplier provides our organization with novel products or services • In previous collaborative innovation projects, the supplier has met cost objectives • The supplier demonstrates significant knowledge and expertise • The supplier interacts frequently with our firm • Purchases from the supplier account for a significant percentage of our total costs of goods sold
Supplier's future innovation potential	• Compared to its competitors, this supplier has better financial performance • The percent of the supplier's sales are from products/services developed in the last three years and is reasonably high • This supplier has an effective project management system to manage new product development projects • Compared to its competitors, this supplier has significantly expanded it product range within the past three years • The strategic goals and technology roadmap of this supplier fit well with those of our company • Compared to its competitors, this supplier is actively involved in collaborating with a wider variety of external partners, such as customers, suppliers, universities, consulting firms, and government, for innovations
Buyer readiness	• Our current corporate strategic plan discusses issues related to supplier innovation • We dedicate resources to attending trade shows or scanning published research and patents for innovations that might be useful to us • We have a formal policy and system for managing intellectual property developed with suppliers • Buyers have annual performance objectives related to their suppliers' performance improvement • We have a formal system for requesting and incentivizing innovation ideas from existing or potential suppliers • We can demonstrate measured improvement in meeting our supplier innovation goals over the last three years

Source: Adapted from Yan, Dooley, and Choi 2018

by entrepreneurialism and competition. That means human creativity is important, which may lead to discovering new ideas that others may not have noticed. Austrian economists (i.e., Hayek 1991; Kirzner 2013; Lachmann 1976, 1986; Schumpeter 1934, 1950) look downstream toward the market and market processes. We may also consider the industrial market that operates on the upstream side of supply chains. Future studies could address the following questions. How does entrepreneurialism translate to upstream linkages? How does entrepreneurialism on the upstream side affect the successes and failures of downstream activities in supply chains? How can the Austrian economic thoughts developed based on downstream market processes be further developed into upstream entrepreneurial activities?

Modularizing Global Supply Networks

Globalization has dominated the world's commerce for the past three decades. We now see how the supply network at the global level has become extremely complex. We hear about how parts crisscross the world multiple times until the product is complete. We all have seen the effects of increased complexity during the pandemic. Some may point to how fragile our supply networks have become. To recap, we have discussed complexity in preceding chapters, most notably in Chapters 5, 7, and 8. In a simplistic sense, we may think of complexity as the number of agents and their interdependencies in a system, where a high number of agents and interdependencies would increase complexity.

If the global supply networks are highly complex, theoretically speaking, the global business landscapes are highly rugged (see Chapter 8). With an increased number of overseas suppliers and increased dependencies on the parts and products they make, we have a highly rugged landscape. That means we have lots of small peaks in our fitness landscape. We would want to see high peaks. The highest peak in the landscape is considered an optimal state of goodness for the system. Choi, Dooley, and Rungtusanatham (2001) provide a way to reduce the small peaks and find a higher peak. The answer is modularization. The concept is akin to the concept of near decomposability (Simon 1962). Modules can be viewed as nearly decomposable units. By themselves, they may not be sold to the consumers, but they can be put together in different combinations to produce products that can be sold. Modules have parts that are highly interdependent, and they remain as nearly independent units. As discussed in Chapter 8, if we could modularize the supply network, that would reduce the number of small peaks in the rugged landscape of a supply network, and many peaks may be combined into fewer but larger peaks. That would lead to a condition for better optimizing the overall supply network.

We saw in our NK simulation models (see Chapter 8) how an increased number of suppliers (N) and their interdependencies (K) lead to global complexity and a rugged landscape. Giannoccaro, Nair, and Choi (2018) suggest that, when such complexity works as a given, focal buying companies should expand their scope of control to help overcome the small peaks. That also means focal companies do not have to increase their scope of control if they could reduce the level of complexity. With modularization, companies may be able to keep interdependencies within their control without necessarily expanding the scope of control. This point comes out in another NK simulation study by Feizabadi, Gligor, and Choi (2021). The reference is made to the modularization concept in Choi, Dooley, and Rungtusanatham (2001) and the concept of near decomposability by Simon (1962). Basically, the density of interdependencies within a regional supply network should be much higher than the density across these regional supply networks. Modularization of the global supply network would give us this type of global supply network structure and nearly decomposable supply networks.

An example comes from German automakers that are re-evaluating their dependencies on China (see https://europe.autonews.com/automakers/germany-auto-industry-would-suffer-trade-war-china). On the one hand, sales in China are strong; on the other hand, there is too much dependence on parts manufactured in China. I recently heard from a personal source that some German automakers are considering separating supply networks for China and Europe. These automakers may build more plants in China, but they want to create separation in their supply networks to reduce dependency. If indeed this is their true intention, then I would say they are taking the right step toward modularizing their global supply networks. Theoretically, they are poised to reduce complexity and create less rugged landscapes. They would increase their chances of finding higher peaks. In a sense, they are re-optimizing their global supply networks. How to modularize global supply networks into regional supply networks will be an important subject to consider by researchers in the coming years. The goal is to help re-optimize and bring more resilience to global supply networks.

The *Harvard Business Review* hosted an online forum in the fall of 2022. This event focused on "Building a More Resilient Supply Chain." They note the U.S.-China trade war and the COVID-19 crisis and how many focal companies are reassessing global supply networks. The online forum explored how to bring resilience without sacrificing competitiveness. Sodhi and Choi (2022) contributed to this forum by taking on the just-in-time (JIT) versus just-in-case (JIC) debate. We propose not abandoning JIT but creating segments in supply chains within which JIT may operate. As uncertainties rise, increasing inventories may be inevitable. However, increasing inventories in a haphazard way via JIC will not help; rather, increasing inventories in a purposeful way will be much more desirable. In a more comprehensive study, Choi, Netland, Sanders, Sodhi, and Wagner (2023) lay out how to do this, first identifying segments of supply networks where we would be able to operate JIT (i.e., matching cycle times, geographical proximity, and close buyer-supplier relationships) and then placing buffers at the points where segments meet. We also suggest that not only inventory but also extra capacity should be viewed as a form of buffer. In essence, we propose to modularize the supply network and place buffers purposefully to allow decoupling between segments or modules representing different parts of supply networks. In this way, the density of interdependencies is high within each module operating in JIT, while the density of interdependencies across the modules would be much lower.

Key Points

- The practice of incomplete contracts can encourage jury-rigging in supply chains and offer more resilience.
- Buyer-supplier relationships may be defined not so much by what exists at the interface *between* two companies but by the supporting social networks that operate *within* each of the two companies.
- The pandemic and other global supply chain disruptions have accelerated the digitization of supply networks and facilitated the emergence of the supplier ecosystem.
- Supply chain digitization is different from digital supply chains, as the former focuses on digitizing the physical supply chain, while in the latter, the service offering is digitally configured and digitally delivered.
- In tetrads, we can study how a network is embedded in a larger network, how subgroups or factions operate in a network, and how strong and weak ties play out in a two-against-two context.
- Supply chain financing looks at how money moves behind the scenes in supply chains, and deep-tier financing is designed to help smaller suppliers in the long tail of the supply chain.

- With over 60% of all known cyber breaches coming through the supply chain, cybersecurity is a supply chain problem, and supply chain professionals will need to work closely with IT professionals.
- Focal companies should look for supplier innovation across the supply chain and not just from their first-tier suppliers.
- Moving toward supply network modularization will offer global supply networks better resilience.

Epilogue

At the moment, I am looking outside a large window at the rear of a big ferry boat. I am taking a ride along with cars, trucks, and other passengers. This particular ferry regularly traverses the freezing waters of the Norwegian Sea between a small port city called Bodo and Lofoten Islands, both north of the Arctic Circle. I have spent the past two nights in this area and am heading back to Trondheim. I decided to take a weekend off to venture out to Lofoten Islands while visiting the Norwegian University of Science and Technology (NTNU) in Trondheim, Norway. It has been adventurous the last few days trying to connect the schedules of the train between Trondheim and Bodo and the ferry between Bodo and Lofoten Islands. It has been tough, but the islands were simply breathtaking with rugged beauty.

Being on a ferry with cars, trucks, and other passengers, I cannot help but think how it is a small piece of the global supply network. While on the islands, I saw lots of wooden racks for drying cods and many small cabins dotted across the shoreline for the workers in the fishing industry. The ferry might be moving cods from the islands that might end up on someone's dinner table in places like Italy or Portugal. Going the other way, it might bring fresh produce and other necessary items like clothes and mobile phones that the islanders require. Yes, it also transports tourists like me back and forth.

Speaking of being a tourist, I almost did not make it to the islands because of the timing issue between the train and ferry schedules. I arrived in Bodo a bit late because the train got stuck somewhere between Trondheim and Bodo for over an hour. So, I missed the last ferry that evening to the islands and was forced to spend the night in Bodo. Then, I learned that the next boat to Lofoten Islands would not be available until the late afternoon the following day, and that meant to get back to Trondheim to make my Monday meetings, I would be getting to the islands and spending the night, only to turn right around the following morning. I looked into alternative modes of transportation like planes, buses, and rental cars, but there was no viable option given my timing constraints. I remember myself slowly realizing that I might not get to the islands even after a 10-hour train ride. Then, a kind staff at the hotel in Bodo pointed out that there was a midnight ferry, catering largely to commercial trucks, that was to leave Bodo at 1 a.m. Yes, I was on that ferry.

In supply networks, linking the right nodes is important, but timing is also important. A hungry person needs food now, the parts in short supply are needed now, and the travelers need to get to their intended destination now. Many timing requisites and many nodes in the network need to link up at the right time and at the right place to make things happen. What things? One answer might be happiness. When the food arrives, a hungry person is happy; when the parts in shortage arrive, the plant manager is happy, and ultimately consumers receive their stuff on time, so they are happy; and when the travelers are able to reach the next point in their travel itinerary, they are happy. Maybe, Santa Clause was one of the first supply chain professionals that brought happiness to people.

Those of us in the tradition of working in supply chain management are engaged in helping goods and services overcome time and space so that those in need can get their stuff and be happy. Supply chain professionals help create products and services that were not there before and take them to where they are needed. We extract raw materials from the earth, process them into the right forms, fabricate them into the right shapes, assemble them into something that can be processed further, and put them together so they can be delivered at the right place, at the right time, and at the right price. A sick person can get the proper medication prescribed by a doctor, a young couple in a budding relationship can share a meal together, and a business executive can make her meeting in a city in a different time zone. We bring happiness. We operate where the rubber meets the road, where stuff happens to make things possible, and where supply meets demand to make people happy.

As I anticipate the closure of this book project, at least for now, I see myself getting a little philosophical. Perhaps, there are two levels of happiness—one with the lowercase "h" and another with the uppercase "H." The lowercase "happiness" is what we all seek as individuals. We need clothes to wear, food to eat, and a roof over our heads. As we all seek our happiness, we find our states of individual happiness are interdependent. I was happy when I made it to the ferry, even though it was one o'clock in the morning; maybe the ferry was also happy, just a bit, it got a passenger. In this particular case, I was closely coupled with this particular ferry, having no other options. When many happinesses at the individual-node level are closely coupled, they lead to a rugged landscape. We can only find small hills, like the early morning ferry ride, and trying to find a tall, single peak would not be possible. I had to make many suboptimal compromises, such as paying the hotel the full rate for staying only a few hours and not getting any sleep that night.

Happiness with an upper case "H" would be equivalent to finding a single peak. We can set up, as a collective goal, finding that elusive single peak, and there is nothing wrong with that. However, my guess is, as much as we would like to find it, we will soon discover that our effort is a futile exercise. We can have as our collective goal a world at peace, a world devoid of sicknesses, and a world with no global warming, all worthy goals, but these are elusive goals attempting to overcome what some call "wicked problems." Many well-meaning individuals that work on these issues I have met, while they were committed and dedicated, also seemed rather frustrated. I would submit that Happiness is not a controlled state that can be attained by planning and execution but an emergent state that needs to be allowed to unfold over time. We do not know what it looks like, but when it happens, we will know. From our end, we just have to better control the interdependencies among happinesses at the individual node level.

We have considered some of the ways to do that in this book—the type of contracts that may provide more flexibility (i.e., incomplete contracts), nearly decomposable supply networks (i.e., modularized supply networks), and innovative technologies to help SME suppliers (i.e., deep-tier financing). Then, we might improve our chances of finding a taller peak in our happiness landscape.

References

Abrahamson, Eric, and Lori Rosenkopf. 1997. "Social Network Effects on the Extent of Innovation Diffusion: A Computer Simulation." *Organization Science* 8 (3): 289–309. https://doi.org/10.1287/orsc.8.3.289.

Agrawal, Narendra, and Steven Nahmias. 1997. "Rationalization of the Supplier Base in the Presence of Yield Uncertainty." *Production and Operations Management* 6 (3): 291–308. https://doi.org/10.1111/j.1937-5956.1997.tb00432.x.

Ahuja, Gautam. 2000. "Collaboration Networks, Structural Holes, and Innovation: A Longitudinal Study." *Administrative Science Quarterly* 45 (3): 425–55. https://doi.org/10.2307/2667105.

Ahuja, Gautam, Francisco Polidoro, and Will Mitchell. 2009. "Structural Homophily or Social Asymmetry? The Formation of Alliances by Poorly Embedded Firms." *Strategic Management Journal* 30 (9): 941–58. https://doi.org/10.1002/smj.774.

Alessio, John C. 1990. "A Synthesis and Formalization of Heiderian Balance and Social Exchange Theory." *Social Forces* 68 (4): 1267–85. https://doi.org/10.1093/sf/68.4.1267.

Ambulkar, Saurabh, Jennifer Blackhurst, and Scott Grawe. 2015. "Firm's Resilience to Supply Chain Disruptions: Scale Development and Empirical Examination." *Journal of Operations Management* 33–34 (1): 111–22. https://doi.org/10.1016/j.jom.2014.11.002.

Andersen, Poul H., Luitzen de Boer, and Thomas Y. Choi. forthcoming. "Within-Organizational Structures and Roots of the Buyer-Supplier Relationship." In *The Oxford Handbook of Supply Chain Management*, edited by Choi, Thomas Y., Julie J. Li, Dale S. Rogers, Tobias Schoenherr, and Stephan M. Wagner. Oxford University Press.

Anderson, Bo. 1975. "Cognitive Balance Theory and Social Network Analysis." In *Perspectives on Social Network Research*, edited by Paul W. Holland and Samuel Leinhardt, 453–69. New York: Academic Press.

Antal, T., P.L. Krapivsky, and S. Redner. 2006. "Social Balance on Networks: The Dynamics of Friendship and Enmity." *Physica D: Nonlinear Phenomena* 224 (1–2): 130–36. https://doi.org/10.1016/j.physd.2006.09.028.

Apple Inc. 2012. "Apple Supplier Responsibility: 2012 Progress Report."

Asanuma, Banri. 1985. "The Contractual Framework for Parts Supply in the Japanese Automotive Industry." *Japanese Economic Studies* 13 (4): 54–78. https://doi.org/10.2753/JES1097-203X130454.

Ashby, Alison. 2016. "From Global to Local: Reshoring for Sustainability." *Operations Management Research* 9 (3–4): 75–88. https://doi.org/10.1007/s12063-016-0117-9.

Ashby, W. Ross. 2015. *An Introduction to Cybernetics*. Mansfield Centre, CT: Martino.

Autry, Chad W., and Stanley E. Griffis. 2008. "Supply Chain Capital: The Impact of Structural and Relational Linkages on Firm Execution and Innovation." *Journal of Business Logistics* 29 (1): 157–73. https://doi.org/10.1002/j.2158-1592.2008.tb00073.x.

Axelrod, Robert. 1984. *The Evolution of Cooperation*. New York: Basic Books.

Bacharach, Samuel B. 1989. "Organizational Theories: Some Criteria for Evaluation." *Academy of Management Review* 14 (4): 496. https://doi.org/10.2307/258555.

Bacon, Glenn C. 1985. "Innovation in the Systems Business: Dynamics of Autonomy and Cooperation." *Journal of Product Innovation Management* 2 (2): 107–12. https://doi.org/10.1111/1540-5885.220107.

Baker, Wayne E., and Robert R. Faulkner. 1993. "The Social Organization of Conspiracy: Illegal Networks in the Heavy Electrical Equipment Industry." *American Sociological Review* 58 (6): 837. https://doi.org/10.2307/2095954.

Balakrishnan, Karthik, Usha Mohan, and Sridhar Seshadri. 2008. "Outsourcing of Front-End Business Processes: Quality, Information, and Customer Contact." *Journal of Operations Management* 26 (2): 288–302. https://doi.org/10.1016/j.jom.2007.08.001.

Baldwin, Carliss Y., and Kim B. Clark. 2000. *Design Rules*. Cambridge, MA: MIT Press.

Ballew, Paul D., and Robert H Schnorbus. 1994. "Realignment in Auto Supplier Industry." *Economic Perspectives* xviii (1).

Bamford, James. 1994. "Driving America to Tiers." *Financial World*.

Barratt, Mark, Thomas Y. Choi, and Mei Li. 2011. "Qualitative Case Studies in Operations Management: Trends, Research Outcomes, and Future Research Implications." *Journal of Operations Management* 29 (4): 329–42. https://doi.org/10.1016/j.jom.2010.06.002.

Bastl, Marko, Mark Johnson, and Thomas Y. Choi. 2013. "Who's Seeking Whom? Coalition Behavior of a Weaker Player in Buyer-Supplier Relationships." *Journal of Supply Chain Management* 49 (1): 8–28. https://doi.org/10.1111/j.1745-493x.2012.03274.x.

Baumann, Oliver, Jens Schmidt, and Nils Stieglitz. 2019. "Effective Search in Rugged Performance Landscapes: A Review and Outlook." *Journal of Management* 45 (1): 285–318. https://doi.org/10.1177/0149206318808594.

Baumann, Oliver, and Nicolaj Siggelkow. 2013. "Dealing with Complexity: Integrated vs. Chunky Search Processes." *Organization Science* 24 (1): 116–32. https://doi.org/10.1287/orsc.1110.0729.

Bavelas, Alex. 1950. "Communication Patterns in Task-Oriented Groups." *The Journal of the Acoustical Society of America* 22 (6): 725–30. https://doi.org/10.1121/1.1906679.

Beauchamp, Murray A. 1965. "An Improved Index of Centrality." *Behavioral Science* 10 (2): 161–63. https://doi.org/10.1002/bs.3830100205.

Bengtsson, Maria, and Sören Kock. 2000. ""Coopetition" in Business Networks—to Cooperate and Compete Simultaneously." *Industrial Marketing Management* 29 (5): 411–26. https://doi.org/10.1016/S0019-8501(99)00067-X.

Benton, W.C., and Michael Maloni. 2005. "The Influence of Power Driven Buyer/Seller Relationships on Supply Chain Satisfaction." *Journal of Operations Management* 23 (1): 1–22.

Beyer, Janice M. 1984. "Ideologies, Values, and Decision Making in Organizations." In *Handbook of Organizational Design*, edited by Paul C. Nystrom and William H. Starbuck. Vol. 2. London: Oxford University Press.

Bhakoo, Vikram, and Thomas Choi. 2013. "The Iron Cage Exposed: Institutional Pressures and Heterogeneity Across the Healthcare Supply Chain." *Journal of Operations Management* 31 (6): 432–49. https://doi.org/10.1016/j.jom.2013.07.016.

Blau, Peter M., and Richard A Schoenherr. 1971. *The Structure of Organizations*. New York: Basic Books.

Bode, Christoph, and Stephan M. Wagner. 2015. "Structural Drivers of Upstream Supply Chain Complexity and the Frequency of Supply Chain Disruptions." *Journal of Operations Management* 36 (1): 215–28. https://doi.org/10.1016/j.jom.2014.12.004.

Bode, Christoph, Stephan M. Wagner, Kenneth J. Petersen, and Lisa M. Ellram. 2011. "Understanding Responses to Supply Chain Disruptions: Insights from Information

Processing and Resource Dependence Perspectives." *Academy of Management Journal* 54 (4): 833–56. https://doi.org/10.5465/amj.2011.64870145.

Boisot, Max, and Bill Mckelvey. 2010. "Integrating Modernist and Postmodernist Perspectives on Organizations: A Complexity Science Bridge." *Academy of Management Review* 35 (3): 415–33. https://doi.org/10.5465/AMR.2010.51142028.

Bolandifar, Ehsan, Panos Kouvelis, and Fuqiang Zhang. 2016. "Delegation vs. Control in Supply Chain Procurement under Competition." *Production and Operations Management* 25 (9): 1528–41. https://doi.org/10.1111/poms.12566.

Bonacich, Phillip. 1972. "Factoring and Weighting Approaches to Status Scores and Clique Identification." *The Journal of Mathematical Sociology* 2 (1): 113–20. https://doi.org/10.1080/0022250X.1972.9989806.

Borgatti, Stephen P., and Martin G. Everett. 2000. "Models of Core/Periphery Structures." *Social Networks* 21 (4): 375–95. https://doi.org/10.1016/S0378-8733(99)00019-2.

Borgatti, Stephen P., Martin G. Everett, and Linton C. Freeman. 2002. *UCINET 6 for Windows: Software for Social Network Analysis*. Natick, MA: Analytic Technologies Inc.

Borgatti, Stephen P., and Xun Li. 2009. "On Social Network Analysis in a Supply Chain Context." *Journal of Supply Chain Management* 45 (2): 5–22. https://doi.org/10.1111/j.1745-493X.2009.03166.x.

Bozarth, Cecil C., Donald P. Warsing, Barbara B. Flynn, and E. James Flynn. 2009. "The Impact of Supply Chain Complexity on Manufacturing Plant Performance." *Journal of Operations Management* 27 (1): 78–93. https://doi.org/10.1016/j.jom.2008.07.003.

Brandenburger, Adam, and Barry Nalebuff. 1996. *Co-Opetition*. New York: Doubleday.

Brandon-Jones, Emma, Brian Squire, and Yvonne G. T. Van Rossenberg. 2015. "The Impact of Supply Base Complexity on Disruptions and Performance: The Moderating Effects of Slack and Visibility." *International Journal of Production Research* 53 (22): 6903–18. https://doi.org/10.1080/00207543.2014.986296.

Brintrup, Alexandra. 2022. "Artificial Intelligence in the Supply Chain: A Classification Framework and Critical Analysis of the Current State." In *The Oxford Handbook of Supply Chain Management*, edited by Choi, Thomas Y., Julie J. Li, Dale S. Rogers, Tobias Schoenherr, and Stephan M. Wagner. Oxford University Press.

Brusoni, Stefano. 2005. "The Limits to Specialization: Problem Solving and Coordination in 'Modular Networks.'" *Organization Studies* 26 (12): 1885–907. https://doi.org/10.1177/0170840605059161.

Brusoni, Stefano, Michael G. Jacobides, and Andrea Prencipe. 2009. "Strategic Dynamics in Industry Architectures and the Challenges of Knowledge Integration." *European Management Review* 6 (4): 209–16. https://doi.org/10.1057/emr.2009.26.

Burkhardt, Marlene E., and Daniel J. Brass. 1990. "Changing Patterns or Patterns of Change: The Effects of a Change in Technology on Social Network Structure and Power." *Administrative Science Quarterly* 35 (1): 104. https://doi.org/10.2307/2393552.

Burt, David N., and Michael F. Doyle. 1993. *The American Keiretsu: A Strategic Weapon for Global Competitiveness*. Homewood, Il: Business One Irwin.

Burt, Ronald S. 1982. *Toward a Structural Theory of Action: Network Models of Social Structure, Perception, and Action*. Quantitative Studies in Social Relations. New York: Academic Press.

Burt, Ronald S. 1995. *Structural Holes: The Social Structure of Competition*. Paperback ed. Cambridge, MA: Harvard University Press.

Burt, Ronald S. 2000a. "The Network Structure of Social Capital." *Research in Organizational Behavior* 22: 345–423.

Burt, Ronald S. 2000b. "Decay Functions." *Social Networks* 22 (1): 1–28. https://doi.org/10.1016/S0378-8733(99)00015-5.

Burt, Ronald S. 2001. "Structural Holes Versus Network Closure as Social Capital." In *Social Capital: Theory and Research*, edited by Lan Lin, Karen Cook, and Ronald S. Burt, 31–56. New York: Routledge.

Burt, Ronald S. 2002. "Bridge Decay." *Social Networks* 24 (4): 333–63.

Cachon, Gérard P., and Martin A. Lariviere. 2005. "Supply Chain Coordination with Revenue-Sharing Contracts: Strengths and Limitations." *Management Science* 51 (1): 30–44. https://doi.org/10.1287/mnsc.1040.0215.

Caplow, Theodore. 1956. "A Theory of Coalitions in the Triad." *American Sociological Review* 21 (4): 489–93.

Caplow, Theodore. 1959. "Further Development of a Theory of Coalitions in the Triad." *American Journal of Sociology* 64 (5): 488–93.

Caplow, Theodore. 1968. *Two Against One: Coalitions in Triads*. Englewood Cliffs, NJ: Prentice-Hall.

Carley, Kathleen. 1991. "A Theory of Group Stability." *American Sociological Review* 56 (3): 331. https://doi.org/10.2307/2096108.

Carr, Chris, and Julia Ng. 1995. "Total Cost Control: Nissan and Its U.K. Supplier Partnerships." *Management Accounting Research* 6 (4): 347–65. https://doi.org/10.1006/mare.1995.1025.

Carter, Craig R., Lisa M. Ellram, and Wendy Tate. 2007. "The Use of Social Network Analysis in Logistics Research." *Journal of Business Logistics* 28 (1): 137–68. https://doi.org/10.1002/j.2158-1592.2007.tb00235.x.

Carter, Craig R., Dale S. Rogers, and Thomas Y. Choi. 2015. "Toward the Theory of the Supply Chain." *Journal of Supply Chain Management* 51 (2): 89–97. https://doi.org/10.1111/jscm.12073.

Carter, Joseph, and Thomas Y. Choi. 2008. *Foundation of Supply Management*. Tempe, AZ: Institute for Supply Management.

Cartwright, Dorwin, and Frank Harary. 1956. "Structural Balance: A Generalization of Heider's Theory." *Psychological Review* 63 (5): 277–93. https://doi.org/10.1037/h0046049.

Carzo, Rocco, and John N. Yanouzas. 1969. "Effects of Flat and Tall Organization Structure." *Administrative Science Quarterly* 14 (2): 178. https://doi.org/10.2307/2391096.

Celly, Kirti Sawhney, Robert E. Spekman, and John W. Kamauff. 1999. "Technological Uncertainty, Buyer Preferences and Supplier Assurances: An Examination of Pacific Rim Purchasing Arrangements." *Journal of International Business Studies* 30 (2): 297–316. https://doi.org/10.1057/palgrave.jibs.8490071.

Chae, Sangho. 2017. "Three Essays on Theorizing Supply Chain-Make Versus Supply Chain-Buy." Tempe: Arizona State University.

Chae, Sangho, Thomas Y. Choi, and Daesik Hur. 2017. "Buyer Power and Supplier Relationship Commitment: A Cognitive Evaluation Theory Perspective." *Journal of Supply Chain Management* 53 (2): 39–60. https://doi.org/10.1111/jscm.12138.

Chae, Sangho, Benn Lawson, Thomas J. Kull, and Thomas Choi. 2019. "To Insource or Outsource the Sourcing? A Behavioral Investigation of the Multi-Tier Sourcing Decision." *International Journal of Operations & Production Management* 39 (3): 385–405. https://doi.org/10.1108/IJOPM-04-2018-0231.

Chase, Richard B., and Nicholas J. Aquilano. 1992. *Production & Operations Management: A Life Cycle Approach.* 6th ed. Homewood, IL: Irwin.

Chen, Fangruo. 2003. "Information Sharing and Supply Chain Coordination." In *Handbooks in Operations Research and Management Science*, edited by Shane Henderson and Barry Nelson, 11:341–421. Elsevier. https://doi.org/10.1016/S0927-0507(03)11007-9.

Chen, Ying-Ju, Stephen Shum, and Wenqiang Xiao. 2012. "Should an OEM Retain Component Procurement When the CM Produces Competing Products?" *Production and Operations Management* 21 (5): 907–22. https://doi.org/10.1111/j.1937-5956.2012.01325.x.

Cheng, Yu-Ting, and Andrew H. Van de Ven. 1996. "Learning the Innovation Journey: Order out of Chaos?" *Organization Science* 7 (6): 593–614. https://doi.org/10.1287/orsc.7.6.593.

Chiles, Todd H., and Thomas Y. Choi. 2000. "Theorizing TQM: An Austrian and Evolutionary Economics Interpretation." *Journal of Management Studies* 37 (2): 185–212. https://doi.org/10.1111/1467-6486.00177.

Chin, Kwai-Sang, Ying-Ming Wang, Gary Ka Kwai Poon, and Jian-Bo Yang. 2009. "Failure Mode and Effects Analysis by Data Envelopment Analysis." *Decision Support Systems* 48 (1): 246–56. https://doi.org/10.1016/j.dss.2009.08.005.

Choi, Thomas Y. 2007. "New Supply Management Frontier: Supplier-Supplier Relationship." *Supply Chain Management Review* 11 (5): 51–56.

Choi, Thomas Y., and Orlando C. Behling. 1997. "Top Managers and TQM Success: One More Look After All These Years." *Academy of Management Executive* 11 (1): 37–47.

Choi, Thomas Y., and Kevin J. Dooley. 2009. "Supply Networks: Theories and Models." *Journal of Supply Chain Management* 45 (3): 25–26. https://doi.org/10.1111/j.1745-493X.2009.03168.x.

Choi, Thomas Y., Kevin J. Dooley, and Manus Rungtusanatham. 2001. "Supply Networks and Complex Adaptive Systems: Control Versus Emergence." *Journal of Operations Management* 19 (3): 351–66. https://doi.org/10.1016/S0272-6963(00)00068-1.

Choi, Thomas Y., and Karen Eboch. 1998. "The TQM Paradox: Relations among TQM Practices, Plant Performance, and Customer Satisfaction." *Journal of Operations Management* 17 (1): 59–75. https://doi.org/10.1016/S0272-6963(98)00031-X.

Choi, Thomas Y., and Janet L. Hartley. 1996. "An Exploration of Supplier Selection Practices across the Supply Chain." *Journal of Operations Management* 14 (4): 333–43. https://doi.org/10.1016/S0272-6963(96)00091-5.

Choi, Thomas Y., and Elsebeth Holmen. 2023. "Ready for Another Leap? Making a Case for Tetrads." *Journal of Purchasing and Supply Management.* DOI: 10.1016/j.pursup.2023.100825.

Choi, Thomas Y., and Yunsook Hong. 2002. "Unveiling the Structure of Supply Networks: Case Studies in Honda, Acura, and DaimlerChrysler." *Journal of Operations Management* 20 (5): 469–93. https://doi.org/10.1016/S0272-6963(02)00025-6.

Choi, Thomas Y., and Yusoon Kim. 2008. "Structural Embeddedness and Supplier Management: A Network Perspective." *Journal of Supply Chain Management* 44 (4): 5–13. https://doi.org/10.1111/j.1745-493X.2008.00069.x.

Choi, Thomas Y., and Daniel R. Krause. 2006. "The Supply Base and Its Complexity: Implications for Transaction Costs, Risks, Responsiveness, and Innovation." *Journal of Operations Management* 24 (5): 637–52. https://doi.org/10.1016/j.jom.2005.07.002.

Choi, Thomas Y., and Jeffrey K. Liker. 1992. "Institutional Conformity and Technology Implementation: A Process Model of Ergonomics Dissemination." *Journal of Engineering and Technology Management* 9 (2): 155–95. https://doi.org/10.1016/0923-4748(92)90003-N.

Choi, Thomas Y., and Jeffrey K. Liker. 1995. "Bringing Japanese Continuous Improvement Approaches to U.S. Manufacturing: The Roles of Process Orientation and Communications." *Decision Sciences* 26 (5): 589–620. https://doi.org/10.1111/j.1540-5915.1995.tb01442.x.

Choi, Thomas Y., and Tom Linton. 2011. "Don't Let Your Supply Chain Control Your Business." *Harvard Business Review* 89 (12): 112–17.

Choi, Thomas Y., Sriram Narayanan, David Novak, Jan Olhager, Jiuh-Biing Sheu, and Frank Wiengarten. 2021. "Managing Extended Supply Chains." *Journal of Business Logistics* 42 (2): 200–206. https://doi.org/10.1111/jbl.12276.

Choi, Thomas Y., Torbjorn Netland, Nada Sanders, ManMohan Sodhi, and Stephan Wagner. 2023. "Just-in-Time for Supply Chains in Turbulent Times." *Production and Operations Management*. http://dx.doi.org/10.2139/ssrn.4378448.

Choi, Thomas Y., Dale S. Rogers, and Bindiya Vakil. 2020. "Coronavirus Is a Wake-Up Call for Supply Chain Management." *Harvard Business Review Online*, March.

Choi, Thomas Y., and Manus Rungtusanatham. 1999. "Comparison of Quality Management Practices: Across the Supply Chain and Industries." *Journal of Supply Chain Management* 35 (1): 20–27. https://doi.org/10.1111/j.1745-493X.1999.tb00052.x.

Choi, Thomas Y., Benjamin B. M. Shao, and Zhan (Michael) Shi. 2015. "Hidden Suppliers Can Make or Break Your Operations." *Harvard Business Review Online*, May.

Choi, Thomas Y, and Nazli Wasti. 1995. "Institutional Pressures and Organizational Learning: American-Owned Automotive Parts Suppliers and Japanese Shop Floor Production Methods." In *Engineered in Japan: Japanese Technology Management Practices*, edited by Jeffrey K. Liker, John Creighton Campbell, and John E. Ettlie. Oxford University Press.

Choi, Thomas Y., and Zhaohui Wu. 2009a. "Go Ahead, Leap: Triads and Their Practical and Theoretical Import." *Journal of Purchasing and Supply Management* 15 (4): 269–70. https://doi.org/10.1016/j.pursup.2009.09.002.

Choi, Thomas Y., and Zhaohui Wu. 2009b. "Taking the Leap from Dyads to Triads: Buyer–Supplier Relationships in Supply Networks." *Journal of Purchasing and Supply Management* 15 (4): 263–66. https://doi.org/10.1016/j.pursup.2009.08.003.

Choi, Thomas Y., and Zhaohui Wu. 2009c. "Triads in Supply Networks: Theorizing Buyer-Supplier-Supplier Relationships." *Journal of Supply Chain Management* 45 (1): 8–25. https://doi.org/10.1111/j.1745-493X.2009.03151.x.

Choi, Thomas Y., Zhaohui Wu, Lisa M. Ellram, and Balaji Koka. 2002. "Supplier-Supplier Relationships and Their Implications for Buyer-Supplier Relationships." *IEEE Transactions on Engineering Management* 49 (2): 119–30. https://doi.org/10.1109/TEM.2002.1010880.

Chou, Yen-Chun, and Benjamin B. M. Shao. 2014. "Total Factor Productivity Growth in Information Technology Services Industries: A Multi-Theoretical Perspective." *Decision Support Systems* 62 (June): 106–18. https://doi.org/10.1016/j.dss.2014.03.009.

Clark, Kim B., and Takahiro Fujimoto. 1991. *Product Development Performance: Strategy, Organization, and Management in the World Auto Industry*. Boston, Mass: Harvard Business School Press.

Coase, R. H. 1937. "The Nature of the Firm." *Economica* 4 (16): 386–405. https://doi.org/10.1111/j.1468-0335.1937.tb00002.x.

Coleman, James S. 2006. *The Mathematics of Collective Action*. New Brunswick, NJ: Aldine Transaction.

Cook, Wade D., Kaoru Tone, and Joe Zhu. 2014. "Data Envelopment Analysis: Prior to Choosing a Model." *Omega* 44 (April): 1–4. https://doi.org/10.1016/j.omega.2013.09.004.

Cook, William, ed. 1998. *Combinatorial Optimization*. Wiley-Interscience Series in Discrete Mathematics and Optimization. New York: Wiley.

Cox, Andrew. 2001. "Managing with Power: Strategies for Improving Value Appropriation from Supply Relationships." *Journal of Supply Chain Management* 37 (2): 42–47.

Crook, T. Russell, and James G. Combs. 2007. "Sources and Consequences of Bargaining Power in Supply Chains." *Journal of Operations Management* 25 (2): 546–55. https://doi.org/10.1016/j.jom.2006.05.008.

Cummins, Tim, Stuart Kauffman, and Thomas Y. Choi. 2021. "How to Navigate Inefficiency and Incomplete Contracts." *Supply Chain Management Review* May/June: 22–27.

Curry, Timothy J., and Richard M. Emerson. 1970. "Balance Theory: A Theory of Interpersonal Attraction?" *Sociometry* 33 (2): 216. https://doi.org/10.2307/2786331.

Daft, Richard L. 2013. *Organization Theory & Design*. 11th ed. Mason, OH: South-Western Cengage Learning.

Das, T. K., and Noushi Rahman. 2010. "Determinants of Partner Opportunism in Strategic Alliances: A Conceptual Framework." *Journal of Business and Psychology* 25 (1): 55–74. https://doi.org/10.1007/s10869-009-9132-2.

Davis, Jason P., Kathleen M. Eisenhardt, and Christopher B. Bingham. 2007. "Developing Theory Through Simulation Methods." *Academy of Management Review* 32 (2): 480–99. https://doi.org/10.5465/amr.2007.24351453.

Demski, Joel S, and Gerald A. Feltham. 1978. "Economic Incentives in Budgetary Control Systems." *The Accounting Review* 53 (2): 336–59.

Deshpande, Vinayak, Leroy B. Schwarz, Mikhail J. Atallah, Marina Blanton, and Keith B. Frikken. 2011. "Outsourcing Manufacturing: Secure Price-Masking Mechanisms for Purchasing Component Parts: Secure Price-Masking." *Production and Operations Management* 20 (2): 165–80. https://doi.org/10.1111/j.1937-5956.2010.01188.x.

Dickson, Gary W. 1966. "An Analysis of Vendor Selection Systems and Decisions." *Journal of Purchasing* 2 (1): 5–17. https://doi.org/10.1111/j.1745-493X.1966.tb00818.x.

DiMaggio, Paul J., and Walter W. Powell. 1983. "The Iron Cage Revisited: Institutional Isomorphism and Collective Rationality in Organizational Fields." *American Sociological Review* 48 (2): 147. https://doi.org/10.2307/2095101.

Dobler, Donald W., and David N. Burt. 1996. *Purchasing and Supply Management: Text and Cases*. 6th ed. International ed. McGraw-Hill Series in Management. New York: McGraw-Hill.

Dong, Binwei, Wansheng Tang, and Chi Zhou. 2018. "Strategic Procurement Outsourcing with Asymmetric Cost Information Under Scale Economies." *Journal of the Operational Research Society* 69 (11): 1751–72. https://doi.org/10.1080/01605682.2017.1409155.

Dooley, Kevin J. 1997. "A Complex Adaptive Systems Model of Organizational Change." *Nonlinear Dynamics, Psychology, and Life Sciences* 1 (1): 69–97. https://doi.org/10.1023/A:1022375910940.

Dooley, Kevin J. 2001. "Organizational Complexity." In *International Encyclopedia of Business and Management*, edited by Malcolm Warner. London: Thompson Learning.

Dooley, Kevin J., and Andrew H. Van de Ven. 1999. "Explaining Complex Organizational Dynamics." *Organization Science* 10 (3): 358–72.

Dore, Ronald. 1983. "Goodwill and the Spirit of Market Capitalism." *The British Journal of Sociology* 34 (4): 459. https://doi.org/10.2307/590932.

Doty, D. Harold, and William H. Glick. 1994. "Typologies as a Unique Form of Theory Building: Toward Improved Understanding and Modeling." *Academy of Management Review* 19 (2): 230. https://doi.org/10.2307/258704.

Dubois, Anna, and Peter Fredriksson. 2008. "Cooperating and Competing in Supply Networks: Making Sense of a Triadic Sourcing Strategy." *Journal of Purchasing and Supply Management* 14 (3): 170–79. https://doi.org/10.1016/j.pursup.2008.05.002.

Durach, Christian F., Frank Wiengarten, and Thomas Y. Choi. 2020. "Supplier–Supplier Coopetition and Supply Chain Disruption: First-Tier Supplier Resilience in the Tetradic Context." *International Journal of Operations & Production Management* 40 (7/8): 1041–65. https://doi.org/10.1108/IJOPM-03-2019-0224.

Dyer, Jeffrey H. 1996. "Does Governance Matter? *Keiretsu* Alliances and Asset Specificity as Sources of Japanese Competitive Advantage." *Organization Science* 7 (6): 649–66. https://doi.org/10.1287/orsc.7.6.649.

Dyer, Jeffrey H., and Nile W. Hatch. 2006. "Relation-Specific Capabilities and Barriers to Knowledge Transfers: Creating Advantage through Network Relationships." *Strategic Management Journal* 27 (8): 701–19. https://doi.org/10.1002/smj.543.

Dyer, Jeffrey H., Prashant Kale, and Harbir Singh. 2001. "How to Make Strategic Alliances Work." *MIT Sloan Management Review* 42 (4): 37–43.

Dyer, Jeffrey H., and Kentaro Nobeoka. 2000. "Creating and Managing a High-Performance Knowledge-Sharing Network: The Toyota Case." *Strategic Management Journal* 21 (3): 345–67. https://doi.org/10.1002/(SICI)1097-0266(200 003)21:3<345::AID-SMJ96>3.0.CO;2-N.

Ebel, Holger, Jörn Davidsen, and Stefan Bornholdt. 2002. "Dynamics of Social Networks." *Complexity* 8 (2): 24–27. https://doi.org/10.1002/cplx.10066.

Eisenhardt, Kathleen M. 1989a. "Agency Theory: An Assessment and Review." *Academy of Management Review* 14 (1): 57–74. https://doi.org/10.5465/amr.1989.4279003.

Eisenhardt, Kathleen M. 1989b. "Building Theories from Case Study Research." *Academy of Management Review* 14 (4): 532. https://doi.org/10.2307/258557.

Eisenhardt, Kathleen M., and Claudia Bird Schoonhoven. 1996. "Resource-Based View of Strategic Alliance Formation: Strategic and Social Effects in Entrepreneurial Firms." *Organization Science* 7 (2): 136–50. https://doi.org/10.1287/orsc.7.2.136.

Ellis, Scott C., Jeff Shockley, and Raymond M. Henry. 2011. "Making Sense of Supply Disruption Risk Research: A Conceptual Framework Grounded in Enactment Theory." *Journal of Supply Chain Management* 47 (2): 65–96. https://doi.org/10.1111/j.1745-493X.2011.03217.x.

Ellram, Lisa M. 1995. "Partnering Pitfalls and Success Factors." *International Journal of Purchasing and Materials Management* 31 (1): 35–44. https://doi.org/10.1111/j.1745-493X.1995.tb00201.x.

Eoyang, Glenda H. 1997. *Coping with Chaos: Seven Simple Tools*. Cheyenne, WY: Lagumo Corp.

Eriksson, Victor. 2021. "Transport Service Triads in Supply Networks." Diss., Gothenburg, Sweden, Chalmers University.

Ethiraj, Sendil K., and Daniel Levinthal. 2004. "Modularity and Innovation in Complex Systems." *Management Science* 50 (2): 159–73. https://doi.org/10.1287/mnsc.1030.0145.

Ettlie, John E., and Paul A. Pavlou. 2006. "Technology-Based New Product Development Partnerships." *Decision Sciences* 37 (2): 117–47. https://doi.org/10.1111/j.1540-5915.2006.00119.x.

Everett, M. G., and S. P. Borgatti. 1999. "The Centrality of Groups and Classes." *The Journal of Mathematical Sociology* 23 (3): 181–201. https://doi.org/10.1080/0022250X.1999.9990219.

Fare, Rolf, Shawna Grosskopf, Mary Norris, and Zhongyang Zhang. 1994. "Productivity Growth, Technical Progress, and Efficiency Change in Industrialized Countries." *The American Economic Review* 84 (1): 66–83.

Feizabadi, Javad, David M. Gligor, and Thomas Y. Choi. 2021. "Examining the Resiliency of Intertwined Supply Networks: A Jury-Rigging Perspective." *International Journal of Production Research*, September, 2432–51. https://doi.org/10.1080/00207543.2021.1977865.

Feldmann, Andreas, and Jan Olhager. 2019. "A Taxonomy of International Manufacturing Networks." *Production Planning & Control* 30 (2–3): 163–78. https://doi.org/10.1080/09537287.2018.1534269.

Ferguson, Ronald J., Michele Paulin, and Jasmin Bergeron. 2005. "Contractual Governance, Relational Governance, and the Performance of Interfirm Service Exchanges: The Influence of Boundary-Spanner Closeness." *Journal of the Academy of Marketing Science* 33 (2): 217–34. https://doi.org/10.1177/0092070304270729.

Fernandez-Giordano, Marisel, Leopoldo Gutierrez, Francisco Javier Llorens-Montes, and Thomas Y. Choi. 2022. "Stratified View of Institutional Fit." *British Journal of Management* 33 (3): 1499–516. https://doi.org/10.1111/1467-8551.12546.

Festinger, Leon. 2001. *A Theory of Cognitive Dissonance*. Reissued by Stanford University Press in 1962, renewed 1985 by author. Stanford, CA: Stanford University Press.

Fine, Charles H. 1998. *Clockspeed: Winning Industry Control in the Age of Temporary Advantage*. Reading, MA: Perseus Books.

Flamholtz, Eric G., T.K. Das, and Anne S. Tsui. 1985. "Toward an Integrative Framework of Organizational Control." Accounting, Organizations and Society 10 (1): 35–50. https://doi.org/10.1016/0361-3682(85)90030-3.

Fleischer, Mitchell, and Jeffrey K. Liker. 1997. *Concurrent Engineering Effectiveness: Integrating Product Development across Organizations*. Cincinnati: Hanser Gardner.

Flynn, Barbara B., Xenophon Koufteros, and Guanyi Lu. 2016. "On Theory in Supply Chain Uncertainty and Its Implications for Supply Chain Integration." *Journal of Supply Chain Management* 52 (3): 3–27. https://doi.org/10.1111/jscm.12106.

Flyvbjerg, Bent. 2020. "The Law of Regression to the Tail: How to Survive Covid-19, the Climate Crisis, and Other Disasters." *Environmental Science & Policy* 114 (December): 614–18. https://doi.org/10.1016/j.envsci.2020.08.013.

Forrester, Jay Wright. 1999. *Industrial Dynamics*. System Dynamics Series. Waltham, MA: Pegasus Communications.

Freeman, Linton C. 1977. "A Set of Measures of Centrality Based on Betweenness." *Sociometry* 40 (1): 35. https://doi.org/10.2307/3033543.

Frenken, Koen. 2000. "A Complexity Approach to Innovation Networks. The Case of the Aircraft Industry (1909–1997)." *Research Policy* 29 (2): 257–72. https://doi.org/10.1016/S0048-7333(99)00064-5.

Friedkin, Noah E. 1982. "Information Flow Through Strong and Weak Ties in Intraorganizational Social Networks." *Social Networks* 3 (4): 273–85. https://doi.org/10.1016/0378-8733(82)90003-X.

Fuhrmans, Vanessa. 2011. "VW-Suzuki Partnership Nears Collapse." *Wall Street Journal.* https://www.wsj.com/articles/SB10001424053111903532804576564671448602578.

Fujimoto, Takahiro. 1999. *The Evolution of a Manufacturing System at Toyota.* New York: Oxford University Press.

Gamson, William A. 1961. "A Theory of Coalition Formation." American Sociological Review 26 (3):373. https://doi.org/10.2307/2090664.

Ganco, Martin, and Rajshree Agarwal. 2007. "Performance Differentials between Diversifying Entrants and Entrepreneurial Start-Ups: A Complexity Approach." *SSRN Electronic Journal.* https://doi.org/10.2139/ssrn.1027904.

Ganco, Martin, Rahul Kapoor, and Gwendolyn K. Lee. 2020. "From Rugged Landscapes to Rugged Ecosystems: Structure of Interdependencies and Firms' Innovative Search." *Academy of Management Review* 45 (3): 646–74. https://doi.org/10.5465/amr.2017.0549.

Gargiulo, Martin, and Mario Benassi. 2000. "Trapped in Your Own Net? Network Cohesion, Structural Holes, and the Adaptation of Social Capital." *Organization Science* 11 (2): 183–96. https://doi.org/10.1287/orsc.11.2.183.12514.

Gavetti, Giovanni, and Daniel Levinthal. 2000. "Looking Forward and Looking Backward: Cognitive and Experiential Search." *Administrative Science Quarterly* 45 (1): 113–37. https://doi.org/10.2307/2666981.

Gaylord, Richard J., and Kazume Nishidate. 1996. *Modeling Nature: Cellular Automata Simulations with Mathematica.* Santa Clara, CA: TELOS.

Gerlach, Michael L. 1992. *Alliance Capitalism: The Social Organization of Japanese Business.* Berkeley: Univ. of California Press.

Gerwin, Donald. 1984. "Relationship Between Structure and Technology." In *Handbook of Organizational Design.* Vol. 2, edited by Paul C. Nystrom and William H. Starbuck. London: Oxford University Press.

Giannoccaro, Ilaria, Anand Nair, and Thomas Choi. 2018. "The Impact of Control and Complexity on Supply Network Performance: An Empirically Informed Investigation Using NK Simulation Analysis: The Impact of Control and Complexity." *Decision Sciences* 49 (4): 625–59. https://doi.org/10.1111/deci.12293.

Gibson, James L., John Ivancevich, and Robert Konopaske. 2011. *Organizations: Behavior, Structure, Processes.* 14th ed. Dubuque, IA: McGraw-Hill.

Gimeno, Javier. 1999. "Reciprocal Threats in Multimarket Rivalry: Staking out 'Spheres of Influence' in the U.S. Airline Industry." *Strategic Management Journal* 20 (2): 101–28. https://doi.org/10.1002/(SICI)1097-0266(199902)20:2<101::AID-SMJ12>3.0.CO;2-4.

Goldstein, Jeffrey. 1994. *The Unshackled Organization: Facing the Challenge of Unpredictability through Spontaneous Reorganization.* Portland, OR: Productivity Press.

Gonchar, Michael. 2021. "Trade Troubles: Learning About the Global Supply Chain and Why It's Broken." *New York Times,* October 21. https://www.nytimes.com/2021/10/21/learning/lesson-plans/trade-troubles-learning-about-the-global-supply-chain-and-why-its-broken.html?searchResultPosition=2.

Goodman, P. S., M. Fichman, F. J. Lerch, and P. R. Snyder. 1995. "Customer-Firm Relationships, Involvement, and Customer Satisfaction." *Academy of Management Journal* 38 (5): 1310–24. https://doi.org/10.2307/256859.

Gottinger, Hans W. 1983. *Coping with Complexity: Perspectives for Economics, Management and Social Sciences.* Holland: D. Reidel.

Granovetter, Mark S. 1973. "The Strength of Weak Ties." *American Journal of Sociology* 78 (6): 1360–80.

Granovetter, Mark. 1985. "Economic Action and Social Structure: The Problem of Embeddedness." *American Journal of Sociology* 91 (3): 481–510.

Gray, John V, Andrea M Prud'homme, and Andrew Barley. 2019. "Emerging Technologies in Supply Management." Tempe, AZ: CAPS Research.

Grimm, Jörg H., Joerg S. Hofstetter, and Joseph Sarkis. 2016. "Exploring Sub-Suppliers' Compliance with Corporate Sustainability Standards." *Journal of Cleaner Production* 112 (January): 1971–84. https://doi.org/10.1016/j.jclepro.2014.11.036.

Grover, Varun, and Manoj K. Malhotra. 2003. "Transaction Cost Framework in Operations and Supply Chain Management Research: Theory and Measurement." *Journal of Operations Management* 21 (4): 457–73. https://doi.org/10.1016/S0272-6963(03)00040-8.

Gualandris, Jury, and Matteo Kalchschmidt. 2014. "A Model to Evaluate Upstream Vulnerability." *International Journal of Logistics Research and Applications* 17 (3): 249–68. https://doi.org/10.1080/13675567.2013.860959.

Gualandris, Jury, and Matteo Kalchschmidt. 2015. "Supply Risk Management and Competitive Advantage: A Misfit Model." *The International Journal of Logistics Management* 26 (3): 459–78. https://doi.org/10.1108/IJLM-05-2013-0062.

Guastello, Stephen J. 2016. *Chaos, Catastrophe, and Human Affairs: Applications of Nonlinear Dynamics to Work, . . . Organizations, and Social Evolution.* Place of publication not identified: Psychology Press.

Gulati, Ranjay. 1995. "Social Structure and Alliance Formation Patterns: A Longitudinal Analysis." *Administrative Science Quarterly* 40 (4): 619. https://doi.org/10.2307/2393756.

Gulati, Ranjay. 1998. "Alliances and Networks." *Strategic Management Journal* 19 (4): 293–317. https://doi.org/10.1002/(SICI)1097-0266(199804)19:4<293::AID-SMJ982>3.0.CO;2-M.

Gulati, Ranjay. 1999. "Network Location and Learning: The Influence of Network Resources and Firm Capabilities on Alliance Formation." *Strategic Management Journal* 20 (5): 397–420. https://doi.org/10.1002/(SICI)1097-0266(199905)20:5<397::AID-SMJ35>3.0.CO;2-K.

Gulati, Ranjay, Nitin Nohria, and Akbar Zaheer. 2000. "Strategic Networks." *Strategic Management Journal* 21 (3): 203–15. https://doi.org/10.1002/(SICI)1097-0266(200003)21:3<203::AID-SMJ102>3.0.CO;2-K.

Guo, Pengfei, Jing-Sheng Song, and Yulan Wang. 2010. "Outsourcing Structures and Information Flow in a Three-Tier Supply Chain." *International Journal of Production Economics* 128 (1): 175–87. https://doi.org/10.1016/j.ijpe.2010.06.017.

Hakansson, Hakan, and Jan Johanson. 1990. "Formal and Informal Cooperation Strategies in International Industrial Networks." In *Understanding Business Markets: Interaction, Relationships, and Networks,* edited by David Ford. London: Academic Press.

Hammer, Michael. 1990. "Reengineering Work: Don't Automate, Obliterate." *Harvard Business Review* 68 (4): 104–12.

Handfield, Robert B., and Christian Bechtel. 2002. "The Role of Trust and Relationship Structure in Improving Supply Chain Responsiveness." *Industrial Marketing Management* 31 (4): 367–82. https://doi.org/10.1016/S0019-8501(01)00169-9.

Handfield, Robert, Thomas Y. Choi, Jaikishen Venkatraman, and Shweta Murthy. 2017. "Emerging Procurement Technology: Data Analytics and Cognitive Analytics." Tempe, AZ: CAPS Research.

Handfield, Robert, Seongkyoon Jeong, and Thomas Choi. 2019. "Emerging Procurement Technology: Data Analytics and Cognitive Analytics." *International Journal of Physical Distribution & Logistics Management* 49 (10): 972–1002. https://doi.org/10.1108/IJP DLM-11-2017-0348.

Handley, Sean M., and W. C. Benton. 2012. "The Influence of Exchange Hazards and Power on Opportunism in Outsourcing Relationships." *Journal of Operations Management* 30 (1–2): 55–68. https://doi.org/10.1016/j.jom.2011.06.001.

Hansen, Morten T. 1999. "The Search-Transfer Problem: The Role of Weak Ties in Sharing Knowledge Across Organization Subunits." *Administrative Science Quarterly* 44 (1): 82–111. https://doi.org/10.2307/2667032.

Harland, Christine M., Richard C. Lamming, Jurong Zheng, and Thomas E. Johnsen. 2001. "A Taxonomy of Supply Networks." *Journal of Supply Chain Management* 37 (4): 21–27. https://doi.org/10.1111/j.1745-493X.2001.tb00109.x.

Hart, Oliver, and John Moore. 1988. "Incomplete Contracts and Renegotiation." *Econometrica* 56 (4): 755. https://doi.org/10.2307/1912698.

Hartley, Janet L., and Thomas Y. Choi. 1996. "Supplier Development: Customers as a Catalyst of Process Change." *Business Horizons* 39 (4): 37–44. https://doi.org/10.1016/S0007-6813(96)90050-6.

Hartley, Janet L., and Thomas Y. Choi. 2020a. "Evolving to Achieve Category Management Success." *Inside Supply Management*, January/February.

Hartley, Janet L., and Thomas Y. Choi . 2020b. "Exploring Category Management: Across Different Business and Organizational Settings." Tempe, AZ: CAPS Research.

Hatfield, Elaine, G. William Walster, and Ellen Berscheid. 1978. *Equity: Theory and Research*. Boston: Allyn and Bacon.

Hayek, Friedrich. 1991. "The Use of Knowledge in Society." In *Austrian Economics: A Reader*, edited by Richard M. Ed. Ebeling, 247–63. Hillsdale, MI: Hillsdale College Press.

Heider, Fritz. 1958. *The Psychology of Interpersonal Relations*. Hoboken: John Wiley & Sons.

Helper, Susan. 1990. "Comparative Supplier Relations in the U.S. and Japanese Auto Industries: An Exit Voice Approach." *Business Economic History* 19: 153–62.

Helper, Susan. 1991. "How Much Has Really Changed Between US Automakers and Their Suppliers?" *MIT Sloan Management Review* 32 (4): 15.

Helper, Susan. 1993. "An Exit-Voice Analysis of Supplier Relations: The Case of the U.S. Automotive Industry." In *The Embedded Firm: On the Socioeconomics of Industrial Networks*, edited by Gernot Grabher, 141–60. London: Routledge.

Helper, Susan, and Mari Sako. 1995. "Supplier Relations in Japan and the U.S.: Are They Converging." *MIT Sloan Management Review* 32 (4): 77–82.

Helper, Susan, and Evan Soltas. 2021. "Why the Pandemic Has Disrupted Supply Chains." White House. https://www.whitehouse.gov/cea/written-materials/2021/06/17/why-the-pandemic-has-disrupted-supply-chains/.

Herrigel, Gary, and Volker Wittke. 2005. "Varieties of Vertical Disintegration: The Global Trend Toward Heterogeneous Supply Relations and the Reproduction of Difference in US and German Manufacturing." In *Changing Capitalisms? Internationalization, Institutional Change, and Systems of Economic* Organization, edited by Glenn Morgan, Richard Whitley, and Eli Moen. Oxford University Press.

Hofmann, Erik, Simon Templer, Dale S. Rogers, Thomas Y. Choi, Rudolf Leuschner, and Rohan Korde. 2021. "Supply Chain Financing and Pandemic: Managing Cash Flows to Keep Firms and Their Value Networks Healthy." *Rutgers Management Review* 6 (1): 1–22.

Holland, John H. 1995. *Hidden Order: How Adaptation Builds Complexity*. Helix Books. Reading, Mass: Addison-Wesley.

Huang, Boray, and Seyed M. R. Iravani. 2005. "Production Control Policies in Supply Chains with Selective-Information Sharing." *Operations Research* 53 (4): 662–74. https://doi.org/10.1287/opre.1040.0203.

Huckfeldt, R. Robert. 1983. "Social Contexts, Social Networks, and Urban Neighborhoods: Environmental Constraints on Friendship Choice." *American Journal of Sociology* 89 (3): 651–69. https://doi.org/10.1086/227908.

Human, S. E., and K. G. Provan. 1997. "An Emergent Theory of Structure and Outcomes in Small-Firm Strategic Manufacturing Networks." Academy of Management Journal 40 (2): 368–403. https://doi.org/10.2307/256887.

Hunt, Shelby D., and John R. Nevin. 1974. "Power in a Channel of Distribution: Sources and Consequences." Journal of Marketing Research 11 (2): 186–93. https://doi.org/10.1177/002224377401100210.

Ireland, R. Duane, and Justin W. Webb. 2007. "A Multi theoretic perspective on Trust and Power in Strategic Supply Chains." *Journal of Operations Management* 25 (2):482–97

Ivanov, Dmitry, and Alexandre Dolgui. 2020. "Viability of Intertwined Supply Networks: Extending the Supply Chain Resilience Angles towards Survivability. A Position Paper Motivated by COVID-19 Outbreak." *International Journal of Production Research* 58 (10): 2904–15. https://doi.org/10.1080/00207 543.2020.1750727.

Jacob, François. 1977. "Evolution and Tinkering." *Science* 196 (4295): 1161–66. https://doi.org/10.1126/science.860134.

Jensen, Michael C. 1983. "Organization Theory and Methodology." *The Accounting Review* 58 (2): 319–39.

Jensen, Michael C., and William H. Meckling. 1976. "Theory of the Firm: Managerial Behavior, Agency Costs and Ownership Structure." *Journal of Financial Economics* 3 (4): 305–60. https://doi.org/10.1016/0304-405X(76)90026-X.

Jeong, Seongkyoon, Adegoke Oke, and Thomas Y. Choi. 2022. "Opportunistic Innovation in the Age of Digital Services." *Journal of Operations Management* 68 (4): 328–52. https://doi.org/10.1002/joom.1181.

Jin, Mingzhou, and S. David Wu. 2006. "Supplier Coalitions in On-Line Reverse Auctions: Validity Requirements and Profit Distribution Scheme." *International Journal of Production Economics* 100 (2): 183–94. https://doi.org/10.1016/j.ijpe.2004.10.017.

Johnson, David W., Geoffrey Maruyama, Roger Johnson, Deborah Nelson, and Linda Skon. 1981. "Effects of Cooperative, Competitive, and Individualistic Goal Structures on Achievement: A Meta-Analysis." *Psychological Bulletin* 89 (1): 47–62. https://doi.org/10.1037/0033-2909.89.1.47.

Johnson, J. David. 2004. "The Emergence, Maintenance, and Dissolution of Structural Hole Brokerage Within Consortia." *Communication Theory* 14 (3): 212–36. https://doi.org/10.1111/j.1468-2885.2004.tb00312.x.

Jones, Gareth R. 2013. *Organizational Theory, Design, and Change.* 7th. ed. Global ed. Always Learning. Boston, Munich: Pearson.

Kalkanci, Başak, Morvarid Rahmani, and L. Beril Toktay. 2019. "The Role of Inclusive Innovation in Promoting Social Sustainability." *Production and Operations Management* 28 (12): 2960–82. https://doi.org/10.1111/poms.13112.

Kamath, Rajan R, and Jeffrey K Liker. 1994. "A Second Look at Japanese Product Development." *Harvard Business Review* 72 (6): 154–58.

Kauffman, Stuart A. 1993. *The Origins of Order: Self-Organization and Selection in Evolution.* New York: Oxford University Press.

Kauffman, Stuart A. 1996. *At Home in the Universe: The Search for Laws of Self-Organization and Complexity.* 1st paperback ed. New York: Oxford University Press.

Kauffman, Stuart, Surya D. Pathak, Pradyot K. Sen, and Thomas Y. Choi. 2018. "Jury Rigging and Supply Network Design: Evolutionary 'Tinkering' in the Presence of Unknown-Unknowns." *Journal of Supply Chain Management* 54 (1): 51–63. https://doi.org/10.1111/jscm.12146.

Kayış, Enis, Feryal Erhun, and Erica L. Plambeck. 2013. "Delegation vs. Control of Component Procurement Under Asymmetric Cost Information and Simple Contracts." *Manufacturing & Service Operations Management* 15 (1): 45–56. https://doi.org/10.1287/msom.1120.0395.

Kellogg, Deborah L., and Richard B. Chase. 1995. "Constructing an Empirically Derived Measure for Customer Contact." *Management Science* 41 (11): 1734–49. https://doi.org/10.1287/mnsc.41.11.1734.

Kembro, Joakim, Dag Näslund, and Jan Olhager. 2017. "Information Sharing Across Multiple Supply Chain Tiers: A Delphi Study on Antecedents." *International Journal of Production Economics* 193 (November): 77–86. https://doi.org/10.1016/j.ijpe.2017.06.032.

Kim, Tai-Young, Hongseok Oh, and Anand Swaminathan. 2006. "Framing Interorganizational Network Change: A Network Inertia Perspective." *Academy of Management Review* 31 (3): 704–20. https://doi.org/10.5465/amr.2006.21318926.

Kim, Yusoon, Yi-Su Chen, and Kevin Linderman. 2015. "Supply Network Disruption and Resilience: A Network Structural Perspective." *Journal of Operations Management* 33–34 (1): 43–59. https://doi.org/10.1016/j.jom.2014.10.006.

Kim, Yusoon, and Thomas Y. Choi. 2015. "Deep, Sticky, Transient, and Gracious: An Expanded Buyer-Supplier Relationship Typology." *Journal of Supply Chain Management* 51 (3): 61–86. https://doi.org/10.1111/jscm.12081.

Kim, Yusoon, and Thomas Y. Choi. 2018. "Tie Strength and Value Creation in the Buyer-Supplier Context: A U-Shaped Relation Moderated by Dependence Asymmetry." *Journal of Management* 44 (3): 1029–64. https://doi.org/10.1177/0149206315599214.

Kim, Yusoon, and Thomas Y. Choi. 2021. "Supplier Relationship Strategies and Outcome Dualities: An Empirical Study of Embeddedness Perspective." *International Journal of Production Economics* 232 (February): 107930. https://doi.org/10.1016/j.ijpe.2020.107930.

Kim, Yusoon, Thomas Y. Choi, and Paul F. Skilton. 2015. "Buyer-Supplier Embeddedness and Patterns of Innovation." *International Journal of Operations & Production Management* 35 (3): 318–45. https://doi.org/10.1108/IJOPM-05-2013-0251.

Kim, Yusoon, Thomas Y. Choi, Tingting Yan, and Kevin Dooley. 2011. "Structural Investigation of Supply Networks: A Social Network Analysis Approach." *Journal of Operations Management* 29 (3): 194–211. https://doi.org/10.1016/j.jom.2010.11.001.

Kirchherr, W. W. 1992. "Kolmogorov Complexity and Random Graphs." *Information Processing Letters* 41 (3): 125–30. https://doi.org/10.1016/0020-0190(92)90040-3.

Kirzner, Israel M. 2013. *Competition and Entrepreneurship. The Collected Works of Israel M. Kirzner.* Indianapolis: Liberty Fund.

Krackhardt, David. 1990. "Assessing the Political Landscape: Structure, Cognition, and Power in Organizations." *Administrative Science Quarterly* 35 (2): 342. https://doi.org/10.2307/2393394.

Krackhardt, David. 1992. "The Strength of Strong Ties: The Importance of Philos in Organizations." In *Networks and Organizations: Structure, Form, and Action*, edited by Nohria, N. and Robert G. Eccles, 216–39. Boston: Harvard Business School Press.

Krause, Daniel R., and Robert B. Handfield. 1999. "Developing a World-Class Supply Base." Tempe, AZ: Center for Advanced Purchasing Studies.

Krause, Daniel R., Robert B. Handfield, and Thomas V. Scannell. 1998. "An Empirical Investigation of Supplier Development: Reactive and Strategic Processes." *Journal of Operations Management* 17 (1): 39–58. https://doi.org/10.1016/S0272-6963(98)00030-8.

Kurpjuweit, Stefan, Stephan M. Wagner, and Thomas Y. Choi. 2021. "Selecting Startups as Suppliers: A Typology of Supplier Selection Archetypes." *Journal of Supply Chain Management* 57 (3): 25–49. https://doi.org/10.1111/jscm.12230.

Lachmann, Ludwig M. 1976. "On the Central Concept of Austrian Economics: The Market Process." In *The Foundations of Modern Austrian Economics*, edited by Edwin G. Dolan, 126–32. Kansas City: Sheed & Ward.

Lachmann, Ludwig M. 1986. *The Market as an Economic Process.* Oxford: Basil Blackwell.

Lahno, Bernd. 2000. "In Defense of Moderate Envy." *Analyse & Kritik* 22 (1): 98–113. https://doi.org/10.1515/auk-2000-0105.

Langfred, Claus W., and Neta A. Moye. 2004. "Effects of Task Autonomy on Performance: An Extended Model Considering Motivational, Informational, and Structural Mechanisms." *Journal of Applied Psychology* 89 (6): 934–45. https://doi.org/10.1037/0021-9010.89.6.934.

LaPorte, Todd R., ed. 2015. *Organized Social Complexity: Challenge to Politics and Policy.* Princeton, NJ: Princeton University Press.

Larsen, Marcus M., Stephan Manning, and Torben Pedersen. 2013. "Uncovering the Hidden Costs of Offshoring: The Interplay of Complexity, Organizational Design, and Experience." *Strategic Management Journal* 34 (5): 533–52. https://doi.org/10.1002/smj.2023.

Larson, Paul D., and Jack D. Kulchitsky. 1998. "Single Sourcing and Supplier Certification." *Industrial Marketing Management* 27 (1): 73–81. https://doi.org/10.1016/S0019-8501(97)00039-4.

Lee, Gwendolyn K., and Mishari A. Alnahedh. 2016. "Industries' Potential for Interdependency and Profitability: A Panel of 135 Industries, 1988–1996." *Strategy Science* 1 (4): 285–308. https://doi.org/10.1287/stsc.2016.0023.

Lee, Hau L., and Corey Billington. 1992. "Managing Supply Chain Inventory: Pitfalls and Opportunities." *MIT Sloan Management Review* 33 (3): 65–77.

Lee, Hau L., V. Padmanabhan, and Seungjin Whang. 1997. "Information Distortion in a Supply Chain: The Bullwhip Effect." *Management Science* 43 (4): 546–58. https://doi.org/10.1287/mnsc.43.4.546.

Leenders, Michiel R., and David L. Blenkhorn. 1988. *Reverse Marketing: The New Buyer-Supplier Relationship.* New York; London: Free Press; Collier Macmillan.

Lenox, Michael, and Andrew King. 2004. "Prospects for Developing Absorptive Capacity Through Internal Information Provision." *Strategic Management Journal* 25 (4): 331–45. https://doi.org/10.1002/smj.379.

Levin, Daniel Z., and Rob Cross. 2004. "The Strength of Weak Ties You Can Trust: The Mediating Role of Trust in Effective Knowledge Transfer." *Management Science* 50 (11): 1477–90. https://doi.org/10.1287/mnsc.1030.0136.

Levinthal, Daniel A. 1997. "Adaptation on Rugged Landscapes." *Management Science* 43 (7): 934–50. https://doi.org/10.1287/mnsc.43.7.934.

Li, Hongmin, Yimin Wang, Rui Yin, Thomas J. Kull, and Thomas Y. Choi. 2012. "Target Pricing: Demand-Side Versus Supply-Side Approaches." *International Journal of Production Economics* 136 (1): 172–84. https://doi.org/10.1016/j.ijpe.2011.10.002.

Li, Mei, and Thomas Y. Choi. 2009. "Triads in Services Outsourcing: Bridge, Bridge Decay and Bridge Transfer." *Journal of Supply Chain Management* 45 (3): 27–39. https://doi.org/10.1111/j.1745-493X.2009.03169.x.

Liker, Jeffrey K. 2021. *The Toyota Way: 14 Management Principles from the World's Greatest Manufacturer*. 2nd ed. New York: McGraw Hill Education.

Liker, Jeffrey K., and Thomas Y. Choi. 2004. "Building Deep Supplier Relationships." *Harvard Business Review* 82 (12): 104–13.

Litwak, Eugene, and Henry J. Meyer. 1966. "A Balance Theory of Coordination Between Bureaucratic Organizations and Community Primary Groups." *Administrative Science Quarterly* 11 (1): 31. https://doi.org/10.2307/2391393.

Lomi, A., and E. R. Larsen. 1996. "Interacting Locally and Evolving Globally: A Computational Approach to the Dynamics of Organizational Populations." *Academy of Management Journal* 39 (5): 1287–321. https://doi.org/10.2307/257000.

Luce, R. Duncan, and Albert D. Perry. 1949. "A Method of Matrix Analysis of Group Structure." *Psychometrika* 14 (2): 95–116. https://doi.org/10.1007/BF02289146.

Luo, Qiuju, and Dixi Zhong. 2015. "Using Social Network Analysis to Explain Communication Characteristics of Travel-Related Electronic Word-of-Mouth on Social Networking Sites." *Tourism Management* 46 (February): 274–82. https://doi.org/10.1016/j.tourman.2014.07.007.

Lv, Fei. 2019. "Should Competing Original Equipment Manufacturers Outsource Procurement Activities Under Asymmetric Cost Information?" *International Journal of Production Research* 57 (14): 4561–78. https://doi.org/10.1080/00207543.2018.1521023.

Madhavan, R., and D. R. Gnyawali. 2004. "Two's Company, Three's a Crowd? Triads in Cooperative-Competitive Networks." *Academy of Management Journal* 47 (6): 918–27. https://doi.org/10.2307/20159631.

Marsden, Peter V. 2002. "Egocentric and Sociocentric Measures of Network Centrality." *Social Networks* 24 (4): 407–22. https://doi.org/10.1016/S0378-8733(02)00016-3.

Martínez-Berumen, Héctor A., Gabriela C. López-Torres, and Laura Romo-Rojas. 2014. "Developing a Method to Evaluate Entropy in Organizational Systems." *Procedia Computer Science* 28: 389–97. https://doi.org/10.1016/j.procs.2014.03.048.

McKelvey, Bill. 1997. "Perspective—Quasi-Natural Organization Science." *Organization Science* 8 (4): 351–80. https://doi.org/10.1287/orsc.8.4.351.

McKelvey, Bill. 1999. "Avoiding Complexity Catastrophe in Coevolutionary Pockets: Strategies for Rugged Landscapes." *Organization Science* 10 (3): 294–321. https://doi.org/10.1287/orsc.10.3.294.

McMillan, John. 1990. "Managing Suppliers: Incentive Systems in Japanese and U.S. Industry." *California Management Review* 32 (4): 38–55. https://doi.org/10.2307/41166627.

Mena, Carlos, Andrew Humphries, and Thomas Y. Choi. 2013. "Toward a Theory of Multi-Tier Supply Chain Management." *Journal of Supply Chain Management* 49 (2): 58–77. https://doi.org/10.1111/jscm.12003.

Meyer, John W, and Brian Rowan. 1977. "Institutionalized Organizations: Formal Structure as Myth and Ceremony." *American Journal of Sociology* 83 (2): 340–63.

Mills, Theodore M. 1954. "The Coalition Pattern in Three Person Groups." *American Sociological Review* 19 (6): 657–67.

Mills, Theodore M . 1958. "Some Hypotheses on Small Groups from Simmel." *American Journal of Sociology* 63 (6): 642–50.

Mintzberg, Henry. 1979. *The Structuring of Organizations: A Synthesis of the Research.* Theory of Management Policy Series. Englewood Cliffs, NJ: Prentice-Hall.

Mizruchi, Mark S. 1994. "Social Network Analysis: Recent Achievements and Current Controversies." *Acta Sociologica* 37 (4): 329–43. https://doi.org/10.1177/000169939403700403.

Moran, Peter. 2005. "Structural vs. Relational Embeddedness: Social Capital and Managerial Performance." *Strategic Management Journal* 26 (12): 1129–51. https://doi.org/10.1002/smj.486.

Morgan, Gareth. 2006. *Images of Organization.* Updated ed. Thousand Oaks: SAGE.

Morrissette, Julian O. 1958. "An Experimental Study of the Theory of Structural Balance." *Human Relations* 11 (3): 239–54. https://doi.org/10.1177/001872675801100304.

Nagel, Kai, and Maya Paczuski. 1995. "Emergent Traffic Jams." *Physical Review* 51 (4): 2909–18. https://doi.org/10.1103/PhysRevE.51.2909.

Nahapiet, Janine, and Sumantra Ghoshal. 1998. "Social Capital, Intellectual Capital, and the Organizational Advantage." *Academy of Management Review* 23 (2): 242. https://doi.org/10.2307/259373.

Nair, Anand, Ram Narasimhan, and Thomas Y. Choi. 2009. "Supply Networks as a Complex Adaptive System: Toward Simulation-Based Theory Building on Evolutionary Decision Making." *Decision Sciences* 40 (4): 783–815. https://doi.org/10.1111/j.1540-5915.2009.00251.x.

Narasimhan, Ram, and Jayanth Jayaram. 1998. "Causal Linkages in Supply Chain Management: An Exploratory Study of North American Manufacturing Firms." *Decision Sciences* 29 (3): 579–605. https://doi.org/10.1111/j.1540-5915.1998.tb01355.x.

Narasimhan, Ram, Srinivas Talluri, and David Mendez. 2001. "Supplier Evaluation and Rationalization via Data Envelopment Analysis: An Empirical Examination." *Journal of Supply Chain Management* 37 (3): 28–37. https://doi.org/10.1111/j.1745-493X.2001.tb00103.x.

Narayanan, Sriram, and Ed Terris. 2020. "Inclusive Manufacturing: The Impact of Disability Diversity on Productivity in a Work Integration Social Enterprise." *Manufacturing & Service Operations Management* 22 (6): 1112–30. https://doi.org/10.1287/msom.2020.0940.

Newcomb, Theodore M. 1961. *The Acquaintance Process.* New York: Holt, Rinehart & Winston. https://doi.org/10.1037/13156-000.

Newcomb, Theodore M . 1981. "Heiderian Balance as a Group Phenomenon." *Journal of Personality and Social Psychology* 40 (5): 862–67. https://doi.org/10.1037/0022-3514.40.5.862.

Nishiguchi, Toshihiro. 1994. *Strategic Industrial Sourcing: The Japanese Advantage.* New York: Oxford University Press.

Nishiguchi, Toshihiro, and Alexandre Beaudet. 1998. "The Toyota Group and the Aisin Fire." *Sloan Management Review* 40 (1): 49–59.

Noordhoff, Corine S., Kyriakos Kyriakopoulos, Christine Moorman, Pieter Pauwels, and Benedict G. C. Dellaert. 2011. "The Bright Side and Dark Side of Embedded Ties in Business-to-Business Innovation." *Journal of Marketing* 75 (5): 34–52. https://doi.org/10.1509/jmkg.75.5.34.

Novak, David C., and Thomas Y. Choi. 2015. "The Role of Geography in Shaping SCM's Professional Identity." *Journal of Business Logistics* 36 (2): 231–32. https://doi.org/10.1111/jbl.12087.

Nowak, Martin A., and Robert M. May. 1992. "Evolutionary Games and Spatial Chaos." *Nature* 359 (6398): 826–29. https://doi.org/10.1038/359826a0.

Obstfeld, David. 2005. "Social Networks, the *Tertius Iungens* Orientation, and Involvement in Innovation." *Administrative Science Quarterly* 50 (1): 100–130. https://doi.org/10.2189/asqu.2005.50.1.100.

Obstfeld, David, Stephen P. Borgatti, and Jason Davis. 2014. "Brokerage as a Process: Decoupling Third Party Action from Social Network Structure." In *Research in the Sociology of Organizations*, edited by Daniel J. Brass, Giuseppe (Joe) Labianca, Ajay Mehra, Daniel S. Halgin, and Stephen P. Borgatti, 40:135–59. Emerald Group. https://doi.org/10.1108/S0733-558X(2014)0000040007.

Oliver, Christine. 1990. "Determinants of Interorganizational Relationships: Integration and Future Directions." *Academy of Management Review* 15 (2): 241–65. https://doi.org/10.5465/amr.1990.4308156.

Olsen, Rasmus Friis, and Lisa M. Ellram. 1997. "A Portfolio Approach to Supplier Relationships." *Industrial Marketing Management* 26 (2): 101–13. https://doi.org/10.1016/S0019-8501(96)00089-2.

Osgood, Charles E., and Percy H. Tannenbaum. 1955. "The Principle of Congruity in the Prediction of Attitude Change." *Psychological Review* 62 (1): 42–55. https://doi.org/10.1037/h0048153.

Ouchi, William G. 1980. "Markets, Bureaucracies, and Clans." *Administrative Science Quarterly* 25 (1): 129. https://doi.org/10.2307/2392231.

Park, Jae Jeok, and Erwin Tan. 2018. "Exploiting Sino-US Geostrategic Competition: The View from Seoul and Singapore." *Asian Studies Review* 42 (3): 537–55. https://doi.org/10.1080/10357823.2018.1478799.

Parkhe, Arvind. 1991. "Interfirm Diversity, Organizational Learning, and Longevity in Global Strategic Alliances." *Journal of International Business Studies* 22 (4): 579–601. https://doi.org/10.1057/palgrave.jibs.8490315.

Pathak, Surya D., Jamison M. Day, Anand Nair, William J. Sawaya, and M. Murat Kristal. 2007. "Complexity and Adaptivity in Supply Networks: Building Supply Network Theory Using a Complex Adaptive Systems Perspective." *Decision Sciences* 38 (4): 547–80. https://doi.org/10.1111/j.1540-5915.2007.00170.x.

Pathak, Surya D., Zhaohui Wu, and David Johnston. 2014. "Toward a Structural View of Co-Opetition in Supply Networks." *Journal of Operations Management* 32 (5): 254–67. https://doi.org/10.1016/j.jom.2014.04.001.

Patrucco, Andrea, Christine Mary Harland, Davide Luzzini, and Federico Frattini. 2022. "Managing Triadic Supplier Relationships in Collaborative Innovation Projects: A

Relational View Perspective." *Supply Chain Management: An International Journal* 27 (7): 108–27. https://doi.org/10.1108/SCM-05-2021-0220.

Paulraj, Antony, Augustine A. Lado, and Injazz J. Chen. 2008. "Inter-Organizational Communication as a Relational Competency: Antecedents and Performance Outcomes in Collaborative Buyer-Supplier Relationships." *Journal of Operations Management* 26 (1): 45–64. https://doi.org/10.1016/j.jom.2007.04.001.

Phillips, Joan M., Ben S. Lin, and Thomas G. Costello. 1998. "A Balance Theory Perspective of Triadic Supply Chain Relationships." *Journal of Marketing Theory and Practice* 6 (4): 78–91. https://doi.org/10.1080/10696679.1998.11501812.

Pich, Michael T., Christoph H. Loch, and Arnoud De Meyer. 2002. "On Uncertainty, Ambiguity, and Complexity in Project Management." *Management Science* 48 (8): 1008–23. https://doi.org/10.1287/mnsc.48.8.1008.163.

Pilling, Bruce K., Lawrence A. Crosby, and Donald W. Jackson. 1994. "Relational Bonds in Industrial Exchange: An Experimental Test of the Transaction Cost Economic Framework." *Journal of Business Research* 30 (3): 237–51. https://doi.org/10.1016/0148-2963(94)90054-X.

Plambeck, Erica, L., and Kamalini Ramdas. 2020. "Alleviating Poverty by Empowering Women Through Business Model Innovation: Manufacturing & Service Operations Management Insights and Opportunities." *Manufacturing & Service Operations Management* 22 (1): 123–34. https://doi.org/10.1287/msom.2019.0844.

Polanyi, Karl. 2001. *The Great Transformation: The Political and Economic Origins of Our Time.* 2nd ed. Boston,: Beacon Press.

Prashant, Kale, and Singh Harbir. 2009. "Managing Strategic Alliances: What Do We Know Now, and Where Do We Go from Here?" *Academy of Management Perspectives* 23 (3): 45–62. https://doi.org/10.5465/amp.2009.43479263.

Price, James L., and Charles W Mueller. 1986. *Handbook of Organizational Measurement.* Marshfield, MA: Pitman.

Provan, Keith G. 1983. "The Federation as an Interorganizational Linkage Network." *Academy of Management Review* 8 (1): 79. https://doi.org/10.2307/257170.

Provan, Keith G. 1993. "Embeddedness, Interdependence, and Opportunism in Organizational Supplier-Buyer Networks." *Journal of Management* 19 (4): 841–56. https://doi.org/10.1177/014920639301900406.

Provan, Keith G., and H. Brinton Milward. 1995. "A Preliminary Theory of Interorganizational Network Effectiveness: A Comparative Study of Four Community Mental Health Systems." *Administrative Science Quarterly* 40 (1): 1. https://doi.org/10.2307/2393698.

Ramasesh, Ranga V., and Tyson R. Browning. 2014. "A Conceptual Framework for Tackling Knowable Unknown Unknowns in Project Management." *Journal of Operations Management* 32 (4): 190–204. https://doi.org/10.1016/j.jom.2014.03.003.

Richardson, James. 1993. "Parallel Sourcing and Supplier Performance in the Japanese Automobile Industry." *Strategic Management Journal* 14 (5): 339–50. https://doi.org/10.1002/smj.4250140503.

Richardson, James, and James Roumasset. 1995. "Sole Sourcing, Competitive Sourcing, Parallel Sourcing: Mechanisms for Supplier Performance." *Managerial and Decision Economics* 16 (1): 71–84. https://doi.org/10.1002/mde.4090160109.

Rivkin, Jan W. 2000. "Imitation of Complex Strategies." *Management Science* 46 (6): 824–44. https://doi.org/10.1287/mnsc.46.6.824.11940.

Robins, Garry, and Malcolm Alexander. 2004. "Small Worlds Among Interlocking Directors: Network Structure and Distance in Bipartite Graphs." *Computational & Mathematical Organization Theory* 10 (1): 69–94. https://doi.org/10.1023/B:CMOT.0000032580.12184.c0.

Rodrigues, Aroldo. 1967. "Effects of Balance, Positivity, and Agreement in Triadic Social Relations." *Journal of Personality and Social Psychology* 5 (4): 472–76. https://doi.org/10.1037/h0024410.

Rodrigues, Aroldo, and José Augusto Dela Coleta. 1983. "The Prediction of Preferences for Triadic Interpersonal Relations." *Journal of Social Psychology* 121 (1): 73–80. https://doi.org/10.1080/00224545.1983.9924469.

Rogers, Dale S., Rudolf Leuschner, and Thomas Y. Choi. 2016a. "Funding the Supply Chain and the Organization." *Inside Supply Management*, March.

Rogers, Dale S., Rudolf Leuschner, and Thomas Y. Choi. 2016b. "The Rise of Fintech in Supply Chains." *Harvard Business Review Online*, June.

Rogers, Dale, Rudolf Leuschner, and Thomas Y. Choi. 2020. *Supply Chain Financing: Funding the Supply Chain and the Organization.* London: World Scientific.

Rogers, Dale S., Todd Taylor, Raymundo Beristain-Barajas, and Thomas Y. Choi. 2018. "Blockchain and Supply Management." Tempe, AZ: CAPS Research.

Rogers, Zachary S., Victor Benjamin, and Mohan Gopalakrishnan. 2018. "Cyber Security in Supply Chains: Understanding Threats and Potential Security Practices." Tempe, AZ: CAPS Research.

Rogers, Zachary S., and Thomas Y. Choi. 2018. "Purchasing Managers Have a Lead Role to Play in Cyber Defense." *Harvard Business Review Online*, July.

Rogers, Zachary S., Thomas Y. Choi, and Seongkyoon Jeong. 2021. "Rethinking Cybersecurity: Hidden Vulnerabilities in the Supply Chain." *Supply Chain Management Review* July/August: 32–37.

Rossetti, Christian L., and Thomas Y. Choi. 2005. "On the Dark Side of Strategic Sourcing: Experiences from the Aerospace Industry." *Academy of Management Executive* 19 (1): 46–60.

Rossetti, Christian L., and Thomas Y. Choi. 2008. "Supply Management Under High Goal Incongruence: An Empirical Examination of Disintermediation in the Aerospace Supply Chain." *Decision Sciences* 39 (3): 507–40. https://doi.org/10.1111/j.1540-5915.2008.00201.x.

Sanders, Nada R., Art Locke, Curtis B. Moore, and Chad W. Autry. 2007. "A Multidimensional Framework for Understanding Outsourcing Arrangements." *Journal of Supply Chain Management* 43 (4): 3–15. https://doi.org/10.1111/j.1745-493X.2007.00037.x.

Schiller, Bradley R., and Karen Gebhardt. 2019. *The Economy Today.* 15th ed. International student edition. McGraw-Hill Series Economics. New York: McGraw-Hill Education.

Schleper, Martin C., Constantin Blome, and David A. Wuttke. 2017. "The Dark Side of Buyer Power: Supplier Exploitation and the Role of Ethical Climates." *Journal of Business Ethics* 140 (1): 97–114. https://doi.org/10.1007/s10551-015-2681-6.

Schoenherr, Tobias, Carlos Mena, and Thomas Y. Choi. 2019. "Measuring and Managing Risks in Supply Chains." Tempe, AZ: CAPS Research.

Schreer, Benjamin. 2019. "Why US-Sino Strategic Competition Is Good for Australia." *Australian Journal of International Affairs* 73 (5): 431–48. https://doi.org/10.1080/10357718.2019.1632261.

Schumpeter, Joseph A. 1934. *The Theory of Economic Development*. Translated by Redvers Opie. Cambridge, MA: Harvard University Press.

Schumpeter, Joseph A. 1950. *Capitalism, Socialism, and Democracy*. New York: Harper & Row.

Scott, John. 1986. *Capitalist Property and Financial Power: A Comparative Study of Britain, the United States, and Japan*. Brighton, Sussex: Wheatsheaf Books.

Scott, John. 2000. *Social Network Analysis: A Handbook*. 2nd ed. Thousands Oaks, CA: SAGE.

Scott, W. Richard. 1987. "The Adolescence of Institutional Theory." *Administrative Science Quarterly* 32 (4): 493. https://doi.org/10.2307/2392880.

Scott, William A. 1963. "Cognitive Complexity and Cognitive Balance." *Sociometry* 26 (1): 66. https://doi.org/10.2307/2785725.

Shao, Benjamin B. M., Zhan (Michael) Shi, Thomas Y. Choi, and Sangho Chae. 2018. "A Data-Analytics Approach to Identifying Hidden Critical Suppliers in Supply Networks: Development of Nexus Supplier Index." *Decision Support Systems* 114 (October): 37–48. https://doi.org/10.1016/j.dss.2018.08.008.

Shi, Guang Victor, James Baldwin, S. C. Lenny Koh, and Thomas Y. Choi. 2018. "Fragmented Institutional Fields and Their Impact on Manufacturing Environmental Practices." *International Journal of Production Research* 56 (1–2): 431–46. https://doi. org/10.1080/00207543.2017.1353712.

Siggelkow, Nicolaj, and Jan W. Rivkin. 2005. "Speed and Search: Designing Organizations for Turbulence and Complexity." *Organization Science* 16 (2): 101–22. https://doi.org/10.1287/orsc.1050.0116.

Simchi-Levi, David, Philip Kaminsky, and Edith Simchi-Levi. 2000. *Designing and Managing the Supply Chain: Concepts, Strategies, and Case Studies*. Irwin/McGraw-Hill Series Operations and Decision Sciences Operations Management. Boston: Irwin/McGraw-Hill.

Simmel, Georg. 1950. "The Triad." In *The Sociology of Georg Simmel*, edited by Kurt H. Wolff. New York: Free Press.

Simon, Herbert A. 1962. "The Architecture of Complexity." *Proceedings of the American Philosophical Society* 106 (6): 467–82.

Simon, Herbert A. 1976. *Administrative Behavior: A Study of Decision-Making Processes in Administrative Organization*. 3d ed. New York: Free Press.

Snell, S. A. 1992. "Control Theory in Strategic Human Resource Management: The Mediating Effect of Administrative Information." *Academy of Management Journal* 35 (2): 292–327. https://doi.org/10.2307/256375.

Sobrero, Maurizio, and Edward B Roberts. 2002. "Strategic Management of Supplier–Manufacturer Relations in New Product Development." *Research Policy* 31 (1): 159–82. https://doi.org/10.1016/S0048-7333(00)00157-8.

Sodhi, ManMohan S. 2015. "Conceptualizing Social Responsibility in Operations Via Stakeholder Resource-Based View." *Production and Operations Management*, June, n/a-n/a. https://doi.org/10.1111/poms.12393.

Sodhi, ManMohan S., and Thomas Y. Choi. 2022. "Don't Abandon Your Just-in-Time Supply Chain, Revamp It." *Harvard Business Review Online*, October.

Spencer, J. W. 2003. "Global Gatekeeping, Representation, and Network Structure: A Longitudinal Analysis of Regional and Global Knowledge-Diffusion Networks." *Journal of International Business Studies* 34 (5): 428–42. https://doi.org/10.1057/palgrave.jibs.8400039.

Stallkamp, Thomas T. 2005. *Score! A Better Way to Do Business: Moving from Conflict to Collaboration*. Philadelphia; London: Wharton School; Pearson Education.

Stevenson, William B., Jone L. Pearce, and Lyman W. Porter. 1985. "The Concept of 'Coalition' in Organization Theory and Research." *Academy of Management Review* 10 (2): 256–68. https://doi.org/10.5465/amr.1985.4278178.

Sting, Fabian J., Merieke Stevens, and Murat Tarakci. 2019. "Temporary Deembedding Buyer-Supplier Relationships: A Complexity Perspective." *Journal of Operations Management* 65 (2): 114–35. https://doi.org/10.1002/joom.1008.

Stouthuysen, Kristof, Hendrik Slabbinck, and Filip Roodhooft. 2012. "Controls, Service Type and Perceived Supplier Performance in Interfirm Service Exchanges." *Journal of Operations Management* 30 (5): 423–35. https://doi.org/10.1016/j.jom.2012.01.002.

Streufert, Siegfried, and Susan C. Streufert. 1978. *Behavior in the Complex Environment*. New York: V. H. Winston & Sons.

Talluri, Srinivas, Hugo A. DeCampos, and G. Tomas M. Hult. 2013. "Supplier Rationalization: A Sourcing Decision Model." *Decision Sciences* 44 (1): 57–86. https://doi.org/10.1111/j.1540-5915.2012.00390.x.

Templar, Simon, Erik Hofmann, and Charles Findlay. 2020. *Financing the End-to-End Supply Chain: A Reference Guide to Supply Chain Finance*. 2nd ed. London; New York: Kogan Page.

Thompson, James D. 2003. *Organizations in Action: Social Science Bases of Administrative Theory*. Classics in Organization and Management. New Brunswick, NJ: Transaction.

Tomlin, Brian. 2006. "On the Value of Mitigation and Contingency Strategies for Managing Supply Chain Disruption Risks." *Management Science* 52 (5): 639–57. https://doi.org/10.1287/mnsc.1060.0515.

Tosi, H. L., J. P. Katz, and L. R. Gomez-Mejia. 1997. "Disaggregating the Agency Contract: The Effects of Monitoring, Incentive Alignment, and Term in Office on Agent Decision Making." *Academy of Management Journal* 40 (3): 584–602. https://doi.org/10.2307/257054.

Treleven, Mark, and Sharon Bergman Schweikhart. 1988. "A Risk/Benefit Analysis of Sourcing Strategies: Single vs. Multiple Sourcing." *Journal of Operations Management* 7 (3–4): 93–114. https://doi.org/10.1016/0272-6963(81)90007-3.

Trent, Robert J., and Robert M. Monczka. 1998. "Purchasing and Supply Management: Trends and Changes Throughout the 1990s." *International Journal of Purchasing and Materials Management* 34 (3): 2–11. https://doi.org/10.1111/j.1745-493X.1998.tb00296.x.

Tsai, Wenpin. 2002. "Social Structure of 'Coopetition' Within a Multiunit Organization: Coordination, Competition, and Intraorganizational Knowledge Sharing." *Organization Science* 13 (2): 179–90. https://doi.org/10.1287/orsc.13.2.179.536.

Tschang, F. Ted. 2007. "Balancing the Tensions Between Rationalization and Creativity in the Video Games Industry." *Organization Science* 18 (6): 989–1005. https://doi.org/10.1287/orsc.1070.0299.

Tully, Shawn. 1995. "Purchasing's New Muscle." *Fortune*, February 20.

Uzzi, Brian. 1996. "The Sources and Consequences of Embeddedness for the Economic Performance of Organizations: The Network Effect." *American Sociological Review* 61 (4): 674. https://doi.org/10.2307/2096399.

Uzzi, Brian. 1997. "Social Structure and Competition in Interfirm Networks: The Paradox of Embeddedness." *Administrative Science Quarterly* 42 (1): 35. https://doi.org/10.2307/2393808.

Uzzi, Brian, and Ryon Lancaster. 2003. "Relational Embeddedness and Learning: The Case of Bank Loan Managers and Their Clients." *Management Science* 49 (4): 383–99. https://doi.org/10.1287/mnsc.49.4.383.14427.

Vachon, S., and R. D. Klassen. 2002. "An Exploratory Investigation of the Effects of Supply Chain Complexity on Delivery Performance." *IEEE Transactions on Engineering Management* 49 (3): 218–30. https://doi.org/10.1109/TEM.2002.803387.

Valente, Thomas W. 1996. "Social Network Thresholds in the Diffusion of Innovations." *Social Networks* 18 (1): 69–89. https://doi.org/10.1016/0378-8733(95)00256-1.

Vedel, Mette, Anne-Maria Holma, and Virpi Havila. 2016. "Conceptualizing Inter-Organizational Triads." *Industrial Marketing Management* 57 (August): 139–47. https://doi.org/10.1016/j.indmarman.2016.01.005.

Vickery, Shawnee K., Jayanth Jayaram, Cornelia Droge, and Roger Calantone. 2003. "The Effects of an Integrative Supply Chain Strategy on Customer Service and Financial Performance: An Analysis of Direct versus Indirect Relationships." *Journal of Operations Management* 21 (5): 523–39. https://doi.org/10.1016/j.jom.2003.02.002.

Villena, Verónica H., Thomas Y. Choi, and Elena Revilla. 2015. "Managing the Dark Side of Close Buyer-Supplier Relationship." *Supply Chain Management Review*, November.

Villena, Verónica H., Thomas Y. Choi, and Elena Revilla. 2019. "Revisiting Interorganizational Trust: Is More Always Better or Could More Be Worse?" *Journal of Management* 45 (2): 752–85. https://doi.org/10.1177/0149206316680031.

Villena, Verónica H., Thomas Y. Choi, and Elena Revilla. 2021. "Mitigating Mechanisms for the Dark Side of Collaborative Buyer–Supplier Relationships: A Mixed-Method Study." *Journal of Supply Chain Management* 57 (4): 86–116. https://doi.org/10.1111/jscm.12239.

Villena, Verónica H., Elena Revilla, and Thomas Y. Choi. 2011. "The Dark Side of Buyer-Supplier Relationships: A Social Capital Perspective." *Journal of Operations Management* 29 (6): 561–76. https://doi.org/10.1016/j.jom.2010.09.001.

Wakolbinger, T., and J. M. Cruz. 2011. "Supply Chain Disruption Risk Management Through Strategic Information Acquisition and Sharing and Risk-Sharing Contracts." *International Journal of Production Research* 49 (13): 4063–84. https://doi.org/10.1080/00207543.2010.501550.

Waldrop, M. Mitchell. 1992. *Complexity: The Emerging Science at the Edge of Order and Chaos*. New York: Simon & Schuster.

Walsh, James P., and Robert D. Dewar. 1987. "Formalization and the Organizational Life Cycle." *Journal of Management Studies* 24 (3): 215–31. https://doi.org/10.1111/j.1467-6486.1987.tb00700.x.

Wang, Yulan, Baozhuang Niu, and Pengfei Guo. 2014. "The Comparison of Two Vertical Outsourcing Structures Under Push and Pull Contracts." *Production and Operations Management* 23 (4): 610–25. https://doi.org/10.1111/poms.12025.

Warren, Roland L. 1967. "The Interorganizational Field as a Focus for Investigation." *Administrative Science Quarterly* 12 (3): 396. https://doi.org/10.2307/2391312.

Wasserman, Stanley, and Katherine Faust. 1994. *Social Network Analysis: Methods and Applications*. Structural Analysis in the Social Sciences 8. Cambridge; New York: Cambridge University Press.

Wasserman, Stanley, and Joseph Galaskiewicz. 1994. *Advances in Social Network Analysis: Research in the Social and Behavioral Sciences*. Thousand Oaks, CA: SAGE.

Weick, Karl E. 2006. *The Social Psychology of Organizing*. 2nd ed. Topics in Social Psychology. New York: McGraw-Hill.

Whipple, Judith M., and Robert Frankel. 2000. "Strategic Alliance Success Factors." *Journal of Supply Chain Management* 36 (3): 21–28. https://doi.org/10.1111/j.1745-493X.2000.tb00248.x.

Wiengarten, Frank. 2019. "Developing Supplier Ecosystem to Create Value." Tempe, AZ: CAPS Research.

Wiengarten, Frank, Thomas Y. Choi, and Di Fan. 2020. "Supplier Ecosystems: Managing Complexities in the Supplier Chain." *Supply Chain Management Review* September/October: 48–55.

Williamson, Oliver E. 1981. "The Economics of Organization: The Transaction Cost Approach." *American Journal of Sociology* 87 (3): 548–77.

Wiseman, Robert M., and Luis R. Gomez-Mejia. 1998. "A Behavioral Agency Model of Managerial Risk Taking." *The Academy of Management Review* 23 (1): 133. https://doi.org/10.2307/259103.

Wolff, Kurt H. 1950. *The Sociology of Georg Simmel*. New York: Free Press.

Wolfram, Stephen. 1986. *Theory and Applications of Cellular Automata*. Singapore: World Scientific.

Womack, James P., Daniel T. Jones, and Daniel Roos. 2014. *The Machine That Changed the World: The Story of Lean Production—Toyota's Secret Weapon in the Global Car Wars That Is Now Revolutionizing World Industry*. Place of publication not identified: Free Press.

Wu, Zhaohui, and Thomas Y. Choi. 2005. "Supplier-Supplier Relationships in the Buyer-Supplier Triad: Building Theories from Eight Case Studies." *Journal of Operations Management* 24 (1): 27–52. https://doi.org/10.1016/j.jom.2005.02.001.

Wu, Zhaohui, Thomas Y. Choi, and M. Johnny Rungtusanatham. 2010. "Supplier-Supplier Relationships in Buyer-Supplier-Supplier Triads: Implications for Supplier Performance." *Journal of Operations Management* 28 (2): 115–23. https://doi.org/10.1016/j.jom.2009.09.002.

Wynstra, Finn, Martin Spring, and Tobias Schoenherr. 2015. "Service Triads: A Research Agenda for Buyer-Supplier-Customer Triads in Business Services." *Journal of Operations Management* 35 (1): 1–20. https://doi.org/10.1016/j.jom.2014.10.002.

Yan, Tingting, Thomas Y. Choi, Yusoon Kim, and Yang Yang. 2015. "A Theory of the Nexus Supplier: A Critical Supplier From A Network Perspective." *Journal of Supply Chain Management* 51 (1): 52–66. https://doi.org/10.1111/jscm.12070.

Yan, Tingting, Kevin J. Dooley, and Thomas Y. Choi. 2018. "Measuring Supplier Innovation." *Supply Chain Management Review* March/April.

Yang, Yang S., Thomas Y. Choi, Craig R. Carter, and Rui Yin. 2022. "Expanding the Boundaries of Buyer-Supplier Agency Problems: Moving from Dyad to Triad." *Journal of Purchasing and Supply Management* 28 (3): 100749. https://doi.org/10.1016/j.pursup.2022.100749.

Yoo, Seung Ho, Thomas Y. Choi, and DaeSoo Kim. 2021. "Integrating Sourcing and Financing Strategies in Multi-Tier Supply Chain Management." *International Journal of Production Economics* 234 (April): 108039. https://doi.org/10.1016/j.ijpe.2021.108039.

Zhao, Kang, Akhil Kumar, and John Yen. 2011. "Achieving High Robustness in Supply Distribution Networks by Rewiring." *IEEE Transactions on Engineering Management* 58 (2): 347–62. https://doi.org/10.1109/TEM.2010.2095503.

Zhao, Kang, Zhiya Zuo, and Jennifer V. Blackhurst. 2019. "Modelling Supply Chain Adaptation for Disruptions: An Empirically Grounded Complex Adaptive Systems

Approach." *Journal of Operations Management* 65 (2): 190–212. https://doi.org/ 10.1002/joom.1009.

Zhao, Xiande, Baofeng Huo, Barbara B. Flynn, and Jeff Hoi Yan Yeung. 2008. "The Impact of Power and Relationship Commitment on the Integration Between Manufacturers and Customers in a Supply Chain." *Journal of Operations Management* 26 (3): 368–88. https://doi.org/10.1016/j.jom.2007.08.002.

Zimmerman, Brenda, Curt Lindberg, and Paul E. Plsek. 1998. *Edge Ware: Lessons from Complexity Science for Health Care Leaders.* Irving, TX: VHA Inc.

Zucker, Lynne G. 1987. "Institutional Theories of Organization." *Annual Review of Sociology* 13: 443–64.

Index

For the benefit of digital users, indexed terms that span two pages (e.g., 52–53) may, on occasion, appear on only one of those pages.

Tables and figures are indicated by *t* and *f* following the page number.